'Safe moor'd in Greenwich ti
A study of the skeletons of Royal Nav
marines excavated at the Royal Hospital ~~~~~~~~

by Ceridwen Boston, Annsofie Witkin, Angela Boyle and David R P Wilkinson

with contributions by

*Leigh Allen, Duncan H Brown, Bethan Charles, Brian Dean,
Lorraine Lindsay-Gale and Nicholas Marquez-Grant*

Illustrations by

Markus Dylewski, Amy Hemingway and Georgina Slater

Oxford Archaeology Monograph 5

Oxford 2008

'Safe moor'd in Greenwich tier': A study of the skeletons of Royal Navy sailors and marines excavated at the Royal Hospital

Designed by Oxford Archaeology Graphics Office

Cover design by Georgina Slater and Lucy Martin

The publication of this volume has been funded by Mount Anvil.

Edited by Ian Scott

The quotation in the title is taken from William Spavens, *Memoirs of a seafaring life: the narrative of William Spavens on the Navy Chest at Chatham*, 1796, Rodger N A M (ed), Folio Society, 2002, London, page 99.

This book is part of a series of books on Burials in London – which can be bought from all good bookshops and Internet Bookshops. For more information visit thehumanjourney.net

Figures are reproduced from the Ordnance Survey on behalf of the controller of Her Majesty's Stationery Office, © Crown Copyright, AL 100005569

Plates 1–9, 11 and 12 © National Maritime Museum, Greenwich London; Plate 10 reproduced by permission of The National Archives.

Typeset by Manila Typesetting Company
Printed by Alden group, Oxfordshire

ISBN 978-0-904220-51-3
© 2008 Oxford Archaeological Unit

Contents

List of Figures vi
List of Plates vii
List of Tables ix
Summary x
Acknowledgements xi

CHAPTER 1: INTRODUCTION 1

PROJECT BACKGROUND 1
Geology and location 1
ARCHAEOLOGICAL AND HISTORICAL BACKGROUND 1
Introduction 1
Prehistoric period 1
Roman period 3
Early medieval period (to AD 1066) 4
Later medieval period (AD 1066-1550) 4
Post-medieval period (AD 1550 +) 4
PROJECT AIMS 4
Archaeological desk-based assessment, October 1999 4
Archaeological evaluation, November 1999 5
Archaeological watching briefs on the sites of the proposed student accommodation, conference facility, and on the site of the electricity substation, January-March 2000 5
Archaeological excavation Areas 1 and 2, June-September 2001 5
FIELDWORK METHODOLOGY 5
Introduction 5
Archaeological watching brief, July 1999 5
Archaeological evaluation, November 1999 6
Archaeological watching briefs on the sites of the proposed student accommodation, conference facility, and on the site of the electricity substation, January-March 2000 6
Archaeological excavation Areas 1 and 2, June-September 2001 6

CHAPTER 2: THE BURIAL GROUND AND GREENWICH PENSIONERS 7

THE BURIAL GROUND 7
THE ROYAL HOSPITAL OVER TIME 10
SOCIAL HISTORY OF THE GREENWICH PENSIONERS 11
Introduction 11
Documentary sources 12
Composition of the Greenwich assemblage 12
    Naval hierarchy in life and death 12
    Manning the Royal Navy 13
    Nationality 14
    Greenwich Pensioners on the Trafalgar Roll 15
    Social class 16
    Life after the Royal Navy 16
    Out-pensioners and in-pensioners 17
LIFE OF IN-PENSIONERS IN THE HOSPITAL 17
WOMEN AND CHILDREN AT THE ROYAL HOSPITAL 18

CHAPTER 3: RESULTS OF THE FIELDWORK 21

INTRODUCTION 21
FIELDWORK RESULTS 21
Archaeological watching brief, July 1999 21
Archaeological evaluation, November 1999 21
    Trench 10 21
    Trenches 11 and 12 22
    Trench 13 22

Trench 14	22
In summary	22
Watching brief on site of student accommodation, February-March 2000	23
Trench 15	23
Archaeological watching brief on site of conference facility, January-March 2000	23
Archaeological excavation - Phase 1 the electrical substation, January 2000	23
Archaeological excavation - Phase 2 Areas 1 and 2, June-September 2001	26
Burials	26
Non-grave features in Area 1	27
Non-grave features in Area 2	30
CHAPTER 4: HUMAN SKELETAL REMAINS	31
INTRODUCTION	31
Osteological methodology	31
Preservation and completeness	31
Skeletal inventory	31
Sex determination	32
Age estimation	32
Stature estimation	32
Comparative assemblages used in the analysis	33
PRESERVATION AND COMPLETENESS	33
PALAEODEMOGRAPHY	34
Age and sex distribution	34
Ancestry	35
STATURE ESTIMATION	35
SKELETAL PATHOLOGY	37
Introduction	37
Trauma	38
Fractures	40
Soft tissue trauma	43
Rupture	43
Osteochondritis dissecans	44
Spondylolysis	44
Os acromiale	44
Infection	44
Non-specific infection	44
Periostitis- multiple element involvement	45
Osteomyelitis	46
Chronic respiratory disease	46
Maxillary sinusitis	47
Treponemal disease (yaws and venereal syphilis)	47
Tuberculosis	51
Joint disease	52
Degenerative joint disease	52
Osteoarthritis	52
Schmorl's nodes	54
Rheumatoid arthritis	54
Diffuse Idiopathic Systemic Hyperostosis (DISH)	54
Metabolic disorders	55
Iron deficiency anaemia	55
Scurvy	56
Rickets	58
Osteoporosis	59
Neoplasms	60
Osteochondroma	60
Osteoma	60
Congenital anomalies	60
Other pathology	60
Pulmonary hypertrophic osteoarthropathy	60
Medical interventions	61
Craniotomy	63

Dental pathology 64
   Dental caries 64
   Periapical abscesses 65
   Ante-mortem tooth loss 65
   Dental calculus 66
   Periodontal disease 66
   Dental enamel hypoplasia 66
   Dental wear 67
DISCUSSION 67
CONCLUSION 69

CHAPTER 5 COFFINS AND COFFIN FITTINGS 71
INTRODUCTION 71
HISTORIC BACKGROUND 71
   18th- to 19th-century funerary practices 71
COFFIN CONSTRUCTION AND DECORATION 71
   Coffin 71
   Upholstery stud-work 72
   Breastplates 72
   Grips and grip plates 73
   Lid motifs and escutcheons 73
DISCUSSION 73
CONCLUSION 73

**APPENDIX 1 SELECTED TRAFALGAR VETERANS WHO DIED IN THE ROYAL HOSPITAL,
GREENWICH (AFTER AYSHFORD AND AYSHFORD 2004)** 75
APPENDIX 2 GRAVE CATALOGUE *by Brian Dean, Lorraine Lindsay-Gale and Ceridwen Boston* 79
APPENDIX 3 SKELETAL CATALOGUE *by Nicholas Marquez-Grant and Annsofie Witkin* 93
APPENDIX 4 COFFIN FITTINGS 128
APPENDIX 5 DETAILED CATALOGUE OF SELECTED METALWORK AND TEXTILE FROM GRAVES
by Lorraine Lindsay-Gale and Ceridwen Boston 139
APPENDIX 6 POTTERY *by Duncan H Brown* 143
APPENDIX 7 CLAY PIPES *by Angela Boyle* 146
APPENDIX 8 GLASS *by Leigh Allen* 148
APPENDIX 9 CERAMIC BUILDING MATERIAL *by Leigh Allen* 149
APPENDIX 10 ANIMAL BONE *by Bethan Charles* 150
APPENDIX 11 RESEARCH PROJECTS UNDERTAKEN ON THE ASSEMBLAGE 152

BIBLIOGRAPHY 153

List of Figures

Figure 1	Site location	2
Figure 2	Location of excavation, evaluation and watching brief trenches	3
Figure 3	Map of the Hundred of Blackheath (1778) (Reproduced courtesy of the Greenwich Heritage Centre)	8
Figure 4	Plan of the (Royal Hospital) Burial Ground, *c.* 1780	9
Figure 5	Ordinance Survey 1st edition 25 inch Map (1865) with the area of proposed development outlined	11
Figure 6	Age-at-death at Greenwich Hospital (data taken from Ayshford and Ayshford, *Trafalgar Roll*); N = 100	15
Figure 7	Trench 15: plan of burials 1565 and 1572	24
Figure 8	Electricity substation trench: plan of burial 2005	25
Figure 9	Area 1- west-facing section at north end of trench	26
Figure 10	Area 2- east-facing section with grave 6032	27
Figure 11	Area 1- plan showing graves and piling trenches	28
Figure 12	Area 2- plan showing graves and piling trenches	29
Figure 13	Age and sex distribution in the Greenwich assemblage (N = 107)	35
Figure 14	Distribution of male stature by percentage of males with measurable left femora, N = 88	36
Figure 15	Stature distribution of the Greenwich pensioners, from left femoral lengths (in feet)	37
Figure 16	Stature distribution of marines collated from Marine Description Books, in feet (taken from Ayshford and Ayshford 2004)	38
Figure 17	Location of fractures in male skeletons by element (N = 97)	41
Figure 18	True prevalence (TPR) of periostitis by element in adult male sample (N = 97)	45

List of Plates

Plate 1	The Royal Hospital Greenwich. Engraving, based on a painting by Clarkson Stanfield. In the background, left to right, are the Queen Anne Court, the present Trafalgar Quarters on Park Row (then Hospital offices) and the Dome of the Queen Mary Court. The print was originally published in Captain Marryat's novel *Poor Jack* (1840). (© National Maritime Museum, Greenwich, London)
Plate 2	Greenwich pensioner (etching and aquatint, hand-coloured, early 19th century) (© National Maritime Museum, Greenwich, London)
Plate 3	Greenwich pensioners (soft-ground etching with aquatint, hand-coloured, 1808) (© National Maritime Museum, Greenwich, London)
Plate 4	Greenwich pensioner (hand-coloured lithograph, 1828) (© National Maritime Museum, Greenwich, London)
Plate 5	'Ah, the Navy is not what it was!'- Greenwich pensioners (hand-coloured lithograph, 1828) (© National Maritime Museum, Greenwich, London)
Plate 6	A Greenwich Pensioner, wearing a cocked hat and apparently with Hospital Boatswain's lace on his cuff (aquatint, hand-coloured and partly glazed with gum-arabic, published 1 December 1834) (© National Maritime Museum, Greenwich, London)
Plate 7	'The Way of the World'- Two battered Greenwich Pensioners, one missing all four limbs, the other an arm and a leg, in conversation outside a building marked 'The Helpless Ward' of the Hospital Infirmary. The inscription reads: ' Ah! Messmate, you are a happy Fish to what I am, you have only got an Arm and a Leg lopp'd off. Whilst I hav'n't a Limb left about me but what's of Timber, with one Eye out and my Nose damaged.'- 'Go it Joe, grumble, grumble. You are like the rest of th' World. Never contented.' (hand-coloured lithograph, 1834) (© National Maritime Museum, Greenwich, London)
Plate 8	John Adams, alias John Wilkinson, Greenwich Pensioner, boatswain's mate of the *Agamemnon* while commanded by Nelson 8 Apr 1793-16 Sep 1798 (watercolour, Frederick Cruikshank, June 1840) (© National Maritime Museum, Greenwich, London)
Plate 9	Two pensioners, one minus a leg, the other minus an arm, sitting drinking and smoking with a woman standing behind them. The Royal Hospital, Greenwich is in the distance (mezzotint, date unknown) (© National Maritime Museum, Greenwich, London)
Plate 10	Discharge Paper of Marine Corporal George Frederick Eller, who had his leg amputated at the Battle of the Nile (1798) (TNA ADM 73-8)
Plate 11	'A Milling Match between Decks'- The lower deck of a man-of-war in port. Note the two black sailors, the fistfight and the many prostitutes on board (coloured etching) (© National Maritime Museum, Greenwich, London)
Plate 12	The dining hall of the Royal Hospital Greenwich (hand-coloured lithograph, mid 19th century) (© National Maritime Museum, Greenwich, London)
Plate 13	Areas 1: General view of excavation looking south-east
Plate 14	Areas 1 and 2: Excavation of graves
Plate 15	Grave 3127: double interment, skeletons 3211 and 3162. The upper pair of two pairs of skeletons within a single grave cut
Plate 16	Skeleton 3103: Poorly reduced but well healed nasal fracture
Plate 17	Skeleton 3164: Poorly reduced fracture of the tibial shaft with considerable overlap and shortening of the element
Plate 18	Skeleton 3229: Bilateral fractures and secondary osteomyelitis of the femoral shafts (possibly compound fractures)
Plate 19	Skeleton 3229: Radiograph showing overlap of the fractured bone and associated osteomyelitis and callus formation. Arrow indicates the sinus for draining of infected material from marrow cavity
Plate 20	Skeleton 3202: Marked exostosis formation on the right femoral shaft secondary to soft tissue injury
Plate 21	Skeleton 3045: Amputation and secondary osteomyelitis of the right femur
Plate 22	Skeleton 3098: Pott's disease (tuberculosis of the spine). Note the crush fractures and the collapse of the vertebrae

Plate 23	Skeleton 3194: Hypervascularity and periostitis on the right pelvis - possibly pulmonary hypertrophic osteoarthropathy
Plate 24	Skeleton 3194: Active periostitis on the proximal shaft of the right femur. Arrow indicates areas of reactive new bone- possible pulmonary hypertrophic osteoarthropathy
Plate 25	Skeleton 6056: periostitis and possible osteitis of the left femur and tibia
Plate 26	Skeleton 3061: Below knee amputation of the right tibia and fibula
Plate 27	Skeleton 3061: Radiograph showing demineralisation of the amputated stump from lack of use
Plate 28	Grave 3118: Skeleton 3119 with post-mortem craniotomy
Plate 29	Grave 6084: Burial 6146: The clear coffin stain and nails indicated a single break coffin. One of a pair of coffined burials in grave 6084
Plate 30	Grave 6069: Burial 6098: Remnants of simple wooden coffin still overlying the chest and arm regions. 6098 is the upper burial of two in grave 6069

List of Tables

Table 1	Devonport Buildings- Phases of archaeological work	1
Table 2	Age-at-death categories used in the osteological analysis	32
Table 3	Skeletal completeness (N = 107)	33
Table 4	Bone preservation (N = 107)	34
Table 5	Summary of age and sex distribution in the total assemblage (N =107)	34
Table 6	Distribution of male stature in the Greenwich assemblage (N = 88)	36
Table 7	Stature estimates from seven contemporary assemblages in England	37
Table 8	Crude prevalence (CPR) of pathology in the adult assemblage (N = 105)	39
Table 9	True prevalence of fractures by element (N = 105)	41
Table 10	Summary of the prevalence of elements showing periostitis (N = 105)	46
Table 11	Summary of skeletons with periostitis on multiple elements (n = 54); L - left; R- right; numbers refer to the number of elements involved.	48–49
Table 12	Prevalence of extra-spinal osteoarthritis by joint in adults (N = 105)	53
Table 13	Pathology present in 12 adult males displaying bony modification of the sphenoid consistent with scurvy (n = 12)	58
Table 14	Summary of skeletons with rickets or possible rickets (n = 10)	59
Table 15	Summary of congenital anomalies (n = 11)	60
Table 16	Dental caries prevalence	64
Table 17	Comparison of dental pathology rates per tooth or socket in seven contemporary English assemblages	65
Table 18	Quantities of pottery in each feature type	143
Table 19	Quantities of ware types present	144
Table 20	Maximum vessel count by ware type and vessel	144
Table 21	Summary of clay pipe fragments	146–147
Table 22	Number of bones according to feature type and species	151

Summary

Between July 1999 and September 2001, Oxford Archaeology (OA) undertook detailed archaeological works at Devonport Buildings, King William Walk, Greenwich, London, on behalf of Mount Anvil. These works were in advance of redevelopment, which comprised a new Conference Facility, Student Accommodation and an electricity sub-station. The proposed redevelopment lay within an area formerly used as the ratings' burial ground of the Royal Hospital Greenwich and originally had contained the remains of an estimated 20,000 retired seamen and marines of the Royal Navy, interred between 1749 and 1856. Most Greenwich pensioners were veterans of Britain's wars with the Dutch, the Americans, the Spanish, the French Republic and Napoleon. This report includes the results of the desk-based assessment, archaeological evaluation, watching briefs and excavation phases of the project.

A total of 107 skeletons were recovered from 55 graves. As may be expected, the majority were older adult males, but a small number of women and adolescents were also present. The assemblage was remarkable for the high prevalence of a wide range of pathological conditions, which included numerous fractures, rickets, tuberculosis, syphilis, scurvy, cancer and a range of non-specific infections. Amputations and craniotomies were also identified. These clearly illustrate the rigours of life in the Royal Navy at this time, and reflect the advance age of the assemblage.

Evidence for wooden coffins and shrouds was recovered from many graves, the former represented by iron coffin fittings and nails. Unfortunately, due to severe iron corrosion, no individuals could be identified from breastplate inscriptions. Small quantities of pottery, ceramic building material, animal bone, glass and clay pipe were recovered from the grave fills but appeared to be residual. In addition to graves, a small number of other features were excavated, including the foundations of a number of brick-built structures, pits and ditches. Most post-dated the use of the cemetery.

Although it was not possible to identify individuals, a wide range of documentary sources on the retired seamen and marines from the Royal Hospital Greenwich were consulted. This has greatly aided in the interpretation of the assemblage.

From the time of the Napoleonic Wars, interest in Nelson and the Royal Navy has remained intense, and military historians have devoted considerable attention to battle tactics, the structure of the ships of the line, and biographical details of Nelson and other commanders. Interest in the social context of the Royal Navy, in particular the daily life of the ratings or common seamen and marines, is relatively recent and is historical in approach. The skeletal sample of the Greenwich pensioners is unique in being the only large assemblage of Royal Navy veterans to undergo systematic osteological analysis. Coupled with the sheer range of pathological conditions, its uniqueness makes this specialist assemblage one of considerable osteological importance, and one that warrants more research in the future.

Acknowledgements

The fieldwork was project managed by David Wilkinson of OA and supervised by Richard Hewitt, Andrew Norton and Annsofie Witkin, also of OA. The project was monitored by Ken Whittaker initially and latterly by Mark Stevenson of the Greater London Archaeological Advisory Service. The post-excavation programme was managed by Angela Boyle and latterly, by Louise Loe. Support was provided by Leigh Allen (finds management) and Nichola Scott (archives management). Osteological analysis was undertaken by Annsofie Witkin. Ceridwen Boston recorded the coffin fittings. Historical research was undertaken by Lorraine Lindsay-Gale, Ceridwen Boston and Jon Chandler. Illustrations were produced by Georgina Slater, Amy Hemingway and Markus Dylewski. Specialists contributing to the report included Brian Dean, Nicholas Marquez-Grant, Leigh Allen, Duncan H Brown and Bethan Charles. Ceridwen Boston compiled the report.

Our thanks goes to the National Maritime Museum, Greenwich, for giving access to their archive of prints of the Hospital and the Greenwich pensioners, and to Geraldine Charles, archivist of the National Maritime Museum for providing maps of Greenwich dated 1869 and 1884. Thanks are also due to the National Archives for permission to reproduce the discharge certificate of Corporal George Frederick Eller, Royal Marines. We are also grateful for the input of Pieter van der Merwe of the National Maritime Museum, Roy and Lesley Adkins, Hedley Swain, Bill White and Roy Stephenson of the Museum of London, and Jane Sidell, Archaeological Scientific Advisor of English Heritage.

The fieldwork and report was undertaken on behalf of Mount Anvil, acting for the University of Greenwich, to whom we are particularly grateful for funding this valuable project. Particular thanks go to Ray Scoins and Julia Tapp, both of Mount Anvil, for their assistance during the fieldwork and subsequent post-excavation phases respectively. The report was copy edited by Ian Scott of Oxford Archaeology.

Thanks are due also to Greenwich Hospital, the Navy's oldest charity, which still operates today providing charitable support and education to serving and retired personnel of the Royal Navy and Royal Marines and their dependants.

Chapter 1: Introduction

PROJECT BACKGROUND

Oxford Archaeology (OA) was commissioned by Mount Anvil, on behalf of the University of Greenwich, to prepare a desk-based assessment and undertake detailed archaeological fieldwork at Devonport Buildings, King William Walk, Greenwich, London, in advance of the construction of a conference facility, student accommodation and an electricity substation (OAU 1995; OA 1999a; OA 1999b; OA 1999c). The development was sited within the precincts of the 18th- to 19th-century burial ground of the Royal Hospital Greenwich (Fig. 1; see also Fig. 2), and included the demolition of the existing southern wing of the Devonport Building (built in 1882). The archaeological works included an evaluation, excavations and watching briefs, which were carried out between July 1999 and September 2001.

Archaeological investigations were undertaken in a number of phases, which are listed in Table 1. The results of each phase of works are discussed within this document.

The archaeological work was carried out in accordance with a number of Written Schemes of Investigation (WSIs) prepared by OA and approved by English Heritage's Greater London Archaeological Advisory Service (GLAAS). The watching brief on engineering test pits undertaken in July 1999 formed the first stage of archaeological assessment of the proposed development area. This was followed by a desk-based assessment, which in turn was followed by further phases of archaeological investigation, which comprised evaluation, excavations and watching briefs. The locations of all areas of archaeological intervention are shown in Figure 2.

Geology and location

The development area is located in the south-western corner of the Royal Hospital at Greenwich, London, beside the Devonport Buildings (NGR TQ 3850 7760) (Fig. 1) and sited on Quaternary Floodplain Gravel (BGS 1981, Sheet 271).

The two proposed buildings cover an area of $c.$ 580 m^2 bounded by King William Walk to the south-west, by the National Maritime Museum to the east, by Romney Road to the north-west and by Greenwich Park to the south-east (Fig. 1). The River Thames lies approximately 350 m to the north of the site. The Royal Naval College lies opposite the Hospital on the northern side of Romney Road. The site of the smaller proposed building (the student accommodation) was occupied by a part of the Devonport Buildings, which subsequently was demolished. The site of the conference facility had been used as tennis courts until redevelopment. An upstanding stone memorial commemorating the naval pensioners buried within the cemetery is located in a grassed area to the south of the proposed conference facility.

ARCHAEOLOGICAL AND HISTORICAL BACKGROUND

Introduction

No archaeological investigations had been carried out within the proposed development area prior to the work undertaken by OA. The following background information relating to the site is derived from the desk-based assessment (OA 1999), which summarises the known archaeological discoveries within a study area measuring 1.5 km square centred on the proposed development. The study area has in the past seen several archaeological investigations, including watching briefs, evaluation trenches, open-area excavations and surveys.

Prehistoric period

Numerous artefacts, including Mesolithic and Neolithic worked flints and Bronze Age weapons, have been retrieved from the southern foreshore of the River Thames beside the Royal Hospital in the latter half of the 20th century. These discoveries indicate the presence of prehistoric activity within the general area of the development.

Greenwich Park, $c.$550 m to the south-east of the proposed development, contains a Bronze Age barrow cemetery comprising approximately 50 round barrows. A geophysical and earthwork survey carried out by the Royal Commission on the Historical Monuments of England (RCHME) in 1993-4 identified 31 barrows but was unable to determine the full extent of the cemetery.

Table 1 Devonport Buildings - phases of archaeological work.

Type of archaeological work	Date
Watching brief – Engineering test pits	July 1999
Desk based assessment	October 1999
Evaluation	November 1999
Watching brief - Student Accommodation	January-March 2000
Excavation of electricity sub-station	January 2000
Excavation of Areas 1 and 2	June-September 2001

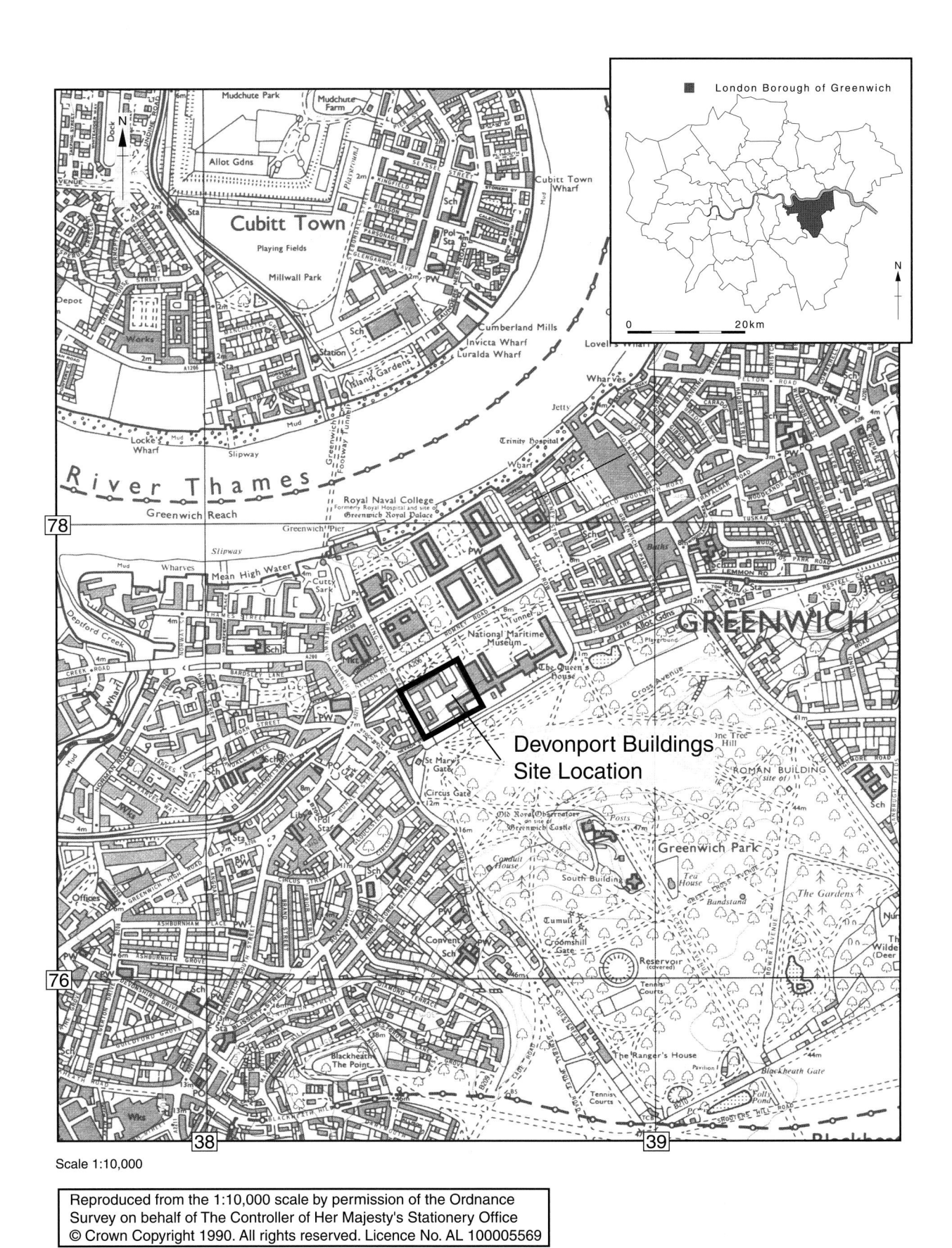

Figure 1 Site location.

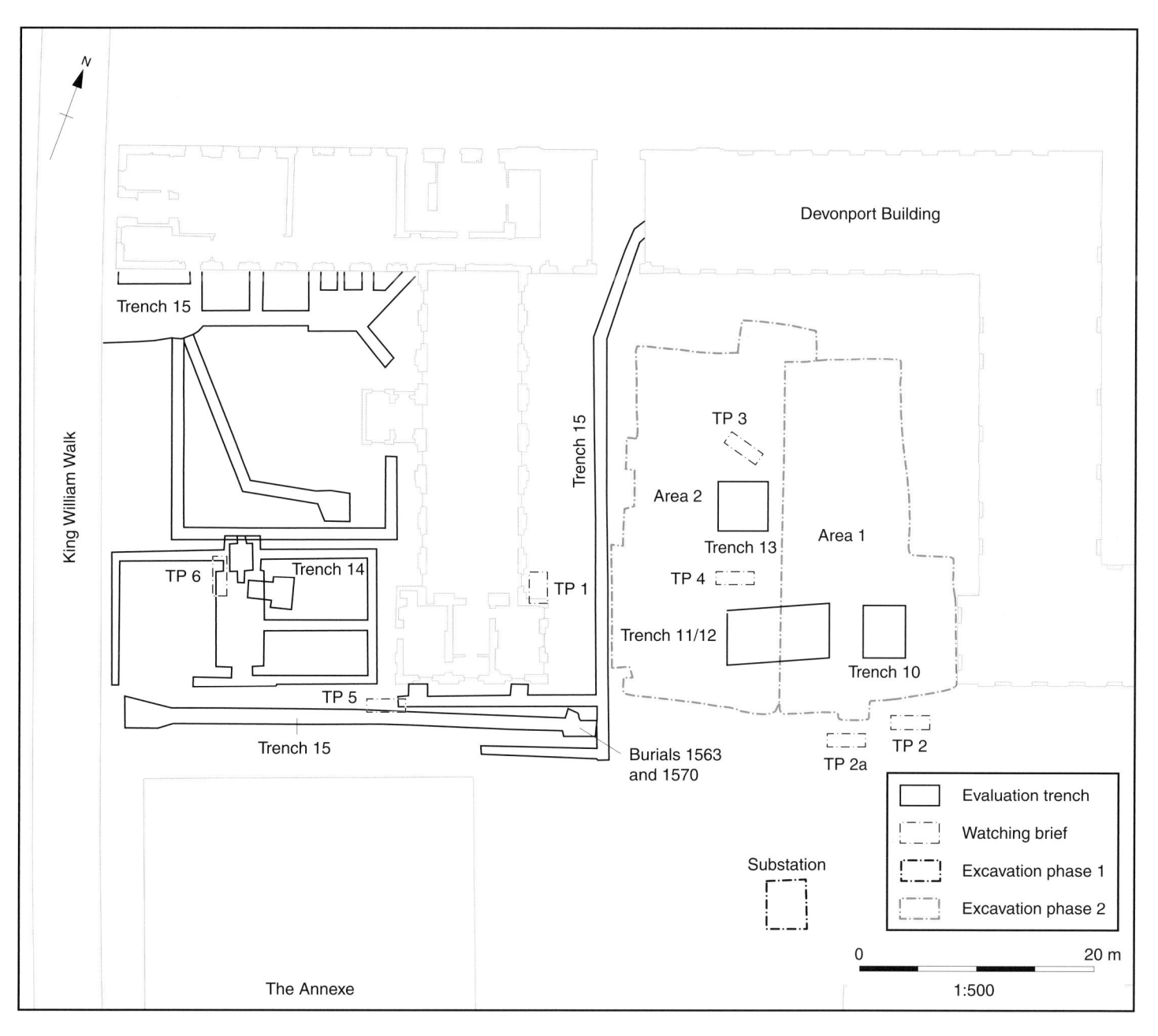

Figure 2 Location of excavation, evaluation and watching brief trenches.

Roman period

In the grounds of the Royal Naval College, Roman remains were found under the hospital before 1928, but no further information is provided in the sources consulted and the exact location of the site is not known. In a nearby residential property *c.* 450 m north-east of the development site, in the immediate vicinity of the college, foundations of a Roman building were found 'some years ago' (before 1990). Three sherds of Roman pottery were found in the latter half of the 19th century *c.* 150 m to the south-west of the development.

In 1902, a possible Romano-British temple was discovered within Greenwich Park, *c.* 750 m south-east of the development. Over 400 Roman coins were found. There were further excavations in 1978-79 when the remains of an earlier Roman rectangular building (possibly a villa) were revealed beneath the temple. The earlier building, dating to *c.* AD 100, had been destroyed by fire and the temple built on the site soon afterwards. Geophysical survey, undertaken as part of the RCHME's park survey in 1993, failed to produce any additional evidence for the nature and extent of the site.

Isolated Roman finds in the vicinity discovered at various times over the last hundred years, include a bronze bowl and a coffin from within Greenwich Park, *c.* 450 m to the south-east of the development site, and a Roman helmet and bronze box possibly of Roman date, which were found on the Thames foreshore *c.* 450 m to the north of the site. These sites and finds indicate clear evidence of Roman activity in the area around the development site.

Early medieval period (to AD 1066)

In 1860, four inhumation burials with grave goods were found at the 'Old Tilt Yard', *c.* 250 m to the north-east of the area of development. One of the graves was probably of 7th-century date. A further skeleton, possibly Saxon in date, was found *c.* 100 m to the east of these burials in 1979. The burials indicate the presence of an Anglo-Saxon cemetery, the size and extent of which is unknown.

Excavations *c.* 600 m to the south-east conducted by Hearne in 1714 and by Douglas in 1784, revealed early medieval inhumation burials, some in coffins and buried with grave goods. The distance between these burials and the burials within the 'Old Tilt Yard' would suggest that these finds were not parts of the same cemetery but represent two separate burial grounds.

The first documentary mention of Greenwich was in AD 964, when Elstrudis, daughter of King Alfred the Great, donated considerable property in Greenwich to the Abbey at Ghent. The place-name Greenwich - 'Grenavic' - is derived from the Anglo-Saxon for 'green port'. The Domesday Book lists arable land, pasture, woodland and four mills attached to the manor, which was held by the Bishop of Lisieux of Bishop Odo of Bayeux.

Later medieval period (AD 1066–1550)

In 1268 the manor of Greenwich was held by the Abbot of Ghent. Documentary sources suggest that the Abbot's land holding was a monastic grange. Excavation in 1970-1 within the Grand Square *c.* 300 m north-east of the site revealed the remains of a rectangular building, which may have formed part of the grange. This 14th-century building probably had two floors and was a part chalk/limestone and part-timber structure. The Abbot of Ghent's lands at Greenwich returned to Royal hands in 1414 when King Henry V suppressed Alien Priories during the war with France.

The Duke of Gloucester built Greenwich Palace on the site of the earlier manor between 1433 and 1439. He also constructed a castle to the south, on the site of the present Royal Observatory, and enclosed the surrounding deer park. The Royal Palace comprised two courts and a hedged garden. It was enlarged and rebuilt in the reigns of Henry VII and Henry VIII (Colvin 1982, 97) and was one of the main royal palaces during the 16th century. A Franciscan friary was established on land beside the palace in 1485. It is believed that remains of the friary survive beneath the King's House.

Post-medieval period (AD 1550 +)

The area of development lies outside the Tudor palace complex which is located *c.* 300 m to the east and north-east. In the 17th century, the Tudor palace was demolished to make way for a new palace. Based on the designs of John Webb, the building of the new royal palace at Greenwich (the King's House) was commissioned after 1661, but due to lack of funds the palace was never completed. In 1692 Christopher Wren was commissioned to convert the unfinished building into a naval hospital.

The need for a hospital and retirement home for disabled and aged seamen of the Royal Navy had long been recognised by the Admiralty. In the 1666, Samuel Pepys wrote of a proposal to build such an establishment at Chatham (Latham 2000, 134). This plan was never realised, and it was some three decades before a hospital was founded at Greenwich on land adjacent to the existing Royal Palace, and east of the borough of Greenwich itself. The Royal Hospital was established by a Royal Charter dated 1694. The hospital took in its first pensioners in 1705.

Originally founded for 100 seamen, demand was such that between 1811 and 1814 the accommodation was enlarged and the maximum number of 'inpensioners' was fixed at 2,710 (Lewis 1960, 415). The hospital was to become one of the grandest, largest and best loved institutions of its time, and to every seamen of Nelson's day, the word 'hospital' meant first and foremost, one thing- the Royal Hospital at Greenwich (ibid., 414) (Plate 1).

PROJECT AIMS

Archaeological desk-based assessment, October 1999

The aims of the desk based assessment were as follows:

- To clarify the extent of the Royal Hospital Burial grounds (the site does not fall within an extension of St Alphege's Church cemetery as previously believed);
- Determine the extent of the disturbance by modern activity including construction of the railway tunnel *c.* 50 m to the north in the 1870s, and the construction of the Devonport Buildings (the Dreadnought Hospital Nurses Home) immediately north of the proposed sites in 1926-9
- Clarify the history and location of earlier buildings in the area of the proposed development site and its immediate vicinity in particular known archaeology associated with the early medieval manor and the later medieval palace.

The desk based assessment concluded that the proposed development site had a high potential to contain multi-period remains dating from the prehistoric to post-medieval periods, although no such sites or finds were located during the OA watching brief of geo-technical test pits in July 1999. The site is located on one of the few areas of gravelly ground beside the river's edge, which would have provided well-drained land conducive to early settlement. The study area contains evidence of activity dating from the prehistoric to post-medieval periods and the location and nature of these finds is discussed above.

It was further concluded that any archaeological deposits in the area and pre-dating the burial ground were likely to have been truncated by post-medieval grave digging. The extent of the damage to archaeological deposits was uncertain and it was thought possible that archaeological features such as the bottoms of ditches cut into the natural ground might have survived. It was possible therefore that the construction of the foundations for the proposed buildings might have an impact on surviving archaeological deposits.

Archaeological evaluation, November 1999

The aims of the evaluation were as follows:

1. To establish the presence or absence of archaeological remains within the development area and to determine the extent, condition, nature, character, quality, date and depth below ground surface of any archaeological remains.
2. To establish the ecofactual and environmental potential of any archaeological features and deposits.
3. To define the research potential, prioritise importance, and to determine corresponding minimum levels of data collection required to explore the demographic structure of the cemetery population; burial rite and undertaking practices; skeletal palaeopathology; topographic structure and development of the cemetery.
4. If significant archaeological remains are discovered, to determine what further mitigation measures may be required and to agree these with Mount Anvil, the local planning authority and English Heritage.
5. To make available the results of the investigation, in the form of a written report.

Archaeological watching briefs on the sites of the proposed student accommodation, conference facility, and on the site of the electricity substation, January–March 2000

The aims of the watching briefs were as follows:

1. To establish the presence or absence of archaeological remains within the area of the proposed substation and to determine the extent, condition, nature, character, quality, date, depth below ground surface and depth of any archaeological remains present within the sites of both the proposed student accommodation and the substation.
2. To establish the ecofactual and environmental potential of archaeological deposits and features within the area of the proposed substation.
3. To define the research potential, prioritize importance, and to determine corresponding minimum levels of data collection required to explore the demographic structure of the cemetery population; burial rites and undertaking practices; skeletal palaeopathology; topographic structure and development of the cemetery.
4. To make available the results of the investigation.
5. To recover evidence of pre-cemetery activities and to consider these in the context of the urban development of Greenwich.

Archaeological excavation Areas 1 and 2, June–September 2001

The aims of the preceding phases of archaeological investigation were refined in advance of the excavation. The specific excavation aims are detailed below:

1. To collect data, which will contribute to the understanding of the history and development of funeral trends.
2. To collect data which will contribute to the understanding of the demography of the small percentage of the population of the graveyard that is being disturbed.
3. To establish the stratigraphic sequence of burials.
4. To provide dating evidence for the surviving burials.
5. To recover evidence of burial rites and undertaking practices.
6. To determine the character and date range of the burials.
7. To recover evidence for the management of the graveyard through time.
8. To recover evidence of coffins and coffin furniture.
9. To recover evidence for the treatment of the dead.
10. To identify individuals with biographical information from coffin plates.

FIELDWORK METHODOLOGY

Introduction

The archaeological work at the Royal Hospital Greenwich involved a watching brief on test pits, an archaeological evaluation, a watching brief and excavation on the sites of the electricity substation and student accommodation, and excavation of Areas 1 and 2 within the footprint of the proposed conference facility. The site description below summarises the findings in these phases, but concentrates on the areas where the skeletons were exhumed. A description of each excavated grave is presented as Appendix 2.

Site procedures were in accordance with the requirements of the *OA Field Manual* (Wilkinson 1992), and the Greater London Archaeology Advisory Service's Guidance Paper No. 3, *Standards and Practices in Archaeological Fieldwork in London*. Detailed recording of burial evidence was as specified in the *OA Field Manual* (Wilkinson 1992), the *MoLAS Archaeological Site Manual*, Section 3.5 'Recording and excavation of skeletons and coffins: Introduction', and in IFA Technical Paper No. 13, *Excavation and post-excavation treatment of cremated and inhumed human remains* (McKinley and Roberts 1993).

Archaeological watching brief, July 1999
(Fig. 2, TP1-2, 2a-6)

Seven engineering test pits were excavated using a mechanical excavator fitted with a toothed bucket.

The trenches were excavated to a common width of 1.0 m but varied in length from 2.0-3.4 m. Depth of excavation was dependent on the revealed deposits and the level of the natural sand/gravel. Their depth precluded any manual cleaning or close visual examination of revealed deposits. Within these constraints, it was possible to produce reasonably accurate records of the stratigraphy. Artefacts were recorded but not retained. The excavation method and the ground conditions meant that it was extremely difficult to distinguish between hitherto undisturbed graves, and scatters of redeposited human bone.

Archaeological evaluation November 1999 (Fig. 2, Trenches 10-14)

Four trenches (Trenches 10-13) measuring 2.5 m by 2 m were located within the footprint of the proposed conference facility and a single trench (Trench 14) of similar dimensions was located within the footprint of the proposed student accommodation buildings. The overburden was removed by mechanical excavator down to the top of archaeological deposits, burials or natural, whichever was the highest. All further investigation was by hand. The skeletons were exposed, cleaned, assessed, planned and photographed, but not lifted.

Archaeological watching briefs on the sites of the proposed student accommodation, conference facility, and on the site of the electricity substation, January-March 2000 (Fig. 2, Trench 15 & Substation)

An archaeological watching brief (Trench 15) was carried out in the area of the proposed student accommodation (*c*. 22 m x 10 m) and associated services and in the area of the proposed electrical substation close to the Maritime Museum.

The area of the proposed substation had not been accessible at the time of the 1999 evaluation as it was then located beneath a bicycle shed. The trench measured 3.36 m x 4.05 m with deep foundations (see Fig. 8). It was anticipated that some skeletons would have to be excavated and removed, but that those burials not suffering direct impact from the new construction would be left *in situ*. As with previous phases, the location of grave groups and surface features (such as coffin wood and human remains) would be planned.

Archaeological excavation Areas 1 and 2, June–September 2001 (Fig. 2, Areas 1 & 2)

Areas 1 and 2 lay within the footprint of the proposed conference facility. Excavation of archaeological features (principally graves) was carried out in designated areas where piling would impact on the archaeological deposits. A total of 29 pile locations of three different sizes (single, double and triple) were investigated (trenches 3000-3015 in Area 1, and trenches 6000-6012 in Area 2). Their locations are shown on Figures 11 and 12. The ground level was reduced until the grave cuts were visible. The locations of the pile trenches were surveyed using an EDM, and marked on the ground.

Any burials lying within or partly within the pile excavation areas were subjected to full excavation. All graves cutting or cut by the grave within the piling trench were also fully excavated. Samples for stomach contents were taken from approximately 25% of the burials. Wooden coffins and any associated fittings, including nails, were recorded on a proforma coffin recording sheet. All surviving coffin fittings were recorded in detail where possible by reference to the published corpus of material from Christ Church, Spitalfields (Reeve and Adams 1998) as well as the unpublished catalogue of material from St Nicholas, Sevenoaks, Kent (Boyle 1995).

All inhumation burials were assigned group numbers. These are shown on the plans (Figs 11-12). Each individual context (eg. grave cut, fill, skeleton and coffin) within the burial group was assigned a unique number from a continuous running sequence. Detailed works, comprising 100% excavation, and geo-referenced photography were undertaken for all inhumation burials. All inhumations were returned to the premises of Oxford Archaeology for processing and assessment.

Bulk soil samples were taken from all graves for the recovery of charred plant remains, human and animal bone and small artefacts.

All discrete non-burial features were excavated and planned at a scale of 1:10 or 1:20 as appropriate. Generally, features were fully excavated, although those of low archaeological significance were half-sectioned. Standard black and white and colour photographs of each feature were taken.

Chapter 2: The Burial Ground and Greenwich Pensioners

THE BURIAL GROUND

The earliest map of the development area is *A Survey of the King's Lordship or Manor of East Greenwich*, dated 1695 (OA 1999b, fig. 3). The development area is located in the south-western corner of the then newly-founded Royal Hospital, within a square plot of open land surrounded by four roads (Romney Road which bounds the northern edge was then called Turpin Lane). Its use as a burial ground dates from the mid 18th century. It was not an extension of St Alphege's church cemetery as was previously believed (OA 1999a, 1).

The architect Nicholas Hawksmoor acquired the plot of land for the hospital, and in 1742, at the end of a long lease, it returned to the full possession of the Royal Hospital and opened as the Royal Hospital Burial Ground. The first pensioner, a John Meriton, was buried there in 1749. A grander vault, the Mausoleum, was made ready for officers by the following year (Newell 1984).

The new burial ground, covering three and a half acres lay between Romney Road and the Park on part of 'Goddard's Ground', and provided a much needed extension to the original hospital cemetery at Maze Hill, *c.* 600 m to the east. The Maze Hill cemetery was by then full (Newell 1984, 73). Re-use of the Maze Hill burial ground had involved a considerable number of exhumations and reburials and required a radical change in the previous burial method. 'The Board considered the present practice of burying 3½ feet [0.91 m] deep and in a very irregular manner' [to be unsatisfactory]. 'In future, [graves were to be dug] 8 feet deep [2.46 m] and in a regular orderly manner.' (loc.cit.). The re-use of the Maze Hill cemetery had to be abandoned following a public outcry. In 1747 it was described by locals as a 'very great nuisance and desired that it should be shut up' (quoted by Newell 1984, 73). The Board's alternative request to extend the hospital cemetery into Greenwich Park was also refused. The new burial practice briefly adopted at Maze Hill prior to its closure does not appear to have been implemented in the new Royal Hospital burial ground on Romney Road.

Rocque's Map of Greenwich (1744) is large-scale and shows a number of buildings (OA 1999b, fig.4). Three rectangular buildings are shown to the east of King Street (now King William Street) on the central/west side of the square plot of ground. It would appear that a rectangular building on the site of the proposed student accommodation block is located near to or on the site of one of the buildings shown on Rocque's map. Archaeological investigation did not reveal any evidence for this building.

On the 1778 Map of the Hundred of Blackheath (Fig. 3) buildings are shown but are only representational. Although there is no indication of a burial ground, the scale of the map is such that it is unlikely that 'burial ground' would be marked. A rectangular building is shown on or near the site of the proposed student accommodation and is probably the same as the building shown on Rocque's Map of 1744.

The first plan of the area that explicitly marks out the development area as a burial ground dates to *c.* 1780. A Plan of the [Royal Hospital] Burial Ground (Fig. 4) shows its exact extent bounded by four roads: King Street (now King William Street); Romney's Road (now Romney Road); Friars Road (a road that once ran along the north-eastern side of the cemetery and mausoleum) and an unnamed road (no longer extant) bordering Greenwich Park. In the middle of the burial ground is a rectangular building marked 'The School', and a square building adjoining marked 'School Master's House', both of which are presumably surrounded by graves. These buildings may be those shown on the maps of 1744 and 1778.

In 1777–1783, a hospital school infirmary was built within the precinct of the Royal Hospital burial ground, possibly following the demolition of the building(s) shown on maps of 1744, 1778 and *c.* 1780. The school infirmary survives as a Grade II Listed Building and is incorporated as a rear wing of the Devonport Buildings (built in 1926-9). The 1999 Trenches 14 and 15 lie immediately west of this building. Construction of the infirmary also involved tree planting, levelling and grassing. At the time the new Royal Hospital burial ground was described as being in 'a very rude and disorderly state due to the quantities of rubbish thrown there during the building of the School Infirmary' (Newell 1984, 100). It is noteworthy that the sandy silt subsoil, in which burials were discovered during the OA watching brief in July 1999, contained frequent brick, tile and mortar fragments, which would appear to support the reference to this dumped material. Residents complained of '. . . an unpleasing disagreeable sight, burials being very frequent and the Graves from necessity being larger and kept open longer than is usually practised' (loc. cit.). Presumably this was for the purpose of multiple interments, a number of which have been excavated (see Chapter 5 and Appendix 2 below).

A plan of the parish of St Alphege, Greenwich (*c.* 1824) shows the infirmary building with 'Hospital Burial Ground' written beside it. There are no other buildings within the burial ground. The map shows

Figure 3   Map of the Hundred of Blackheath (1778). (Reproduced courtesy of the Greenwich Heritage Centre).

St Mary's church just south of the burial ground. The church, which was demolished in 1936, was a 'daughter' church to St Alphege to the east and is not known to have had a separate cemetery.

In just over a century the Hospital burial ground was full, and was closed in 1857. Daniel Drewett (aged 60 years) was the last pensioner to be buried there. A poem by George Hewens (1857) commemorates the closure of the burial ground, and is reproduced here. A new cemetery was opened well to the east of the hospital at East Greenwich Mount Pleasaunce.

Figure 4   Plan of the (Royal Hospital) Burial Ground, c. 1780.

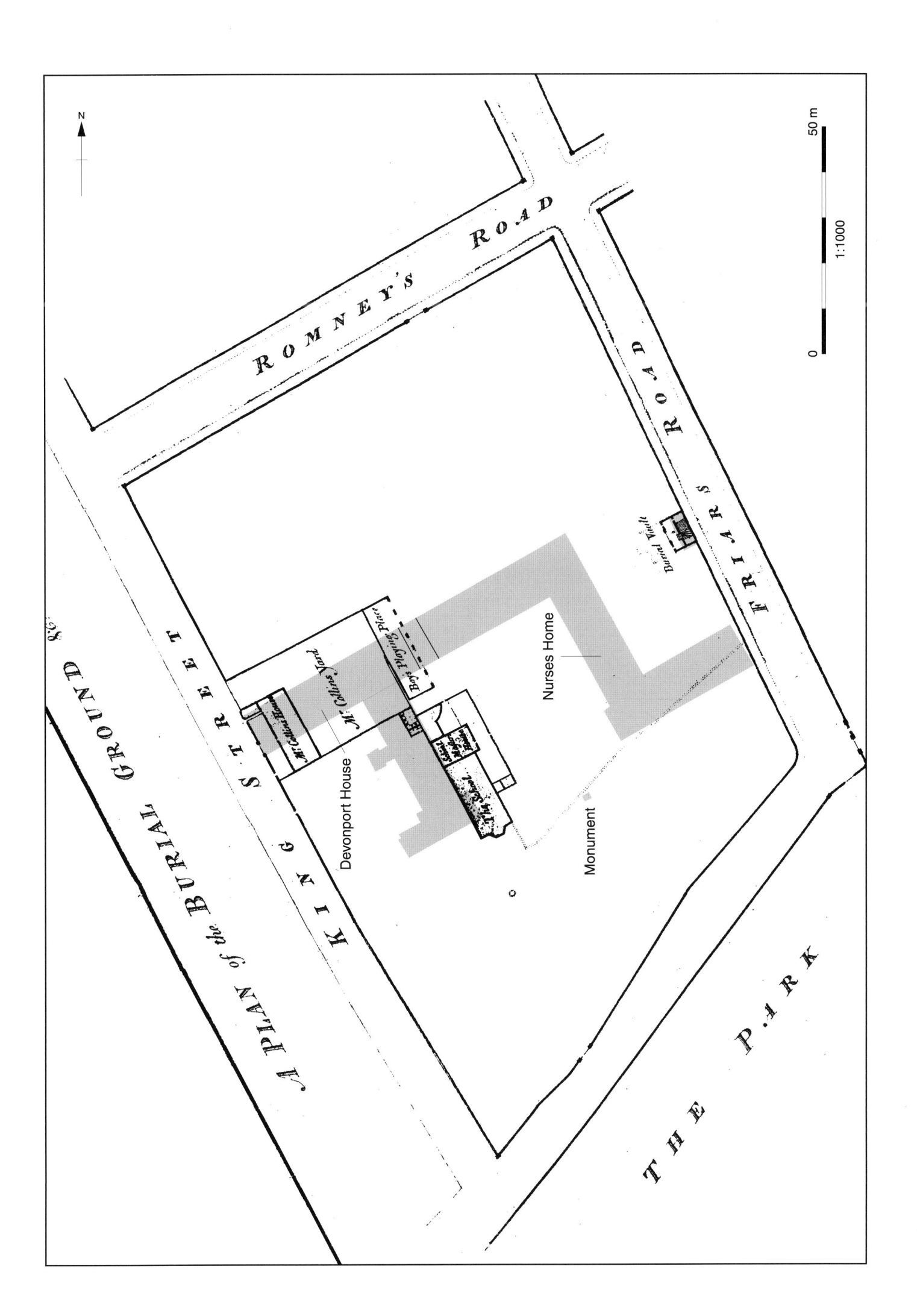

A PLAN of the BURIAL GROUND &c.

ROMNEY'S ROAD

KING STREET

FRIARS ROAD

THE PARK

Mr Collins House
Mr Collins Yard
Devonport House
Boys Playing Place
Nurses Home
Monument
Burial Vault

N

50 m

1:1000

0

> **OF CLOSING THE CEMETERY OF GREENWICH HOSPITAL (ROMNEY ROAD)**
>
> *Monday, August 31st, 1857*
>
> *Daniel Drewett, aged 60.-Finis.*
> *'Per Mare. Per Terram'*
> *'Tis finished! Now his corse must close the scene,*
> *And, undisturbed, the grass shall flourish green;*
> *No more a friend deplored we here may trace,*
> *We seek their exit in a distant place;*
> *On the dread locale here the gates we close,*
> *And leave their brethren to their last repose.*
> *Could one historic candidate be found*
> *From Nature's page to cull their work around,*
> *What golden legend would the spot then unfold!*
> *What tales of heroism might be told!*
> *How many a hoary veteran here laid low,*
> *What patriotic furor once could glow.-*
> *The humble shipmate here, the chieftain great,*
> *Their dust commingled in a common fate;*
> *All animation once in England's cause,*
> *And bade the inveterate foe respect her laws;*
> *They fought, they bled, and privations groan,*
> *And braved the storm for country and their home.*
> *Ah! Many a gallant head, reclined in death,*
> *With animation fraught, with kindled breath,*
> *To wonder-stricken, eager, motley, few,*
> *Some ancient battle strife would oft renew;*
> *And youthful aspirants, with ardour beam,*
> *Drink in his eloquence, and court the stream,*
> *And so, with watchful ear, they list' and learn*
> *How they, time hence, might laurels earn;*
> *And thus, full many a votary of fame*
> *Have passed away and left behind A NAME!*
> *In peace they rest, and on this bourne no more*
> *Will they be harrass'd by the clangs of war!*
> *Yet unborn ages shall their names revere*
> *And say "England's patriots lie buried here!"*
>
> **GEORGE HEWENS.**

The Ordnance Survey (OS) 1st Edition 25inch map of 1865 is the earliest detailed map of the area of development (Fig. 5). The map shows the area marked as the 'Grave Yard' as a landscaped area with trees, footpaths and a monument. Two further maps of Greenwich dated 1869 and 1884 show the words 'burial ground' across the whole area beside the Infirmary.

The burial ground is estimated to have contained the burials of 20,000 Royal Navy pensioners- a mixture of retired seamen and marines (Newel 1984, 217). The remains of many were disturbed by later development. In the 1870s, a tunnel for the London-Greenwich railway was cut east-west across the northern half of the Royal Hospital Burial Ground *c.* 50 m north of the area of the development. It necessitated the exhumation of an estimated 1,400 bodies. In 1925 statutory consent was given for the exhumation of bodies prior to the construction of the Devonport Nurses Home for the Dreadnought Hospital. Over 4,000 bodies were removed and reburied in the Mount Pleasaunce burial ground (Newell 1984, 217). In 1991, developments undertaken by the National Maritime Museum to the south of the west wing of the Queen's House revealed undated burials. No further details are known.

Today there are no upstanding memorials to the ratings in the burial ground, and no grave markers or the cuts for the bases of such memorials were discovered during the excavation. Although many memorials were destroyed in the Blitz, transcriptions of some have survived in the National Archives (Greenwich Hospital Memorial Inscriptions). It appears that some memorials from the earlier and later burial grounds are still extant. One of half a dozen such memorial stones commemorates the colourful life of the seaman and Greenwich pensioner Edward Harris (Memorial number M2415). Today it lies in the floor of the Devonport Mausoleum. The inscription reads as follows:

> Here lyeth interred ye body of / Edward Harris Born at Dover / in Kent, Mariner / A man just in his actions / Kind to his family / was 18 years a slave in Barbary / & steadfastly kept to ye Church/ of England, Served the Government / at sea faithfully / Received His Majs Royal Bounty / of this Hospital / & died in ye faith of ye said church ye 27 day of June 1797 aged 75 years Ex dono . . .

Like so many other pensioners Edward Harris died at an advanced old age.

THE ROYAL HOSPITAL OVER TIME

Just as the size of the Royal Navy varied over time, so too did the number of seamen and marines eligible for a pension. Numbers rose during the wars with the Spanish, Dutch and French from the mid-18th to early 19th centuries, as the number of enlisted fighting men increased, and those injured in service became more numerous. In 1708 there were 300 pensioners and 40 staff (Newell 1984, 32). By 1729 there were 700 pensioners (Newell 1984, 64). The capacity of the hospital was increased by 200 in 1731, and by 1738 there were 1,000 pensioners (ibid., 66, 71). By 1750 the number of pensioners had risen to 1,100 (ibid. 76). In 1763, the out-pensioner scheme was established by Act of Parliament. Out-pensioners could live at home and draw a pension of £7 per year (Newell 1984, 84-5). At this time there were 1,800 in-pensioners. By 1811, there were 12,000 out-pensioners. The number of in-pensioners peaked at 2,710 pensioners in 1814. Enlistment of seamen and marines into the Royal Navy fell following the 1815 peace with France. However, veterans of the war continued to require aid, and this need became more acute with their increasing age. The hospital was fullest in the 1830s when many veterans of the Napoleonic Wars were in their dotage.

Veterans from earlier conflicts, however, were beginning to die off. For example, at the 1836 commemoration of the Glorious First of June (Lord Howe's naval victory over the French Republic in 1794) attended by William IV, all the pensioners who had fought in the battle were paraded before the King him. Of the original 1,700 servicemen, only 176 were

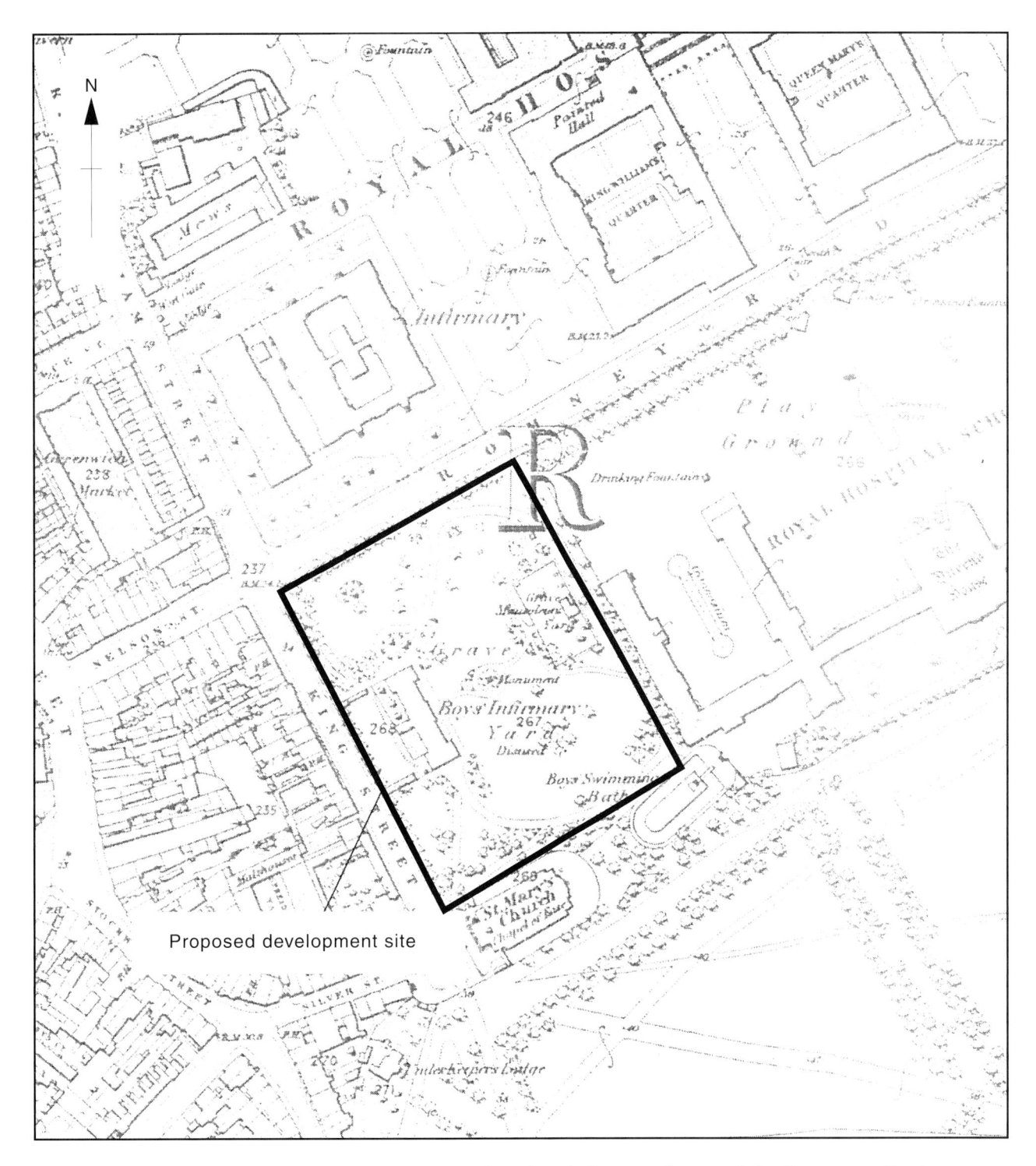

Figure 5 Ordinance Survey 1st edition 25 inch Map (1865) with the area of proposed development outlined.

present. Between 1815 and the 1830s the hospital was full, but by 1851 there were only six candidates for 88 vacancies, by 1857, five for 835, and by 1859 only three for 956 vacancies. The hospital had clearly outlived its function, and in 1869 the few remaining pensioners were paid to find alternative accommodation, and the hospital was closed (Newell 1984, 178). By that time the Romney Road burial ground had been closed for 11 years. The Royal Naval College took over the hospital buildings in 1873 and remained there until 1998.

SOCIAL HISTORY OF THE GREENWICH PENSIONERS

Introduction

The Royal Hospital at Greenwich was intended as the Royal Naval counterpart to the Chelsea Hospital for soldiers. In the words of its Royal Charter, it was an institute for 'the reliefe and support of Seamen serving on board the Ships and Vessells belonging to the Navy Royall . . . who by reason of Age, Wounds or other disabilities shall be uncapable of further service . . . and unable to maintain themselves.' Other aims stated in its Royal Charter of 1694 were 'the sustenance of the widows of seamen', and the 'maintenance and education of children of seamen'. The hospital was funded by a number of sources, including the proceeds of confiscated lands, unclaimed prize money, wages of men who 'ran' (ie. deserted) and a regular collection from both Royal Navy and merchant navy seamen of 6d per month, deducted automatically from their wages (Lavery 1989, 130). Royal patronage was also courted. A statue of George II was unveiled in the Great Court of the Hospital in August 1735. The same year George II granted the Hospital the estates of the disgraced Jacobite Earl of Derwentwater, who had been executed in 1716, and the Hospital entered a phase of real prosperity.

From 1705, the Hospital housed and cared for those long-serving seamen and marines who were mentally and/or physically unable to look after themselves. It should be stressed that the Hospital served a very different function from the other three major Royal Navy hospitals of the day at Gosport, Chatham and Plymouth. These hospitals had been established to care for injured and diseased sailors still on active service, rather than old and retired sailors. For this reason, it comes as no surprise that a large proportion of the skeletal sample excavated at Greenwich comprised older adult males. This contrasts strongly with the much wider age distribution of skeletons buried in the Paddock, Haslar Hospital, Gosport. The latter ranged from 16 to 50 years, the majority being 20–30 years old (Boston 2005).

Documentary sources

A wide range of documents pertaining to the Greenwich pensioners was consulted by Lorraine Lindsay-Gale (2002). These are held in the National Archives at Kew and the National Maritime Museum at Greenwich. Although this research is of considerable value in vividly bringing to life some of the individuals who comprised the pensioner population of the Hospital, it must be stressed that her work was not exhaustive, and that considerably more research in the future will undoubtedly prove highly valuable. The sources consulted by Lindsay-Gale are listed below:

- ADM 73 Pensioners' Admission Papers; files 1–69
- ADM 73 Register of Graves at Royal Hospital from 1857; file 463
- ADM 73 Hospital Burial Registers 1844 – 1860; file 460
- ADM 65 Letters relating to Pensioners Admissions; files 81–97
- ADM 36–39 Admiralty Ships Musters
- ADM 97–99 Sick and Wounded Seamen 1702–1862, 1742–1833, 1698–1816
- ADM 102 Naval Hospitals and Hospital Ships, Musters and Journals 1740–1860

The *Ayshford Complete Trafalgar Roll* (Ayshford and Ayshford 2004) was also consulted. This roll lists the records of all officers and ratings, who fought at the Battle of Trafalgar. Although highly useful, this record only covers a very small proportion of the seamen who eventually became Greenwich pensioners, the roll being limited to protagonists of a single battle. Nevertheless, it offers a useful snapshot of the lives of seamen and marines during the Napoleonic Wars, 703 of whom later became Greenwich pensioners. The Ayshfords used many of the sources listed above, but consulted other records, such as the Index of Seamen's affects; Index of the Wills of Seamen; Royal Marine description books; Wage Remittances; Wage Allocations; Naval medals; Royal Marines Effective and Subsistence records, and Chatham Chest contributions.

A number images of Greenwich pensioners and sailors are reproduced in Plates 2 to 9. They clearly reflect the advanced age and many mutilations and disabilities recorded in the written sources. The discharge certificate of Corporal George Frederick Eller (Plate 10), 'earnestly recommended [him] as a proper object of His Majesty's Royal Bounty of Greenwich Hospital'. Eller, who had been a marine corporal on board *Orion* was discharged following the amputation of his right leg at the Battle of the Nile. It should be noted that Eller was only 21 years old. Historical accounts of injuries and diseases will be discussed below (Chapter 4).

Composition of the Greenwich assemblage

Naval hierarchy in life and death

In interpreting both the burial archaeology and the osteology of this assemblage it is essential to place the men in their social context, both within the Royal Navy and the wider society. Burials at the Royal Hospital include both marines and seamen, and a small proportion of officers, the most famous being Admiral Sir Thomas Masterman Hardy, who was Nelson's flag captain at Trafalgar and who served as Governor of the Hospital until his death in 1839. Officers were interred in a separate burial ground from the ratings. The OA excavation investigated part of the ratings' burial ground.

The skeletal population examined in this report largely comprised the rank and file of the Navy (the ratings or 'the lower deck') – including landmen, ordinary and able seamen – and petty officers, and amongst the marines, privates and non-commissioned officers. Gunners and gunner's mates, cooks, carpenters and other skilled workmen were also part of this fraternity. The investigated graves also included a small number burials of women and these will be considered further below.

On coming aboard ship, seamen were assigned a rating by the first lieutenant on the basis of their sailing experience and ability (Lavery 1989, 129). 'Landmen' had no previous experience of the sea and performed uncomplicated tasks, and provide muscle power for hoisting and lowering sails, swabbing decks and moving loads such as barrels from one part of the ship to another. A man rated as an 'ordinary seamen' was 'useful on board, but is not an expert or skilful sailor' (Burney 1815, 327). An 'able seaman' was 'not only able to work, but is also well acquainted with his duty as a seaman' (loc.cit.). Pay and prize money was dependent on grade (Ayshford and Ayshford 2004; Fremont-Barnes 2005, 12). Ratings were overseen by warrant officers and commissioned officers.

Marines were not generally employed in handling the ship, although they often manned the capstan when raising the anchor (Lavery 1989, 170-71), and would provide extra muscle power for hauling on braces when tacking ship (ibid., 196). Most of the marines were assigned to the ship's gun crews in action (ibid., 199). Nonetheless, they were essentially sea-going soldiers whose principal role was to fight using virtually the same tactics and weaponry as soldiers on land, their standard weapon being the flintlock musket or 'Brown Bess' (Lavery 2004). Captain William Glascock drew attention to the different skills of marines and sailors:

> But in most of the affairs we were able to relate, marines and seamen were able to work most perfectly together; the former, efficient soldiers as they were, holding the enemy's troops and covering the no less efficient cutting out and demolition work of the seamen. (quoted by Lavery 1989, 152)

Onboard duties of marines included acting as guards and preventing desertion amongst the sailors. They were berthed separately from the seamen in order to reduce fraternisation (Lewis 1960, 273). They were also sometimes employed for impressment duties. Marines were deployed in small detachments aboard ship, and comprised a relatively small proportion of the ship's crew. For example, the total proportion of marines in the ships' crews at Trafalgar was 15.6% (calculated from the Trafalgar Roll, Ayshford and Ayshford 2004). In the 1790s and 1800s a 74 gun ship would have had a detachment of 100-120 marines out of a complement of some 590 to 640 men; that is about 17% of the crew would be marines.

Manning the Royal Navy

With the nation's defences almost entirely dependent on the strength and readiness of the Royal Navy, the need for seamen was insatiable, and even at the height of the Napoleonic Wars the force was never able to achieve full manning of all its ships (Fremont-Barnes 2005). The Royal Navy easily constituted the nation's largest employer. There is no single source that can provide figures for the numbers of sailors and marines serving with the Royal Navy during the late 18th and early 19th centuries, but two series of figures are available, one series presented by the Hardwick Commission in 1859 (hereafter HC), and the second compiled and published by Lloyd (1968, 286-90) (hereafter LL) (see also Rodger 2004, appendix vi). The manpower figures in the Naval estimates voted during the Revolutionary and Napoleonic Wars, give a sense of the scale of naval operations, although they cannot be taken to give the exact number of sailors and marines in service at any one time since the figures were a 'financial abstraction' that 'bore no fixed relation to the number of real men actually serving' (Rodger 2004, 198). In 1793 Parliament voted monies for 45,000 sailors and marines (Clowes 1899, 153) when there were between 59,042 (HC) and 69,868 (LL) men on ships' books. By 1801 the figure in Parliamentary estimates had risen to 130,000 men, and the number of men serving was between 131,959 (HC) and 125,061 (LL). With the resumption of hostilities in May 1803 after the brief Peace of Amiens, Parliament voted funding for 50,000 sailors and marines rising to 100,000. The numbers serving were 67,148 (HC) / 49,430 (LL). By 1810 when the numbers serving peaked at 146,312 (HC) or 142,098 (LL); the annual estimates allowed for 145,000 sailors and marines (Clowes, 1900, 9). In 1805, the year of the Battle of Trafalgar, numbers of men entered on ships' books stood at 114,012 (HC) / 109,205 (LL) (Rodger 2004, 639) in a year when the naval estimates allowed for 120,000 sailors and marines.

Manning the fleet to meet the increasing demands made upon it was a problem. There was no system for training sailors for the Royal Navy, and it had to compete with the merchant fleet for men from the finite pool of available sailors (Rodger 2004, 499). The Navy's pay rates were poor by comparison with merchant rates, but in some other respects – better food and conditions – service in the Royal Navy was advantageous (Rodger 2004, 499).

It took years of experience to train an able seaman and most expert seamen were 'bred to the sea', starting a sailing career in their early teens. Nonetheless, because the Revolutionary and Napoleonic Wars lasted 20 years, the pool of sailors did increase to meet in part the increased demand from merchant fleet and Royal Navy. Many sailors were from seafaring families or at least lived in ports and were familiar with ships (Lavery 2004, 47). Admiral Collingwood considered that the ideal age for recruitment was fourteen to sixteen years, when boys were strong enough to begin to work hard, but young enough to learn. 'Such boys soon become good seamen: landsmen very rarely do, for they are confirmed in other habits' (cited in Lavery 2004, 48). It seems that seamanship was rather like a language best learnt early.

Seamen were recruited by a number of means, some were volunteers, others were pressed into the service through the Impress Service (Rodger 2004, 496-500; Lloyd 1968, 124-49), and others were recruited under the Quota Acts (Rodger 2004, 443-44). Men volunteered for a number of reasons, to escape the poverty so widespread amongst the rural and working classes of this period, some to escape creditors and the debtors' prison, and some were in search of adventure and the possibility of prize money (Fremont-Barnes 2005, 6-8).

In 1795 and 1796 five successive Quota Acts were passed to raise fixed numbers of volunteers for the Navy. The 1795 acts imposed quotas on English and Welsh counties (35 George III, c. 5), English, Welsh and Scottish ports (35 George III, c. 9), and Scottish counties, burghs and cities (35 George III, c. 29). The two 1796 acts levied the English and Welsh counties, and Scottish counties, cities and burghs, respectively.

The Admiralty had to rely on impressment to maintain the manning of the fleet. In theory, foreigners, boys under 18 or men over 55 years, apprentices, harvesters, merchant seamen in their first two years at sea, and fishermen could not be taken up by press gangs. Although there were undoubtedly abuses, it is nonetheless true that press gangs were after the experienced seamen essential for the successful operation of a ship (Rodger 2004, 497). It is difficult to ascertain true proportion of 'pressed men' within the Royal Navy from ship's musters and other records, as many pressed men were encouraged to 'volunteer', thereby making themselves eligible for the Bounty, to which pressed men were not otherwise entitled. (Lewis 1960, 137; Lloyd 1968, 132).

Because of the real threat to the health of the crews by disease – epidemics could spread like wildfire in the crowded confines of a ship – newly pressed men, quota men and volunteers had be passed by a naval surgeon to ensure that they were not infectious (Kemp 1970).

Away from home, Royal Navy captains often supplemented their crew with foreign and/or merchant seamen. Foreign seamen were often pressed men or volunteers 'recruited' in foreign ports or taken from enemy prizes. Another not uncommon but unofficial means of gaining new or better sailors was to commandeer parts of the crews of merchant ships, often British or American, but sometimes foreign. A Royal Navy captain might exchange his inferior hands for more able seamen by this means. Merchant crews, whence many Royal Navy seamen were drawn, had an eclectic mixture of origins, and hence, many such exchanges included foreign nationals. For example, in July 1803, the distinguished Royal Navy captain Sir Edward Pellew (who otherwise preferred his native Cornishmen aboard) intercepted the merchant ship *Rushdale* of Hull, taking three able seamen; then the *Coromandel* returning from China was stopped and nine mostly prime seamen 'volunteered'. In the following two months, Pellew 'acquired' seven indifferent hands from the *Recovery* and *Ramble* of London, and the *Walker*, a Spanish ship; three from a privateer, the *Speculation*, and four excellent men from the battleship *Spenser*. Pellew recaptured an East Indiaman, the *Lord Nelson* from the French on the 27th August 1803 with her prize crew of 42 Frenchmen. From her crew he took two Americans, a Swede, a Norwegian and a German, and two of his French prisoners who volunteered (Clayton and Craig 2004, 42-3).

Unlike the recruiting of experienced seamen, recruiting marines for the Royal Navy was much easier. In comparison to sailing a ship, the duties of marines required relatively little training. Posters stuck up in market places advertised the service, and sergeants roamed the land trying to recruit young men with tales of adventure and prize money. Men were offered a substantial bounty, which had reached the princely sum of £26 per man by 1801. Most marines were recruited from the unskilled working classes, a large proportion being listed as 'labourers' in the Marine Musters (Ayshford and Ayshford 2004).

Nationality

Despite the Admiralty's prohibition on enlisting foreigners, most Royal Navy ships contained a significant proportion of foreign seamen. Lindsay-Gale (2002) found that Britain's 'hearts of oak' were not entirely manned by loyal British patriots. The 'place of origin' of sailors recorded in ships' musters revealed that the majority of seamen originated from England, Wales and Scotland, but these were by no means the exclusive source. Often a captain favoured officers and crew from his own place of origin, so crews might be predominantly Scottish, Irish or Cornish, depending on the captain in question (Clayton and Craig 2004, 41). For example, Sir Edward Pellew, the famous Cornish frigate captain whose squadron took numerous prizes in the wars with the French Republic, brought with him a core of followers who always sailed with him, moving with him from ship to ship. This core (officers, seamen and marines) was predominantly West Country in origin. The muster books of one of his ships, the *Tonnant*, reveal that of the 272-strong crew whose place of origin was stated, 57 came from Devon and 52 from Cornwall. The remainder was from Lancashire, Wales, Cumberland and Scotland. Marines were drafted from the Plymouth division (Clayton and Craig 2004, 41-42).

Amongst natives of the British Isles, a very large contingent of seamen was Irish (particularly from Cork and Dublin) and far fewer were Scots or Welsh. The next largest group was European: Dutch, Germans, Swedish, Danish, a few Portuguese, Prussians, Hungarians, Swiss and Italians. Interestingly, a small proportion of seamen fighting with the Royal Navy at Trafalgar were French and Spanish in origin (Ayshford and Ayshford 2004). Rodger (2004, 498) gives a breakdown by nationality for a sample of men from ships commissioned at Plymouth in 1804-5: 47% were English, 29% Irish, 8% Scots, 3% Welsh and 1 % from the Isle of Man or Channel Islands. Other nationalities comprised 11%. There were a few Americans from East Coast states, who at this time were counted as being British, and quite a number from the West Indies. Several individuals came from Africa. Sometimes 'a black' or 'blk' was written alongside their name in the register. Interestingly, though, not all Africans or West Indians were identified as black, making it probable that racial identity was not systemically recorded. 'Blacks' were also recorded as coming from Bengal and Madras, East Indies, and from Macao, China. This suggests that this was a general term applied to non-Caucasians. Cartoons and illustrations of seamen of the Royal Navy of this period often depict negroid seamen at work or play with their white colleagues (Plate 11).

Most marines were recruited from within the British Isles, the south-west counties (particularly Devon) contributing the largest numbers (from Ayshford and Ayshford 2004). An exception is the Prussian marine discussed below. Examples of foreign seamen and marines included:

- **Joel Britain**, aged 63 in 1803. Height 5ft 3in. He was injured in the head whilst serving on the *Victory*. His previous ship was the *Tremendous*. He was born in New York, and had a wife called Mary.
- **Phoebus Sandwich**, a 5ft 7in tall 'black' who came from Africa; had a wife in the West Indies; and was hurt in the loins whilst serving on the *Victorious*.
- **Frederick Dalwick** was 5ft 5in tall with light brown hair, blue eyes and a fair complexion. He originated from Wesel, Prussia (now Germany). In 1804 he enlisted as a private in the Royal Marines in the 134th company of the Plymouth Division. He had previously been a labourer. Frederick served in the *Swiftsure* at the Battle of Trafalgar and was awarded a Naval General Service Medal with Trafalgar Clasp. He was 27 years old. He was injured in the left hand whilst 'cutting out' when serving on the HMS *Defence*. He served in the Royal Navy for 16 years and 6 months, and was admitted to Greenwich Hospital in 1833, aged 55 years.

Lewis (1960, 129) notes that on the evidence of the Ship's Books in May 1808 14% of the 563 strong crew of *Implacable* were foreigners, and in 1812 17% of the crew of the *Warspite* were foreigners (ibid., 131). Even the crew of the *Victory*, Nelson's flagship at Trafalgar, contained 8% of foreign seamen and marines (ibid., 129).

Greenwich Pensioners on the Trafalgar Roll

A sample of 100 Trafalgar veterans who died at the Greenwich Hospital was compiled from the Trafalgar Rolls (Ayshford and Ayshford 2004), and is summarised in Appendix 1. From these records it is apparent that most of these in-pensioners survived into old age, despite many suffering severe injuries from enemy action, and prolonged exposure to the hazards of life at sea (such as scurvy, accidents and infections). The majority of the men in the sample died in their late 60s and 70s, the mean age of death being 70.01 years (Fig. 6). There was considerable variation in their length of service in the Royal Navy, which ranged from 2 years to 25 years with an average of 14 years. Lewis (1960, 415-6) reports an even greater average age of Greenwich pensioners and length of service. He found that in 1803 there were 96 pensioners over 80 years, 16 over 90 years and one more than 100 years of age. In his sample of 100 pensioners, the mean age-at-death was 82.5 years, and the average length of service was 25 years, with six having served for over 50 years (ibid., 416). The impact of such longevity of service and the advanced age of the pensioners is clearly reflected in the skeletal remains found in the cemetery (Chapter 4 below). The difference in results between the two samples

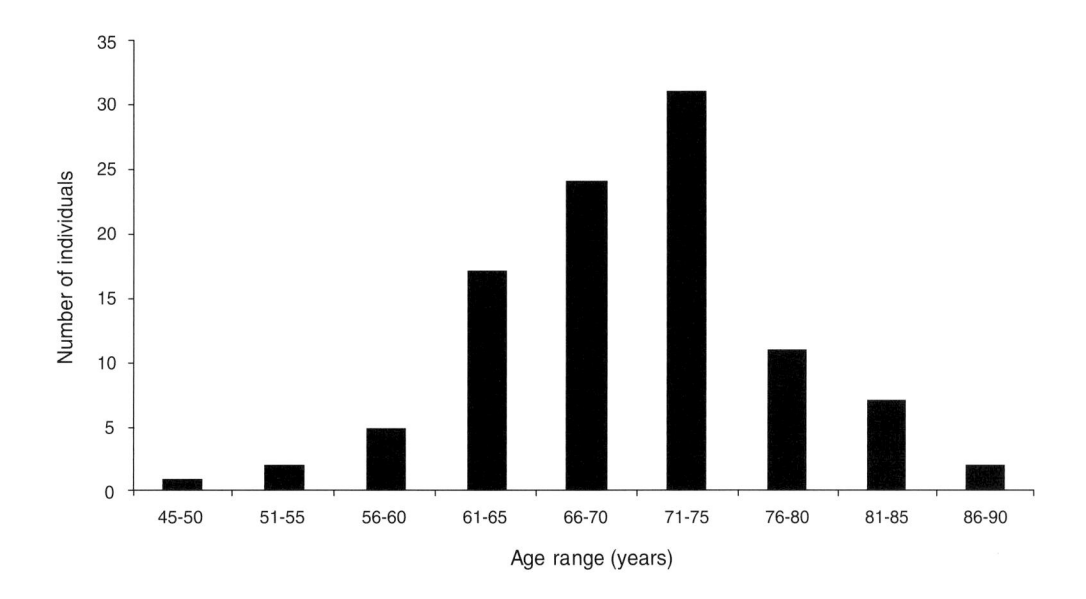

Figure 6   Age-at-death at Greenwich Hospital (data taken from Ayshford and Ayshford, Trafalgar Roll); N = 100.

above reveals that considerably more documentary work is required.

Many servicemen were demobilised following Napoleon's defeat at Waterloo in 1815. The Trafalgar Roll records that many marines with a stature below 5ft 4in were discharged at this time on the grounds that they were 'undersized'. During the conflict this had not appeared to be an issue. Older marines (over 40–45 years) were discharged on the grounds of advanced age.

Social class

Georgian society was highly stratified, and although some fluidity in movement did exist between the social classes, the majority of the population conformed to the roles, occupations, wealth and status prescribed by the class into which they were born. The vast bulk of the seamen and marines serving in the Royal Navy were working class in origin. This is evident from documentary sources that record the occupations of seamen and marines before joining and after leaving the Royal Navy. These were mostly working class occupations, which included many labourers but also skilled workmen. A few were artisans, such as carpenters, bakers or tailors.

The working classes of late Georgian England were exposed to considerable hardships brought about by the social changes that accompanied the Industrial Revolution and the mechanisation of agriculture. For many, life was precarious, with men, women and children working long arduous hours in unhealthy and often dangerous conditions. In the cities, the poorer sort of people populated crowded, polluted slums, where sanitation was poor and infectious diseases rampant. Poverty was widespread and food and clean drinking water was often in short supply. Even by the end of the Victorian age, 30,000 people did not have access to water from a communal pump or tap (Roberts and Cox 2003, 297). In the countryside, the enclosure of common land, the abandonment of partible inheritance, and agricultural mechanisation, all contributed to widespread rural poverty (ibid.). The physical effects of social depravation are reflected in skeletal assemblages of working class origin of this period, as for example from the Cross Bones burial ground, Southwark (Brickley *et al.* 1999) and St Martin's churchyard, Birmingham (Brickley *et al.* 2006). Childhood deprivation was also identified in the Greenwich assemblage (see Chapter 4 below).

Life after the Royal Navy

In the two decades following the Napoleonic Wars, these social hardships were made even more acute by economic depression, a succession of poor harvests and the spiralling cost of grain. Large numbers of men were discharged from the army and navy within months of Waterloo, often without pensions or other provisions to ease their way back into the society that they had left years earlier. Servicemen returning from the wars struggled to find employment in these difficult times, in many cases impaired by physical injuries they had sustained during the conflict. Of those who did find work, many returned to their previous occupations or used skills acquired during their time in the Royal Navy, whilst the more far-sighted saved their prize money and wages and started small businesses on discharge. Many other Royal Navy sailors continued their roving, seafaring way of life, and joined the merchant navy. A conspicuous number did not find employment, however, and drifted from place to place doing such work as they chanced upon.

Injured seamen were sometimes assisted officially from the Chatham Chest, a pension to which all seamen contributed 6d per month throughout their time in the Navy (Ayshford and Ayshford 2004). Assistance from the Chatham Chest was dependant upon the presentation of a smart-ticket or certificate of relief, which needed to be regularly renewed (yearly to five yearly) at a review held monthly. In his memoirs, William Spavens (2000, 98) described the scene at one such review:

> Here you may behold perhaps 500 mutilated creatures of different ages and appearances, some clean and decently appareled; some dirty and almost naked, so that all the cloaths on their backs would scarcely make a kitchen-girl a mop; some with meager and emaciated looks, appear as if they never had a good meal of meat, while here and there one [sic] indeed retain some faint vestiges of their former likeness; some have lost an eye, and others both; some have a hand, some an arm off; some, both near their wrists, some, both close to the shoulders; others, one at the wrist and the other above the elbow; some are swinging on a pair of crutches; some with a wooden leg below the knee; another above the knee; some with one leg off below the knee and the other above; some with a hand off and an eye out; another with an eye out and his face perforated with grains of battle-powder, which leave as lasting an impression as though they were injected by an Italian artist [ie. tattoo artist]; some with their limbs contracted; others have lost part of a hand or part of a foot; some have a stiff knee from a fracture of the petella bone; some have lost the tendons, and others the flesh from their arm-pits; while another has lost a piece from the back of his neck; another has had his skull fractured and trepanned, and a silver plate substituted in the room of what was taken out; some with their noses shot off; others with a piece torn from the cheek; another with his jaw bone of chin shot off, &c. &c. &c.

In Grose's *Dictionary of the Vulgar Tongue* of 1811, one of the slang terms given for a seaman was 'Jack Nastyface'. For so many of the above, this term was sadly very apt. Despite their disfigurements and disabilities, only a small proportion of these maimed and debilitated men eventually gained a place in the Hospital.

The Lloyd's Patriotic Fund was a private charity that assisted wounded seamen and marines (Ayshford and Ayshford 2004) and was set up by civilians enraged that Britain's conquering heroes could be brought so low. The government's heartless treatment of veterans was heavily criticised in many spheres of British society, and was perceived as a sign that something was seriously wrong with the Establishment (Erickson 1996, 206). Fuelled by economic hardship and Radical ideals, this widespread social and political dissatisfaction became overt amongst the masses. The resultant large-scale political meetings and demonstrations gravely alarmed the government (the example of the French Revolution being in the not-so-distant past). Its heavy-handed armed suppression of these rallies culminated in the notorious Peterloo Massacre of 1819.

It is remarkable, given the social background of the Greenwich pensioners, that so many survived into a ripe old age, far surpassing most of their contemporaries. Age at death estimates compiled from the London Bills of Mortality from the 1740s to 1840s by Roberts and Cox (2003, 304) showed that only 13.19-20.58% of the total London population (including all social classes) survived beyond 60 years of age, whilst only 7.56–11.03% survived beyond 70 years. Clearly, the Greenwich pensioners were amongst those few hardened survivors. In the words of Lewis (1960, 416) 'they were mostly the picked, brine-pickled survivors of a gruelling existence from which the weaklings had long since faded.'

Out-pensioners and in-pensioners

Whilst some of the Greenwich pensioners recorded in the General Register of Pensioners and their Families (ADM73/42) and in the Greenwich Hospital Records resided within the hospital, and were buried in the hospital burial ground on their deaths, a much higher proportion were out-pensioners. Out-pensioners lived in the community, many pursuing trades. A large proportion were married and some lived with their wives, although records suggest that many a man and wife did not reside in the same town. Some out-pensioners lived as far away as Dublin and Devon, whilst others appear to have elected to settle much closer to hand, often living in Greenwich itself (Ayshford and Ayshford 2004).

The Trafalgar Rolls (Ayshford and Ayshford 2004) record that most pensioners were initially out-pensioners, but moved into Hospital accommodation in the last few years of life, presumably when the effects of old age made coping with civilian life untenable. It would appear that the more debilitated individuals did enter the hospital at a younger age, however, with a few living as many as 25 years in the hospital. It was much more common, however, to spend only the last 5 to 10 years as an in-pensioner. Only a small proportion of injured and disabled seamen gained a place in the hospital as in-pensioners.

LIFE OF IN-PENSIONERS IN THE HOSPITAL

In his memoirs, William Spavens (2000, 99) described Greenwich Hospital in the following laudatory terms:

> which magnificent building is not to be equalled in the world, and its endowment is equal to its magnificence; its situation is eligible, close by the fine river Thames, where ships pass and repass; the air is salubrious, the park delightful, the chapel elegant, the clothing for the pensioners comfortable, and the provision wholesome and plentiful; all which conspires to render life, loaded with infirmities, tolerable if not happy in its decline, 'when safe moor'd in Greenwich tier'.

Like the Chelsea Pensioners, the Greenwich pensioners were supplied with a characteristic uniform. This comprised blue coat and breeches, a cocked hat of felt, blue worsted stockings, (three pairs to last two years), two pairs of shoes and three shirts. They also received two nightcaps, nightgowns, neckerchiefs and bedding, and the frail and aged were provided with a great coat (Lewis 1960, 415). Pensioners who breached discipline even in minor ways were sometimes required to wear their coats inside out, the bright yellow lining marking them out conspicuously. Special yellow coats with red sleeves or some other badge of disgrace were also designed to identify delinquents until they had 'worked their passage back to grace' (Lewis 1960, 415; Spavens 2000, 99). Punishment duties were also inflicted, such as having to sweep the Grand Square of the Hospital (Spavens 2000, 99). A few in-pensioners were expelled outright for bad behaviour. These included Trafalgar veterans James Bagley, a retired Royal Marine and stocking-maker (for striking a boatswain when drunk), George Baker (for 'misconduct'), Redmond Cafferty and John Ford (crimes not specified) (taken from Ayshford and Ayshford 2004).

Although housed in magnificent buildings, there were complaints about poor food, mismanagement and the pettiness on the part of the trustees. In addition, corruption and jobbery periodically surfaced. In 1771 Captain Thomas Baillie, one of the four captains of the hospital complained that the Secretary John Ibbotson was displacing pensioners from their 'cabins' to make office space for civilian clerks (Newell 1984, 86-7). In 1774 Baillie was appointed Lieutenant Governor of the Hospital. In 1778, Baillie went into print detailing 'the several Abuses that have been introduced into that great National Establishment' (Baillie 1778). An enquiry followed and the result of the enquiry was that Baillie was dismissed from his post. The case became something of a cause célèbre, there was even a debate in the House of Lords. Not satisfied that Baillie had been dismissed some of the Directors of the Hospital brought a case of libel against Baillie.

Baillie won the case thanks to speech by a young lawyer called Thomas Erskine (Newell 1984, 86-92). The speech made Erskine's reputation; he went on to defend Thomas Paine, he was briefly Attorney General and later to become Lord Chancellor. An earlier survey of abuses of Hospital accommodation led to the expulsion of 800 servants (footmen, coachmen and other menial servants) who had never served at sea.

Another scandal involved cheating the pensioners out of basic rations. The pewter tableware, probably made materials from the Hospital's northern estates, became the subject of a scandal and dispute when it was discovered that the depth of the bowls were altered, so as to reduce the daily food rations (Newell, 1984, 72).

Overall, by the standards of the day, however, the Greenwich pensioners were very well fed, and made extra money by selling what they could not eat to the poor of Greenwich. Food was served in a communal dining hall (Plate 12). The usual daily ration was 1 lb of bread, and 2 quarts (4 pints) of beer, with 1 lb of meat (boiled or sometimes roasted) (beef three days a week and mutton two days a week), 4 oz cheese. On Wednesdays and Fridays instead of meat each pensioner had pease pottage, 8 oz cheese, and 2 oz butter (Newell 1984, 82). This diet bore an uncanny resemblance to that aboard ship, but presumably was fresher. Small luxuries included an allowance of one shilling a week for tobacco, and on holidays and naval anniversaries, the daily intake of two quarts of beer was doubled. All in all, the life of an in-pensioner was happy and carefree, and, as Lewis (1960, 416) suggests, may have contributed towards their considerable longevity.

The pensioners were housed in wards. In the early days these were named after the famous ships, battles and military commanders of the day: *Royal Charles, Monk, Restoration, Royal William, Nassau, Barfleur, Marlborough, Blenheim* and *Ramilles*. In the same tradition, later ward names commemorated Admirals and naval commanders, such as Anson, Hardy, Sandwich, Rodney and Duke. The pensioners of each ward selected from amongst their numbers a 'Boatswain' and two 'Boatswain's mates', who were in charge of the ward and received a crown rather than a shilling a week (the pocket money of an ordinary seaman) for their troubles.

At the enormous state funeral of Nelson, on 8th of January 1805, the Greenwich pensioners received national recognition of their role in defeating the French in several recent wars. The funeral was a huge outpouring of national grief, on a scale not seen before and probably only equalled by the funerals of Churchill and of Princess Diana in the 20th century. Nelson's remains were brought home from Spain and lay in state in the Painted Hall of Greenwich Hospital. The hall had originally served as the dining hall for the Hospital but had proved too small for the purpose. Fifteen thousand paid their respects here, whilst many thousands more could not get in (Clayton and Craig 2004, 366). During the funerary procession, as the coffin left the Hall, 500 pensioners who had served under Nelson marched in front. Captain Hardy carried the standard. Other pensioners lined up in double rows. The coffin was rowed up the Thames by Royal Navy seamen, and a great procession accompanied it to St Paul's cathedral. Forty-eight pensioners took part in this part of the procession dressed in black gowns and carrying black staves.

There were many official visits to the Hospital in later years as Greenwich was the quay from which many embarked or disembarked when making trips to and from the Continent. On these occasions, pensioners were lined up on parade. Visitors included King William (1834), Marshal Soult (one of Napoleon's commanders), Queen Victoria and Prince Albert (1840), the King of Prussia (1842), Tzar Nicholas of Russia (1844) and Ibrahim Pasha, Khedive of Egypt (1846). Clearly, Greenwich Hospital was an institution of which the Establishment was proud. In a less generous moment, Dr Johnson commented that the Hospital was 'too magnificent a place for charity, and that its parts were too detached to make one great whole' (Newell 1984, 83). There were many who did not share these sentiments.

WOMEN AND CHILDREN AT THE ROYAL HOSPITAL

In addition to helping aged and disabled seamen, the hospital also provided some support widows and offspring, who were unable to support themselves. Widows or spouses, and offspring or orphans of in-pensioners were not permitted to live in the Hospital (Newell 1984, 31), but often took private lodgings nearby. It was not until the 19th century that thought was given to the plight of the wives and families of pensioners, or to the provision of married quarters (Newell 1984, 175, 177, 260). Indeed in 1857, the new First Lord of the Admiralty noted that parishes were obtaining the release of pensioners from the Hospital so that they could support their families which were being admitted to workhouses (Newell 1984, 175).

However, some widows who were employed as nurses in the hospital and school at Greenwich, did live in (Ayshford and Ayshford 2004). This may well explain the presence of the seven females in the skeletal assemblage. The offspring of pensioners were also provided for, and a school was opened for these children in the Queen's House, which had been adapted for use between 1807 and 1816 (Newell 1984). The Queen's House was converted into the National Maritime Museum in 1937-9. It is highly probable that the two sub adults in the skeletal assemblage were the issue of pensioners.

It is highly unlikely that the female skeletons are those of women who had served in the Royal Navy. Much has been made by ballad-mongers, and in popular literature and on film of women assuming male identities in order to serve as seamen in the Navy.

Motivations are said to have varied from a desire to be reunited with a sweetheart, as a means of shaking off social and sexual mores governing the behaviour of women at this time, or like men, the thirst for adventure and/or the means of gaining untold wealth from prize money. By its very clandestine nature, it is impossible to get a true approximation of the number of such women serving in the Navy, although it is doubtful that it exceeded a few individuals (Lewis 1960, 286).

Historically known figures include Elizabeth Bowden, a black woman known as 'William Brown', and Hannah Snell. Elizabeth Bowden served six weeks aboard the *Hazard* in 1807 as a boy third class (Fremont-Barnes 2005, 48-9). The 'little female tar' was one of the principal witnesses at the court martial of a Lieutenant Berry, at which she appeared garbed in a long jacket and blue trousers (Lewis 1960, 286; Rodger 2004, 506). 'William Brown' was an impressive female who served for at least 11 years during the Napoleonic Wars as an able seaman and captain of the foretop - a post given to the most skilled and agile members of the crew - in the 110-gun *Queen Charlotte* (Harvey 1994, 114). Her true gender was only revealed after the end of the Wars in 1815 (Rodger 2004, 506). Slightly earlier in the 18th century, Hannah Snell (1723-1792), already a mother, had embarked on a career as a soldier, marine and seaman (Harvey 1994, 114). She served at least five years, during which time she was reputedly wounded in twelve places at Pondicherry. She had to remove one of the bullets herself in order to avoid detection. Her stoicism paid off and her true gender wasn't discovered until she returned home and revealed it herself. She was awarded an annuity (Lewis 1960, 286), and eventually married three times (Harvey 1994, 114).

Females aboard ship more commonly lived openly as women, and were usually the wives or lovers of seamen, marines and officers on board. Although some captains forbade women in their ship, it appears to have been an unusual position to take, and there are numerous passing references to wives of both officers and ratings (Lewis 1960, 280-87; Rodger 2004, 505). Captain's order books often prescribe regulations for women belonging to the ship (Lewis 1960, 280-82). Because these women were not entered on the muster books (ibid., 282), it is impossible to quantify their numbers, but their presence is often overlooked in many modern historical accounts of the Royal Navy.

Women attached to members of the lower deck generally performed traditional female roles of cleaning, cooking and ministering to the sick and injured, but also often acted as 'powder-monkeys', bringing gunpowder to the gundecks during battle (Lewis 1960, 283).

In his memoir, John Nichol described the courage of the women on board the *Goliath* at the Battle of the Nile (1798). His station during the battle the powder magazine of the *Goliath*. He recorded that:

> Any information we got was from the boys and the women who carried the powder. The women behaved as well as the men . . . I was much indebted tot eh Gunner's wife who gave her husband and me a drink of wine every now and then. . . Some women were wounded, and one woman belonging to Leith died of her wounds. One woman bore a child in the heat of the action: she belonged to Edinburgh. (quoted in Lewis 1960, 283)

In 2000, Dr Paolo Gallo's team excavated a number of burials on Nelson's Island in the Bay. Interestingly, these fatalities included a woman buried in her dress, who was interred within a wooden coffin marked with a large metal 'G' [possibly for *Goliath*]. This may well have been the unfortunate woman from Leith, or one of women attached to army regiments, who are known to have died aboard ships moored in Aboukir Bay in 1801 (Slope 2004).

In addition to the female burial on Nelson's Island there two newborns and one infant a few months old, the former either stillborn or having died in childbirth or soon afterwards. Childbirth aboard ship was not unknown in the Royal Navy, as already noted, with one woman giving birth in the heat of the Battle of the Nile (Lewis 1960, 283). The fear and excitement of engagement may well have precipitated labour. Another instance, is the birth of Daniel Tremendous MacKenzie aboard the *Tremendous* during the battle of the Glorious First of June. At the age of 53 he received the Naval General Service Medal engraved with his name, rating and ship: 'Daniel T. MacKenzie - Baby - H.M.S. *Tremendous*'.

Women who actually fought in these sea battles were excluded from this honour. Two women - Ann Hopping and Mary Ann Riley - later claimed the Naval General Service Medal for their actions in the battle, and although their claims were not denied, their applications were rejected on the grounds that it would 'leave the Army open to innumerable applications' (cited in Lewis 1960, 283).

Jane Townshend who had served in the *Defiance* at Trafalgar applied for the medal with the support of certificates from Philip Durham, Captain of the *Defiance*. Initially her application was accepted

> The Queen in the Gazette of the 1st of June directs that all who were present in this action shall have a medal, *without any reservation as to sex*, and as this woman produces from the Captain of the *Defiance* strong and highly satisfactory certificates of her useful services during the action she is fully entitled to a medal.

However subsequently the decision was reversed and the Naval General Service Medal Roll annotated accordingly:

> Upon further consideration this [application] cannot be allowed - there were many women in the

fleet equally useful, and it will leave the navy exposed to innumerable applications of the same nature. (TNA, ADM 171/1, ff 131v-132r)

It is far from certain whether any of the seven women buried in the rating's burial ground of Greenwich Hospital had ever sailed in a Royal Navy ship as the consorts of seamen, or whether they had remained on land throughout their lives. It is unlikely that isotope analysis will shed light on this question, as most women do not appear to have remained aboard ship for prolonged periods.

Chapter 3: Results of the Fieldwork

INTRODUCTION

The results of all phases of fieldwork are presented below, with the watching briefs and evaluation results briefly summarised, and the excavation presented in more detail. Most work was concentrated within the footprint of the proposed Conference Centre - an area previously used as tennis courts - and included Test Pits 1, 3 and 4 of the Watching Brief phase, Trenches 10-13 of the Evaluation, and Areas 1 and 2 of the excavation phases (Fig. 2).

Test Pits 2 and 2a of the Watching Brief were located immediately south of this area, close to the seamen's memorial, whilst Test Pit 5 was further west. Test pit 6 and Trenches 14 and 15 were located to the west in the area of the proposed Student Accommodation. The site of the proposed electrical substation lay to the south of Areas 1 and 2 and north-west of the Maritime Museum (Fig. 2).

Plans of the graves revealed in Areas 1 and 2 during the excavation phase are shown in Figures 11 and 12. The plans also show the location of the piling trenches (numbered trenches 3000-3016 in Area 1; and 6000-12 in Area 2). Excavated graves are indicated with hachures. Similarly, the two excavated graves located within Trench 15, just south-west of Area 2, and the excavated grave in the proposed substation site are shown in Figures 7 and 8 respectively. The character and contents of these graves are summarised in the Grave Catalogue (Appendix 2).

FIELDWORK RESULTS

Archaeological watching brief, July 1999

The watching brief maintained on the excavation of seven engineering test pits located within the vicinity of the Infirmary and Devonport Buildings. Test pits 3 and 4 and Test pit 5 were excavated to a maximum depth of 3 m. Test pits 1, 2 and 2a were excavated to a depth of 1.8 m below the present ground surface.

Undisturbed natural was revealed in each of the test pits and was commonly yellowish gravelly sand. A dark reddish silt layer seen in Test pit 5 was interpreted as the silting of a north-south orientated palaeochannel of uncertain date.

With the exception of Test pit 5, where a modern brick drain had truncated earlier deposits, every test pit revealed a substantial layer of disturbed or dumped sandy silt subsoil commonly containing fragments of 18th- and 19th-century brick, tile and mortar fragments. The presence of this building debris was noted in historical sources discussed above.

Evidence of human burial was recorded in the four eastern test pits: Test pits 2 and 2a on the site of the memorial commemorating Greenwich pensioners, and Test Pits 3 and 4 in the area of the tennis courts. The burials lay within, or were sealed by a substantial layer of accumulated graveyard soil, containing post-medieval building debris.

Although *in situ* articulated burials were only clearly seen in Test pit 2, it is probable that some of the disarticulated bones found in the other test pits were intact burials disturbed by the machining of the test pits. The considerable accumulation of grave soil and the lack of visible grave cuts suggested that the area had been heavily used for burials (OA 1999a, 4). A similar density of burial was noted slightly further to the south on the site of the electrical substation (see below), suggesting particularly dense burial activity in the central part of the burial ground. Grave cuts were more clearly visible in Areas 1 and 2 following machining to a far greater depth.

No evidence of activity clearly pre-dating the Royal Hospital was identified, with the exception of a possible palaeochannel in Test pit 5.

Archaeological evaluation, November 1999

Four trenches (Trenches 10-13) were excavated within the footprint of the proposed Conference Facility and one (Trench 14) within the footprint of the proposed student accommodation block (Fig. 2). The description below is based on the evaluation report (OA 1999c). Trenches 10-13 lay within the areas which were excavated in 2001, and the results from these evaluation trenches are only briefly outlined. (For full details see the unpublished client report, OA 1999c). Trench 14 lay outside the excavation area, but was within the area investigated during a watching brief in February–March 2000 (see below).

Trench 10

Trench 10 measured 4.5 m by 4 m at ground level (8.35 m OD) and was excavated to a maximum depth of 1.4 m (6.95 m OD) below the top of the trench. The trench was stepped to create a safe working area. An area 2.5 m by 3 m was investigated at the base of the trench. Natural gravel (1018) was identified at a depth of 7.18 m OD, 1.17 m below the top of the trench. Five WNW-ESE aligned grave cuts (1000, 1010, 1013, 1032 and 1045) were revealed cut into the natural.

The grave cuts had all been truncated prior to the laying of a concrete slab 1031, and the surviving skeletons were 0.10 m below this. The slab may have formed a courtyard for the Maritime Museum. Overlying this concrete were various rubble dumps sealed by make-up layers (1067 and 1068) and the tarmac of the tennis court (1072).

Four graves (1000, 1023, 1032 and 1045) contained well preserved articulated adult skeletons and were filled with orange brown silty sand containing some ceramic building material (CBM) and interpreted as disturbed redeposited natural. A fifth grave (1010) was excavated no further than a layer of disarticulated charnel remains, presumably within the backfill of a further inhumation. Three skeletons were identified as adult males, and the fourth was adult, but of indeterminate sex. None of the skeletons displayed any obvious palaeopathology, and where present the teeth were in very good condition. This data has not been included in the osteological analysis presented Chapter 4. The skeletons and coffin fittings were left *in situ*, and the graves were covered with a cushioning layer of natural sand prior to backfilling of the trenches. Trench 10 was subsequently re-excavated as part of Area 1 in 2001.

Trenches 11 and 12

The two trenches were combined into a single excavation at surface level and stepped for safety because of the unstable deposits. An area 9 m by 4.5 m was excavated to natural gravel (1118) at a depth of 1.40 m below ground level. Trench 11 to the east and Trench 12 to the west both measured 2 m by 2.5 m, and were excavated to a maximum depth of 2.10 m below ground level (6.53 m OD).

In Trench 11, four grave cuts (1113-1116) were noted, graves 1113 and 1116 each containing a fully articulated skeleton and coffin fittings, and graves 1114-1115 each with two burials. All were backfilled with redeposited natural gravel. Grave 1113 contained an adult male, and grave 1116 a skeleton of indeterminate sex. Grave 1115 contained two adult skeletons, one male and one female. Grave 1114 also contained two skeletons, one an adult female, but second skeleton was obscured by the female skeleton. None of the skeletons exhibited obvious pathology. Trench 11 was re-excavated as part of Area 1 in 2001.

In Trench 12, two graves filled with redeposited natural were revealed. The redeposited natural was overlaid by a dark brown sandy silt with ceramic building material (CBM) inclusions. Grave 1207 had no surviving skeleton. Grave 1204 contained a fully articulated adult female skeleton and coffin fittings, including coffin handles of Spitalfields type 2a (Reeve and Adams 1993), dating from 1763-1837, and a corroded illegible coffin plate. No palaeopathology was seen. The concrete surface (1122 and 1215) was 0.15 m above the shallowest inhumation, and was overlaid by a series of rubble dumps which in turn were overlaid by the tarmac tennis court (1209) and its make-up layers. Trench 12 was re-excavated as part of Area 2 in 2001.

Trench 13

The trench measured 4.5 m by 4.5 m at ground surface, stepping down to an area of 2 m by 2.5 m, and excavated to a maximum depth of 1.89 m (6.70 m OD) below ground level. The natural gravel (1327) was observed at a depth of 7.10 m OD. No burials were seen in this trench, but deposits of animal bone were observed. The features seen consisted of several ditches and pits containing post-medieval pottery, filled with homogenous brown sandy silt, overlying natural gravels which had collapsed or slipped from the edges of cuts. The latest features were pit 1317, measuring c 2 m in diameter and 0.30 m in depth, and another pit (1315), which was 0.45 m deep and over 0.20 m wide. They truncated two linear ditches which were aligned north-south. Ditch 1312 measured 1.25 m wide and 0.36 m deep – it contained a sherd of Coarse Borderware AD 1350-1500, and this in turn cut away ditch 1320 measuring over 0.45 m wide and 0.26 m deep.

These features were overlain by a make-up layer (1310) of dark brown sandy, silt, with occasional CBM fragments and small rounded pebbles. Overlying this was a possible make-up layer (1308) of lighter brown silty sand. Make-up layers and the tarmac tennis court (1300) completed the sequence.

Trench 14

Trench 14 was located west of the other four trenches. The trench base measured 2 m by 2.5 m, with a step added for access. The trench was excavated to a depth of 2.10 m (6.43 m OD) below ground level, revealing the level of natural gravel (1421). No features were observed in the base of the trench, but cutting the gravel to this depth were a number of post-medieval pits and a foundation cut (1412). The earliest feature was a pit (1419) which was 1 m deep and 2.40 m wide, backfilled with various rubble and mortar layers. The pit cut away a crude brick built foundation (1410) one skin thick and 0.40 m high. The bricks were a dark red colour and measured 0.23 m by 0.11 m by 0.07 m. A pit (1405), 0.60 m deep and over 2.30 m wide truncated both these features. This was backfilled with two layers of orange brown clay silt sandwiching dark grey clay silt with 10% CBM. All the fills contained redeposited natural pebbles and gravel. This pit was partially removed by a pit (1407) 1 m deep and over 1 m wide, backfilled with dark grey clayey silt with 1% CBM and 2% rounded pebbles. Overlying these features was a possible garden soil (1401), 0.40m thick, made up of dark grey brown clayey silt loam with 5% CBM and 10% pebbles and gravel, in turn overlaid by the tarmac car park and concrete base (1400).

In summary

It was clear that only the lower part of the graves, including skeletons and coffin remains, survived. The upper parts of the graves, and any shallower graves that may have existed, had been truncated in preparation for laying a concrete yard surface in the 20th century. Neither the original depth of the graves, nor the height of the original ground surface could therefore be reconstructed with confidence. In parts of the cemetery, it was evident that more than one skeleton occupied a single grave cut. Stacking of two burials on top of one another was noted, but there was no evidence for deeper stacking.

Inhumations were predominantly older adult males, presumably retired sailors or marines. Female burials were found within graves also containing the remains of an adult male, presumably their spouse. No sub adult remains were uncovered in this phase. The remnants of plain wooden coffins were present. These had been decorated with iron *departum* plates, most of which were severely corroded. Grave 1204 was the only grave with recognisable coffin handles. The simplicity of the coffins suggest that the burials in this area were of low-ranking men, perhaps ratings, and their families.

No earlier archaeological deposits was found below the graves, with the exception of a possible medieval ditch in Trench 13. This may have been part of a field boundary or garden feature associated with Greenwich Park. The post-medieval ditches from the same trench are interesting in that they may have served to define areas within the cemetery.

The crude brick wall in Trench 14, of which only a small remnant was found, is likely to be part of one of the buildings shown on the 1778 Map of the Hundred of Blackheath (Fig. 3). The buildings were not present on the 1695 map, and were probably demolished by 1783 prior to the construction of the hospital school infirmary (OA 1999b, 6). It appears that the wall was of 18th-century date. The area was much disturbed by later services, and south of the trench the existing building would have truncated most of the archaeology. Within the footprint of the proposed student accommodation block, the archaeological potential was therefore very limited.

Watching brief on site of student accomodation, February-March 2000 (Fig. 7)

Trench 15

Trench 15 was excavated in February and March 2000. In part, the trench was located within the footprint of the proposed student accommodation facing King William Walk, in the location of the demolished southern wing of the Devonport Building. In this phase, a watching brief on a drainage trench excavation was also undertaken. This extended south and west of the Devonport Building into the area lying immediately the south-west of Area 2 (Fig. 2). A hexagonal area (roughly measuring 2.5 x 2.8 m) was cleared to accommodate a manhole, and two graves (1564 and 1571), and a possible third grave cut (1568), were identified in the north-eastern area of the trench (Fig. 7). Graves 1564 and 1571 lay within the level of impact and the burials were removed. Grave 1571 (of Grave group 1570) cut the natural gravels (1518) and contained one coffined skeleton (1572). The upper part of the grave backfill (1573) was cut by the later grave 1564 (Grave group 1563), without disturbing the underlying skeleton. Grave 1564 contained coffined skeleton 1565. The absence of grave cuts to the east of the three graves suggested that they may have marked out the western limit of the burial ground. Certainly, no burials were discovered between the manhole trench and King William Walk in any of the previous phases of archaeological works.

Within the footprint of the proposed student accommodation building and in the courtyard area to the west of the existing Devonport Building, a number of structures, drains and culverts were uncovered, which mostly related to that building. Pipe trenches 1502, 1507, 1523 and 1543 were recorded. Two brick-built culverts 1524 and 1534 were also identified. Thirteen brick-and-mortar wall foundations were located in different parts of the trench. On the basis of brick and mortar characteristics, all appeared to be either modern or later post-medieval in date. The foundations and/or the lower courses of walls 1505, 1508, 1511, 1524, 1527 and 1552 comprised modern brick (machine- made, stamped and/or frogged) that were bonded with hard, dark grey mortar or cement.

Six of the remaining foundations were later post-medieval in date (probably 18th- to 19th-century). These included north - south orientated wall foundation 1555 and north-west - south-east orientated wall foundation 1548 within the courtyard area facing onto King William Walk; wall 1531 in the area of the demolished south wing; north-west - south-east orientated walls 1556 and 1558 to the south-east of the south wing, and the surviving remnants of a north-west - south-east orientated wall variously numbered 1575, 1578, 1579 and 1577 located along the length of the service trench between the Infirmary building and Area 2.

Linear cut 1527 was vertical sided and flat based, at least 9.3 m in length and 1.8 m deep. It was filled with clay sand containing a high proportion of gravel and building rubble (1528). Its position on the perimeter of the site aligned on King William Walk suggested that this was the foundation for the outer perimeter wall of the Infirmary and graveyard.

Archaeological watching brief on site of conference facility, January-March 2000

Nothing of archaeological significance was revealed.

Archaeological excavation - Phase 1 the electrical substation, January 2000 (Fig. 8)

A trench measuring 3.6 m x 4.5 m was excavated following the demolition of a cycle shed in the area of the proposed substation. The trench was excavated to the impact level between 1.6 m and 2.4 m beneath the present ground surface. The natural geology (2002), a loose yellow gravelly soil, was cut by 26 approximately west-east orientated graves. The graves were closely packed and there was considerable intercutting of features (Fig. 8). The density of burials exceeded all other areas revealed during archaeological works. Interestingly, in Area 1 the greatest grave density and intercutting was discovered in the southern part of the trench (see below) and dense burial was also seen within watching brief on engineering

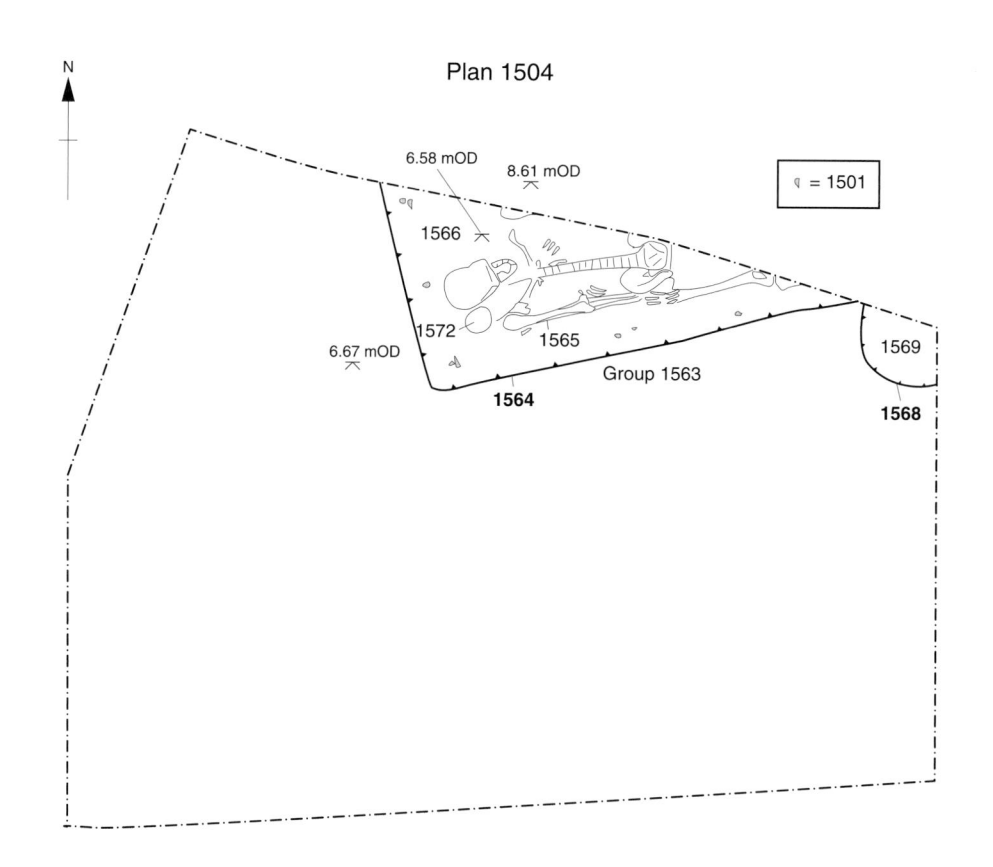

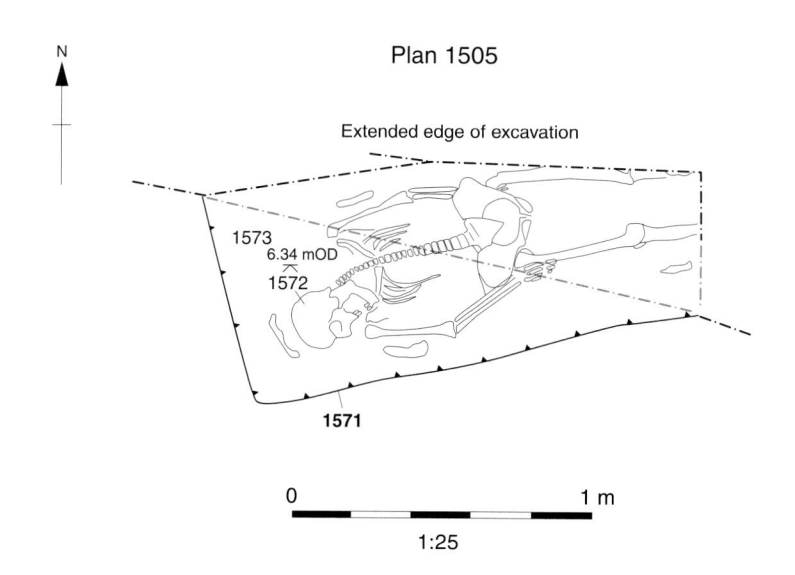

Figure 7 Trench 15: plan of burials 1565 and 1572.

test pit 2, which suggests that burial density across the whole site was greatest in the central part of the burial ground.

Proposed developments did not impact on the burials within the trench with the exception of skeleton 2005 (grave group 2003). Details of this burial are presented in Appendix 2. The skulls of two skeletons were visible at the western ends of grave groups 2010 and 2067, although the former was not discovered within the coffin stain (2012) and may have been charnel from a disturbed grave. With the intercutting of so many graves, such charnel is inevitable. Disarticulated long bones of at least two individuals and a mandible were found dumped in the western end of grave 2025 (grave group 2024). This grave had cut at least five other graves, and this charnel probably originated from at least two of these features. Grave 2025 was in turn cut by grave group 2007.

The only non-burial feature to be excavated within the trench was a modern pit 2082 (diameter 1.7 m;

Chapter Three

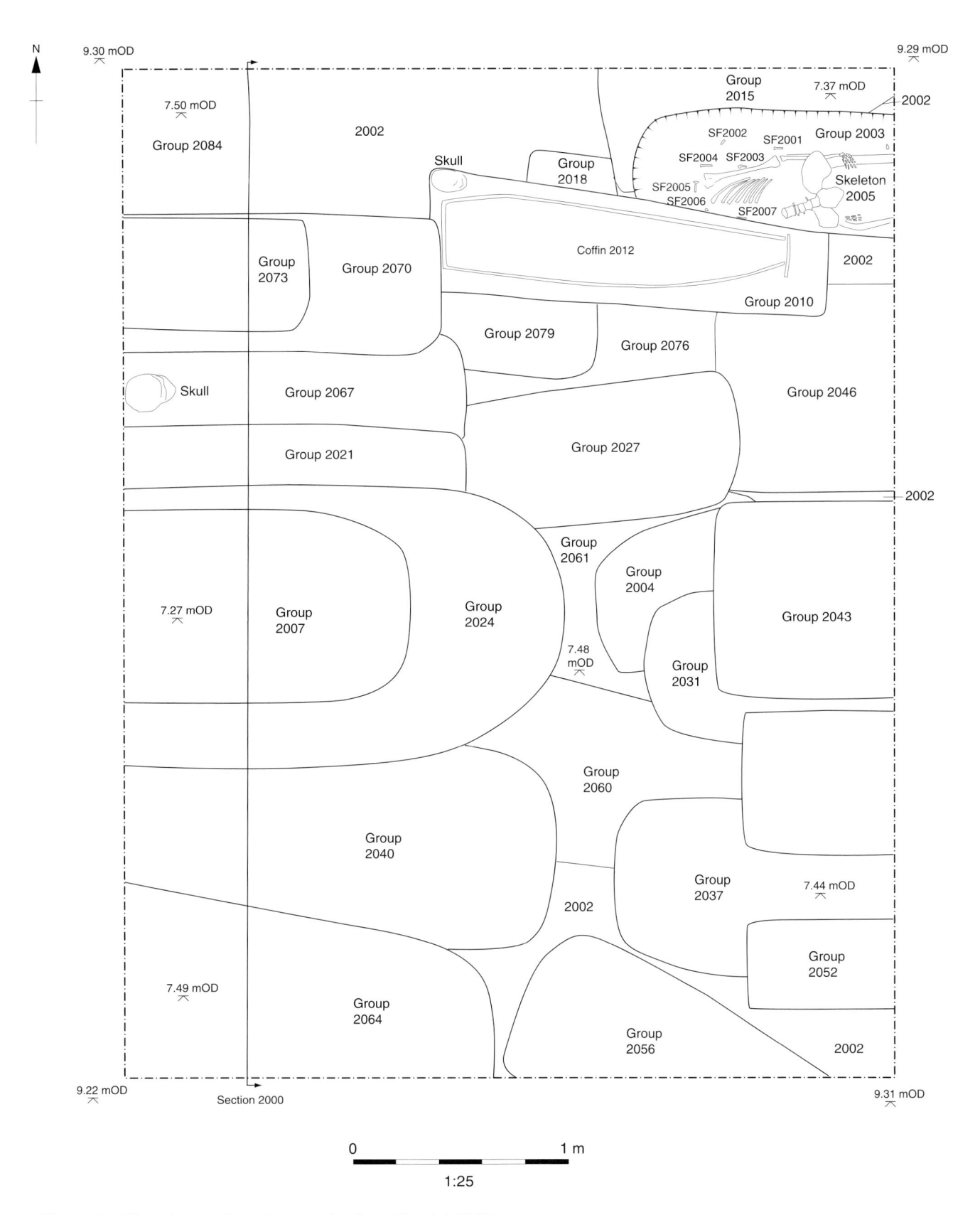

Figure 8   Electricity substation trench: plan of burial 2005.

depth 0.9 m). This not only truncated several grave fills but also cut the made ground (2001) and it was only overlaid by the modern tarmac and a levelling layer 2000. The tarmac and levelling, together with a layer of building debris (2001) sealed the graves. Pit 2082 contained a grey black sandy-clay (2083) with inclusions of slag and scrap metal.

Archaeological excavation - Phase 2 Areas 1 and 2, June-September 2001 (Figs 9–12)

Areas 1 and 2 lay within the footprint of the conference facility (Fig. 2), in a location previously used as tennis courts. Machine stripping revealed graves over the whole of both areas (Plates 13–14). At least 104 grave cuts were visible in Area 1 (Fig. 11) and 60 in Area 2 (Fig. 12).

The natural geology (3000) comprised river gravels in a matrix of loose red-yellow sand. This layer was encountered approximately 1.6 m below the present ground surface. In Area 1 it was sealed by dark grey brown silty sand (3005), approximately 0.4 m in depth, interpreted as a graveyard soil. The graves cut layer 3005 and the natural gravels. The graves were sealed by four layers of made ground (3002, 3003, 3004 and 3011), and by a levelling layer and modern tarmac (3001) (Fig. 9).

Building rubble within these layers probably originated from the demolition and construction of buildings in the vicinity. Eyewitness accounts described the burial ground as being in a disreputable state because demolition debris thrown there during construction of the School Infirmary in the 1770s and 1780s. The area was subsequently landscaped. Layer 3184 was located in the southern central part of Area 1 and extended into Area 2 as layer 6049. Layer 3184 was 0.4 m deep and comprised bands of orange sand (natural) and dark brown silty sand (cemetery soil), and included much disarticulated human bone (c. 10%). It was noted that the upper levels of many graves were truncated over this area, and the layer and associated truncation is interpreted as evidence of the landscaping work. A similar deposit sequence was present within Area 2 (Fig. 10). Layer 6049 was overlaid by graveyard soil 6048 (equivalent to 3005, Fig. 9), which in turn was covered by made ground (6043-6047) and tarmac (6042). (In Figure 10 layer 6049 seals grave 6032 and its fill 6033.)

Burials

Only graves that would be disturbed by piling were excavated. Sixteen piling trenches were located in Area 1 (Fig. 11, T3000-T3015) and 13 in Area 2 (Fig. 12, T6000-T6015). A total of 55 grave cuts containing 104 skeletons were excavated. (Each excavated grave and grave group is described in Appendix 2.) A small quantity of CBM, pottery, clay pipe, glass and a few metal objects were recovered from features. These appeared to have been residual. Specialist reports on artefacts are in Appendices 6 to 10.

The graves were not orientated on the west-east axis so common in Christian burial sites, but were aligned SW-NE at right angles to the long axis of the southern wall of the Devonport Building, and parallel to King William Walk. This suggests that the desire for a neatly laid out graveyard took precedence over burial conventions. Similarly, at the Royal Hospital Haslar, Gosport, Hants., burials were orientated with the NE-SW alignment of the buildings and walls of the hospital, and not W-E as would be expected in a Christian cemetery (Boston 2005).

A similar desire for order was expressed in the northern half of Area 1 and in Area 2, with graves arranged in neat rows, with broadly even spacing between them. It would appear that the locations of these burials were marked above ground. Indeed, a

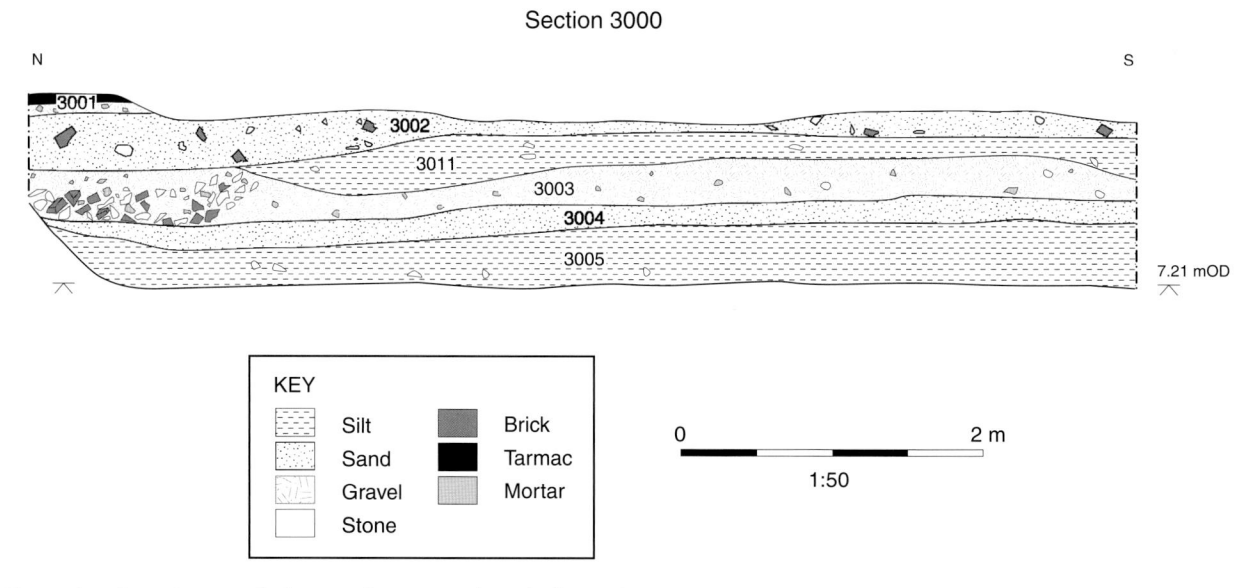

Figure 9 Area 1- west-facing section at north end of trench.

Chapter Three

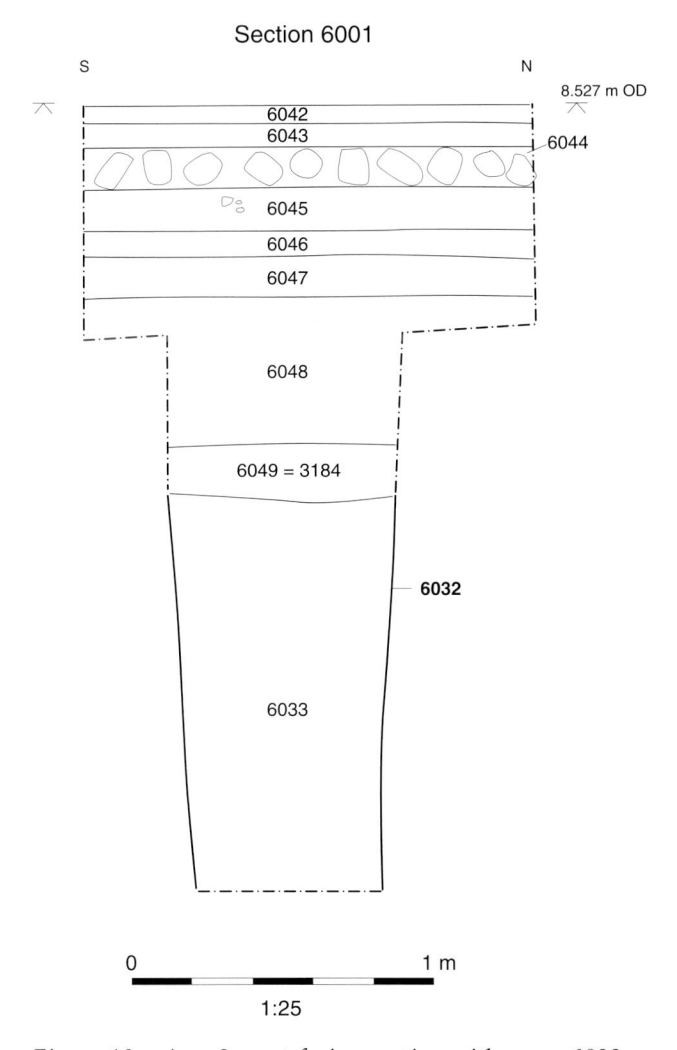

Figure 10 Area 2- east-facing section with grave 6032.

few headstones were present until destroyed in the Blitz. Records of some inscriptions are held by the National Archives, Kew. In the south-western part of Area 1, the regular organisation of earlier graves in rows may be discerned, but many of these were cut or overlaid by later burials, resulting in considerably more truncation of the skeletons. The densest area of intercutting was within the southern part of the trench as noted above.

All the excavated graves were bottomed. Many graves contained multiple interments. The number of inhumations per grave varied from one to six, a mean of three burials per grave (Plate 15).

The vast majority of skeletons were male, but five females, and two possible females and two adolescents (skeleton 3132 aged 12–14 years, and skeleton 3249 aged 16–18 years) were also excavated (Chapter 4, Palaeodemography). A single infant burial was identified but not removed. Most of the remains were males older than 40 years. Thus, the assemblage appeared to have been comprised almost exclusively of pensioners. Assuming that the females of the assemblage were spouses, it is reasonable to suppose that they would be interred within the same grave as their husbands. This was not necessarily the case, however. Female skeleton 3072 was the last of four vertically stacked burials in grave group 3450. The other three burials were elderly males, one of whom may well have been her husband. In grave group 6150, two pairs of skeletons were buried one above the other. Skeleton 6027 was a possible woman buried as one of a pair with male skeleton 6053, but overlaying male skeleton 6056. It is uncertain whether the man next to her or beneath her was her spouse, or indeed, whether either was her husband. The remaining three females (skeletons 3174, 3245 and 6132) and possible female (skeleton 3223) were each individually interred. It is impossible to know whether males in the adjacent graves were their spouses, however. Married couples could not be identified from spatial relations with any degree of confidence.

No difference in burial treatment was accorded to the two adolescents. Skeleton 3132 (aged 12–14 years) was the earliest of three burials within grave group 3410, being overlaid by two older males. An older adolescent 3249 was interred in grave group 3250 above skeleton 3255 (a 35–40 year old male). Like the female burials, it is impossible to know whether these sub adults were related to the other burials within the grave. In the case of group 3410, there were no non-metric traits present that would suggest a familial relationship between skeletons 3249 and 3255. Skeleton 3132 was not analysed for non-metric traits, being too immature, and hence, no osteological evidence exists to suggest a father-child relationship in either case.

Dark staining of the backfill of many graves, remnants of wood within the graves and the presence of iron fixing nails and coffin fittings were associated with 86 burials, indicating that most, if not all of the deceased had been coffined. Where the coffin stain was well preserved, the single break shape could clearly be seen (Plate 29). No legible breastplates were present, and hence, the individual identity of the deceased remains unknown. The coffins and fittings are consistent with working class burials of the time, but were considerably more ornate than those of the Haslar Hospital burial ground, Gosport (Boston 2005). The coffins and fittings are discussed more fully in Chapter 5 below and the fittings summarised in Appendix 4.

Within the graves, the lack of clothes fastenings, such as buttons, toggles or buckles, suggested that the dead had been laid out in shrouds rather than in their personal clothes (in keeping with the prevailing custom in civilian burial). A few copper alloy pins, verdigris staining on the skeletons and the occasional scraps of textile all support this interpretation (Appendix 5).

Non-grave features in Area 1

A limited number of non-grave features were discovered during the excavation of Areas 1 and 2, including the foundations of structures, ditches and pits. Most were post-medieval or modern, post-dating the burials.

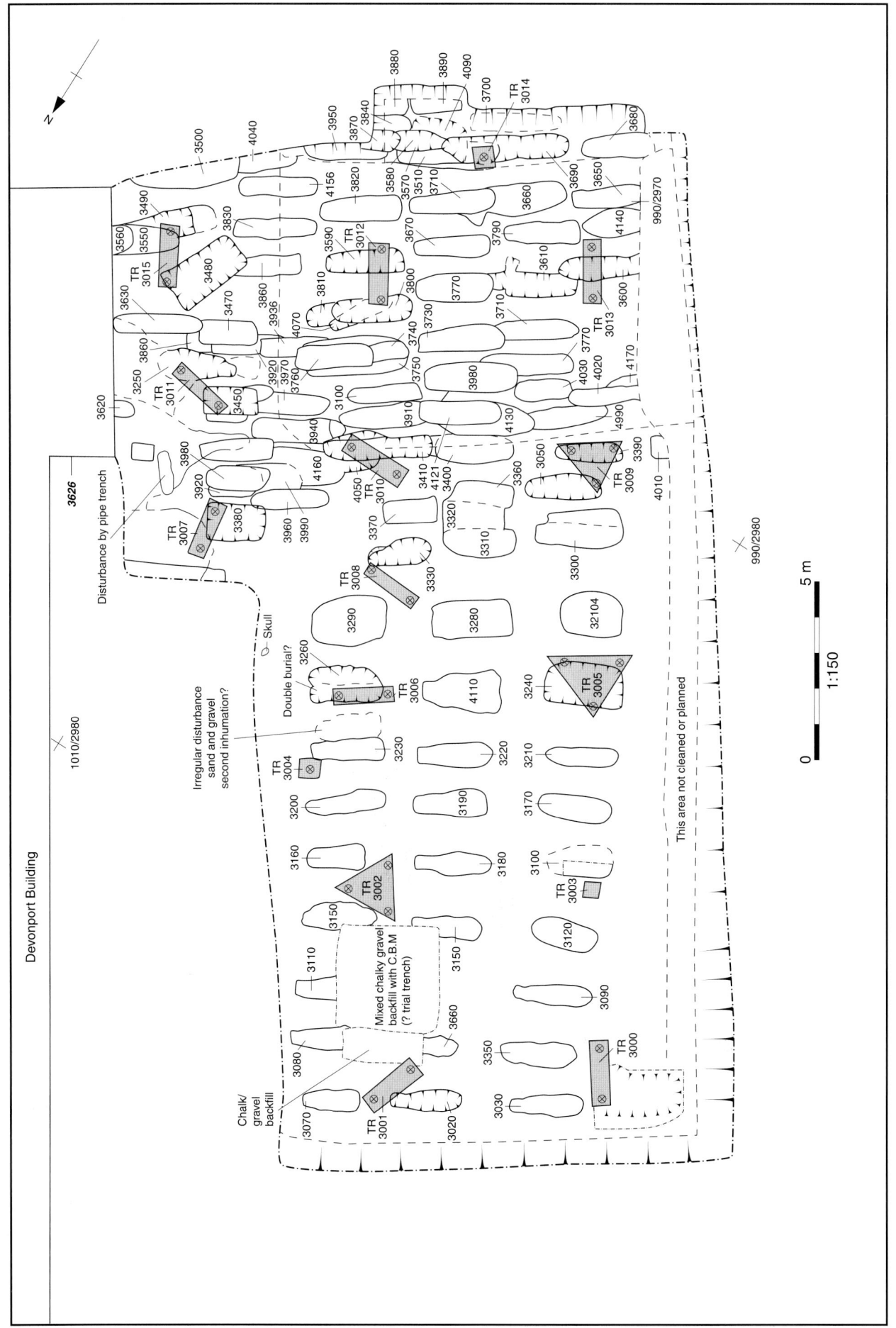

Figure 11 Area 1- plan showing graves and piling trenches.

Chapter Three

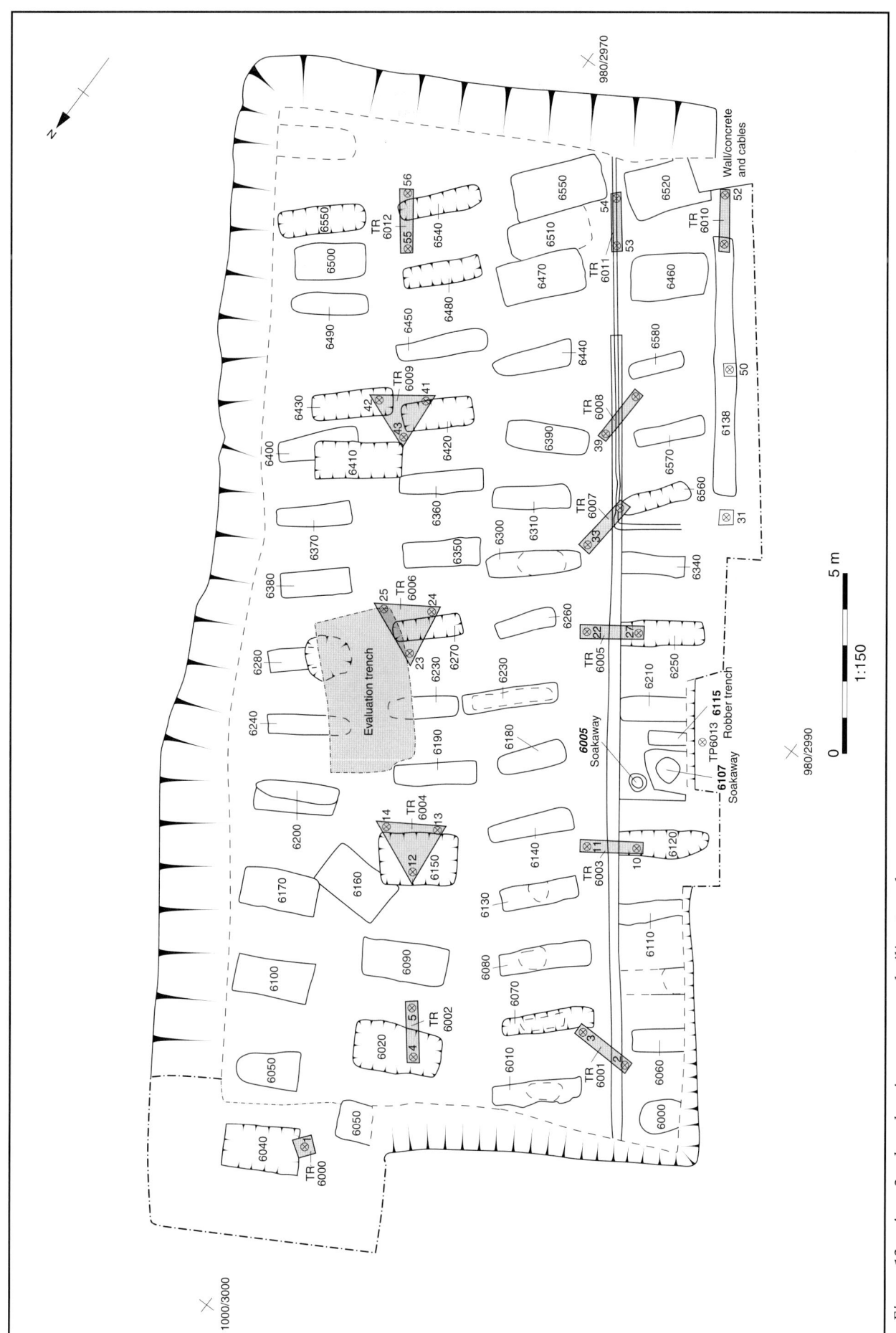

Figure 12   Area 2- plan showing graves and piling trenches.

A rectangular flat based feature (3233) measuring 0.6 m x 0.56 m, was interpreted as a small charnel pit. It contained the pelvis and femora of possible female adult (3232). This feature was truncated by grave cut 3114 (group 3490).

A similar rectangular feature with vertical sides and a flat base (measuring 0.23 m x 0.63 m x 0.11 m) had been dug into the natural gravels (3000) in the eastern end of grave 3215 (group 4090). It contained part of a skull and a right humerus, which was assigned to possible female skeleton 3223.

Also in the south-eastern part of Area 1 was a large area of modern truncation 3147, which was not fully excavated but which extended 12 m in a north-south direction at an acute angle to the southern wall of the Devonshire Building. Its maximum extent in Area 1 was 13 m wide and 1.1 m deep. It remains uncertain if it comprised a single or several cuts. This modern disturbance cut through modern overburden and partly truncated all the graves in the area. It was backfilled with modern building debris (3146).

The foundation trench (3625) and the southern wall of the Devonport Buildings (3626) truncated a number of the south-eastern burials, including groups 3620, 3550 and 3560, removing the lower parts of the skeletons.

Non-grave features in Area 2

A north-south ditch (6008, 6122 and 6124) was found within the northern part of Area 2. This was a shallow feature cutting the natural gravels (3000), but was overlain with graveyard soil (3045) and modern levelling layers and tarmac. Along its length it was truncated by at least three graves (6002 (group 6020), 6026 (group 6150), and unexcavated grave group 6090), and clearly predated them. The ditch ranged in depth from 0.2 m to 0.32 m, becoming shallower towards the south. It appears to have been truncated altogether south of the above interventions. The ditch varied in width from 0.52 m to 0.7 m. In profile, it had moderately sloping sides and a flat base. Its single fill (variously 6007, 6123 and 6125) contained little to date the feature, bar a tile fragment of late post-medieval date, which may itself be residual.

One foundation trench (6139) containing the base of a brick and mortar wall was revealed in the south-western part of Area 2. The remains of the wall survived to four courses. The bricks were red, orange and yellow (measuring 96 mm x 211 mm x 61 mm) bonded by lime mortar in English and Flemish bonds. The total eastern extent of the structure was revealed within the trench (measuring 7.02 m long and 0.6 m in width). The return of the wall towards the west was seen at its northern and southern extent. The function of this structure is not understood.

A number of modern service trenches and soakaways crossed the site truncating burials. Pipe trench 6006 in the western part of the trench truncated burials 6110, 6210, 6250, 6340 and 6560. Modern brick built soakaways with associated drains were also present in this area (6005 and 6107).

Chapter 4: Human Skeletal Remains

INTRODUCTION

A total of 107 skeletons were osteologically analysed. These comprised 104 skeletons excavated from Areas 1 and 2, one from the electrical substation trench and two from Trench 15. The high level of completeness and good overall bone preservation make this a particularly valuable assemblage. It is remarkable for the high prevalence of a wide range of pathologies, which clearly reflect the prevailing social depravation of their working class upbringing, the hardships and dangers aboard ship, and the advanced age of the group. The results of the osteological analysis for each skeleton are presented in the skeletal catalogue (Appendix 3).

Unlike many skeletal assemblages, the Greenwich assemblage dates to a known and restricted time period (AD 1749- 1856). It is unusually homogenous in terms of age and sex, and most individuals are of known occupation. Such specialist populations are extremely rare, and offer a unique opportunity to investigate aspects of osteological methodologies and pathology, whilst controlling for age and sex that otherwise may bias interpretation.

It must be stressed that this osteological report covers only the basic demography and pathology observed during fairly rapid analysis of the bones. The assemblage has considerable potential for further research, particularly in the areas of ancestry, activity-related changes, 18th-century naval surgery, and a range of palaeopathologies. A number of post-graduate dissertations addressing aspects of the osteology not covered by the standard client report have been undertaken already using the Greenwich material. A list of these studies is presented in Appendix 11.

Osteological methodology

The following methods were employed during osteological analysis.

Preservation and completeness

Bone preservation may vary considerably between burials as a result of differences within the immediate micro-environment surrounding each skeleton. These include a wide range of environmental factors such as the pH of the surrounding soil, the coffin material and substances and objects placed within the coffin. These factors may interact, creating a unique niche environment for each skeleton (Henderson 1987, 43). Principal factors that affected preservation within the present assemblage were the soil type, the wood of the coffins, the possible use of absorbent material such as sawdust and bran within the coffin - a common practice in this period - all of which may accelerate diagenesis. Pathological conditions such as osteoporosis may also influence bone survival.

Bone preservation was scored on a four point scale - destroyed, poor, good and excellent - on the following basis:

- *Destroyed* - bone severely leached and fragmented with most elements of the skeleton completely destroyed, trabecular bone not surviving, making it impossible to undertake most osteological examinations.
- *Poor* - cortical bone was soft, leached, flaking or eroded particularly relating to trabecular bone; it was not possible to identify most pathologies.
- *Good* - there was some damage to cortical bone, but large areas sufficiently well preserved to identify pathology and non-metric traits and to undertake metrical analysis; trabecular bone preservation was good with most epiphyses and joint surfaces intact, and good representation of ribs, vertebrae and pelvii.
- *Excellent* - cortical and trabecular bone was pristine, not having undergone the above taphonomic changes, making it possible to undertake full osteological analysis.

Completeness was also scored on a four point scale, based on the percentage of the total skeleton present. The four categories were 5–25%; 26–50%; 51–75%, and 76%-near complete. Completeness was affected by bone preservation and to some extent by the intercutting of graves (particularly in the southern part of Area 1) and truncation by later features. Where charnel within one grave could be clearly identified as originating from an earlier truncated grave, these elements were re-united with their skeleton. Where this was not possible, the charnel was analysed separately. This osteological analysis was kindly undertaken by Dr Peter Hacking, and forms part of the site archive but has not been included in this report.

Skeletal inventory

An inventory of each skeleton was created by shading in the skeletal elements that were present on a pictorial representation. In addition, the presence or absence of skeletal elements was recorded in tabular form and entered into an Access database. This recording formed the basis of the calculated true prevalence of pathological lesions described below.

Dental inventories were made following the Zsigmondy system (as cited in Hillson 1996, 8–9). Dental notations were recorded by using universally accepted recording standards and terminology (after Brothwell 1981).

Sex determination

Sexually dimorphic traits emerge after the onset of puberty, and hence, can only be ascribed with any degree of certainty to skeletons aged greater than 16–18 years. The pelvis is the most sexually dimorphic element, exhibiting features that directly relate to functional evolutionary differences between the sexes (Meindl, Lovejoy, Mensforth, *et al.* 1985; Mays 1998; Mays and Cox 2000), most significantly childbirth in females. Blind studies of individuals of known sex reveal that ascribing sex using this element alone had a reported accuracy as high as 96% (Mays 1998; Sutherland and Suchey 1991).

The skull is the next most sexually dimorphic element, from which it is claimed that sex may be correctly inferred in up to 92% of cases (Mays 1998, 38). It has been claimed that sex estimation from the cranium alone has an accuracy of 88% (St Hoyme and Iscan 1989, 69) whilst 90% accuracy is achieved when the mandible is also present (Krogman and Iscan 1986, 112). This observed sexual dimorphism arises as the result of the action of testicular hormones on the bones of the male skull (ibid., 38), which cause a general increase in robusticity and enlargement of muscle attachment sites. Blind studies undertaken on the named assemblage of Christ Church, Spitalfields, revealed that in skeletons where both complete skulls and pelvii were present, sex determination had an accuracy as high as 98% (Molleson and Cox 1993).

Six cranial features and a maximum of ten pelvic features were used for sexing adults. On the cranium, the features used were selected from Ferembach *et al* (1980) and Buikstra and Ubelaker (1994). Sexually diagnostic features of the pelvis included the greater sciatic notch and preauricular sulcus (Ferembach *et al* 1980), as well as several features of the pubic bone described by Phenice (1969).

Metrics used in the assignment of sex are based on the generalisation that males (under the influence of male hormones) tend to be taller and more robust than their female counterparts. Metrics used were the diameters of the femoral, humeral and radial heads, the clavicular length, and the width of the glenoid fossa (Chamberlain 1994). This method is limited by the fact of considerable interpersonal and interpopulation variation. A substantial zone of intermediate values exists between the sexes, rendering sexing using metrical analysis alone very unhelpful in most cases. In the Greenwich assemblage, sex was thus determined principally by cranial and pelvic morphology.

Sex may be ascribed to skeletons with differing levels of certainty, depending on the extent of sexual dimorphism present and the number of sexually dimorphic sites available for study. Sex categories used in this study reflect this uncertainty. Probable male (= '? Male') or probable female (= '? Female') is used where the sex could be ascribed but where some uncertainty exists, and 'male' or 'female' is used where there is considerable certainty of the sex of an individual.

Age estimation

Macroscopic estimation of age establishes the biological age of the skeleton and not the individual's chronological age. Disparity between the two may develop as a result of factors such as nutrition and lifestyle, which may impact on skeletal growth and degeneration (Schwartz 1995, 185). Limitation in ageing methods, particularly in older individuals, was particularly significant in this ageing population, and was probably most responsible for the great disparity between biological age and the age at death range known from historical records.

In order to increase the accuracy of age estimations, multiple methods were employed. Age estimation of the two sub adults was based on the sequence and timing of epiphyseal fusion (Ferembach *et al.* 1980; Schwartz 1995) and on dental development of permanent dentition (Moorees *et al.* 1963). Adults were aged from the extent of degeneration of the ilial auricular surface (Lovejoy, Meindl, Pryzbeck, *et al.* 1985) and the pubic symphysis (Todd 1921a and 1921b; Brooks and Suchey 1990). Age estimation based on the timing of ectocranial suture closure (Meindl and Lovejoy 1985) was also used but was not as rigorously applied as the aforementioned, as the accuracy and precision of this method is believed not to be high (Cox 2000). Dental attrition models (such as Miles 1962) were not used as considerable discrepancies between this method and other ageing methods have been identified. In general, the Greenwich pensioners' dentition showed greater overall wear than that found in contemporary skeletal populations. Nonetheless considerable under-ageing using dental attrition methods (eg. Miles 1962) was still present. This probably reflects the more refined diet and milling techniques in this time period compared with earlier agricultural societies on which such ageing methods were based. Table 2 presents the age categories employed in this analysis.

Stature estimation

Adult stature was calculated from the maximum length of the left femur by applying the regression formulae for white males and females devised by Trotter and Gleser (1952) and revised by Trotter (1970). Skeletons of ambiguous sex and those displaying marked pathology of the femur were excluded.

Table 2 Age-at-death categories used in osteological analysis.

Skeletal age at death
Adolescent : 13–18 yrs
Young Adult : 19–25 yrs
Middle Adult : 26–35 yrs
Mature Adult: 36–45 yrs
Older Adult: 45+ years
Adult: age undetermined

Comparative assemblages used in the analysis

The results of the osteological analysis of the Greenwich pensioner sample were compared to seven broadly contemporary English skeletal assemblages of differing socio-economic backgrounds. This facilitated comparisons between different social classes with regards to their patterns of health and disease. These assemblages were from the Newcastle Infirmary, Newcastle-upon-Tyne (Boulter *et al*. 1997), the Cross Bones burial ground, London (Brickley *et al*. 1999), St Martin's, Birmingham (Brickley *et al*. 2006); Christ Church, Spitalfields, London (Cox 1996; Molleson *et al*. 1993), St Luke's church, Islington (Boyle *et al*. 2005), St George's crypt, Bloomsbury (Boston *et al*. 2006; Boston *et al*. forthcoming) and from an archaeological evaluation at the Royal Hospital Haslar, Gosport, Hampshire (Boston 2005).

Burials from the Newcastle Infirmary dated to between 1745 and 1845, and were those of patients who died in the hospital. Medical treatment in public hospitals was reserved for the poor, as the more affluent classes were treated privately at home. Hence, the burial assemblage comprised the poor of the city, who were eligible for medical care under the Poor Law (Nolan 1997). The assemblage is particularly interesting as it included a number of merchant seamen, perhaps accounting for 35% of the assemblage (ibid).

The Cross Bones burial ground was in use from the middle of the 19th century. The inhumations comprising the sample were interred within a 10 to 30 year time span. Around 18% of those buried there were from the workhouse. Overall, the dead were the poorest members of the underprivileged community of Southwark, London (Brickley *et al*. 1999, 48).

The skeletal assemblage from St Martin's churchyard, Birmingham, dated to the post-medieval period, with the bulk of the burial population being interred during the period from the later 18th century to the 1860s. The bulk of the population comprised the working classes of the parish, with some middle class elements.

The named sample from Christ Church, Spitalfields, was buried within the church crypt between 1729 and 1852. Trade directories and burial records indicate that most individuals were artisans and master craftsmen (Cox 1996, 69), many of whom had achieved considerable affluence in the silk trade, but remained resolutely middle class. Very few were professionals or independently wealthy. Still fewer were indigent.

The named assemblage from the crypt of St George's church, Bloomsbury, London, comprised 72 skeletons retrieved from open wood and lead coffins (Boston *et al*. 2006; Boston *et al*. forthcoming). The assemblage contained few sub adults, and many individuals fell within the mature to older adult age categories. The assemblage was principally upper middle class, with professions such the Law, medicine, politics, the military and the Church being well represented. Paleodemographics and disease profiles were consistent with an affluent population. Burials dated from 1812 to 1856.

An evaluation in the grounds of Haslar Hospital, Gosport, Hants., one of the three Royal Navy hospitals devoted to treating the sick and hurt on active service revealed 167 graves of seamen and soldiers who died at the hospital (Boston 2005). The remains of 19 servicemen were examined *in situ*, but not lifted. All were male, and most were young to prime age adults. Relatively little pathology was noted on the skeletons, suggesting that many had died of acute diseases or injuries that left little evidence on the bone. The burials dated from 1753 to 1826.

PRESERVATION AND COMPLETENESS
(Tables 3–4)

The integrity of the majority of Greenwich skeletons had been largely maintained, with 71.96% of the skeletons being more than 75% complete; and 93.46% being more than 50% complete (Table 3). Only one skeleton was represented by less than 25% of its elements. Although many grave cuts contained more than one skeleton, the burials had been neatly stacked one above the other, such that the integrity of each skeleton was easily maintained during excavation. It is probable that some mixing of smaller bones (such as phalanges) did occur, although the excavators were certain that this was limited in extent. In some cases, where a burial had been truncated by a later grave - more common in Area 1 than Area 2 - the disturbed elements of the earlier skeleton were often included in the backfill of the new grave. It was with a high degree of confidence that this charnel was re-united with the skeleton of which it had originally been part. Otherwise, the bones were assigned as charnel and excluded from the analysis below.

Overall, bone preservation was good (63.55% of assemblage) to excellent (14.02%). In 22.43% of skeletons, however, it was rated as poor (Table 4). With more than three-quarters of the assemblage so well preserved, there was considerable potential for identification of pathological and non-pathological bone modification, and for the presence of non-metric traits. Fragmentation was also relatively minor, allowing a large proportion of crania and long bone measurements to be taken.

Table 3 Skeletal completeness (N = 107).

Completeness	N (skeletons)	%
76–100%	77	71.96
51–75%	23	21.50
26–50%	6	5.61
0–25%	1	0.93
Total	**107**	

Table 4 Bone preservation (N = 107).

Bone condition	N (skeletons)	%
Excellent	15	14.02
Good	68	63.55
Poor	24	22.43
Destroyed	0	0
Total	107	100

PALAEODEMOGRAPHY

Age and sex distribution (Table 5)

The assemblage comprised 107 skeletons, of which 105 were adult and two (skeletons 3132 and 3249) were sub adult (Fig. 13). The sub adult skeleton 3132 was aged between 12 and 14 years, and skeleton 3249 between 16 and 18 years. Skull and pelvic morphology did suggest that skeleton 3249 was male, but due to its sub adult classification, it was categorised as sex unidentified. It is possible that these two adolescents were the offspring of pensioners living in the hospital. Skeleton 3249, however, showed degenerative changes of the vertebral bodies consistent with one who had undertaken prolonged strenuous physical activities, particularly the carrying of heavy weights. It is possible therefore that this individual was a young recruit - boys as young as 12 years were recruited - who had been debilitated in active service at an early age, and was pensioned to Greenwich. However, this interpretation does not accord with historical records, and furthermore there was no evidence of traumatic injury to the skeleton.

One older adult skeleton (6019) could not be sexed. There were five females in the adult assemblage (4.76%; n = 105) and two possible females (3223 and 6027). Three female skeletons were mature adults: skeleton 3245 aged 35–45 years; 3072 aged 40+ years, and 6132 aged 40–50 years. Two skeletons (2005 and 3174) were of older adults aged 50+ years. One possible female skeleton (3223) was aged 40+ years and the other possible female (6027) was aged as 50+ years. It is probable that these were the wives or widows of in-pensioners. Historical documents reveal that such women were often employed within the hospital as domestic servants or nurses (see Chapter 2 above).

Unsurprisingly, given the nature of the assemblage, the vast majority of the adult population (n = 105) was sexed as male (83.8%; n = 88) or possibly male (8.57%; n = 9). In the following analysis possible males and females were treated as definitely male and female.

Most males and possible males were mature or older adults. The exceptions were 4 adult males skeletons (3061, 3108, 3164 and 3261) and a possible male (3274) of 30–40 years, and 10 skeletons aged at 35–40/45 years. It was possible to identify 34 male individuals from Greenwich as being aged over 40 years, 12 as over 45 years, and 35 as greater than 50 years and one greater than 60 years.

Most older individuals could not be more precisely aged due to the limitations of osteological methodologies that are most accurate in skeletons aged 30 years or less at death, but become increasingly imprecise with advancing age (Mays 1998). Unfortunately, the sternal rib end ageing method devised by Iscan et al. (1984), that Loth (1995), and Witkin and Boston (2005; 2006) demonstrated to be so useful in ageing older post-medieval skeletons beyond 50 years of age and up to the age of 78 years, could not be employed on the Greenwich material due to the poor preservation of the fourth sternal rib end.

Ageing methods used in this analysis (such as degeneration of the ilial auricular surface and the pubic symphysis) do not allow for the identification of individuals older than 50 to 60 years, as variation in the rate of degeneration of these joints becomes increasingly varied with advancing age (Cox 2000). Historical data collated from a sample of 100 individuals listed in the Ayshford Trafalgar Rolls (Appendix 1) indicated that the mean age of death of pensioners dying at the hospital was 70.1 years, with the age range tightly clustered about the mean (see below). Due to the limitations in osteological ageing methods, it was impossible to precisely determine biological age at death, or for this age distribution to accurately reflect the chronological age distribution known from historical data, other than to concur that this was an aged population.

Table 5 Summary of age and sex distribution in the total sample (N = 107).

Age categories	Unknown sex	Male	? Male	% male & ? male	Female	? female	% females & ? females	Total	% population
Adolescent	2	0	0	0.00	0	0	0	2	1.87
Young adult	0	0	0	0.00	0	0	0	0	0
Prime adult	0	1	0	1.03	0	0	0	1	0.93
Mature adult	0	13	5	18.56	1	0	14.29	19	17.76
Older adult	1	73	5	80.41	5	1	85.71	85	79.43
Total	3	87	10	100.00	6	1	100.00	107	100.00

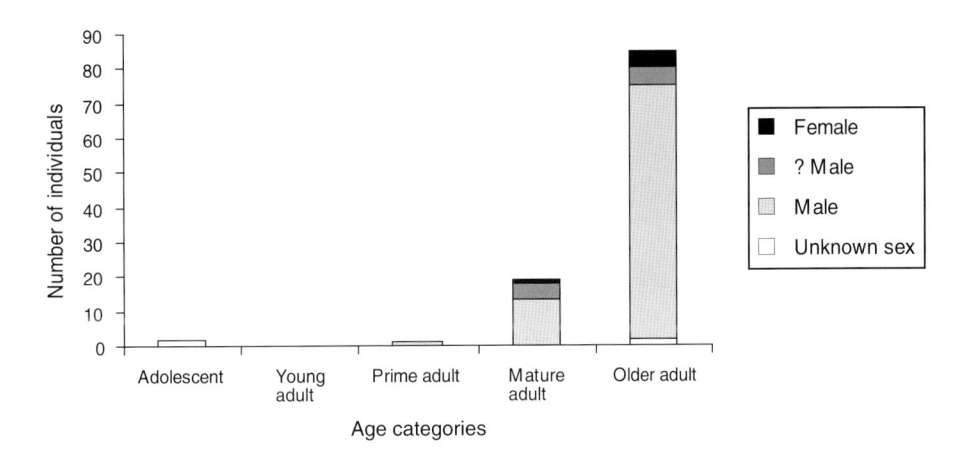

Figure 13 Age and sex distribution in the Greenwich assemblage (N = 107).

Ancestry

Given the wide geographical catchment for recruitment for the Royal Navy (see Chapter 2 above), it is not altogether surprising that the craniometry and morphology of some individuals was indicative of non-Caucasian ancestry. No systematic osteological analysis of ancestry using methodologies employed by forensic anthropologists (e.g. Byers 2005) was undertaken on this assemblage. During the course of the analysis, however, two individuals (skeletons 3061 and 3164) were tentatively ascribed negroid ancestry on the basis of cranial (Gill and Rhine 1990) and femoral morphology (Gilbert 1976). Limited craniometrics (Giles and Elliot 1962) were undertaken, which substantiated the morphological findings. Computer programmes using discriminate function analysis, such as FORDISC (Ousley and Jantz 2005) and CRANID (Wright 2005), were not utilised in this initial analysis. A more systematic and detailed analysis of ancestry is warranted, but unfortunately lay beyond the scope of this report.

Interestingly, both negroid males were aged between 30 and 40 years, and hence were amongst the younger age categories. Skeleton 3061 had undergone a below knee amputation, whilst skeleton 3264 had suffered a comminuted fracture of the left tibia. Both injuries were well healed at the time of death. Skeleton 3061 was the subject of a National Geographic documentary in 2003. As part of the programme, strontium, oxygen and lead isotope analysis was undertaken on the dentine and enamel of a tooth from the skeleton in order to investigate his place of origin (Evans and Chenery 2004). Interestingly, the results indicated that he was not of Caribbean or African origin as expected, but had isotope signatures consistent with a British origin, particularly Eastern Britain.

The presence of significant numbers of blacks in Georgian Britain, particularly in the large cities, has only been acknowledged recently by historians, and because systematic osteological analysis of ancestry is seldom undertaken on post-medieval skeletal populations in Britain, identification of these individuals may be often overlooked. One exception was an adult male of negroid ancestry identified in the assemblage of St Luke's church, Islington, London (Boyle *et al.* 2005). The true number of blacks in Georgian England is difficult to quantify, but in 1764, the *Gentleman's Magazine* estimated the number in London to be as high as 20,000. Other authors (for example Fryer 1984) estimate that the black population was much higher with at least 70,000 black people living in Britain. Most were male and most worked in menial occupations, such as domestic servants or labourers, whilst others were professional boxers and sailors. The possible presence of a black Briton amongst the Greenwich pensioners should thus not come as a great surprise.

STATURE ESTIMATION

Stature is determined by the interplay of inherited and environmental factors. Whilst we all have a maximum genetic potential to attain a certain adult stature, physical and emotional stressors during childhood and adolescence may prevent us achieving this potential (Lewis 2007, 66–68). If such stressors (eg. malnutrition, infection or chronic illness) are too severe or prolonged for the growing body to 'catch-up' growth later, the individual will become permanently stunted. Chronically deprived adolescents may prolong their growth well into their twenties and sometimes even thirties through the delayed fusion of the epiphyses of the long bones, thereby maximising their final adult stature.

Stature has been used as a rough yardstick to indicate the overall health of individuals during the growing years. When analysed in conjunction with indicators of childhood stress, such as dental enamel hypoplasia and cribra orbitalia, adult stature may be a useful indicator of health in individuals and in assemblages as a whole, commonly reflecting the socio-economic nature of that population. As discussed in

Table 6 Distribution of male statures in the Greenwich sample (N = 88).

Stature (m)	N (skeletons)	%
1.50–1.54	1	1.1
1.55–1.59	5	5.6
1.60–1.64	21	23.8
1.65–1.69	32	36.3
1.70–1.74	22	25.0
1.75–1.79	6	6.8
1.80–1.84	1	1.1
1.85+	0	0
Total	**88**	**100%**

Chapter 2, the vast majority of ratings in the Royal Navy were drawn from the working classes, among whom poor nutrition and disease was widespread. It is thus interesting to compare the stature of this assemblage with other recently analysed skeletal assemblages of this period (see Table 7).

It was possible to estimate the stature of 88 adult males and 5 females in the Greenwich assemblage. Female stature ranged from 1.563 to 1.617 m (5ft 1in – 5ft 3in), with a mean stature of 1.595 m (5ft 2in), [sd 1 of 2.19]. Male stature showed a much wider distribution, ranged from 1.542 m - 1.83 m (5ft – 6ft), with a mean of 1.679 m (5ft 5in) [sd 1 of 5.57] (Table 6; Fig. 14).

Although the stature of seamen was not systematically recorded in naval records, one private study undertaken by a Captain Rotheram is held in the National Maritime Museum at Greenwich. Rotheram measured the heights of seamen aboard his ship, and calculated their mean stature as 5ft 5ins (Adkins and Adkins pers. comm.) - a figure that neatly concurs with osteological stature estimates of the Greenwich pensioners.

The mean stature of the Greenwich assemblage was compared with that of seven other contemporary English skeletal populations (Table 7). Although all estimations were undertaken using the equations of Trotter (1970), there are differences in long bones which were used in the analysis. Inevitably, this will introduce subtle differences in stature estimation. In addition, the long bone lengths of 19 male skeletons from the Haslar Hospital were measured whilst the skeletons were *in situ*, undoubtedly introducing a greater margin of error than in laboratory analysed specimens. Notwithstanding these caveats, it is interesting to compare the stature of the two contemporary Royal Naval assemblages, with one another and with contemporary civilian populations.

Table 7 shows that the mean stature of the five females of Greenwich was comparable with the stature of the working class assemblage of the Newcastle Infirmary and the upper middle class assemblage of St George's, Bloomsbury, and was 10 mm greater than that of St Martin's, Birmingham. However, inadvertent bias may have been introduced by the small sample size of the Greenwich females.

Unlike female stature, the pensioners' mean male stature was noticeably less than even that of the pauper assemblage of the Cross Bones, Southwark (by 10 mm), 30 mm less than the mean stature of the other working class assemblage of the Newcastle Infirmary (which included many merchant seamen), and 40 mm less than St Martin's, Birmingham. Interestingly the mean stature of the seamen and soldiers from the Haslar Hospital, Gosport, was the lowest of all the assemblages. It must be acknowledged, however, that the statures of the Greenwich pensioners were not adjusted in accordance with their advanced age (as recommended by Trotter 1970).

The short stature of the ratings appears to reflect their deprived working class origins, where growth stunting during childhood and adolescence had resulted in permanently reduced adult stature (Fig. 15). Marine musters taken on enlistment record many physical characteristics, including stature. Although useful, we cannot know how accurately their heights were taken. Ayshford and Ayshford (2004) collated stature measurements from all musters kept during the Napoleonic Wars, presenting them as distribution graphs (the raw data was not presented). This has been reproduced below as Figure 16. Their pop-

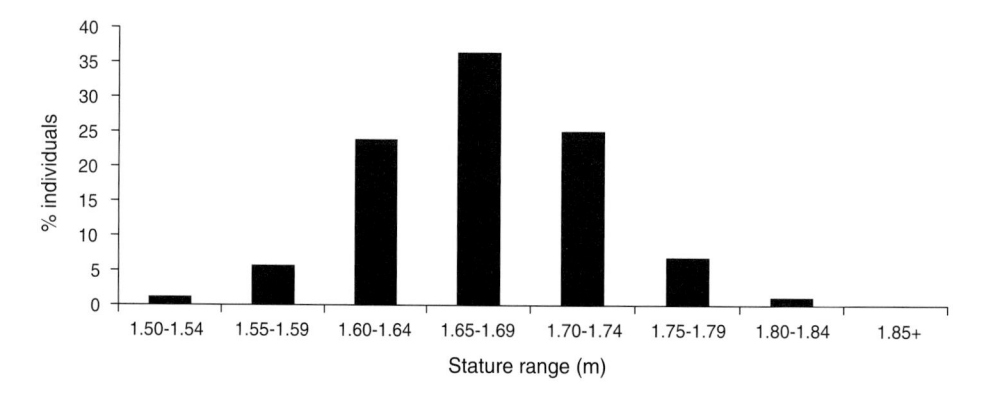

Figure 14 Distribution of male stature by percentage of males with measurable left femora, N = 88.

Table 7 Stature estimates from seven contemporary assemblages in England.

Assemblage	Male (Mean)	Male (Range)	Female (Mean)	Female (Range)
Royal Hospital, Greenwich	1.68 m	1.54–1.83 m	1.60 m	1.56–1.62 m
Haslar Hospital, Gosport	1.64 m	1.54–1.68 m	-	-
St Martin's Church, Birmingham	1.72 m	1.56–1.85 m	1.59 m	1.39–1.71 m
St George's Church, Bloomsbury	1.72 m	1.52 m–1.85 m	1.60 m	1.49 m–1.72 m
St Luke's Church, Islington	1.70 m	1.55 m–1.93 m	1.58 m	1.49 m–1.72 m
Newcastle Infirmary, Newcastle-upon-Tyne	1.71 m	1.60 m–1.83 m	1.60 m	1.50 m–1.76 m
Christ Church, Spitalfields	-	1.68 m–1.70 m	-	1.54 m–1.59 m
Cross Bones, Southwark	1.69 m	1.53 m–1.80 m	1.58 m	1.42 m–1.72 m

ulation included boy recruits who would not have reached their full adult height, and may account for some of the very low statures (some less than 4ft 6in) recorded in the musters. The majority of marines had statures between 5ft 2in and 5ft 8in, and peaked at 5ft 4in. The distribution about the mode is broadly symmetrical. Unfortunately, the stature of seamen was not similarly recorded in the Naval records and it is not known if it differed significantly from marines with whom they sailed.

In the years following Napoleon's defeat at Waterloo, large numbers of servicemen were discharged from the Army and Navy. Marine discharge papers of that time reveal that being 'undersized' was a criterion for the exclusion of privates. In practice this meant that marines shorter than 5ft 4in were discharged. Being 'undersized' did not appear to have been an impediment when the Navy was desperately recruiting men during the French and Napoleonic Wars. In implementing this rule, the Navy effectively excluded between a quarter to a third of the marine force.

Interestingly, the peak stature of marines recorded in the musters broadly concurs with the mean stature (5ft 5in) of the skeletal assemblage from Greenwich Hospital calculated from femoral length. It must be remembered that many marines enlisted in their late teens and early twenties, when they may still have been growing (given the probable delayed fusion of epiphyses), which may in part account for the one inch discrepancy. Methodological limitations also are probably responsible for the differences between historical and osteological stature.

SKELETAL PATHOLOGY

Introduction

The skeletal assemblage from the Royal Hospital burial ground was remarkable for the high prevalence

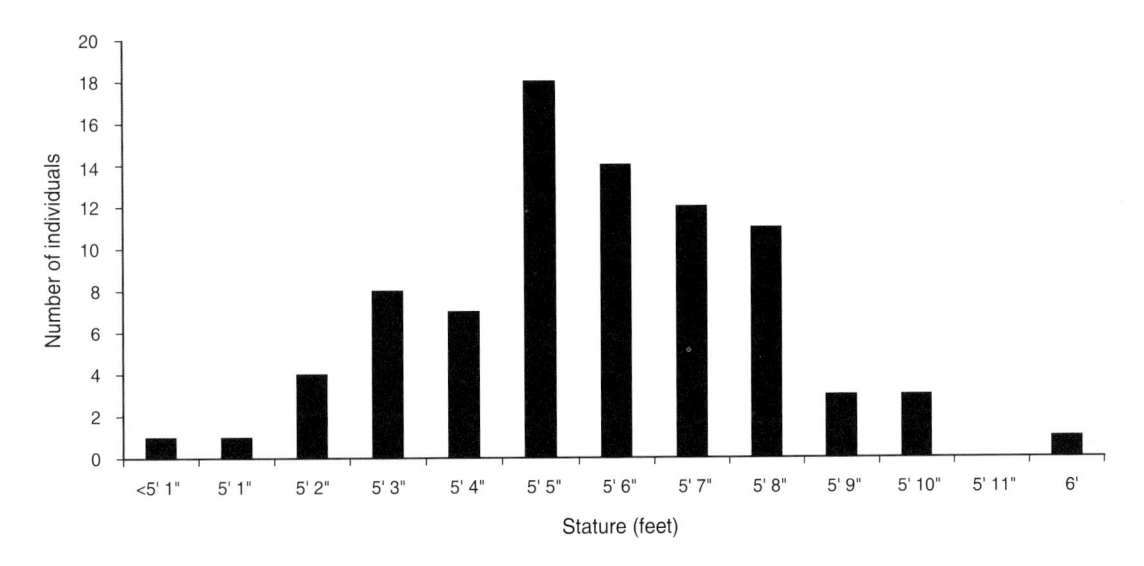

Figure 15 Stature distribution of the Greenwich pensioners, from left femoral lengths (in feet).

Known height of marines on enlistment - all on musters

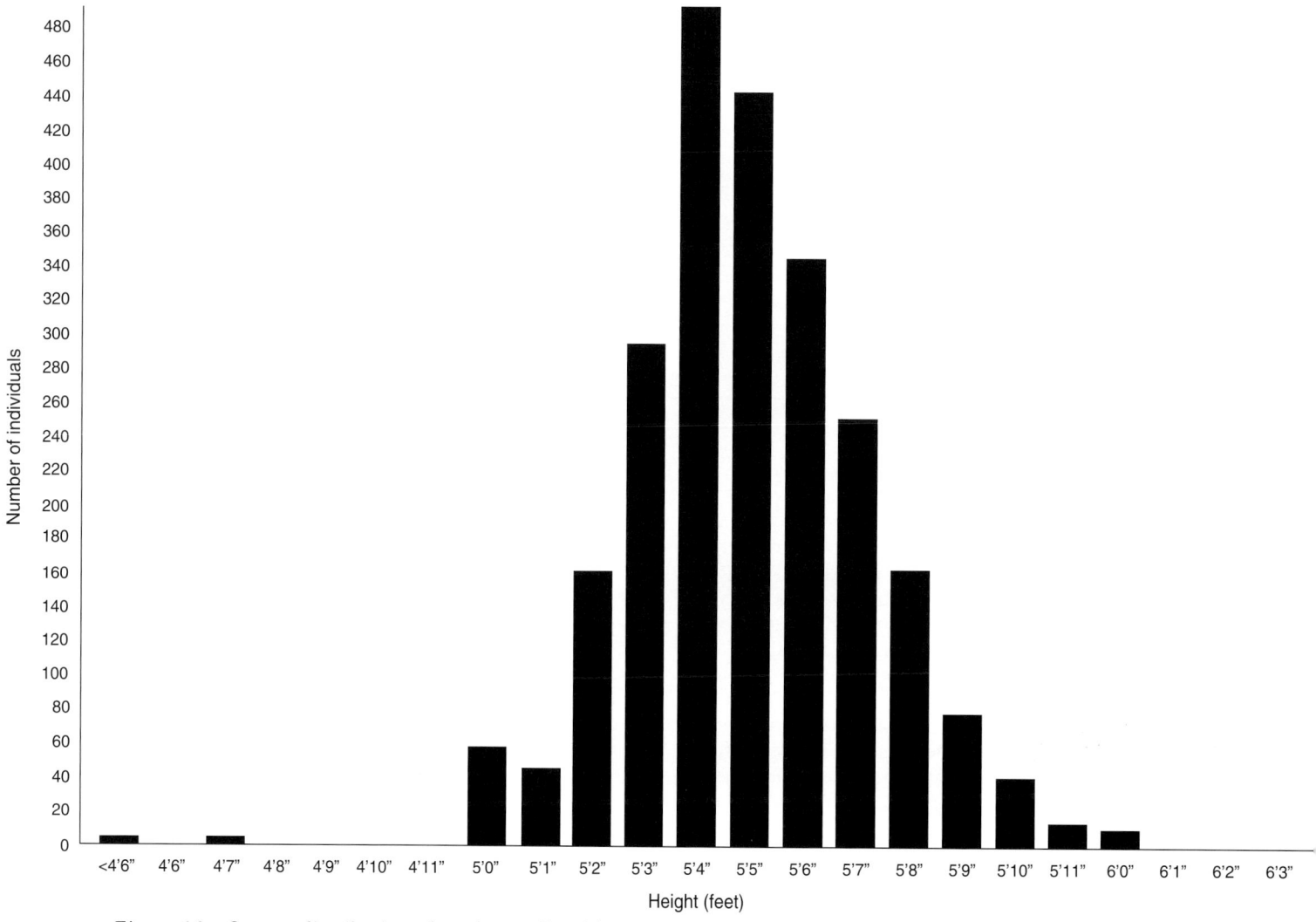

Figure 16 Stature distribution of marines collated from Marine Description Books, in feet (taken from Ayshford and Ayshford 2004).

and wide range of pathologies displayed on the skeletons. Disease and trauma patterns vividly reinforce what is known historically about the origins, on board conditions and dangers faced by the seamen and marines comprising Nelson's Navy. Degenerative joint diseases, such as osteoarthritis, are both reflective of the advanced age group of this assemblage and their physically rigorous lives.

Although it must be acknowledged as an oversimplification of the complex and multiple aetiologies of many of the injuries and diseases, pathologies were classified into seven major categories: trauma, infection, joint disease, metabolic disorders, neoplasms, congenital anomalies and 'other pathologies' that did not fall into any of the above groups. Medical interventions (amputations and craniotomies) and dental pathology are discussed separately below.

Skeletal pathology prevalences were calculated as crude prevalences per skeleton (CPR) and as true prevalences per skeletal element present (TPR). Table 8 summarises the CPR of major categories of disease and trauma noted on the adult skeletons of the assemblage. TPR by skeletal element is presented for the most common pathologies, namely fractures (Table 9) and non-specific bone infection (Table 10).

It should be stressed that the osteological analysis and pathology identification was tightly constrained by time, and that it is the opinion of the examining osteologist, Annsofie Witkin, that some of more subtle bony modifications were missed during analysis. It is therefore probable that the prevalences presented below may slightly under-represent the true picture.

Trauma

The Greenwich assemblage is remarkable for its high rates of trauma, particularly fractures. More of these injuries were probably sustained during everyday life aboard ship than during enemy action, although injury due to the latter could be considerable. As Lewis

Table 8   Crude prevalences (CPR) of pathology in the adult assemblage (N = 105).

Pathology categories	Male (n = 97) N (%)	Female (n = 7) N (%)	Indeterminable sex (n =1) N (%)	Total Adults (n= 105) N (%)
Joint disease				
Osteoarthritis	62 (63.9)	2 (28.57)	0 (0)	64 (60.65)
Rheumatoid arthritis	1 (1)	0 (0)	0 (0)	1 (0.95)
Seronegative spondyloarthropathy	16 (16.4)	0 (0)	0 (0)	16 (61.3)
DISH	3 (3)	0 (0)	0 (0)	3 (2.86)
Osteophytosis (all joints excluding vertebrae)	92 (94.8)	6 (85.7)	0 (0)	98 (93.33)
Schmorl's nodes	67 (69)	2 (28.57)	1 (100)	70 (66.67)
Spinal Degenerative Joint Disease	94 (96.9)	5 (71.43)	1 (100)	100 (95.23)
Spondylolysis	5 (5.1)	0 (0)	0 (0)	5 (47.62)
Other spine conditions	14 (14.4)	0 (0)	0 (0)	14 (13.33)
Other joint diseases	7 (7.2)	2 (28.57)	1 (100)	10 (9.52)
Trauma				
Ante-mortem fracture	82 (84.5)	2 (28.57)	1 (100)	85 (80.95)
Skull wound/injury	52 (53.6)	0 (0)	0 (0)	52 (49.52)
Ligament trauma	6 (6.1)	0 (0)	0 (0)	6 (5.71)
Osteochondritis dissecans	6 (6.1)	0 (0)	1 (100)	7 (66.67)
Cortical defects	1 (1)	0 (0)	0 (0)	1 (0.95)
Other trauma	12 (12.3)	0 (0)	0 (0)	12 (11.43)
Infection				
Maxillary sinusitis	5 (5.1)	1 (14.29)	0 (0)	6 (5.71)
Periostitis	61 (62.8)	2 (28.57)	0 (0)	63 (60.0)
Osteomyelitis	3 (3)	0 (0)	0 (0)	3 (2.86)
Infective arthropathies	1 (1)	0 (0)	0 (0)	1 (0.95)
Tuberculosis	2 (2)	0 (0)	0 (0)	2 (1.90)
Treponemal disease	3 (3)	0 (0)	0 (0)	3 (2.86)
Other infectious diseases	3 (3)	0 (0)	0 (0)	3 (2.86)
Metabolic disorders				
Cribra orbitalia	34 (35)	1 (14.29)	0 (0)	35 (33.33)
Scurvy	12 (12.37)	0 (0)	0 (0)	12 (11.43)
Rickets	10 (10.3)	0 (0)	0 (0)	10 (9.53)
Osteoporosis	2 (2)	0 (0)	0 (0)	2 (1.90)
Other metabolic conditions	1 (1)	0 (0)	0 (0)	1 (0.95)
Neoplastic disease				
Neoplastic disease	9 (9.2)	0 (0)	0 (0)	9 (85.71)
Congenital disorders				
Congenital anomalies	9 (9.2)	1 (14.29)	1 (100)	11 (10.483)
Medical interventions				
Amputations	5 (5.16)	0 (0)	0 (0)	5 (4.76%)
Craniotomies	3 (3.09%)	0 (0)	0 (0)	3 (2.86)

(1960, 361) phrased it battle casualties 'were small compared with those inflicted by causes other than the hand or wit of man'. Falling from the rigging, injuries from swinging booms, and crush injuries during violent storms were probably responsible for a great many injuries. Seamen were aloft in the rigging at all times of day or night and in all weathers, often performing feats that could only be expected of an acrobat or steeplejack. A fall from the rigging onto the deck some 100 feet below was often fatal, and there was also the distinct possibility of killing or injuring another seaman on the crowded decks below (Lewis 1960, 392). Able seaman George Gamsby (Trafalgar veteran and Greenwich pensioner) was one seaman who suffered major disability by falling from the hatchway into the cockpit during the Battle of Trafalgar. His injuries left him with impaired use of both legs and constant back and leg pain (Ayshford and Ayshford 2004).

Skeleton 3241 of the Greenwich assemblage was remarkable for the sheer number of fractures he had sustained. The majority was to the right side of his body and involved the left parietal, the clavicle, four ribs, the humerus, distal radius, pisiform, neck of femur, fibula and distal tibia. All were well healed, although many showed considerable malalignment and overlapping of the broken elements. The most probable explanation for this suite of injuries was a fall onto the deck from a great height. In spite of this multiple trauma, he survived to a ripe old age of 50+ years.

On deck or below deck, landmen and ordinary seamen spent much of their days raising or lowering sails, hauling or pushing out heavy, awkward or dangerous loads, often within confined spaces. Guns that broke loose during firing (either in practice or during enemy action) or during violent storms were responsible for many crush injuries, sometimes fatal (hence the term 'a loose cannon'). On deck, falling or being flung against the ship's sides or contents during bad weather and heavy seas was also a significant cause of injuries. Loose cables and lifeboats and falling rigging also presented a risk of crushing (Lewis 1960, 391–96; Fremont-Barnes 2005).

Injuries sustained during enemy action were often severe, leaving many individuals with permanent disfigurement or disability. Direct hits from small arms fire and cannon balls were a major source of injury during bombardment by the enemy, but flying wooden splinters from enemy cannon balls smashed into the sides of the vessel were an even greater source of injury and subsequent infection (Fremont-Barnes 2005). In the sample of 100 Trafalgar veterans who died at Greenwich Hospital (Appendix 3), trauma suffered at Trafalgar included major injuries from splinters and musket fire; rupture; loss of sight and hearing (probably during the cannonade); fractured arms and skulls, and the loss of limbs. For example, Thomas Chapman, a Royal Marine who died in Greenwich Hospital in 1851 aged 72 years, received a musket ball through the head during the battle. Wounds to both cheeks left him with a rigid lower jaw, which subsequently caused considerable difficulties in eating and speaking. He was one of the lucky ones, however. Memoirs of both seaman 'Jack Nastyface' (Robinson 2002) and ship's surgeon James Lowry (2006) describe balls completely taking off the heads or bodies of seamen that they stood alongside during a bombardment.

Fractures

At least one fracture was observed on 85 adult skeletons: 84.5% (n = 97) of the males, 28.57 % (n = 7) of the females, and in the one of unknown sex. Many male skeletons had sustained multiple fractures, all of which were well healed. Due to the advanced age and prolonged retirement of most of the pensioners, it is reasonable to assume that the majority of these injuries were sustained during active service. Some injuries may well have been of more recent date, however. Interpersonal violence between inpensioners in the Hospital was not unknown. An entry in the Trafalgar Rolls (Ayshford and Ayshford 2005) records that one James Bagley (retired private in the Royal Marines and former stocking maker) was discharged from the Hospital in 1856 for '*being drunk and striking Boatswain Morris*'. He was 71 years old at the time of this misdemeanour.

Table 9 summarises the location of fractures on the male skeletons. These data are presented in Figure 17. The skull (including calvarium, face and mandible) was the most common part of the skeleton to display fractures (TPR 57.1%). In her study of more than 6,000 archaeological skeletons from Britain, Roberts (1991) also found that the skull was most commonly affected. In the Greenwich assemblage, injuries included nasal bone fractures (TPR 61.8%), depression fractures of the cranial vault (frontal bone, n = 4; parietal bones, n = 4) and fractures of the face (zygomas, n = 4; maxillae, n = 12) and mandible (n = 1). In a study of 2280 individuals from Siberia, Spain, the United Kingdom and the U.S.A. undertaken by Walker (1997), it was found that nasal bones were the most commonly fractured bone (7.0%), followed by the frontal (4.6%) and parietal bones (3.9%). Nasal fractures were also the most common fracture location on the skull in the Greenwich pensioner assemblage, but this type of injury and injuries to the face were considerably more common than in Walker's study. Cranial vault fracture prevalence does not appear to differ considerably from Walker's assemblage.

Further analysis on a sample of 43 adult male skulls from Greenwich undertaken by Turnbull (2004) revealed an average of 1.92 fractures per skull, of which the vast majority were radiating fractures (79.26%). Ten depressed fractures of the cranial vault and one of the right zygoma (13.12% of skull fractures) were also identified. Both were attributed to blunt force trauma.

One example of sharp force trauma was identified on the right ascending ramus of the mandible of skeleton 3032, the blow had entirely removed the

Table 9 True prevalence of fractures by element (n = 105).

Elements	Males	Females	Total Adults (including one unsexed skeleton)
Total skull	57.1% (52/91)	0% (0/5)	53.6 % (52/97)
Nasal fractures	61.8 % (47/76)	0% (0/5)	57.3 % (47/82)
Vertebra	1.1 % (21/1880)	0% (0/90)	1.0 % (21/1994)
Ribs	5.1 % (74/1425)	0% (0/64)	4.8 % (74/1513)
Clavicles	4.0 % (7/174)	0% (0/9)	3.7 % (7/185)
Scapulae	1.1 % (2/180)	0% (0/13)	1.0 % (2/195)
Humeri	0.5 % (1/187)	7.6% (1/13)	0.9 % (2/202)
Radii	4.2 % (8/188)	0% (0/13)	3.9 % (8/203)
Ulnae	2.1% (4/189)	0% (0/15)	1.9 % (4/206)
Carpals	0.5 % (4/799)	0% (0/53)	0.4 % (4/863)
Metacarpals	2.6 % (20/763)	0% (0/51)	2.4 % (20/822)
Phalanges	0.3 % (4/1216)	0% (0/84)	0.3 % (4/1307)
Femora	3.7 % (7/185)	0% (0/17)	3.4 % (7/204)
Patella	1.4 % (2/142)	0% (0/10)	1.2 % (2/154)
Tibiae	8.8 % (16/180)	0% (0/12)	8.2 % (16/194)
Fibulae	11.1 % (20/180)	0% (0/12)	10.3 % (20/194)
Tarsals	1.7 % (17/988)	0% (0/69)	1.6 % (18/1071)
Metatarsals	1.2 % (10/772)	0% (0/54)	1.1 % (10/836)
Phalanges	0.9 % (7/705)	0% (0/59)	0.8 % (7/778)

mandibular angle at a 30° to 40° angle to the ramus. Soft tissue damage and resulting loss of function had lead to considerable atrophy of the mandible on that side. This low prevalence is somewhat surprising given that cutlasses and knives were issued to both the French and English before boarding an enemy vessel (Fremont-Barnes 2005), and may well suggest that hand-to-hand combat was less common than has been previously believed. There were no examples of projectile trauma in the assemblage.

In modern western populations, nasal fractures are most commonly caused by blunt trauma in the form of automobile accidents, interpersonal violence and falls, and are the third most frequently broken bone in the body (Vipul *et al.* 2006). Many skeletons displayed fractures of more than one facial bone. For example, skeleton 3103 had fractured both nasal bones, both maxillae and the right zygoma (Plate 16). Considerable deviation of the nose to the right is apparent.

Falls and interpersonal violence were highly probable causes of fractures amongst the ratings. As described above, falls were a common feature of everyday life aboard ship, whilst the social life below decks was anything but decorous, particularly where alcohol was involved.

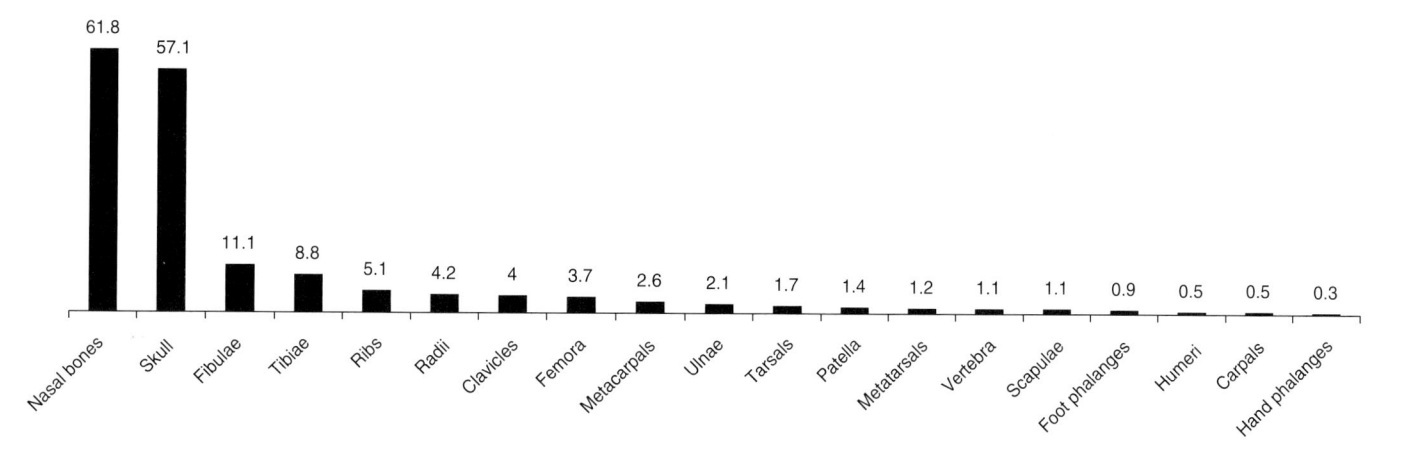

Figure 17 Location of fractures in male skeletons by element (N = 97).

Drunkenness was a perennial problem amongst seamen, but given the conditions and monotony of the service it is hardly surprising that seamen chose this method of escapism (Fremont-Barnes 2005, 27; Lewis 1960, 398–401). According to Leech (cited in Fremont-Barnes 2005, 27)

> to be drunk is considered by almost every sailor as the acme of sensual bliss; whilst many fancy that swearing and drinking are necessary accomplishments in a genuine man-of-war's man.

Lord Keith of the Admiralty, writing in 1812 lamented that

> almost every crime except theft originates in drunkenness, and that a large proportion of men who are maimed or disabled are reduced to that situation by accidents that happen from the same abominable vice (cited in Rodger 2004, 495).

Whilst this may well be somewhat of an overstatement, drunkenness was certainly perceived as being extremely threatening to the ordered regulation of life aboard ship, and the wellbeing of the crew, and officers made considerable efforts to curtail excesses. The extremely generous daily Navy issue of one gallon of beer or half a pint of spirits (most commonly rum or grog) was carefully regulated, and drunkenness was treated as a serious and punishable offence (Fremont-Barnes 2005, 27–8). It was occasionally tolerated, however, and a general free-for-all was often permitted at Christmas and when ships were in home ports. Due to the ever-present risk of desertion, seamen were seldom allowed to celebrate on land. Instead, swarms of bumboats that plied the major seaports brought food, drink, and women to the ships. Plate 11 shows such a scene of revelry in the lower deck. In the foreground is a boxing contest between two seamen (note the cords around their waists limiting their movement), whilst other seamen dance or consort with the prostitutes who have been allowed on board. The scene underlies the potential for both organised and spontaneous brawling. It is highly probable, that the very high prevalence of nasal and facial fractures may well be attributed to interpersonal violence on such occasions. The high prevalence of first metacarpal fractures may be explained in the same way (discussed below).

The prevalence of nasal bone fractures (TPR 61.8%; CPR 35.51% of total population) is particularly startling when compared to the contemporary predominantly working class population of St Martin's, Birmingham. Brickley *et al* (2006) report a CPR of 1.98% for the whole population. However, there was a significance difference between groups within the churchyard, with 11.1% of adult males from vaults displaying nasal fractures compared to 2.11% from earthcut graves. This was interpreted as culturally induced interpersonal violence (Brickley *et al.* 2006).

In the Greenwich assemblage rib fractures were also very common (TPR 5.1%), and was observed in 26 males (CPR 28.87%). This is considerably higher than the CPR of 2.3% identified at St Martin's, Birmingham (Brickley *et al.* 2006). In the Greenwich assemblage, rib fractures per capita varied between 1 and 11. Like nasal fractures, the most common aetiology in modern populations is falling or interpersonal violence.

Injury to the hands, particularly the metacarpals featured frequently (metacarpals, TPR 2.6%), with six fractures to the first metacarpal; three to the second; seven to the third; three to the fourth, and two to the fifth. Sidedness of the injury was apparent in the third metacarpal (two on the left and five on the right), suggesting a greater prevalence of injury to the dominant hand. The distribution of injuries does not reflect the clear preference for the first metacarpal (Bennet's fractures) noted at St Martin's, Birmingham (Brickley and Smith 2006). Bennet's fractures have been associated with the style of boxing popular in the earlier 19th century before the introduction of the Queensbury Rules in 1867, and the wearing of gloves. Styles of professional boxing were copied by the masses, who often undertook bare knuckle fist fighting as a socially acceptable way of settling disputes (ibid.). This boxing style is illustrated by the two pugilist sailors in Plate 11. Interpersonal violence may well be the cause of many first metacarpal fractures. However, Brickley and Smith (2006) also noted that the most common modern cause of Bennet's fracture is falling onto an outstretched hand - undoubtedly a likely hazard aboard ship.

In the Greenwich assemblage fractures to the third metacarpal (CPR 7.2%; n = 7) showed a preference for the right side (although admittedly the sample was small). The cause of these fractures is unclear but injury whilst grasping and pulling on heavy ropes may well have precipitated this damage.

Fractures of the appendicular skeleton occurred with equal frequency on the left and right in the Greenwich assemblage (Galer 2002). The lower leg bones were the most commonly affected (fibulae TPR 11.1%; tibiae TPR 8.8%), and humeri the least affected (TPR 0.5%). In archaeological populations, femoral shafts are infrequently fractured due to the large force required to break this dense bone, but in 3.7% of males this bone had been broken. One example was skeleton 3229, which had suffered bilateral fractures of the femoral shafts with extensive overlapping of the fractured parts, resulting in considerable foreshortening of both bones (Plates 18 and 19). Radiography revealed extensive callus formation and associated osteomyelitis. Clearly this had been an open fracture that had become infected. Neither bone had been set competently, possibly suggesting the lack of effective medical care or that associated soft tissue injury made reduction and fixation unfeasible or problematic soon after the injury was sustained. This is also suggested by the fractured tibial shaft of skeleton 3164 (Plate 17), although no infection was associated with the latter.

Fractures to the vertebrae largely involved crush or wedge fractures of the vertebral bodies (TPR 1.1%).

Systematic analysis of the location of these fractures in the spinal column was not undertaken, but overall, the thoracic and lumbar regions appeared most affected. Compression fractures often occur as a result of weakening of the bone by osteoporosis, causing collapse of the body, and hence, are particularly prevalent in older individuals. Vertebral collapse may involve the whole body or may be restricted to one aspect (most commonly anterior or lateral), resulting in a wedge fracture (Roberts and Manchester 1995, 69–70). Wedge fractures often cause malalignment of the spine, most commonly kyphosis (hunchback) (Aufderheide and Rodríguez-Martín 1998, 24), but rarely produce a neurological deficit (Browner *et al*. 2003, 886). Unequal weight-bearing often precipitates secondary osteoarthritis, and fusion of the affected bodies. Other causes of compression fractures include trauma (usually when the force is applied vertically downwards, or due to hyperflexion), and as secondary to other pathological disorders, such as tuberculosis of the spine (discussed below) and metastatic carcinoma. The advanced age of the Greenwich pensioners make it probable that osteoporosis played a significant role. Macroscopic diagnosis of osteoporosis is particularly problematic in archaeological skeletons (Roberts and Manchester 1995, 179), and hence, this must remain just a hypothesis. Trauma may also have been significant.

Although all long bone fractures had knitted together, many were poorly aligned and often considerable overlap of the broken elements was present. Radiography of some of the long bones was undertaken by Galer (2002) but a more comprehensive programme is still outstanding. Due to extensive callus formation at many fracture sites, it was thus not possible to diagnose different fracture types in this report. Many individuals had suffered multiple fractures. One of the more dramatic cases was the bilateral femoral shaft fractures in skeleton 3229 (Plates 18 and 19), where the left and right femora showed a shortening of 4.5 cm and 5.5 cm respectively. Whilst malalignment of the broken fragments was negligible on the left, the distal portion of the right was rotated laterally, with an apposition of 25%. Poor reduction with resultant overlap was also present in the left tibia of skeleton 3164 (Plate 17). Degenerative joint changes were noted in the hip, knee, ankle and foot joints, such that the medial and intermediate cuneiforms were fused. This was probably secondary to uneven weight distribution due to the shortening of the left leg. Although the proportion of poorly reduced fractures was not quantified in this analysis, the general impression was that many fractured elements had healed but were malaligned. This suggests that reduction of the fracture had been unsuccessful, indicating that splinting of the affected element had been ineffectual or had not been undertaken (Grauer and Roberts 1996).

Neither of the subadults showed evidence of trauma, whilst amongst the seven females, two displayed fractures (CPR 28.57%). This is considerably lower proportion than the adult male population.

Soft tissue trauma

Trauma to the soft tissues overlying the skeleton may sometimes manifest on the bones, particularly where it involves damage to the ligaments and to the tendons by which muscles attach to the bone. Such damage may manifest as enthesophytes (bony projections at the point of insertion) where ossification of the damaged tissue occurs, or as cortical defects, which manifest as depressions of the bone surface, where bony resorption took place (Resnick 1995). The former may have other aetiologies, however, including ankylosing spondylitis and DISH (see below). A particularly marked exostosis was noted on the distal two-thirds of the right femoral shaft of skeleton 3202 (Plate 20). This bony projection is likely to have formed by soft tissue damage to part of the Vastus intermedius muscle.

Analysis of the prevalence and location of soft tissue injury, together with other bony changes associated with repetitive muscle use may be used to identify handedness and suggest occupation (Steele 2000). Unfortunately, such detailed recording was not systematically undertaken during the analysis. Six particularly marked cases of enthesophytes and one cortical defect were noted in passing, but are not representative of the much higher prevalence seen but not recorded during analysis. Soft tissue injury to the upper limb appeared particularly marked, as were muscle markings, and extension of the anterior aspect of the joint surface of the distal humerus (possibly the result of hyperflexion of the elbow joint during hauling on ropes, or moving up and down the ratlines of the ship's rigging principally using the arms). Further systematic analysis of these bony changes would be very valuable to our understanding of this population but lies beyond the scope of this report.

Rupture

Another common soft tissue injury that left no trace on the skeleton, but which was responsible for major disability was 'rupture' (Lewis 1960, 394–396). Endless hauling on ropes, heaving on capstans, and the lowering and hoisting of heavy barrels (particularly water butts) resulted in often permanent damage to the abdominal muscles, which required the wearing of trusses, sometimes for life. Thousands of single and double trusses were issued by the Navy, the injury being so common that they were something like standard issue to all ships (Lewis 1960, 395). By the end of the Napoleonic Wars (1815), 29,712 seamen had been issued with trusses - approximately one in nine of all those in active service during the wars (loc. cit.). Fragments of poorly preserved leather were discovered beneath the back and around the right side in the torso region of the skeleton 6037 (grave 6039, group 6270). Although the leather was too poorly preserved to identify the garment confidently, it had perhaps formed parts of a truss worn for long-term rupture.

Osteochondritis dissecans

Osteochondritis dissecans is a fairly commonly diagnosed osteological disorder of the joint surfaces of the major long bones (Rogers and Waldron 1995). Physically active young males (such as modern athletes) are most often affected in the first two decades of life (ibid.; Aufderheide and Rodríguez-Martín 1998). This disease is due to a significant localised obliteration of the blood supply, causing necrosis of small areas of joint tissue (Roberts and Manchester 1995, 87). Repeated, low-grade, chronic trauma or micro-trauma is thought to play a role in this injury to the blood vessels (Aufderheide and Rodríguez-Martín 1998, 81). The necrotic bone plaque breaks off from the joint surface and may remain loose in the joint (a so-called 'joint mouse'), causing chronic pain and often precipitating osteoarthritis. Alternatively, the fragment may reattach in its original position or be resorbed, and no further symptoms will be experienced.

Six males and the one adult of indeterminate sex (CPR 6.67%; n = 105) displayed this pathology. Its presence is not surprising in this physically active population. From the Trafalgar Rolls (Ayshford and Ayshford 2004), it is apparent that many seamen joined the Navy in their early 20s, as did many marines. It was possible, however, to be a boy recruit joining as young as 12 or 13 years of age. Thus, the age profile of this condition concurs with the young age of recruitment into the Royal Navy of most servicemen.

Spondylolysis

Spondylolysis was present in the lumbar vertebrae of four adult males (CPR 4.12%, n = 97; CPR 3.81% of the adult population). Spondylolysis is the term given to separation of the vertebral arch from its body at the pars interarticularis. The site of predilection of this condition is the fifth lumbar vertebra (Mays 2006). Spondylolysis was identified in the fifth lumbar vertebra in all four individuals from Greenwich (CPR 4.12%, n = 97; CPR 3.81% of the adult population).

Formerly spondylolysis was considered a congenital anomaly of vertebral ossification (Newell 1995), but today the more favoured interpretation is a stress or fatigue fracture that fails to heal (Adams 1990, 191; Standaert and Herring 2000). The cause of the fracture is thought to be the result of sustained strenuous activity involving loading of the spine (Mays 2006, 352). Very few cases develop before the age of five years (Hensinger 1989). A study of a medieval rural population of Wharram Percy, Yorkshire, did not indicate that adult spondylolysis rates increased with increasing age, and thus, injury appeared to have been sustained in late adolescence or early adulthood (Mays 2006). At this young age the neural arches of the vertebrae have not reached their full structural strength, and are least able to resist the heavy biomechanical load placed on lower back during strenuous manual labour (Mays 2006). It is thus more probable that spondylolysis in the three Greenwich pensioners was sustained in early life, possibly before or during their shipboard years. As described above, lifting heavy weights (such as water butts and ammunition) formed a large component of everyday work aboard ship, particularly for landmen. It is thus not surprising that the condition manifested in these individuals.

Os acromiale

In os acromiale, the final epiphyseal element of the acromial process of the scapula fails to unite with the rest of the bone, a union that normally occurs in males by 18–19 years (Stirland 2000; 2005, 533). Whilst this non-fusion was thought to be heredity in origin, evidence from the human remains aboard the sunken Tudor warship the Mary Rose strongly suggested that strenuous use of the upper limb from a young age may induce this condition. Stirland found that 13.6% of individuals (or 12.5% of scapulae present) had os acromiale - a significantly higher rate than the 3–6% that normally occurs in modern populations. She attributed this phenomenon to long bow archery (ibid. 536).

Three adult male Greenwich skeletons (3098, 3218 and 6063) showed evidence of os acromiale. In the first, it was bilateral, but in the other two it was present on the left side only. The CPR of 3.09% is similar to normal variation found within modern populations (Stirland 2005). This finding was somewhat surprising given that most seamen were engaged in strenuous activities involving the upper body. An explanation may lie in the age at which most seamen joined the Royal Navy. The age at which the Greenwich pensioners began their seafaring lives is of considerable significance, however, and it is highly probable that the acromial epiphyses had already fused before these individuals embarked on a seafaring way of life.

Infection

Non-specific infection was identified in a large proportion of the adult males, whilst several cases of specific infections, such as tuberculosis and syphilis, were also present. Adolescent skeleton 3132 (aged 12–14 years) also showed lesions typical of tubercular spine. The extent of healing was classified as active (woven bone), partly healed (striated or lamellar bone) or fully healed (smooth bone) at the time of death.

Non-specific infection

In the Greenwich assemblage, most cases of bone infection could not be identified to a specific microorganism, and hence, have been categorised as non-specific infection. Most lesions were classed as periostitis where reactive new bone was observed on the bone surface. Thickening of the bone was often observed in these cases, and it would appear that the infection had penetrated to the cortical bone beneath. In the absence of a systematic radiology programme, a diagnosis of osteitis was not tenable, and such lesions were classified as periostitis. Where a cloaca or sinus was present to clearly demonstrate drainage of infective material from the marrow cavity, the bony changes were classified as osteomyelitis. The prevalence of periostitis by element is summarised in Table 10. Although the bones of the skull are not in fact covered by periosteum, superficial surface bone changes have been included in this table.

Periostitis is an inflammation of the periosteum, the fibrous sheath that covers bony tissue. This inflammation stimulates a response in which new bone is deposited on the extra-cortical surface as a result of increased osteoblastic activity. This is often secondary to infection (most commonly tracking from the overlying soft tissue, or less commonly from blood-borne microorganisms in systemic infection, or from adjacent infected compact or trabecular bone). One of the Greenwich pensioners displaying periostitis, or possibly osteitis, secondary to trauma was skeleton 3164 (Plate 17). An oblique fracture involving the right distal tibial shaft had healed but was poorly reduced, with considerable overlap and had left the distal part considerably displaced medially and posteriorly. Reactive new bone on the bone surface and thickening around the fracture showed signs of advanced healing, indicating an injury of long standing.

Periostitis may not necessarily be infective in origin, however, as inflammation may also occur in response to mild trauma, local haemorrhage, nutritional imbalances (eg scurvy or from very high levels of Vitamin A), chronic skin ulcers and in some autoimmune disorders (Aufderheide and Rodríguez-Martín 1998, 179).

Periostitis was present in 61 adult males (62.8%, n = 97) and two females (28.57%, n = 7) in the Greenwich assemblage (Fig. 18). In female skeleton 3072, lesions were distributed bilaterally on the femoral shafts, tibiae and fibulae. Skeleton 3174 also showed a wide distribution, involving both tibiae and fibulae and the left ribs (the former being well healed and the latter active).

By far the most common site of periostitis was the tibial shaft (TPR 34.5%), of which four were of females (TPR 33.3%, n = 12) and 63 were of males (TPR 35%, n = 180). Periosteal reactions were also common on the fibulae (TPR 18.2%), often found in association with lesions on the adjacent tibia, probably the result of localised infection (Table 10). In most archaeological assemblages, the tibia is the most common site of periostitis, largely because the anterior tibia is not covered by much soft tissue and lies almost directly beneath the skin. Its location on the lower legs also makes it susceptible to recurrent minor trauma (Roberts and Manchester 1995, 130). Peripheral vascular disease (sometimes associated with diabetes mellitus) may also lead to venous or arterial ulcers. Due to the poor blood supply, these are slow to heal and may become infected. If the soft tissue damage reaches the underlying bone, an inflammatory reaction of the periosteum may occur. Considering the older age of this sample, this aetiology is probable in some of the lesions present. It is important to note, however, that most lesions were well healed at the time of death.

Periostitis - multiple element involvement

Periostitis was present on more than one bone in 53 skeletons. The distribution on different elements is summarised in Table 11. Such distribution patterns aid in differential diagnosis, particularly of systemic diseases. The picture is complicated, however, by the advanced age of the assemblage. As insults accumulated over time, it is difficult to determine whether different lesions comprised a single syndrome or disease or whether different lesions had completely different aetiologies and/or occurred at very different times in

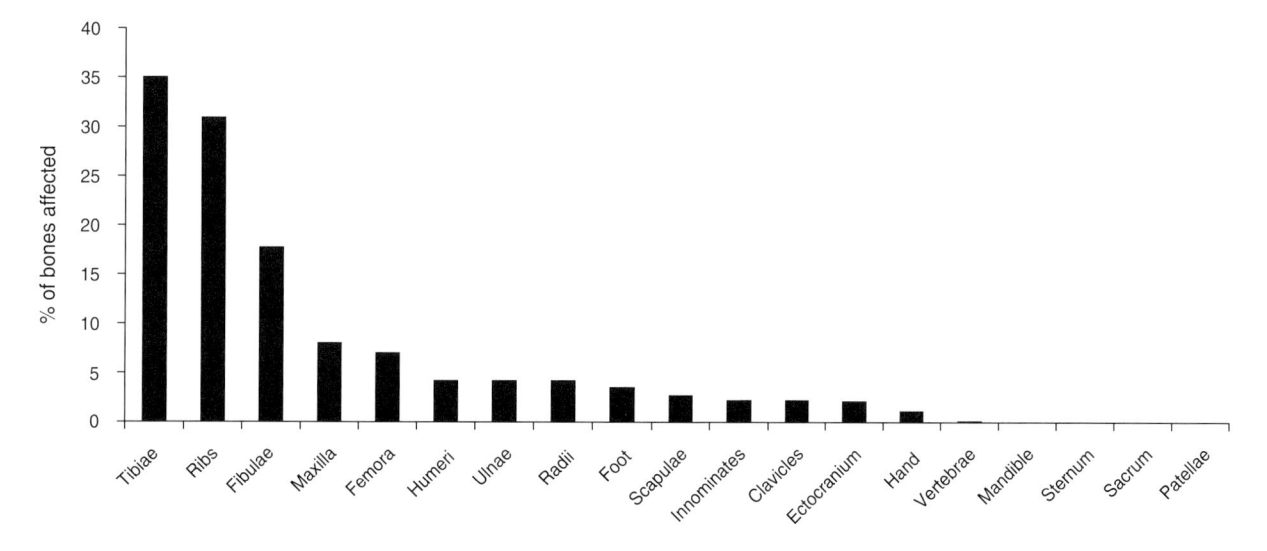

Figure 18   True prevalence (TPR) of periostitis by element in adult male sample (N = 97).

Table 10   Summary of the prevalence of elements showing periostitis (N = 105).

Elements	Males n = 97	Females n = 7	Total Adults (including one unsexed skeleton) n = 105
Endocranium	2.1% (2/91)*	0% (0/5)*	2.0% (2/97)*
Ectocranium	2.1% (2/91)*	0% (0/5)*	2.0% (2/97)*
Maxilla	8.0% (7/87)	20.0% (1/5)	8.6% (8/93)
Mandible	0% (0/88)	0% (0/5)	0% (0/94)
Sternum	0% (0/58)	0% (0/3)	0% (0/62)
Vertebrae	0.1% (2/1880)	0% (0/90)	0.1% (2/1994)
Sacrum	0% (0/85)	0% (0/8)	0% (0/94)
Ribs	30.9% (26/84)*	20.0% (1/5)*	28.8% (26/90)*
Innominates	2.2% (4/181)	0% (0/14)	2.0% (4/197)
Clavicles	2.2% (4/174)	0% (0/9)	2.1% (4/185)
Scapulae	2.7% (5/180)	0% (0/13)	2.5% (5/195)
Humeri	4.2% (8/187)	0% (0/13)	3.9% (8/202)
Ulnae	4.2% (8/189)	0% (0/15)	3.8% (8/206)
Radii	4.2% (8/188)	0% (0/13)	3.9% (8/203)
Hand bones	1.1% (1/89)*	0% (0/7)*	1.0% (1/97)*
Femora	7.0% (13/185)	11.7% (2/17)	7.3% (15/204)
Patellae	0% (0/142)	0% (0/10)	0% (0/154)
Tibiae	35.0% (63/180)	33.3% (4/12)	34.5% (67/194)
Fibulae	17.7% (32/180)	30.0% (3/10)	18.2% (35/192)
Foot bones	3.5% (3/85)*	0% (0/7)*	3.2% (3/93)*

*Rates are of skeletons with one or more ribs/ hand/ foot bones present. The number of elements were not counted here. The cranial vault was treated as a single element, rather than separating it into its different compnents.

that individual's life. For example, most periostitis of the long bones and all cases of osteomyelitis secondary to trauma and amputation were well healed and hence appeared to be of long standing. Most rib lesions, on the other hand were active at the time of death, and evidently affected these individuals up to the time of their deaths (if not actually being fatal).

Differential diagnosis has been attempted on a number of the more florid cases or where the character and distribution of lesions supported a specific diagnosis. A more detailed analysis is warranted but is beyond the scope of this report.

Osteomyelitis

Osteomyelitis was identified in adult male skeletons 3045, 3148, 3229 and 3241 (CPR 4.12%, n = 97) from the presence of cloacae draining the marrow cavity. All four were secondary to major trauma. Skeleton 3045 had undergone an above-knee amputation of his right leg. The entire element, including the head and neck and shaft, was thickly encased in new bone, which was a mixture of healed and active woven bone at the time of death (an involucrum) (Plate 21). The entire original femoral shaft was thinned and necrotic (sequestrum), the enlarged lumen being connected to the surface of the bone by five cloacae. Clearly the infection was long standing and ongoing. It is unclear if the infection had taken hold pre-operatively or was introduced during or after the operation. Amputation in the Royal Navy is discussed in greater detail below.

Skeleton 3229 also displayed osteomyelitis secondary to trauma (Plate 18). In this skeleton, both femora had suffered oblique fractures of the shafts, with associated overlap and callus formation. Whilst the left femoral shaft showed only slight periostitis, two cloacae near the right femoral fracture indicate that secondary osteomyelitis had been present. The smoothness of the callus suggests that both fractures had healed well before death.

Skeleton 3241 had the dubious distinction of having sustained more fractures - at least 16 - than any of the other pensioners examined. Whilst most bones appeared to have healed without becoming infected, fracture of the femoral shaft did result in the bone becoming infected (possibly osteomyelitis), although the shaft had not become thickened. A cloaca had not been identified, however. Unlike the other skeletons in which the femora were affected, the location of osteomyelitis in skeleton 3148 was the right tibial shaft. This infection was probably secondary to fractures of the tibial shaft and of the right fibula.

Chronic respiratory disease

A total of 26 adults with ribs present displayed new woven bone overlying the visceral surface of the ribs (CPR 28.8%, n = 90). These included one female (skeleton 3174). Active woven bone was also present on the ribs of subadult 3132, and may have been tubercular in origin (discussed below). Interestingly, three-quarters of the adults displayed lesions that were active at the time of death. This is in contrast with the bulk of other periosteal reactions which were well healed, and had occurred some time before death. Woven bone was present on multiple ribs on most of the skeletons (sometimes unilateral but often bilateral) and ranging in number from 1 to 15 affected ribs per skeleton.

The vast majority of respiratory disease leaves no trace on the skeleton. However, where a lesion (such as a bulla or abscess) approximates the ribs, resorption or new bone proliferation on the visceral surface of the rib may occur (Roberts *et al.* 1998, 56). Traditionally, such lesions were associated with tuberculosis, but Roberts *et al.* (1998) concluded that no differential diagnosis was possible without the presence of tubercular lesions in other parts of the skeleton. Acute lobar pneumonia, brochiectasis (eg emphysaema), and less likely, metastatic carcinoma, non-specific osteomyelitis and syphilis are all possible causes. In the Greenwich assemblage none of these lesions were associated with rib fractures, all of which were well healed.

The advanced age of many of the pensioners would have rendered them more vulnerable to respiratory diseases such as pneumonia and lung cancer, as did long standing social practices such as smoking or exposure to industrial pollutants that some may have encountered in civilian occupations after leaving the Royal Navy. Tobacco smoking would have predisposed many to developing lung cancer and emphysaema, and was undoubtedly a highly popular pastime amongst pensioners. Plates 6–9 all show pensioners 'blowing a cloud'. Indeed, the Hospital provided each pensioner with a ration of tobacco. Skeletally, the predilection of pensioners for smoking was revealed by the high prevalence of pipe notches in their dentition. Gibson (2002) found that of the 90 individuals he examined, 14 had pipe notches (15.56%), with some individuals showing more than one (a mean of 1.71 per person). Smoking tobacco aboard ship was prohibited, due to the high risk of fire and was inadvisable on a wooden ship packed with explosives. Seamen chewed tobacco instead (Fremont-Barnes 2005, 45). The habit of smoking tobacco probably developed after leaving active service. Given the longevity of most pensioners, many years had elapsed between discharge and death, leaving ample time for pipe notches to develop, a process that may only take a few years (Ogden pers. comm.).

Maxillary sinusitis

Maxillary sinusitis was observed in seven adult males and one female (TPR 8.6%). Lesions within the maxillary sinuses were only observed where the maxilla was already broken to reveal the cavities. In the Greenwich assemblage, a large proportion of the crania was intact, and hence, the sinuses remained unexamined. Maxillary sinusitis is therefore likely to be considerably under recorded.

The aetiology of maxillary sinusitis is multifactoral and may be caused by allergies, smoke and upper respiratory tract infections (Aufderheide and Rodríguez-Martín 1998; Roberts and Manchester 1995, 131). Air pollution in urban areas became severe during the Industrial Revolution, such that much of 18th-century London was 'cover'd by a cloud of smoke, most people being employed in lighting fires' (Werner cited in Roberts and Cox 2003). Although slightly removed from the centre of the industrial East End, air pollution in Greenwich was probably still considerable. It is also likely that after discharge from the Royal Navy many found work in the smoky industrial cities of the age, and some may also have found employment in industrial processes that generated considerable air pollution. It is thus not surprising to find chronic sinusitis in this population.

Treponemal disease (yaws and venereal syphilis)

Three adult male skeletons (3102, 3151 and 3229) showed bony modification consistent with treponemal disease (CPR 3.09%, n = 97), although it was impossible to differentiate between yaws and venereal syphilis. Treponemal bacteria are responsible for a group of closely related diseases that includes yaws, pinta, endemic syphilis and venereal syphilis. Although the above diseases are characterised by different pathological processes, it is virtually impossible to distinguish between the causative micro-organisms under the microscope, leading some researchers to conclude that it is one and the same in all four diseases (Kiple 2003, 331).

Skeleton 3102 displayed new bone formation with marked thickening of shaft of both tibiae ('sabre shins') and fibulae. Active periostitis was also present on the medial aspects of the distal humeral shafts. Unfortunately, the cranium was not present. Bony changes in skeleton 3151 suggestive of treponemal disease included caries sicca on the frontal bone and also possibly on a parietal bone. Healed periostitis was present on the shafts of the humeri, ulnae and radii, and mixed woven and striated bone overlying the femoral and fibular shafts. Both tibiae showed marked shaft thickening and new bone deposition characteristic of 'sabre shins' (Aufderheide and Rodríguez-Martín 1998). Skeleton 3229 also displayed widespread active and healed periostitis, involving the proximal ulnar shafts, the distal radial shafts, mixed lesions on the fibulae and marked thickening and new bone deposition on the shafts of the tibiae. The anterio-superior aspect of the frontal bone had an uneven appearance with three discrete sunken areas, possibly healed caries sicca.

'Safe moor'd in Greenwich tier'

Table 11   Summary of skeletons with periostitis on multiple elements (N = 54); L = left; R = right; numbers refer to the number of elements involved.

Skeleton	Cranium	Vertebrae	Clavicle	Ribs	Scapula	Humerus	Ulna	Radius	Metacarpals	Ilium	Ischium	Femur	Patella	Tibia	Fibula	Tarsals	Metatarsals
1572														LR			
3019														LR	LR		
3029														LR			
3035				2R, 3 L										LR	LR		
3039	maxillary sinus														L		
3045												R		L			
3068				4R, 7 L										LR			
3072	maxillary sinus											LR		LR	L		LR
3083														LR			
3098		13		6R, 8L										LR			
3099	supra-orbital ridge			7R, 5L											L		
3101				5L										LR			
3102				4L		LR								R	R		
3105												L		LR			
3106														R	R		
3108				6R, 5L	L	LR	LR	LR	L2, R2			LR		LR	R	1L	
3115				5R		LR											
3119				6R, 5L								LR		LR	R		
3143				6R; 6L										LR			
3144	LR maxillary sinuses														R		
3148														R			
3151	frontal, parietal, palate					LR	LR	LR				LR		LR	LR		
3152				3R													
3162				5R, 6L										LR			

48

Chapter Four

3164										L1, R2
3168	L zygomatic									
3174		5R, 10L							LR	
3176		6L							LR	
3189									LR	
3194			LR	LR	LR					
3208		6L, 11R	LR						LR	
3211									LR	
3212	endocranial	2R							LR	
3229	frontal	1R		LR	LR			R	LR	
3241		5L, 4R							L	
3243		5L, 6R								
3258		3L, 5R								
3261		10R								
3268		2L, 4R								
3272	maxilla	2L, 7R							LR	
3274	R maxillary sinus	5L, 3R								
3623		3L, 4R								
3628		4L, 4R								
6003									LR	
6023			LR	LR	LR				LR	
6035									LR	
6056					LR	LR		LR	LR	
6058									LR	
6073									LR	
6089		4L		LR	L	L		LR	LR	
6094									L	LR
6105									LR	
6151	palate								L	

The prevalence of 3.1% is broadly comparable with the 2.99% found at St George's crypt, Bloomsbury (Boston 2006) and at the Newcastle Infirmary (3.7%), another assemblage that comprised a large proportion of sailors (Nolan 1997). Contemporary assemblages (such as Christ Church, Spitalfields (Cox 1996), and the Quaker burial ground, Kingston-upon-Thames (Bashford and Pollard 1998) reported rates of 0.21% and 0.28%.

Yaws is restricted to tropical regions, and thus is rarely considered as a possible disease in European archaeological populations. The possibility of yaws in the Greenwich assemblage must be taken into account, however, as a small proportion of individuals are known historically to have originated in the tropics, and many saw service in these regions. As yaws most commonly develops in childhood, the former group was more likely to have been sufferers, particularly those originating from Africa and the West Indies, where yaws was endemic. Yaws was a well-recognised health problem amongst plantation slave children in the Caribbean in the 18th century (Brothwell 2003, 362–4). Indeed, early experimentation of vaccination against yaws was carried out by plantation doctors, who claimed some success in its treatment. Royal Navy ships operating in America and the Caribbean are known historically to have included escaped and freed slaves in their crews (Rodger 1986, 159–61), some of whom may well have been suffering from this infection.

In 18th-century Europe, venereal syphilis had long been regarded as the most serious and dreaded of the sexually transmitted diseases. Although the origin of the disease in the Western world is still not well understood, it appears that the presence of syphilis was first felt in the 15th century AD, and that it rapidly spread across Europe (Roberts and Cox 2003, 340). By the post-medieval period, the 'Great Pox' (or the 'French pox' as syphilis was known in England) had become a significant health problem. Prevention of contagion using early forms of condoms and treatments using mercury and guaiacum were largely unsuccessful (loc. cit.). It was really only with the invention of penicillin in the 1930s that any serious inroad was made into control of this disease.

Venereal syphilis is a sexually transmitted infection caused by the bacterium *Trepanima pallidum*, and is the only treponemal disease that may have a fatal outcome. It is transmitted by sexual contact or may be passed from an infected mother to her foetus. The latter is known as congenital syphilis. Surprisingly, no dental evidence of congenital syphilis (such as Hutchinson's incisors or mulberry molars) was noted in the Greenwich assemblage. Venereal syphilis is a chronic infection characterised by three clinical stages separated by latent stages with no visible symptoms (Arrizabalaga 2003, 316). In primary syphilis, a small painless ulcer or chancre appears on the genitals (and less commonly elsewhere) within 2–6 weeks of infection. In most cases, after a brief latent period, there is a secondary stage characterised by widespread lesions on the skin and in the internal organs, a painless rash, fever, malaise and bone ache. These symptoms disappear after a few weeks, but in 25% of sufferers they recur during the first two years (ibid.). The tertiary stage only develops in a third of untreated cases, and only following a latent phase that may vary in length from one to more than 20 years. It is this tertiary stage that causes such profound systemic damage that results in insanity and death. The bacterium causes progressive destruction of a number of systems of the body, including the skin, mucous membranes, bones, the heart and blood vessels and the nervous system. Nervous system involvement causes a loss of positional sense and sensation that manifests as locomotor ataxia (a stumbling, high stepping gait), and bouts of insanity, known as general paralysis of the insane (ibid.; Roberts and Manchester 1995, 153). Death from tertiary syphilis occurs through cardiovascular involvement, such as a ruptured aneurysm or cardiac valve failure.

The problem of venereal disease was widespread in the Royal Navy, and until 1795 ships' surgeons were entitled to 15 shillings deducted from the infected man's wages (Lloyd 1968, 262; Lavery 1989, 215). The diagnosis of sexually transmitted diseases was itself far from refined, with venereal diseases being confused with that other great naval scourge of the 18th century, scurvy. The lifestyle of seamen and marines made them particularly vulnerable to contracting sexually transmitted diseases, including the 'Pox'. Separation for prolonged periods from wives and sweethearts, the only women available to seamen were the prostitutes who plied their trade in the seaports of Britain and abroad. In his memoir 'Jack Nastyface' (Robinson, 2002, 89, 92) describes these women in the following terms:

> Of all the human race, these poor young creatures are the most pitiable; the ill-usage and the degradation they are driven to submit to, are indescribable. . . .

He concludes with the following reflection:

> I am now happily laid up in matrimonial harbour, blest in a wife and several children, and my constant prayer to heaven is, that my daughters may never step a foot on board of a man-of-war.

Plate 11 shows a scene of revelry below decks in such a ship. On these occasions, literally hundreds of prostitutes were allowed on board. The potential for transmission of venereal diseases was huge. Whilst there was little comeback for seamen in these situations, Picard (2000, 128) reports that on land the usual punishment inflicted by sailors on prostitutes, who had infected them, was to turn the girl out into the street naked except for her stays. This punishment was poor consolation for contracting one of these incurable, painful and sometimes fatal diseases.

Chapter Four

Tuberculosis

Bovine tuberculosis (or scrofula) may be spread to humans by the ingestion of infected meat and milk. The strain responsible is Mycobacterium bovis. Alternatively, the disease may be spread from person to person by inhalation of airborne bacilli present in expectorated phlegm. The seat of the primary lesion in this form of tuberculosis is most commonly the lungs, and is caused by the strain Mycobacterium tuberculosis. Known as 'consumption' in the 18th and 19th centuries, the latter route was more common, the spread of infection being facilitated by high population density, poor nutrition and housing, and inadequate hygiene so prevalent amongst the urban poor (Roberts and Cox 2003). The privileged of society were not immune to this terrible scourge, and famous fatalities from tuberculosis included Keats, Chopin, and Emily and Ann Bronte (Dormandy 1999). These were contemporaries of many of the Greenwich pensioners. As the most vulnerable time to contract tuberculosis is in adolescence, the disease was given a romantic sheen by the young people who were tragically cut down before their time. The physical symptoms of elegantly wasting away added to this notion. Yet the reality of the disease for the majority of affected people was far from romantic, and the disease hit the working class the hardest. Tuberculosis was the leading cause of death amongst the poor in the 19th century (Humphreys 1997, 137). Bills of Mortality from the late 18th and early 19th century show a mortality rate due to consumption of around 25% (Roberts and Cox 2003, 338).

Bone involvement is not present in the majority of tubercular cases. Recent clinical studies have shown that this is present in only 1% of patients (Roberts and Manchester 1995). Before the availability of antibiotics, this figure averaged 5–7% (Aufderheide and Rodríguez-Martín 1998, 133). Most cases of tuberculosis therefore go unrecognised in palaeopathology, and this was undoubtedly the case with the Greenwich pensioners. The true prevalence of the disease was probably much higher.

On the skeletons, new bone growth on the ribs of 26 individuals may be suggestive of tuberculosis, but on their own it is not possible to differentially diagnose tuberculosis from other respiratory diseases. Characteristic lesions in other parts of the body are required. For example, lesions involving the spine have been reported in 25–50% of cases of skeletal tuberculosis (Roberts and Manchester 1995, 138). These smooth-walled lytic lesions in the vertebral bodies are caused by tubercular abscesses, which eventually cause the vertebral body to collapse, causing compression fractures. A profound hunch back (kyphosis) may result. These spinal changes are known as Pott's disease.

Two adult males (3098 and 3099) and one subadult (3132) showed lesions heavily suggestive of tuberculosis (CPR 2.8% of total population; or CPR 2.06% of adult males). A severe case of Pott's disease was manifest in the spinal column of skeleton 3098 (Plate 22). Cortical destruction of the anterior vertebral bodies was present in thoracic vertebrae 1 to 5, with multiple lytic lesions present on the anterior and/or right sides of vertebral bodies of thoracic vertebrae 2 to 5 (most severe in thoracic vertebrae 4 and 5). Similar lesions were noted on thoracic vertebrae 6 to 10, with vertical collapse and wedging of thoracic vertebra 8 and complete destruction of thoracic vertebra 7. Thoracic vertebrae 11 and 12 and lumbar vertebra 1 were ankylosed. The resultant deformity was a kyphosis or Pott's deformity, characteristic of spinal tuberculosis. Incomplete ankylosis of the sacro-iliac joint may be secondary to this deformity. Tubercular lesions were also noted in lumbar vertebra 4. Rib involvement was bilateral, with active woven bone deposited on the visceral surfaces of right ribs 5 to 10, and left ribs 3 to 11. Erosive lesions at the head and neck of six ribs are characteristic of the disease.

Subadult skeleton 3132 also displayed costal and spinal lesions indicative of tuberculosis in thoracic vertebrae 4 to 12 and lumbar vertebrae 1 and 2. Large lytic lesions were present in thoracic vertebra 4 to 12 and lumbar vertebrae 1 and 2, with collapse of the vertebral bodies of thoracic vertebrae 7 to 11. Ankylosis of many thoracic bodies and secondary deformation of many ribs resulted in a marked kyphosis, with an exaggerated anterior curvature of 45–60°. As with skeleton 3098 both new woven bone and erosive lesions were present on the ribs. Skeleton 3132 was only 12–14 years old when he died.

Skeleton 3099 did not display spinal changes, but the smooth rounded erosive lesions present on the necks of right ribs 3 to 11, coupled with new bone deposition on the visceral surfaces of seven right and five left ribs (mixed woven and lamellar bone) were suggestive of tuberculosis.

A CPR of 2.8% in the total Greenwich population was higher than the mean prevalence of 0.62% found in four post-medieval sites discussed by Roberts and Cox (2003, 339). It is considerably greater than the highest rate of 1.6% reported from Newcastle Infirmary, not unexpected in this working class assemblage. The high rate at Greenwich may reflect the working class origins of this population in which the disease was rife. Aboard ship, seamen slept cheek by jowl in their hammocks (each with an allowance of 14 inches). The close quarters of the lower decks where fresh air was often assiduously kept out to create a 'good fug', may well have facilitated the spread of the disease from an infected seamen to his mates. Chaplain Edward Mangin referred to the heat in the 'cavern' of the lower deck as 'so entirely filled with human bodies' as to be 'overpowering' (cited in Lavery 2004, 50). He wrote this in spring on the North Sea when the gunports were usually kept closed, but even in more clement weather when these were opened (dependent on the acquiescence of the captain), ventilation was never very good. It is thus not surprising that the spread of infectious disease was an ever-present threat to the wellbeing of the ship. In these conditions, droplet infection would have been particularly rife.

Joint disease

General wear and tear of the joints over years often results in degenerative joint disease (DJD) and osteoarthritis with increasing age. These changes may also occur in response to repeated stress on joints brought about by strenuous exercise. For example, carrying heavy weights may result in spinal joint degeneration, particularly the lower spine. The presence of these disorders in the Greenwich population reflects both their advanced age and the hard manual labour most undertook whilst aboard ship in the Royal Navy, on merchant ships, and in other occupations in the years preceding and following this service. Marine record papers reveal that many were labourers before joining the Navy, whilst servicemen often took up physically demanding jobs on discharge. In addition, many arthropathies may have developed secondary to trauma and amputations.

Degenerative joint disease

Degenerative joint disease (DJD) and associated osteoarthritis (OA) are two of the most common pathologies found in both living (Meisel and Bullough, 1984) and archaeological populations (Ortner and Putschar 1981, 419-33; Rogers and Waldron 1995, 32). DJD is a multifactoral systemic non-inflammatory disorder, with clinical symptoms of pain and stiffness in movable joints, which may cause major disability in severe cases (Denko 2003, 234). Symptoms, however, are not necessarily proportional to the severity of bony changes on the skeleton. Bony outgrowths or osteophytes often occur on or around the articular surfaces of joints, but resorption of bone (manifesting as porosity of the joint surface, and as subchondral cysts beneath the joint surfaces) are also common features of this disorder (Roberts and Manchester 1995). DJD is diagnosed when the above bony changes occur, but these may occur as part of the normal ageing process, being uncommon in under 30 year olds, but found in 80–90% of modern individuals over 75 years of age (Aufderheide and Rodríguez-Martín 1998, 96). Alone these changes are not necessarily diagnostic of osteoarthritis (Roberts and Manchester 1995). Waldron and Rogers (1991) recommended that osteoarthritis may only be identified if eburnation and/or at least two bony changes are present. The loss of cartilage lining covering the joint surfaces leads to eburnation (polishing of the exposed bone surfaces where they rub together). In the Greenwich assemblage, identification of osteoarthritis was based on eburnation alone.

The aetiology of degenerative joint disease is not fully understood, but its prevalence does increase with advancing age (Doyle 1986). Everyday 'wear-and-tear' over the years is believed to underlie this disorder, but may be accelerated by repeated strenuous activity, such as carrying heavy loads, throwing projectiles, and pushing and pulling heavy objects (Gunn 1974; Jurmain 1999), particularly relating to upper limb joints. Genetic predisposition to this disorder may also influence disease development (Rogers and Waldron 1995). The advanced age and the lifestyle aboard ship would have rendered the Greenwich pensioners particularly vulnerable to developing DJD. In addition, joint disease may develop as a secondary response to trauma (such as a fracture) and metabolic diseases (such as osteoporosis), amongst others. A number of examples of this secondary DJD were apparent in the Greenwich assemblage.

DJD was present in at least one vertebra of the spines of the adult males (CPR 96.9%), in five of the women and in the one adult of unknown sex (CPR 95.23% of the adult population). These took the form of osteophytes or macroporosity. The severity and distribution of these lesions were recorded during the analysis, but analysis of these data lies beyond the scope of this report. In a number of cases, osteophyte formation was so extensive that ankylosis of adjacent vertebrae resulted. Wedge fractures of vertebrae were also present (either as a result of trauma or secondary to osteoporosis), and were frequently associated with DJD or osteoarthritis.

Osteoarthritis

Osteoarthritis was diagnosed where eburnation was present on at least one surface of the joint. The prevalence of extra-spinal osteoarthritis per joint present is summarised in Table 12. The overall crude prevalence was 60.65% (n = 107).

In the Greenwich males, the joints of the elbows, wrists, hand and feet showed the greatest prevalence. Two women with the disorder suffered osteoarthritis of the hands. It is interesting that in the males, the major weight-bearing joints of the hips and knees showed little involvement. In modern western populations, osteoarthritis most commonly occurs in the hips and lower spine of males (particularly white males), and in the cervical spine, knees and finger joints of women (Denko 2003, 235; Weiss and Jurmain 2007).

The aetiology underlying the development and severity of osteoarthritis is notoriously complex and poorly understood. Genetics, build, body mass index, sex, age and mechanical loading from strenuous repeated activities may all play a role in its development (Weiss and Jurmain 2007). The advanced age of most Greenwich pensioners may account, in part, for the high rate of the disease in this assemblage. However, mechanical loading due to specific repetitive and strenuous actions was also very likely to have played a significant role, particularly in osteoarthritis of the upper limbs, and possibly, also of the feet. In the upper body, most affected were the wrists (TPR left, 16%; right, 11.11%) and hands (left, 20%, right, 24.29%), followed by the elbows (left, 12.8%, right, 9.18%). There did not appear to be a clear pattern of handedness, with the left wrist and shoulder more affected than the right, whilst the right hand showed greater involvement than the left.

Table 12   True prevalence of extra-spinal osteoarthritis by joint in adults (N = 105).

Joint	Bones considered	Males n/N (%)	Females n/N (%)	Adults n/N (%)
Left Temporo-mandibular joint	Temporal, mandible	1/76 (1.0%)	0/4 (0%)	1/80 (1.25%)
Right Temporo-mandibular joint	Temporal, mandible	0/75 (0%)	0/4 (0%)	0/79 (0%)
Left shoulder -gleno-humeral joint	Humerus (PE), scapula	5/86 (5.49%)	0/6 (0%)	5/92 (5.32%)
Right shoulder (gleno-humeral joint)	Humerus (PE), scapula	10/84 (6.67%)	0/6 (0%)	10/92 (10.87%)
Left elbow	Humerus (DE), radius (PE), ulna (PE)	10/78 (12.8%)	0/6 (0%)	10/84 (11.9%)
Right elbow	Humerus (DE), radius (PE), ulna (PE)	9/89 (9.18%)	0/6 (0%)	9/95 (9.47%)
Left Wrist (radiocarpal joint)2	Radius (DE), ulna (DE), scaphoid, lunate and triquetral	12/63 (16%)	1/6 (16.67%)	13/69 (18.84%)
Right Wrist (radiocarpal joint)2	Radius (DE), ulna (DE), scaphoid, lunate and triquetral	9/72 (11.11%)	0/5 (0%)	9/77 (11.69%)
Left Hand	All joint surfaces of carpals, metacarpals and phalanges	17/68 (20%)	1/6 (16.67%)	18/74 (24.32%)
Right Hand	All joint surfaces of carpals, metacarpals and phalanges	17/70 (24.29%)	0/6 (0%)	17/76 (22.37%)
Left Hip	*Os coxa* (acetabulum), femur (PE)	4/86 (4.44%)	0/6 (0%)	4/92 (4.35%)
Right Hip	*Os coxa* (acetabulum), femur (PE)	4/88 (4.35%)	0/6 (0%)	4/94 (4.26%)
Left Knee	Femur (DE), patella, Tibia (PE)	3/83 (3.49%)	0/5 (0%)	3/88 (3.41%)
Right Knee	Femur (DE), patella, Tibia (PE)	3/83 (3.49%)	0/5 (0%)	3/88 (3.41%)
Left Ankle	Tibia (DE), fibula (DE), talus	3/82 (3.53%)	0/5 (0%)	3/87 (3.45%)
Right Ankle	Tibia (DE), fibula (DE), talus	1/83 (1.19%)	0/5 (0%)	1/87 (1.14%)
Left Foot	All joint surfaces of tarsals, metatarsals and phalanges.	19/63 (30.16%)	0/6 (0%)	19/69 (27.54%)
Right Foot	All joint surfaces of tarsals, metatarsals and phalanges.	19/61 (31.15%)	0/5 (0%)	19/66 (28.79%)

During the analysis, it was remarked that a number of the skeletons displayed extension of the anterior aspect of the distal humeral joint, a change consistent with hyperflexion of the elbow. This, together with marked muscle attachments to the long bones of the arms and hands, does suggest strenuous use of the arms in this population, particularly of flexion. This interpretation is consistent with the high prevalence of elbow osteoarthritis in this group, a location thought to be more closely associated with activity, due to the specific bio-mechanical properties of the joint (Resnick and Niwayama 1995). The repetitive and strenuous activity of pulling on ropes or stays during the general sailing of a ship, and moving aloft in the rigging, (propelled principally by the arms) may explain these phenomenon in the Greenwich pensioners.

Interestingly, the highest prevalence of osteoarthritis was not in the upper body, but in the feet, where at least one bone of 19 left and 19 right feet showed eburnation (TPR 30.16% and 31.15%, respectively). The first metatarsal was most commonly affected. The reason for this distribution is unclear, but may relate to the seamen's practice of going barefoot whilst aboard ship, and from abnormal weight distribution whilst maintaining their balance aloft. In contrast, osteoarthritis of the hip, knee, and ankle joints was low.

There has been little work undertaken on joint disease in seafarers. No discussion on the distribution or prevalence of osteoarthritis was forthcoming in Stirland's osteological analysis of the crew of the 16th century flagship, the Mary Rose, the only other report on a British ship's crew in the Age of Sail (Stirland

2005). In contemporary civilian populations, such as the named and unnamed assemblages from St Luke's church, Islington, and St George's crypt, Bloomsbury, the distribution of lesions was very different. Amongst the males of the former, the hips, knee joints, lumbar spine and big toe joints were most affected (Boyle *et al.* 2005), whilst in the latter it was the hands and feet (Boston et al. 2006; Boston *et al.* forthcoming). Overall the crude prevalence in both these populations was much lower than Greenwich: 10.1% in the former and 39% in the latter, older population. Non-spinal osteoarthritis was 13.79% in the Newcastle Infirmary assemblage (quoted in Roberts and Cox 2003, 252) a population thought to comprise a high proportion of merchant seamen.

Unfortunately, a more detailed analysis of the distribution patterns of osteoarthritis and activity-related changes in the Greenwich assemblage lay beyond the scope of this report. Further research in this specialist population is certainly warranted.

Schmorl's nodes

Schmorl's nodes are identified as indentations on the superior and inferior surfaces of the vertebral bodies, and are most common in the thoracic and lumbar regions (Rogers and Waldron 1995, 27). These are caused by the herniation of the intervertebral disc through the end plates and are therefore, in effect, pressure defects. In the Greenwich assemblage 70 adults (CPR 66.67%) displayed Schmorl's nodes, and of these, 67 were adult males (CPR 69%, n = 97), 2 were females, and 1 an unsexed adult. In addition, subadult 3249 (aged 16–18 years) also showed Schmorl's nodes on T12, L2 and L5, in the absence of other degenerative changes. There was insufficient recording to identify this condition more specifically (eg Scheierman's disease).

Schmorl's nodes are often a feature of spinal DJD, and are frequently found associated with osteophytes and porosity. Like these other lesions, Schmorl's nodes become increasingly common with age, and are present in most individuals over 45 years of age (Aufderheide and Rodríguez- Martín 1998, 97). This may account for its high prevalence in the Greenwich sample, although the carrying of heavy weights and a strenuous physical lifestyle undoubtedly exacerbated this condition.

Rheumatoid arthritis

One adult male skeleton (3265) had erosive lesions to joints of the hands and feet consistent with rheumatoid arthritis. The changes were bilateral. In both hands, the carpals, distal metacarpal joints one to three, and the proximal and inter-phalangeal joints of digits one to four were affected. The joint surface of the left interphalangeal joints two to three were completely destroyed, presenting a very ragged appearance. Bilaterally the feet showed erosive lesions to the distal first metatarsal and to the proximal joint surfaces of metatarsals one to four. The picture was somewhat complicated by co-existing osteoarthritis in this skeleton.

Rheumatoid arthritis is an autoimmune disease and affects approximately 1% of modern populations (Roberts and Manchester 1995, 116). It is three times more common in females than in males. The disease has its onset in the fourth or fifth decades (Rogers and Waldron, 1995, 55–56). Rheumatoid arthritis is a chronic inflammatory disease, which affects multiple synovial joints bilaterally, most commonly involving the hands, feet, wrists and elbows (Roberts and Manchester 1995, 116). The lesions on skeleton 3265 are consistent with this distribution. The synovial membranes of the joints are initially affected, becoming thickened and granulated. This spreads to the cartilage of the joint, eventually destroying it. The underlying bone is also eroded and ankylosis may occur. The joints become swollen, stiff and very painful. Additional physical symptoms include anaemia, weight loss and fever (Roberts and Manchester 1995, 116; Aufderheide and Rodríguez-Martín 1998, 100). A famous sufferer, who was a contemporary of many of the Greenwich pensioners, is thought to have been the poet Samuel Taylor Coleridge. His liberal use of laudanum to contain the pain caused by his affected hands led to his opium addiction, and hence, to the penning of such memorable poems as 'Kubla Khan- a fragment in a dream' and (appropriately enough in this context) 'The Rime of the Ancient Mariner' (Lefebure 1974).

Diffuse Idiopathic Systemic Hyperostosis (DISH)

Diffuse Idiopathic Systemic Hyperostosis (DISH) is characterised by the ossification of the anterior longitudinal spinal ligament causing a flowing candle-wax-like new bone formation, most commonly on the right side of the vertebral bodies (Rogers and Waldron 1995, 48–49). At least four consecutive vertebrae should be involved to warrant this diagnosis (ibid.). There is also enthesophyte formation at major ligament insertion points, and ossification of cartilage (Roberts and Manchester 1995, 120). The symptoms produced by the disease are generally mild but include stiffness and aching. Modern prevalence of the disease varies between 6 and 12%, affecting more males than females. Prevalence increases with age, 85% of cases being found in individuals aged over 50 years. There is also an association with diabetes and obesity (Rogers and Waldron 1995, 48), and hence, DISH has come to be regarded as a disease of affluence and fine living. The association of DISH with over-indulgence was borne out by the prevalence of the condition in more affluent 18th-century populations. In the upper middle class assemblages of Christ Church, Spitalfields (Molleson *et al.* 1993) and St George's, Bloomsbury (Boston *et al.* 2006; Boston *et al.* forthcoming), the rates were 5.79% and 4.17%, respectively. In the more mixed population (but still with a high proportion of the well-to-do) of St Luke's Church, Islington, the prevalence was 2.28% (Boston and Witkin 2005) whilst in the working class population of the Cross Bones burial ground, Southwark, no cases were identified (Brickley *et al.* 1999). At St Martin's Church, Birmingham, the overall prevalence was 2.42%, with a higher rate in skeletons buried within brick-lined shaft graves and vaults compared to earth-cut graves (Brickley *et al.* 2006). Clearly, affluence influenced the prevalence of this condition.

In the light of this aetiology, it is surprising that DISH was present amongst the Greenwich pensioners, given their social class and occupations. It was recognised in two adult males (CPR 2.06%, n = 97; or 1.87% of the total population). Of the Greenwich pensioners, 90 skeletons had at least four thoracic vertebrae preserved (2.22%). Fifteen of the 1016 thoracic vertebrae present were affected (TPR 1.48%), whilst only 0.423% of lumbar vertebrae (2 of 473) were involved.

Skeleton 3182 showed the characteristic dripping candle wax lesions and ankylosis of the right side of vertebrae T7-L1, and enthesophytosis of the proximal ulnae, calcanei and tibiae. In skeleton 6085, the characteristic 'dripping candle wax' osteophyte formation was present on the right side of the vertebral bodies of T4-L1, resulting in ankylosis of these joints. Large enthesophytes were present on the anterior tibiae.

The crude prevalence of 2.06% is broadly comparable with St Martin's, Birmingham (Brickley *et al.* 2006). However, the high proportion of aged males (the highest risk group for DISH) in the Greenwich assemblage must be borne in mind when undertaking inter-population comparisons, as this may lead to erroneous interpretations.

Metabolic disorders

Iron deficiency anaemia

Thirty-four males and one female (33.33% of adults, n = 105; or 32.71% of the total population, n = 107) showed lesions characteristic of cribra orbitalia (CPR). All lesions were healed. Neither subadult displayed these lesions. Forty-nine skeletons showed pitting and thickening of the diploë of the parietal and/or frontal bones of the skull (CPR 45.79%, n = 107). Although the diagnosis was not confirmed using radiography, these changes were interpreted as porotic hyperostosis. Twenty-seven individuals with porotic hyperostosis also had cribra orbital (CPR 55.1%). Cribra orbitalia and porotic hyperostosis are thought to occur widely in response to a deficiency of iron during childhood, most commonly the result of inadequate dietary intake of iron, and/or as a result of severe intestinal parasite infestation (Stuart-Macadam 1991, 101). Iron is a central component of haemoglobin, the molecule necessary for the transportation of oxygen in the red blood cells of the blood. Red blood cells are produced within the red bone marrow of a number of bones of the body, which include the diploë of the cranial vault, the sternum and the pelvis. In childhood, the diploë are particularly important, but become a secondary site of red blood cell production later in life. In iron deficiency anaemia, the body attempts to compensate for low serum iron levels by hypertrophy of these bones (Aufderheide and Rodríguez-Martín 1998, 346). In children, this manifests osteologically as an increased porosity and thickening of the diploë of the cranial vault (known as porotic hyperostosis) and of the orbital sockets (cribra orbitalia). The latter is often used as a generic indicator of physical stress in childhood. The physical symptoms of anaemia are shortness of breath, fatigue, pallor and palpitations (Roberts and Manchester 1995, 167). Another disease that manifests similarly to iron deficiency anaemia is scurvy (a severe deficiency of vitamin C), and much of the so-called cribra orbitalia described below, in fact, may have been the result of scurvy.

The crude prevalence of cribra orbitalia in the Christ Church, Spitalfields assemblage was 14.57% (Molleson and Cox 1993), whilst in the named assemblage of St Luke's, Islington, it was 9.5% (Boyle *et al.* 2005, 235) and at St Martin's, Birmingham, it was 9.64% (Brickley *et al.* 2006, 126). Interestingly, the lowest prevalence (4.05%) was noted in the paupers of the Cross Bones, Southwark assemblage (Brickley *et al.* 1999). The association between cribra orbitalia and higher social class may reflect infant feeding practices of the day, in which pap or panada (a gruel of flour and water) were substituted for breast milk early in infancy (Roberts and Cox 2003, 307). The poor of Southwark, who through economic necessity were forced to breastfeed longer than their more affluent counterparts, appear to have spared their children some of the illnesses afflicting children of the middling sort. Historical documentation on the Greenwich pensioners attests to their working class origins, and being a childhood disorder, a similar prevalence of cribra orbitalia to the Cross Bones assemblage might be expected. The Greenwich assemblage showed by far the highest prevalence of this disorder amongst the assemblages named above.

In examining the age distribution of cribra orbitalia in the St Martin's, Birmingham, assemblage, Brickley, Buteux, *et al.* (2005, 134) found a prevalence of 20.79% in subadults compared to 5.80% in adults. This difference may be due to remodelling of lesions over time, and the possible association of iron deficiency with greater childhood morbidity and mortality. Their research makes the crude prevalence of 33.33% in the ageing adult population of Greenwich even more remarkable.

A significant proportion of the seamen of the Royal Navy were 'recruited' from seaports, and many had grown up 'using the sea'. It is to be assumed that they had a ready access to fresh fish, but their intake of meat and iron-rich vegetables was probably fairly low. Regular meat consumption lay beyond the means of most poorer families, whilst traditional diets rarely comprised much fresh fruit and vegetables (Roberts and Cox 2003). Once aboard ship, the supply of fresh vegetables and fruit was erratic, depending on the ship putting into port, as fruit and vegetables were highly perishable, and preservation by pickling,(e.g. sauerkraut) was unpopular. Vegetable supplies most commonly mentioned in ships' logs are onions and cabbages. 'Greens', pumpkins, carrots and turnips were also listed (MacDonald 2006, 38). Harvie (2002) comments that by the later 18th century some enlightened captains, such as Captain Cook, attempted to introduce these victuals into the seamen's diet in an attempt to combat scurvy. They were met with considerable resistance from their crews, who regarded these foodstuffs as foreign to a normal diet. However, it should be noted that in the *Additional Regulations and Instructions*, published with the 1790 edition of *Regulations and Instructions relating to His Majesty's Service at Sea* it is noted that it had long been the practice of pursers, when fresh meat was served, to include 'such a quantity of greens and roots to . . . give sufficient satisfaction to the men . . .' (Macdonald 2006, 36–7; see also Rodger 2004, 484–86).

Once in the Royal Navy, a seaman could enjoy a regular supply of red meat (mostly salted), the standard issue being 2lb of beef twice a week and 1lb of pork twice a week (Fremont-Barnes 2005, 25; see also Macdonald 2006, 10, 15–44). Unless compromised by disease (eg. bleeding gastric ulcers, malaria or 'the bloody flux' - dysentery) or blood loss from trauma or rampant intestinal parasitic infestation, it is unlikely that he would develop anaemia. Given the adult age of most seamen, it is also doubtful that such deficiency would manifest on the skeleton as cribra orbitalia or porotic hyperostosis.

The most probable explanation for the high prevalence of cribra orbitalia may lie more in differential diagnosis, and it is highly possible that some of the lesions ascribed to iron deficiency anaemia were in fact scurvy (see next section).

Scurvy

The 15th-century Portuguese explorer Vasco Da Gama referred to scurvy as 'death's dire ravage'. This description was no exaggeration, for during his voyage of discovery around the tip of Africa to the East Indies, 100 of his 160 seamen are thought to have died of this disease (Harvie 2002, 14). In the 18th century, scurvy became a major problem for the Royal Navy, which had hitherto sailed mostly in home waters but who increasingly undertook long transoceanic voyages in pursuit of colonial aspirations and in protection of the merchant navy, so seminal to successful trade (ibid., 18). Scurvy and fevers were the two greatest killers of seamen. As the philosopher and evolutionary theorist, Herbert Spenser (cited in Harvie 2002, 197) commented that:

> the mortality from scurvy during this long period [the 17th and 18th centuries] has exceeded the mortality by battle, wrecks, and all the casualties of sea life, put together.

But against this Rodger (1986, 100–3) has argued that scurvy had been a widespread problem, but that few had actually died from the disease, and further that scurvy largely ceased to be a real problem for the Navy from the time of the Seven Years War. Rodger (2004, 308) also suggests that the effects of scurvy have been exaggerated. He quotes the physician Edward Strother who wrote in *An essay on sickness and health*, 1725 that

> It is yet a sufficient Answer to Patients when they enquire into their ailments to give this Return to a troublesome Enquirer, that their Disease is the Scurvy, they rest satisfied that they are devoured with a Complication of bad Symptoms . . .

Rodger argues that scurvy used as a convenient catch-all term by naval surgeons.

Scurvy is a dietary deficiency disease arising from a prolonged lack of Vitamin C (ascorbic acid), and usually develops in the absence of vegetables and fruit in the diet (French 2003, 295). Vitamin C deficiency results in defective hydroxylation of proline and lysine, two amino acids of collagen, a major structural component of blood capillaries and bone matrix (Follis 1954, cited in Maat 2004, 78). Defective collagen results in fragile capillaries and weakened bone tissue, such that minor trauma (such as a knock on the shin) will precipitate bleeding and bone infractions (fractures limited to the cortex of bone). Weight-bearing extremities (the legs and feet), the heart and digestive tract are particularly vulnerable to major haemorrhaging, which may be fatal (ibid.).

Modern experiments have revealed the following pattern of the disease: after 12 weeks without Vitamin C, a feeling of lethargy develops; by 19 weeks, the skin becomes dry and rough, and hair follicles form lumps; at 23 weeks small haemorrhages in the legs begin, and slightly later, fresh wounds will not heal. The classic symptom of swollen purpled gums appears at 30 weeks, and the potentially fatal cardiac haemorrhages at 36 to 38 weeks (French 2003, 295). This description of the disease broadly concurs with eyewitness accounts of scurvy afflicting sailors on long voyages. In 1535, Jacque Cartier exploring the St Lawrence River in Canada wrote this description of scurvy afflicting his crew (cited in Harvie 2002, 15):

> the unknownen sicknes began to spread itselfe amongst us after the strangest sott that ever was eyther heard of or seene, insomuch as some did lose all their strength, and could not stand on their feete, then did their legges swel, their sinews shrinke as black as any cole. Others had all their skins spotted with spots of blood of a purple coulour: then did it ascend up to their ankles, knees, thighes, shoulders, armes and necke: their gummes so rotten, that all the flesh did fall off, even to the roots of the teeth, which also almost fell out. With such infection did this sicknes spread itself in our

three ships, that about the middle of February, of a hundred and ten persons that we were, there were not ten whole.

Cartier's expedition was only saved by the intervention of some friendly Indians who made them a concoction of the sap and leaves of an indigenous tree. This is one of the first successful cures for scurvy in the long history of misunderstanding of the nature of the disease and its treatment. Some naval surgeons and physicians of the 17th and 18th centuries felt that scurvy was a symptom of venereal disease, whilst others ascribed it to the 'bloody flux' (dysentery). Treatments included bleeding and cupping (a favourite treatment of a wide range of disorders at that time); cinchona bark (the source of quinine); spruce beer; molasses; fumigations of tobacco and tar; burying the sufferer up to his neck in warm sand; numerous quack remedies (some ineffective but innocuous, and some downright toxic), and the consumption of scurvy grass, strong cider, sauerkraut and citrus fruit (Harvie 2002). There were some real benefits in the last four as all contain varying amounts of ascorbic acid, but it was really only with the belated introduction of citrus fruit, particularly lemons, into the diet of seamen that significant inroads were made into the disease.

Discovering an effective cure was slow in coming, despite the merchant and Royal Navy losing large numbers of men to the disease. Famously, Commodore Anson's Pacific expedition which set out in 1740 with six warships and two supply ships and nearly 2000 men, suffered great loses from scurvy and typhoid. After circumnavigating the globe, only one ship the *Centurion* returned in 1744 with less than 200 men. One ship - the *Wager* - had been wrecked – and another – *Gloucester* – was burnt because there were not enough men to sail her.

The influence of ignorant but highly influential physicians to the Admiralty significantly delayed systematic research into treatment, and it was only when a relatively humble naval surgeon, James Lind, conducted more scientific experiments using different 'curatives' than any real progress was made. In 1753 Lind published his results, in which he recommended the use of citrus fruit, but his findings were largely ignored. It took a further four decades, and championing by two more influential surgeons, Blane and Trotter, before the Admiralty introduced the compulsory consumption of lemon juice aboard ship (Harvie 2002; French 2003, 296). From then on lemon juice was issued with the daily rum ration. The mixture of rum and lemon juice sweetened with sugar became known as 'grog' (Fremont-Barnes 2005), the drink so associated in the public mind with sailors of this period. The effect of the compulsory introduction of lemon juice was dramatic, and by 1795 the scourge of scurvy was eliminated in the Royal Navy. 'Limey', the American nickname for English seamen (from the word *limone* or lemon, *not* lime), refers to this practice.

Whilst the ubiquitous nature of scurvy in the Royal Navy of the 18th century is well recognised in documentary sources, identification of diagnostic lesions on the skeleton is less straightforward, and differential diagnosis of lesions is often problematic (Ortner *et al*. 1999). This is because many other conditions produce similar changes (Stirland 2005, 525). Deficiency in Vitamin C results in defective collagen, which in turn retards normal growth in subadults, and small blood vessel wall integrity, resulting in haemorrhage (Aufderheide and Rodríguez-Martín 1998, 312). Subperiosteal haemorrhages from minor trauma in both adults and subadults manifest as diffuse but localised new bone deposition on the diaphyses of long bones when ossification of the haemorrhage occurs (ibid.). Maat's (1982) work on Dutch sailors found that such lesions were the hallmark of scurvy, but they may be readily mistaken for periostitis associated with localised infection or other causes (such as venous ulcers or varicose veins), as discussed above. It is highly probable that some periostitis recorded in the Greenwich assemblage was scorbutic in nature, particularly where it occurred bilaterally or in multiple elements. An unusually large number of pensioners suffered multiple element involvement, particularly of the lower extremities (Table 11). It is uncertain how many of these were precipitated by scurvy.

Another skeletal indicator of scurvy is the sievelike lesions in the eye sockets (Aufderheide and Rodríguez-Martín 1998). These are often difficult to distinguish from cribra orbitalia, and it is probable that some lesions ascribed to iron deficiency may well be scorbutic in nature. Stirland (2005, 526) attributed pitting on the parietal bones observed in 16th-century sailors of the Mary Rose to scurvy. The ectocranial surface had a thickened orange peel appearance. This appeared to be similar to cranial lesions recorded on skeleton 3255 of the Greenwich assemblage. New bone deposition on the bone surface had resulted in a nodular, bumpy appearance. The diploë were slightly hypertrophied. Of course, such lesions may not be scorbutic in nature, and may be attributed to a number of other disorders, such as iron deficiency anaemia, the presence of porotic hyperostosis being thought to be differentially diagnosis. Skeleton 3255 showed no other bony changes that might suggest a diagnosis of scurvy.

Ortner and Ericksen (1997) recognised that bony changes on the greater wing of the sphenoid were indicative of scurvy. Fine foramina were observed on these bones in 12 pensioners (CPR 12.37% of males; 11.21% of total population), and formed the basis for diagnosis of the disease in this report (Table 13). Skeleton 3152 also showed pitting and new bone formation on the infra-temporal surfaces of the maxillae, located at the insertion sites of the Pterygoid medialis and lateralis muscles. As scurvy may manifest on the bones and teeth in a number of ways, it is not unreasonable to assume that a scorbutic individual may display multiple diverse lesions. Table 13 summarises the presence of sphenoid and

Table 13 Pathology present on 12 adult males displaying bony modification of the sphenoid consistent with scurvy (N = 12).

Skeleton	Sphenoid/ pterygoid plates	Periostitis of long bone shafts	Cribra orbitalia	Porotic hyperostosis	AMTL (N = 376 sockets)
3016	healed foramina	-	-	healed	31
3024	healed foramina	-	-	-	2
3029	healed foramina	L & R tibiae	-	-	1
3035	healed foramina	L & R fibulae & tibiae	healed Grade 1	healed	28
3103	healed foramina	L tibia	-	-	32
3152	healed foramina; also lesions on maxillae	R tibia	healed Grade 1	-	1
3241	healed foramina	L & R tibiae; R femur	healed Grade 2	-	24
3272	healed foramina	L & R tibiae	healed Grade 2	healed	21
6056	healed foramina	L & R tibiae, fibulae, femora, radii, ulnae, humeri clavicles, scapular blades	-	healed	6
3086	healed foramina	-	healed Grade 2	healed	1
3144	healed foramina	R fibula	-	-	32
3253	healed foramina	-	-	-	28
Total	**12**	**8**	**5**	**5**	**207 (55.05%)**

pterygoid lesions, periostitis, cribra orbitalia, porotic hyperostosis and ante-mortem tooth loss (AMTL) in the above 12 individuals. Eight displayed periostitis, of which five involved more than one bone, usually the lower limb bones. Skeleton 6056 showed gross involvement of most of the upper and lower limb bones, the mixture of healed, lamellar bone, spicules and active bone clearly indicating a condition of long standing, which was still active at the time of death. The characteristics of the lesions and the ongoing nature of the disease in this 50+ year old male makes it unlikely that this was scorbutic in origin, as he had undoubtedly been ashore for many years prior to his demise. In this case, alternative diagnoses, such as pulmonary arthropathy, should be considered. Similarly, given the rough-and-tumble lifestyle of so many seamen (even in their dotage), periostitis may be due to a wide range of another causes. The crude prevalence of periostitis in the 12 scorbutic individuals is nevertheless higher than for the total adult male population.

Cribra orbitalia was present in five of the 12 individuals, and as would be expected in ageing adults, was healed and manifested as low grades of severity (Grades 1 and 2 according to Stuart-Macadam's criteria (1991). Five cases of 'porotic hyperostosis' were also present. Tooth loss secondary to gum involvement has been reported historically. In the 12 individuals, a true prevalence of AMTL was 55.05% of alveolar sockets present - almost 10% higher than the adult male population average (TPR 44.67 %). Whilst this is only a small group, and the presence of each individual pathology may be attributed to different diseases and advanced age, it is nevertheless interesting that all these individuals, with the exception of skeleton 3024 showed more than one pathology that may have been scorbutic in origin.

Rickets

Rickets is due to a childhood deficiency of Vitamin D (Roberts and Manchester 1995, 173). In adults, this deficiency is known as osteomalacia. Vitamin D is mainly synthesised by the skin when it is exposed to sunlight, but may also be obtained from foods, such as eggs and oily fish. The vitamin is needed for the uptake of calcium, and hence, the normal mineralisation of bone. In rickets, the bones soften, allowing them to distort, particularly the major long bones. Bowing of the weight-bearing bones of the legs (tibiae and femora) manifests most commonly in the skeletal record, but if rickets develops early in life when an infant is still crawling, the arm bones may be similarly affected (ibid.). In severe cases, the individual may become markedly knock-kneed, making locomotion difficult and painful. Large nodules of bone may also grow on the end of the ribs producing a concave or pigeon chest. The pelvic bone may also deform, making childbirth impossible later in life. Other symptoms include muscle and joint pain, abdominal pain and muscle spasm (Beck 1997, 130). A deficiency in Vitamin D in adulthood may cause osteomalacia, which results in osteopenia, bone softening and distortion (including vertebral body compression and kyphosis) and fractures (Aufderheide and Rodríguez-Martín 1998, 308).

The industrialisation of Britain caused a substantial increase of this condition in urban areas, due to the persistent pall of smoke and smog overhanging the cities. In the overcrowded slums with their overhanging buildings, sunlight was largely blotted out. Children of the poor also had to work indoors for most of the daylight hours and were therefore even more susceptible to developing the condition. To the people of the Continent, which was less industrialised, rickets was known as the 'English Disease'. The children of the more privileged classes were also at risk from the pervasive air pollution, but infants were not helped by fashionable feeding practices described above (Roberts and Cox 2003, 308).

Skeletal evidence for rickets was present in ten adult males from Greenwich (CPR 10.3% of adult males; 9.35% of the total population). Anterior bowing of the femora was recorded in all ten cases, whilst medio-lateral bowing of the tibiae present in seven cases, and in one case, the fibulae also (Table 14). In all cases, the extent of bowing was described as slight or moderate. No other bones were affected in these individuals.

Given the predominantly working class and urban origins of the Greenwich pensioners, it is not surprising that the prevalence of rickets was relatively high in this population. It exceeded the CPR of 6.76% recorded for the Cross Bones burial ground assemblage (Brickley *et al.* 1999) and the CPR of 5.07% at St Bride's lower churchyard (West 1982 cited in Roberts and Cox 2003, 310) assemblage, both in London, and the CPR of 7.5% of the St Martin's, Birmingham assemblage (Brickley *et al.* 2006, 132). These working class populations show considerably higher CPR than the mean of 3.65% for the post-medieval period cited in Roberts and Cox (2003, 310), which included large numbers of middle class individuals.

Clearly, once aboard seamen and marines were exposed to an abundance of sunlight, in fact they were renowned for their tanned and leathery complexions. Even officers were not immune, as is vividly illustrated in Jane Austen's *Persuasion*, when Sir Walter Elliot, father of the heroine Anne Elliot, comments disgustedly on the appearance of Royal Navy officers, and one Admiral Baldwin, in particular:

> a sailor grows old sooner than any other man . . . they are all knocked about, and exposed to every climate and weather until they are not fit to be seen. It is a pity they are not all knocked on the head when they reach Admiral Baldwin's age [a man in his 40s].

He describes the unfortunate Admiral Baldwin as

> the most deplorable looking person you can imagine, his face the colour of mahogany, rough to the last degree, all lines and wrinkles. . .

One assumes with two brothers as admirals (one an Admiral of the Fleet), Jane Austen was writing this description from first hand experience. With such prolonged exposure to the elements, it is thus not surprising than osteomalacia was not present in the Greenwich assemblage.

Osteoporosis

Osteoporosis is a proportional decrease of both the bone mineral and the bone matrix, leading to bone which is light and brittle, and liable to fracture after minimal trauma (Steinbock 2003, 236). There are two types of osteoporosis: Type 1 or post-menopausal osteoporosis (affecting women over 50 years of age), and is commonly the underlying condition in vertebral crush fractures, and fractures of the distal radius; and Type 2 or senile osteoporosis, which affects both males and females over the age of 60 years equally, and predisposes individuals to vertebral wedge fractures and fractures of the femoral neck. Being so closely associated with advancing age, it is somewhat surprising that in the Greenwich assemblage only two older males (3241 and 6013) are recorded as suffering from this disorder. This apparent under-representation may be due to the difficulty in differentiating between bone mineral loss as a result of the disorder, and bone mineral loss due to taphonomic processes (such as leaching).

Skeleton 3241 had experienced 16 fractures, including the right distal radius and the right femoral neck, the head being forced inferiorly towards the greater trochanter. In addition, the bodies of thoracic vertebra 8 and lumbar vertebrae 2 and 3 showed severe vertical compression. The bone was brittle and very light in weight. Due the excessive trauma suffered by this individual, it is unclear which fractures, if any, were osteoporotic in origin, or which

Table 14 Summary of skeletons with rickets or possible rickets (N = 10).

Skeleton	Element affected	Severity
3051	tibiae; femora	slight
3103	tibiae; femora	slight
3189	tibiae; femora	slight
3211	femora	moderate
6016	tibiae; femora	slight
6037	femora	slight
6098	tibiae; femora	slight
6146	femora	moderate
6023	tibiae; femora	very slight
6105	tibiae; fibulae; femora	slight to moderate

had resulted from injuries incurred during his sailing career. The lightness of the bone does tentatively suggest that osteoporosis may have been responsible for at least some of the fractures. In the second recorded case, skeleton 6013, the bodies of thoracic vertebrae 8 - 12 and lumbar vertebra 4 had suffered wedge fractures, resulting in kyphosis of the spine. This was ascribed to osteoporosis, but will require further specialist analysis (eg. dual energy X-ray absorptiometry) to confirm the diagnosis.

Neoplasms

Osteochondroma

The left proximal femoral shaft of skeleton 6037, immediately inferio-medial to the lesser trochanter displayed an oval lesion of dense bone (measuring 25 mm x 19 mm) diagnosed as a juxtacortical chondroma. The surface of the lesion was rugose in appearance with irregular bony nodules protruding. Inferior to the lesion the shaft appeared flattened and smoothed, possibly due to the pressure of the tumour.

Osteochondromas account for nearly half of all benign tumours (Aufderheide and Rodríguez-Martín 1998, 381). They are minor clinical significance and rarely undergo malignant degeneration (ibid.).

Osteoma

A bony outgrowth or nodule on the lateral shaft of the left fifth metatarsal of skeleton 3269 (measuring 8.3 mm in diameter and 4.9 mm high) has tentatively been diagnosed as an ecchonchroma or osteoma. Both are benign tumours.

Button or ivory osteomas were present on the parietal or frontal bones of six older adults. These benign tumours manifest as small, dense, smooth oval or round outgrowths on the skull vault, and are more common in older individuals (Aufderheide and Rodríguez-Martín 1998, 375). They are of no clinical significance.

Congenital anomalies

Minor congenital anomalies were observed in 11 individuals, and are of little, if any, clinical significance (Table 15). In eight cases, these involved minor anomalies of the lowest lumbar vertebra (L5) and the sacrum. Complete or partial sacralisation, where L5 fuses with the first sacral vertebra was the most common anomaly (n = 5), whilst S1 in skeleton 3072 remained unfused to S2 on the right side. The left side morphologically resembled L5. Another midline defect present in the sacra of four individuals was spina bifida occulta. This anomaly is identified from non-union of the spinous processes of the sacrum. Unlike more severe forms of spina bifida, it is asymptomatic.

One of the right mid-thoracic ribs of skeleton 3229 was bifid at the costal end. It is unlikely that this would have had any functional effects.

Table 15   Summary of congenital anomalies (n = 11).

Skeleton	Diagnosis	Element involved
3072	S1 partly unfused; L side like L5 in morphology	S1
3098	os acromiale	L & R acromia
3099	spina bifida occulta; partial sacralisation	L5, S1-5
3176	partial sacralisation; slight spina bifida occulta	L6, S1 & 2
3194	spina bifida occulta	sacrum incomplete
3213	sacralisation	L5, S1-5
3229	sacralisation; partial spina bifida occulta	L5; S3-5
	bifid R rib (mid-thoracic) at costal end	R Rib
6019	abnormal shortening of bone- congenital dysplasia	L & R 4th metatarsal
6063	os acromiale	L acromial process
6073	os acromiale	L acromial process
6113	sacralisation (near complete)	L5

The epiphysis of the acromial process of the scapulae of three skeletons (3098, 6063 and 6073) remained unfused. This condition is known as os acromiale and may be congenital or activity-related in aetiology. The condition is discussed more fully above.

Other pathology

Pulmonary hypertrophic osteoarthropathy

Numerous elements of skeleton 3194 displayed hypervascularity and considerable periostitis, forming large plaques of active woven bone on the bone surfaces (Plates 23 and 24). This was particularly apparent at the insertion points of muscles (such as the *Supra-* and *Infraspinatous*, *Subscapularis*, *Subclavius* and *Trapezius* of the shoulder joint; the *Triceps brachii* (right only); at the intertubercular groove of the right humerus (possibly for the *Pectoralis major*); *Iliacus* and *Gluteus medius* and *minimus* on the pelvis; the *Pectineus*, *Vastus lateralis*, *medius* and *intermedius* on the femora). Woven bone was also present at the insertion points of ligaments (such as the sternoclavicular ligament of the clavicle, and the ilio-femoral and pubo-femoral ligaments of the pelvis). All of the ribs that were present displayed active woven bone, particularly at the intercostal muscle insertion sites. Hypervascularity (pitting) was evident on the head and neck and costal ends of the ribs. Similar pitting was present on the scapulae adjacent to the glenoid cavity, and around the acetabulum of the pelvis. The thoracic and lumbar vertebral bodies were also very porous.

A second skeleton (6056) also presented with periostitis of multiple elements, which involved the diaphyses of all the major long bones (including clavicles) and the scapular bodies. The hands, feet and skull were unaffected. These lesions manifested very differently from those seen on skeleton 3194, and comprised prolific new bone growth consisting of areas of woven, lamellar bone, plaques and spicules. Spicules were most commonly sited at the insertion points of large muscles, such as at the interosseus borders of the arms and legs, and the deltoid tuberosity, the soleal line and linea aspera. Thickening of the lower limb bones was marked. Little joint involvement was noted, with the exception of moderate lipping of the glenoid fossa.

Differential diagnosis of these systemic conditions is somewhat uncertain. The original diagnosis of fluorosis in skeleton 3194 has since been revised. One strong possibility is secondary hypertrophic osteoarthropathy. This appears also true for skeleton 6056 (Plate 25). The skeletal hallmark of this disease is periostitis, usually involving the diaphyses of all the major and minor long bones, and more occasionally the scapulae, clavicles, ribs and spine (Resnick 1995, 4429–30). Unlike other conditions, such as fluorosis and syphilis, secondary hypertrophic osteoarthropathy rarely affects the skull (Aufderheide and Rodríguez-Martín 1998, 91). The appearance of the lesions varies between individuals, but the 'irregular solid areas of periosteal cloaking with a wavy contour' described by Resnick (1995, 4430) is consistent with lesions seen in skeleton 3194, whilst the 'tree bark' described by Ortner and Putschar (1981) aptly describes the appearance of lesions on skeleton 6056. Intensive overgrowth of vascular tissue surrounding tendons and joints is also a feature of this disease, and may be the cause of hypervascularity and pitting observed at insertion sites and around the acetabulae of skeleton 3194 (Plate 23), and the porosity and new bone deposition along tendon sites in skeleton 6056. Neither skeleton displayed other common features of the disease, however, such as joint involvement and tufting of the distal hand phalanges.

In modern western populations, secondary or pulmonary hypertrophic osteoarthropathy most commonly affects males in older age categories (Aufderheide and Rodríguez-Martín 1998, 91). The age and sex of skeletons 3194 (40+ years) and 6056 (50+ years) is consistent with this epidemiology. The skeletal lesions resolve when the primary disease is treated (Aufderheide and Rodríguez-Martín 1998, 91), but this remodelling may take months or years (Resnick 1995, 4429).

Traditionally associated with pulmonary disease (bronchogenic carcinoma, bronchiectasis, pulmonary fibrosis, empyema, and pleural neoplasia), this condition is less commonly also caused by diseases of other systems, including the gut (eg. ulcerative colitis, intestinal neoplasia and dysentery), kidneys (pyelonephritis), the endocrine system (thyroid disease), the liver (cirrhosis, biliary atresia), and the circulatory and lymphatic systems (Hodgkin's disease, aortic aneurysm). Bronchogenic carcinoma remains by far the most common cause, however (Resnick 1995, 4429).

This cancer of the lung epithelium most commonly develops as a result of tobacco smoking, followed by prolonged exposure to industrial pollutants, such as asbestos, and heavy metals - uranium, gold, nickel and chromate - in mining (Chandrasoma and Taylor 1995, 537). Whilst some ex-Royal Navy seamen did become miners, for example John Nichol, who wrote a memoir of his experiences in Nelson's Navy, tobacco smoking is the most probable cause. As noted above (see Chronic respiratory disease), pipe smoking was a popular pastime of the Greenwich pensioners, and carried the same health risks as it does today.

Medical interventions

The Navy had very few physicians - in 1797 there were only 15, including those on half pay (Lavery 1989, 212) - but every man-of-war was provided with a surgeon and his mates (Porter 2002, 117), the quality of medical treatment in the Royal Navy was very variable. Rated as warrant officers, ships surgeons of the 18th century were poorly paid. Amongst their peers on land they were professionally despised (Harvie 2002, 27). Prior to 1795, ship's surgeons were poorly paid. But they remuneration improved dramtically during the War with France. The pay of surgeon in 1797 was less than a ship's lieutenant, but by 1815 surgeons were paid only a little less than post Captains (Lewis 1960, table viii) although they received fewer allowances.

Like other surgeons of their day, naval surgeons did not undertake the rigorous academic medical training that was required to practice as a physician. But the Royal Navy required more of its surgeons, and they were expected to deal with medical matters other than surgery, and the Navy required its surgeons to undertake a qualifying course in medicine before they could be admitted into a man-of-war (Rodger 2004, 196).

The actions of the surgeon, like all else aboard ship, fell under the jurisdiction of the captain. As a means of quality control, all surgeons were also required to keep records minutely detailing their cases, treatment and outcomes (see Lavery 1998, 481–539 for extracts from surgeons' journals). These had to be submitted to the Sick and Hurt Board at the end of the surgeon's tour of duty. Surgeons deemed as wanting in skill or knowledge would have their warrant withheld. Surgeon's assistants or mates were entirely self-taught and were even lower down the ship hierarchy. Smollett, a surgeon's mate - cum - novelist, wrote that 'the captain is too much of a gentleman to know a surgeon's mate by sight' (cited in Harvie 2002, 27).

Despite these deficiencies in training and a frequent lack of drugs and equipment, most ship's surgeons worked hard under trying conditions, which were particularly acute during outbreaks of disease (eg typhus, yellow fever or dysentery) and during and following a naval engagement. Indeed, many innovations and new techniques in surgery and medicine were developed by army and naval surgeons during this period. Sick and injured seamen were seen by the surgeon in their hammocks on the lower deck or in the sick berth. Basic nursing care was undertaken by the surgeon's mate or by inexperienced boys (loblollies), and often left much to be desired. In his memoir, 'Jack Nastyface' (Robinson 2002, 115–6) describes how 'a steady and much respected seaman' who had stoically and wordlessly suffered the amputation of both legs and whose wounds were healing well, died 'from lying in one position for such a length of time that his back mortified' (ie. he died of bedsores, that may be easily prevented by regularly changing the patient's position).

During a battle, a temporary operating theatre was set up in the cockpit on the orlop deck, in the area normally designated as the dining area of midshipmen. The dining table or midshipmen's sea chests lashed together served as the operating table, and the wounded were seen in the order in which they appeared for attention. Surgeons were often faced with overwhelming casualties and had to work rapidly to attend to all cases. One seaman, Samuel Leech (1844, 142–43) described the cockpit in the middle of battle:

> The surgeon and his mate were smeared with blood from head to foot. They looked more like butchers than doctors ... The task was painful to behold, the surgeon using his knife and saw on human flesh and bones as freely as a butcher in the shambles.

The principal aim was to arrest haemorrhage, initially by applying a tourniquet and later by tying off large arteries and veins with ligatures, and where limbs were badly damaged, amputation was the quickest and most effective way to save a man's life. A skilful surgeon could perform an amputation with remarkable speed - sometimes in as little as two or three minutes (Fremont-Barnes 2005, 41). Another reason for speed was the intensity of pain suffered by the soon-to-be amputee, as such battle operations were performed without anaesthetic or analgesia. The former was still unknown, and there was not the time or sufficient supplies of rum or laudanum to deaden the pain, and most patients had only a leather-covered chain to bite down upon during the procedure (Fremont-Barnes 2005, 42). Following surgery, the greatest cause of mortality was infection.

Loss of a limb or an eye was a common fate in the Royal Navy at this time (as is illustrated in Plates 2–5, 7 and 9), it's prevalence leading Princess Caroline (daughter of George III) to exclaim whilst visiting the fleet which had been fighting the Dutch off Dogger Bank in 1781: 'What! Have all the English lost either an arm or a leg?' In the Greenwich pensioner population alone, six individuals (CPR 6.19%) were missing a leg or a hand. They were in good company; the great naval hero Lord Nelson had suffered amputation of his right lower arm after being hit during an assault on Santa Cruz on Tenerife in 1797. Previous to that in 1794, Nelson had lost the use of his right eye as a result of damage from stones and sand thrown up by a French cannonade before Calvi.

In the Greenwich assemblage, skeletons 3032, 3045, 3086 and 3261 had undergone above knee amputations, skeleton 3061 a below-knee amputation and skeleton 6089 had a possible amputation of the left hand at the wrist. In the first four, the distal third or midshaft of the femur had been amputated (three left and one right), whilst in skeleton 3061, both the right fibula and tibia had been sawn off just distal to the tibial tuberosity. A partial bone cap had begun to form over the stump in skeleton 3061, but this was thin and fragile, and unlikely to have withstood weight-bearing. Bony resorption was evident in the stumps of all five leg amputees, possibly due to secondary infection and/or due to the probable lack of weight-bearing of the limbs. In skeletons 3032 and 3061, the bone was thin and porous, resorption resulting in the bone of the stump being thin and tapering to a point (Plate 26). Radiography of 3061 (Plate 27) revealed the extent of bone loss (manifesting as black on the X-ray; note the difference in density between the stump and the healthy left tibia). This demineralisation would suggest that the stump had not been used for weight-bearing and had atrophied. It is unlikely that skeleton 3061 had used a peg leg, so ubiquitous in contemporary depictions of Greenwich pensioners. He may have used under-arm crutches instead. Bony modification to the shoulder joints was not noted, but the left humerus did weigh 15g more than the left, very, very tentatively suggesting densification due to increased use. Handedness or slight variations in taphonomy of the burial environment may equally be responsible for this difference, however. Skeleton 3086 showed more convincing bony changes to the shoulder joints suggestive of crutch use. Articular facets were present on the superio-lateral aspect of the lesser tubercle and the superio-posterior aspect of the greater tubercle. Unfortunately the scapulae were too damaged to identify any morphological changes. Similar changes to the humeri were present in skeleton 3261. Better preservation of the scapulae allowed the identification of a small articular facet on the inferior surface of the right scapula, located laterally and latero-posteriorly.

Amputation was usually undertaken as a life-saving measure and little attention could be spared to form the stump carefully in order to maximise even weight-bearing and the comfortable wearing of a prostheses, although the principle of removing more bone whilst preserving the maximum amount of soft tissue, thus permitting the skin to mend over the bone, and in due course form a useable stump was understood as early as the Middle Ages (Porter 2002, 112). Prostheses were basic and consisted of a peg leg strapped to the residual stump, or a hook to replace a hand (ibid.). Balance was difficult enough in a below- knee amputation where the knee joint was still preserved, but far more problematic in higher amputations (which also were more risky to perform due to the greater risk of major haemorrhage (ibid.). Illustrations of seamen with peg legs almost always depict below knee amputees, but in his memoirs Spavens (2000, 98) described the wearing of peg legs by above knee amputees (see Chapter 2 above). In part, this may explain why all three femoral amputees showed demineralisation suggestive of a lack of weight-bearing following amputation.

Wastage of bone may result from severe infection at the stump site, as occurred most dramatically in skeleton 3045 (Plate 21). Here very severe osteomyelitis had caused major remodelling of the femoral shaft, with the shaft been reduced to a sequestrum (see above). A sharp bony spur protruded distally beyond the limit of the prolific new bone growth. This, together with ongoing infection of the bone and overlying soft tissue, would probably have rendered weight-bearing too painful. Demineralisation is suggested by reduced weight of the affected element relative to the unaffected side in all four lower limb amputees. In skeletons 3032 and 3261, this demineralisation was thought to include the pelvic bones on the affected side also. Only in skeleton 3061 was this observation investigated using radiography, however.

During excavation and during osteological analysis, it was noted that the left hand of skeleton 6089 was missing, and that its absence could not be attributed to taphonomy or poor archaeological recovery (Witkin pers. comm.). No cut or saw marks were evident on the distal ulna joint. Severe longstanding but active periostitis / osteitis on the left distal radius and ulna suggest that the loss of the hand had been associated with severe secondary infection. The infection was still active at the time of death. Skeleton 6089 was much younger than the majority of pensioners, being 35–45 years at the time of his death. It is possible that he had died of complications from his surgery, such as septicaemia, the infection spreading from his affected arm, but this is of course pure speculation.

As was evident in three of the five amputees, secondary infection was commonly associated with amputation, not surprising given that the operation would not have been performed in antiseptic conditions. Aseptic technique during surgery had yet to be invented, and surgical implements were not cleaned between patients. It was really only with Lister's introduction of the antiseptic technique as late as the 1860s that amputation mortality rates reduced dramatically. He claimed a dive from 45.7% to 15% when his antiseptic technique was implemented (Porter 1997, 372). Many - possibly including such as skeleton 3045 - suffered lingering infections, often resulting in chronic ill health and death (Sournia 1992, 345).

Following surgery, the aftercare of the wounds and general nursing of bedridden patients left much to be desired by modern standards, but probably compared with contemporary treatment of civilian patients. Injured ratings were either nursed in the sick bay aboard ship, or transferred to hospital ships (when a large fleet had assembled), which in theory, offered better care than a lone surgeon and his mate could manage (Rodger 2004, 214). Mortality aboard these ships was high, but one surgeon serving in a hospital ship claimed that they were better than the rates that 'candid physicians in London own' (cited in Rodgers 2004, 214). Following a major sea battle, the staff on hospital ships were badly overstretched. Depending on location, the sick and injured were sometimes transferred to hospitals in port, such as Port Mahon, Minorca, and Gibraltar in the Mediterranean (where many of the injured in the Battle of Trafalgar were rehabilitated), or the three Royal Navy hospitals at home at Portsmouth, Chatham and Plymouth. Survivors were either discharged if their injuries were too severe to continue in service, pensioned off, or returned to active service in occupations where their disability was less restricting (eg ship's cooks) (Fremont-Barnes 2005, 25).

Craniotomy

Post-mortem craniotomies had been performed on four skeletons of the Greenwich assemblage (3105, 3106, 3119 and 3159). The skulls of all four had been sawed in the horizontal plane, across the frontal, parietal and occipital bones just superior to the temporal bones and the supra-orbital ridges (Plate 28). No other saw marks were present in the cranial or post-cranial skeletons. Why these three were selected for anatomisation is unclear. Two (skeletons 3105 and 3106) had porotic hyperstosis and cribra orbitalia but no other cranial pathologies were noted that might suggest why these individuals were targeted.

In the Georgian period, post-mortem dissection was an uncommon procedure, and usually one over which the deceased and their relatives exercised little control. In the 18th century, medical institutions had a growing need to be provided with cadavers on which students might learn anatomy and practice dissection. In 1752 the Company of Surgeons was granted the corpses of all executed felons (Porter 1997, 292). However, demand far outstripped supply, and many additional cadavers were supplied to anatomy halls by 'resurrectionists', who raided graveyards, exhumed corpses and sold them on for a handsome profit (Porter 1997, 317–18). Public outrage at this practice reached a height in 1829 with the notorious case of Burke and Hare. The outcome of this sentiment was the passing of the Anatomy Act (1832), which permitted the medical profession to take for dissection all 'unclaimed bodies' of those dying without family, or those dying in the workhouse or hospitals. As a result of the Act, there was a reduction in body-snatching, but it also served to deepen the fear and shame of dying on the parish amongst the poor (Rugg 1999, 222).

The antipathy to the notion of being dissected was based on religious and social perceptions. The Christian belief in the resurrection of the whole body on Judgement Day led to fears that dissection would damage the spiritual state of the dissected person. A deep-seated solicitude for the corpse causes reactions of revulsion at the indignity that the body suffered during exhumation and dissection. Particularly with regard to female corpses, the physical exposure of the naked body to the gaze of young men was perceived as harrowing, a process tantamount to sexual assault (ibid.). It is to be assumed that most of the Greenwich pensioners ascribed to these views, and the anatomisation of four of the pensioners is surprising, given the care taken in their burial. It is of course possible that they had consented to the procedure, as was occasionally the case.

Dental pathology

Dental caries

Dental caries involves the destruction of the enamel surface, the dentine (internal part of the tooth) and the cement (outer layer of the roots) of a tooth. This is caused by the acid produced by bacteria present in dental plaque (Hillson 1996, 269). The association of acidogenic bacteria and sugars in the diet is a well established cause of cavitations (Lukacs 1989, 265). Classified as an infectious disease, caries usually progresses gradually. Oral hygiene is also a significant factor in the development of caries.

The size of each carious lesion was classified according to the universally used grading system produced by Lukacs (1989). The location of the lesion was also recorded. However, due to time constrains, frequencies pertaining to location on the tooth, the size of the lesions, and the identity of the tooth affected are not discussed here.

The prevalence of caries was calculated by dividing the total number of caries by the total number of permanent teeth present. A total of 147 caries was recorded on 1202 permanent teeth of the adult males (TPR 12.2%) and five in 56 permanent teeth of the subadults (TPR 8.93%). No caries were recorded in the female skeletons. The overall caries rate of the total population was therefore 11.67% (Table 16). The mean number of carious lesions per skeleton was 1.41 (n = 108). All lesions were located on the posterior dentition.

This prevalence compared exactly with the mean of seven late Georgian/ early Victorian assemblages (Table 17). It correlated most closely to the predominantly working class assemblage of the Newcastle Infirmary, which interestingly was partly composed of merchant sailors. Rates were higher than other working class assemblages, with the exception of the Cross Bones burial ground, Southwark, and lower than the middle class assemblages of St George's, Bloomsbury, and Christ Church, Spitalfields (Table 17).

Given the advanced age of most skeletons in the Greenwich assemblage and the progressive nature of the disease, it is surprising that the caries rate was not higher. This relatively low prevalence probably relates closely to the amount of sugar (particularly refined sugar) consumed by the pensioners throughout their lives. In the civilian population, the consumption of cane sugar gradually increased over the 18th and 19th centuries. In the 16th and 17th centuries sugar was an expensive high status luxury available only to the most wealthy (Musgrave and Musgrave 2000, 60). However, the development of sugar plantations in the West Indies in the 18th century made sugar more readily available and created a more affordable supply of the commodity to markets in Europe. As the price of sugar fell, so consumption gradually spread down the social classes, until by the latter half of the 19th century it was available to all but the most indigent (ibid.). By the early 19th century, sugar was widely available to the middle classes, but not readily accessible to the lower classes.

The amount of sugar consumed by seamen and marines aboard ship is unclear, but was not generally cited in accounts of ships rations, which comprised bread or ship's biscuit (a very hard biscuit of wholewheat flour, salt and water) every day; pease (dried peas) four times a week; pork and beef twice a week (usually salted); oatmeal three times a week (usually served as skilygalee, a gruel boiled up in fatty water); and butter and cheese three times a week (if not too rancid) (Macdonald 2006, 10; Fremont-Barnes 2005, 24–25). Fresh meat and vegetables and fruit augmented this monotonous diet when ships came into port, or when livestock aboard ship were slaughtered. In the 1808 edition of the *Regulations and Instructions*, sugar was include in the allowance of provisions to be issued at the rate of 2oz three times a week (Lewis 1960, table xiv).

The first formal set of *Regulations and Instructions relating to His Majesty's Service at Sea* published in 1733, replaced fish with a ration of oatmeal. Part of the oatmeal ration might comprise sugar or molasses, usually as a substitute for oatmeal at the rate of one pound of sugar for two quarts of oatmeal, or five and threequarter pounds of molasses for one gallon of oatmeal (McDonald 2006, 9, 35). Presumably, like other food, this depended on availability, with those ships operational in the West Indies probably receiving a larger proportion of sugar in their oatmeal ration.

Small amounts of sugar were added to 'Scotch coffee' (burnt bread boiled in water), tea and cocoa, and in the later 18th and 19th centuries to sweeten the lemon juice added to the daily grog ration (Fremont Barnes 2005). The daily oatmeal porridge or 'burgoo'

Table 16   Dental caries prevalence (N = 1303).

Teeth	Age and sex distribution				
	Females	Males	Unsexedadults	Subadults	Total (%)
All anterior	0/24	43/502	0	0/22	43/548 (7.85%)
All posterior	0/21	104/655	0	5/34	109/710 (15.35%)
Total	0/45	147/1202	0/0	5/56	152/1303 (11.67%)

Plates

Plate 1   The Royal Hospital Greenwich.

Plate 2   Greenwich pensioner (early 19th century)

Plate 3   Greenwich pensioners (1808)

Plate 4   Greenwich pensioner (1828)

Plate 5   'Ah, the Navy is not what it was!'- Greenwich pensioners (1828)

Plate 6   A Greenwich Pensioner, wearing a cocked (1834)

Plate 7   'The Way of the World'- Two battered Greenwich Pensioners (1834)

Plate 8   John Adams, alias John Wilkinson, Greenwich Pensioner. (June 1840)

Plate 9   Two pensioners, one minus a leg, the other minus an arm (date unknown)

Plate 10   Discharge Paper of Marine Corporal George Frederick Eller, who had his leg amputated at the Battle of the Nile (1798)

Plate 11   'A Milling Match between Decks'- The lower deck of a man-of-war in port.

Plate 12   The dining hall of the Royal Hospital Greenwich (mid 19th century)

Plate 13   Areas 1: General view of excavation looking south-east

Plate 14   Areas 1 and 2: Excavation of graves

Plate 15   Grave 3127: double interment, skeletons 3211 and 3162. The upper pair of two pairs of skeletons within a single grave cut.

Plate 16   Skeleton 3103: Poorly reduced but well healed nasal fracture

Plate 17   Skeleton 3164: Poorly reduced fracture of the tibial shaft with considerable overlap and shortening of the element.

Plate 18   Skeleton 3229: Bilateral fractures and secondary osteomyelitis of the femoral shafts (possibly compound fractures)

Plate 19   Skeleton 3229: Radiograph showing overlap of the fractured bone and associated osteomyelitis and callus formation.

Plate 20   Skeleton 3202: Marked exostosis formation on the right femoral shaft secondary to soft tissue injury.

Plate 21   Skeleton 3045: Amputation and secondary osteomyelitis of the right femur

Plate 22   Skeleton 3098: Pott's disease (tuberculosis of the spine). Note the crush fractures and the collapse of the vertebrae

Plate 23   Skeleton 3194: Hypervascularity and periostitis on the right pelvis

Plate 24   Skeleton 3194: Active periostitis on the proximal shaft of the right femur.

Plate 25   Skeleton 6056: periostitis and possible osteitis of the left femur and tibia

Plate 26   Skeleton 3061: Below knee amputation of the right tibia and fibula

Plate 27   Skeleton 3061: Radiograph showing demineralisation of the amputated stump from lack of use

Plate 28   Grave 3118: Skeleton 3119 with post-mortem craniotomy.

Plate 29   Grave 6084: Burial 6146: The clear coffin stain and nails indicated a single break coffin

Plate 30   Grave 6069: Burial 6098: Remnants of simple wooden coffin still overlying the chest and arm regions

GREENWICH.

Greenwich Pensioners.

A Greenwich Pensioner.

Ah! the Navy arn't what it was!

THE WAY OF THE WORLD

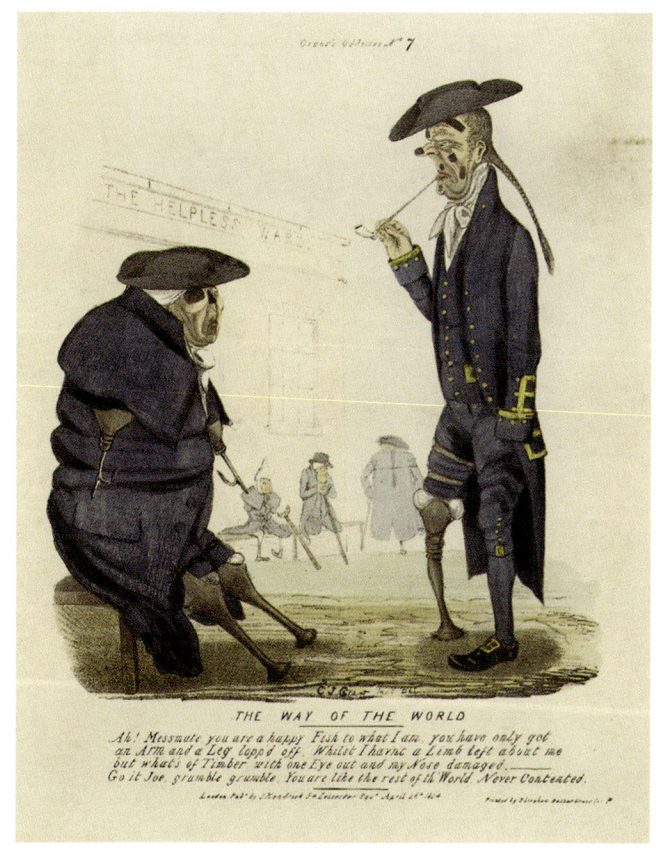

Ah! Messmate you are a happy Fish to what I am, you have only got
an Arm and a Leg lopp'd off. Whilst I have a Limb left about me
but what's of Timber with one Eye out and my Nose damaged.——
Go it Joe, grumble grumble. You are like the rest of the World Never Contented.

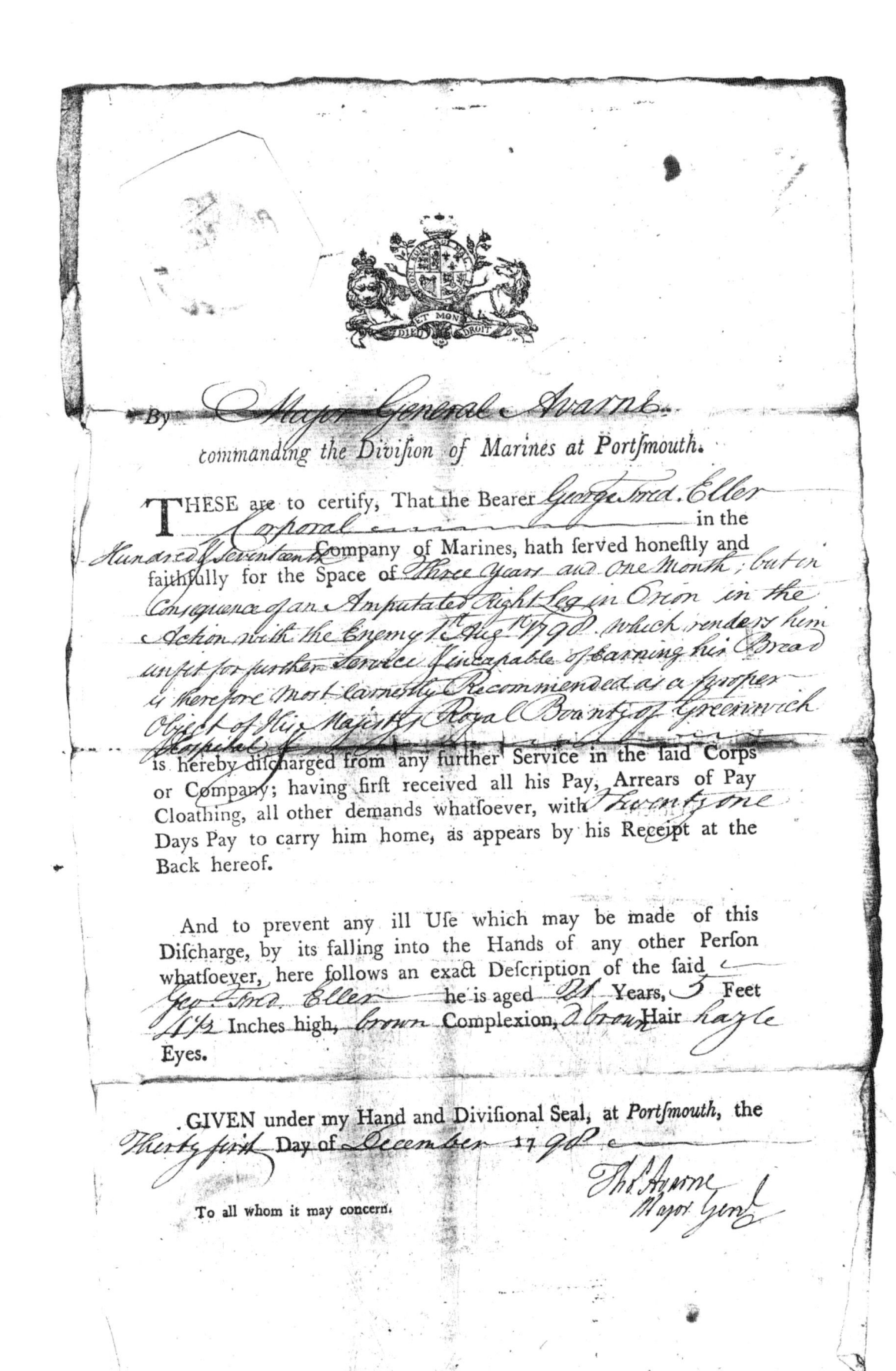

By *Major General Avarne*
commanding the Division of Marines at Portsmouth.

THESE are to certify, That the Bearer *George Fred. Eller* in the *Corporal* *Hundred & Seventeenth* Company of Marines, hath served honestly and faithfully for the Space of *Three Years and One Month; but in Consequence of an Amputated Right Leg in Orion in the Action with the Enemy 1st Aug 1798 which renders him unfit for further Service & incapable of earning his Bread is therefore most earnestly Recommended as a proper Object of His Majesty's Royal Bounty of Greenwich Hospital* is hereby discharged from any further Service in the said Corps or Company; having first received all his Pay, Arrears of Pay Cloathing, all other demands whatsoever, with *Twenty one* Days Pay to carry him home, as appears by his Receipt at the Back hereof.

And to prevent any ill Use which may be made of this Discharge, by its falling into the Hands of any other Person whatsoever, here follows an exact Description of the said *Geo. Fred. Eller* he is aged *21* Years, *5* Feet *4½* Inches high, *Brown* Complexion, *Brown* Hair *hazle* Eyes.

GIVEN under my Hand and Divisional Seal, at Portsmouth, the *Thirty first* Day of *December* 1798

Th. Avarne
Major Genl

To all whom it may concern.

A MILLING MATCH Between Decks.

DINING HALL, GREENWICH.

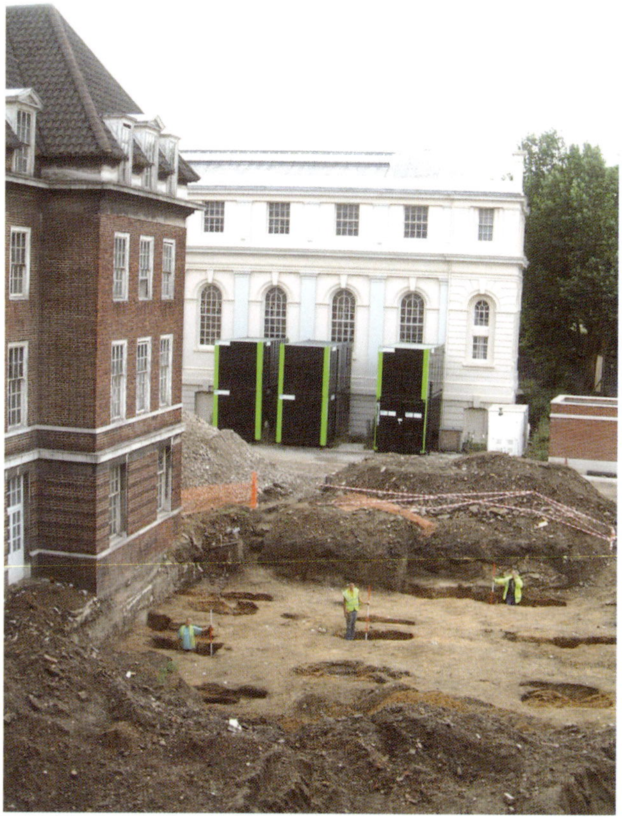

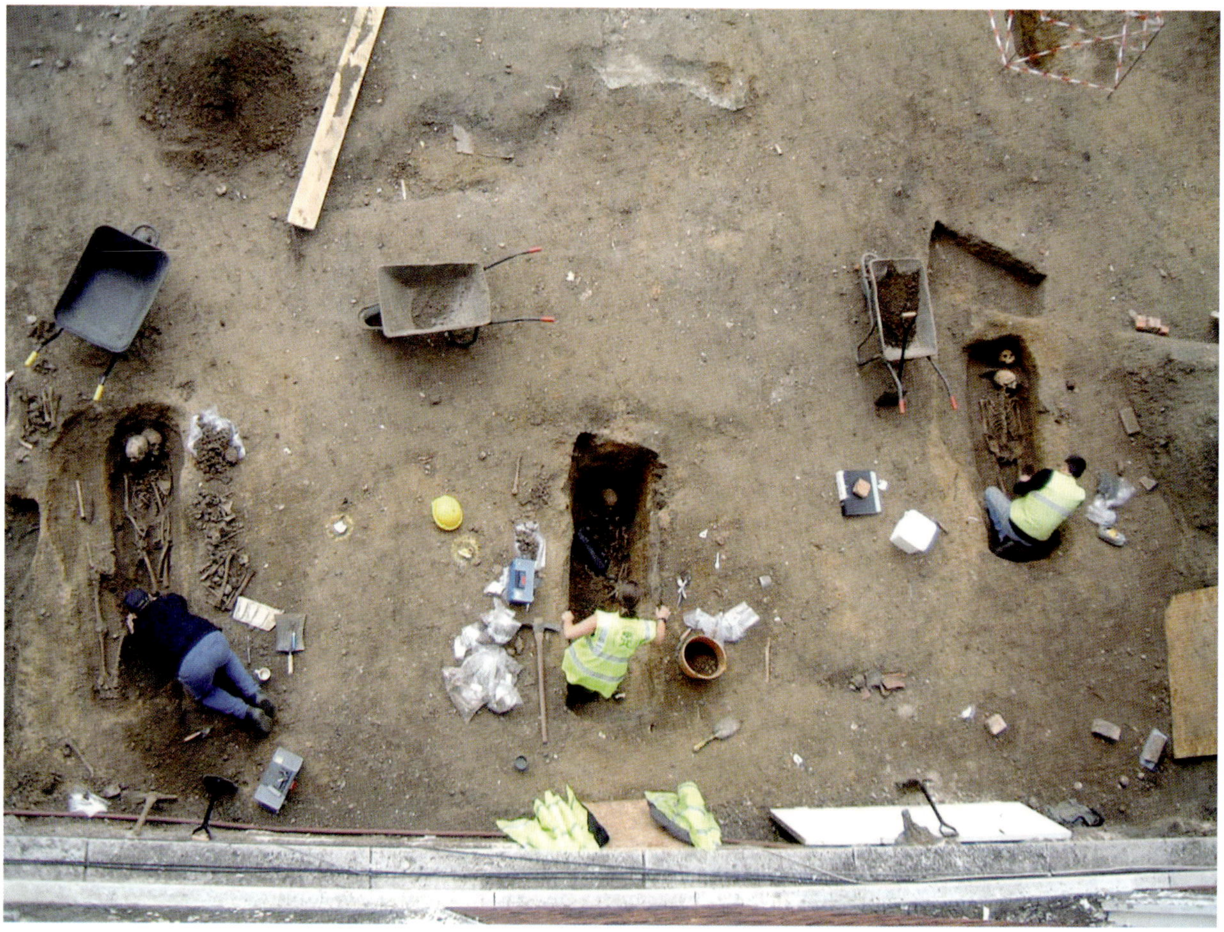

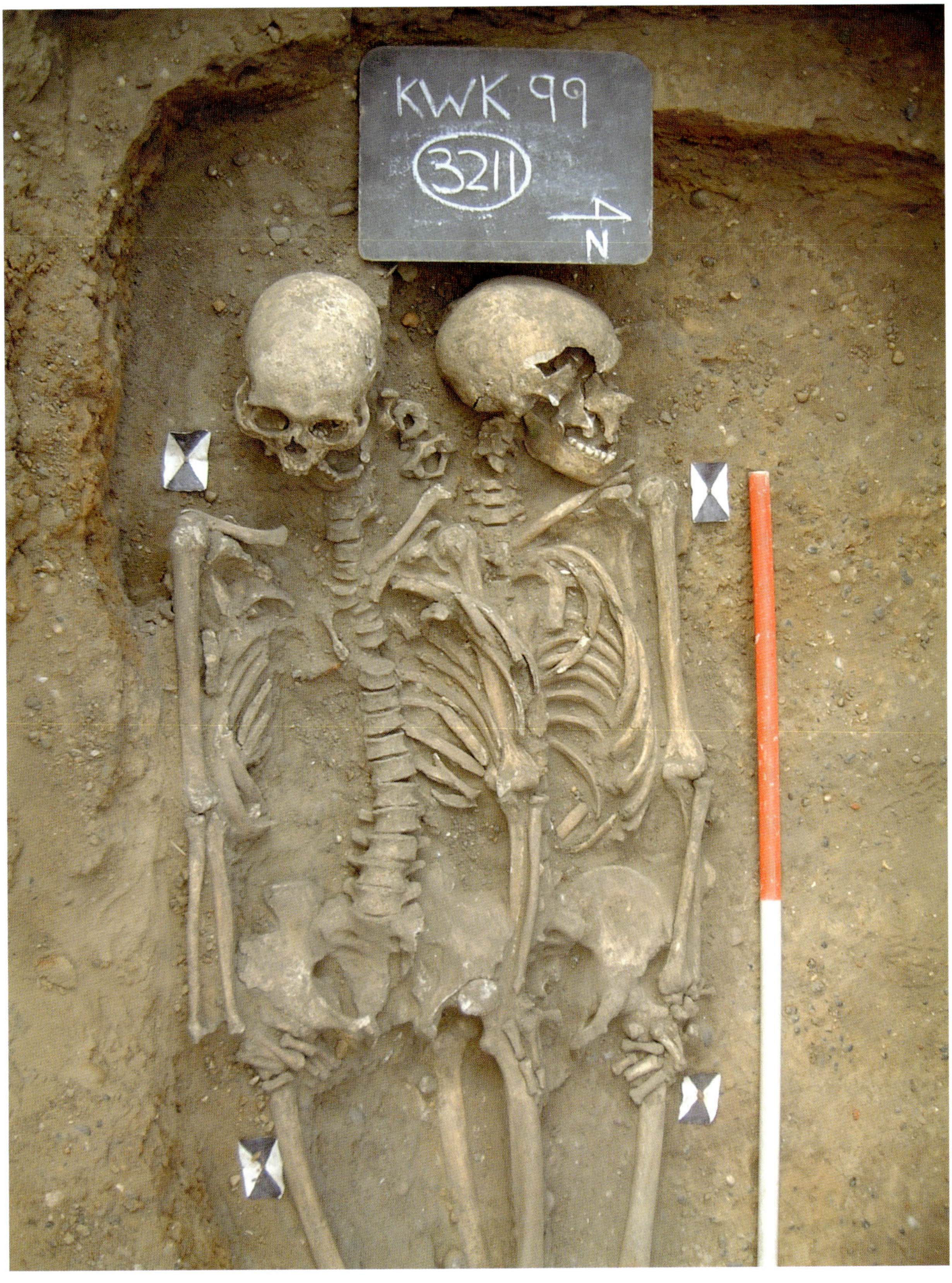
KWK 99
3211
N

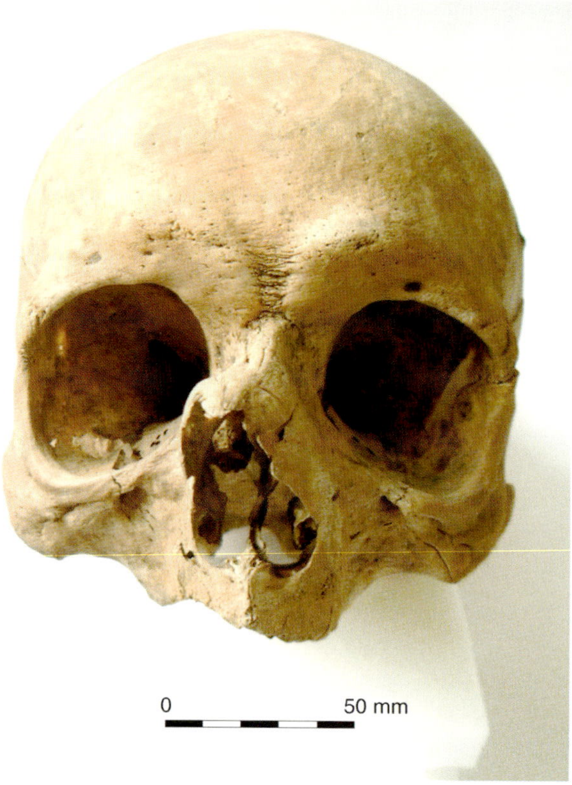
0
50 mm

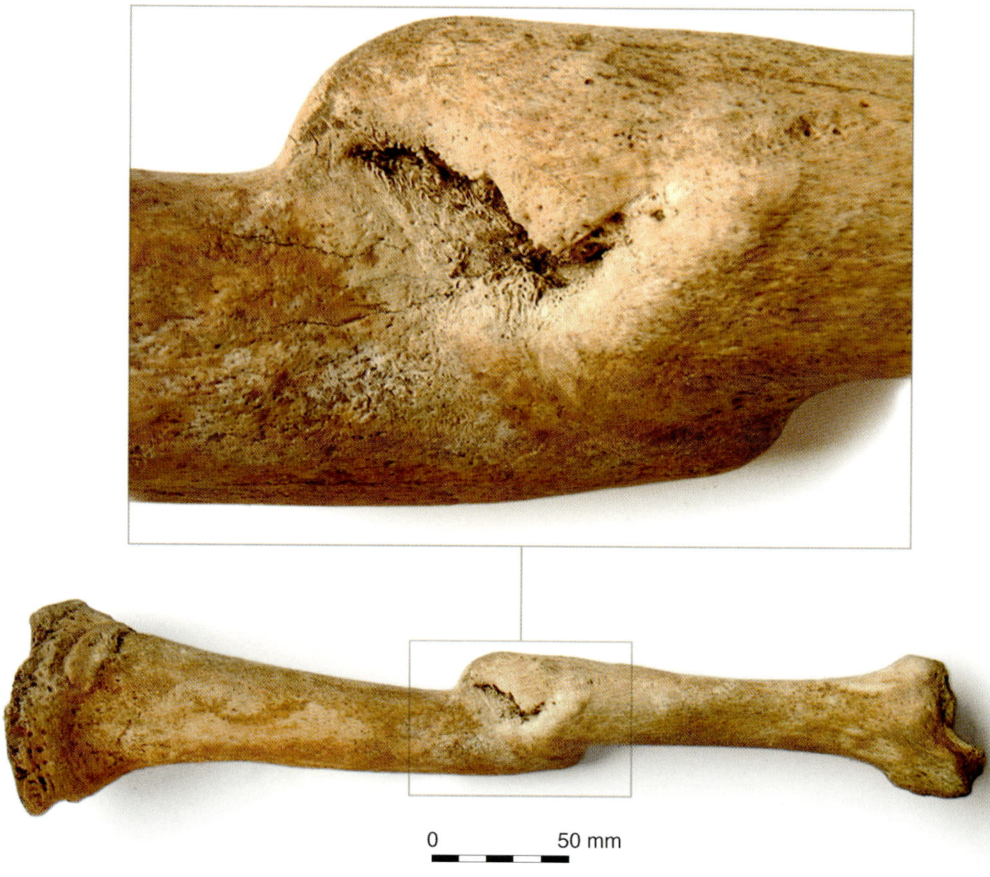
0
50 mm

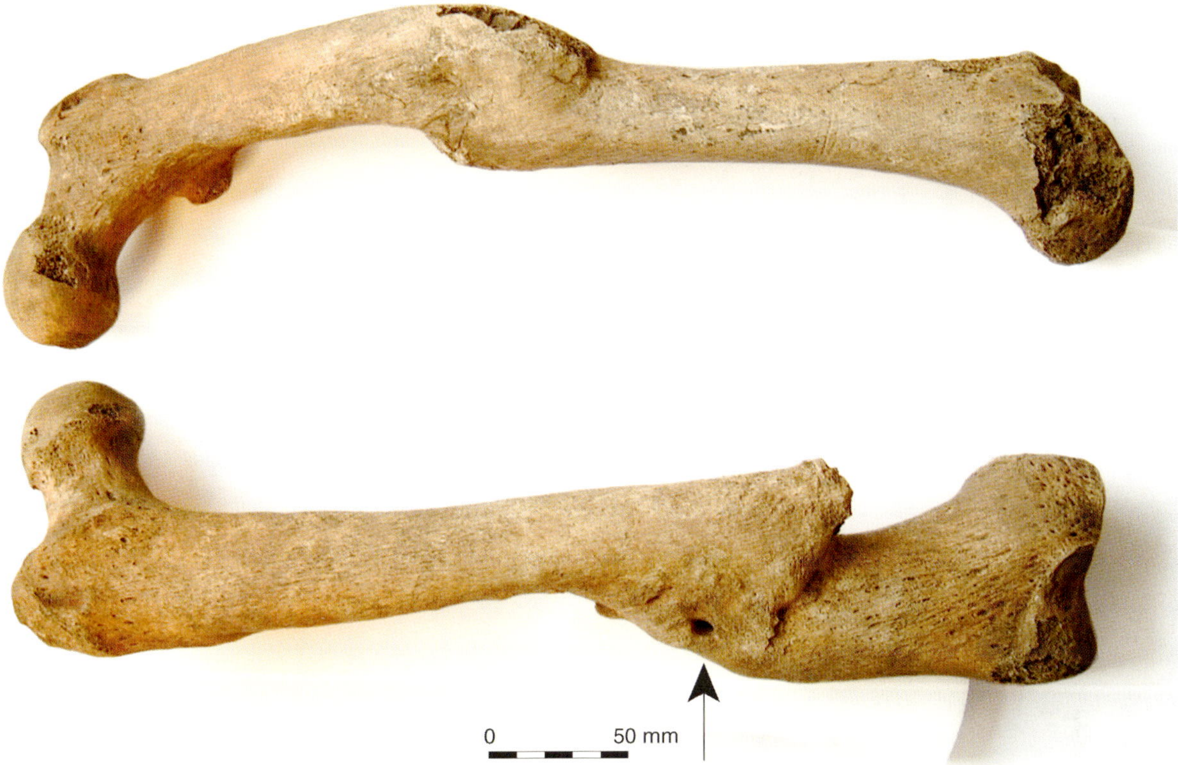
0
50 mm

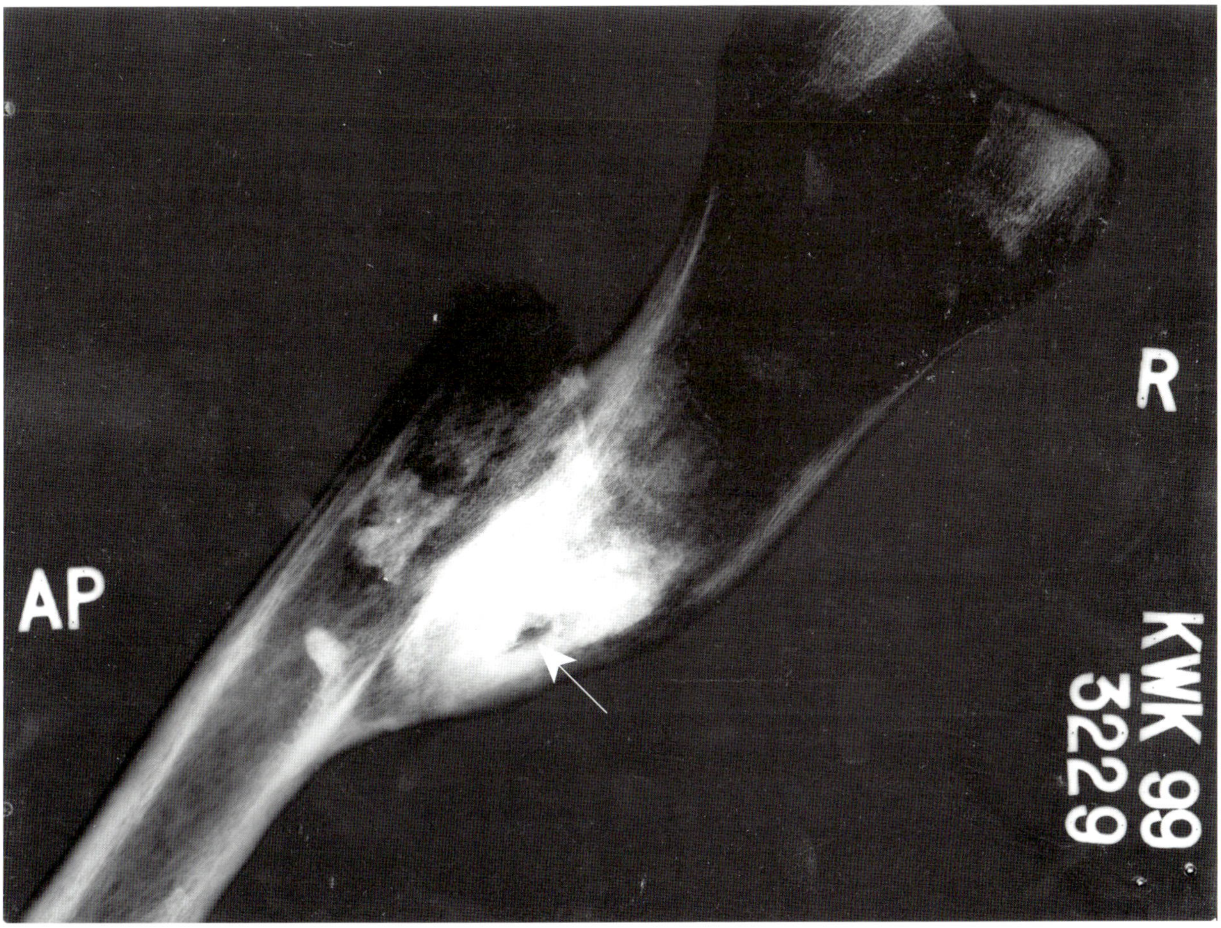
R
AP
KWK 99
3229

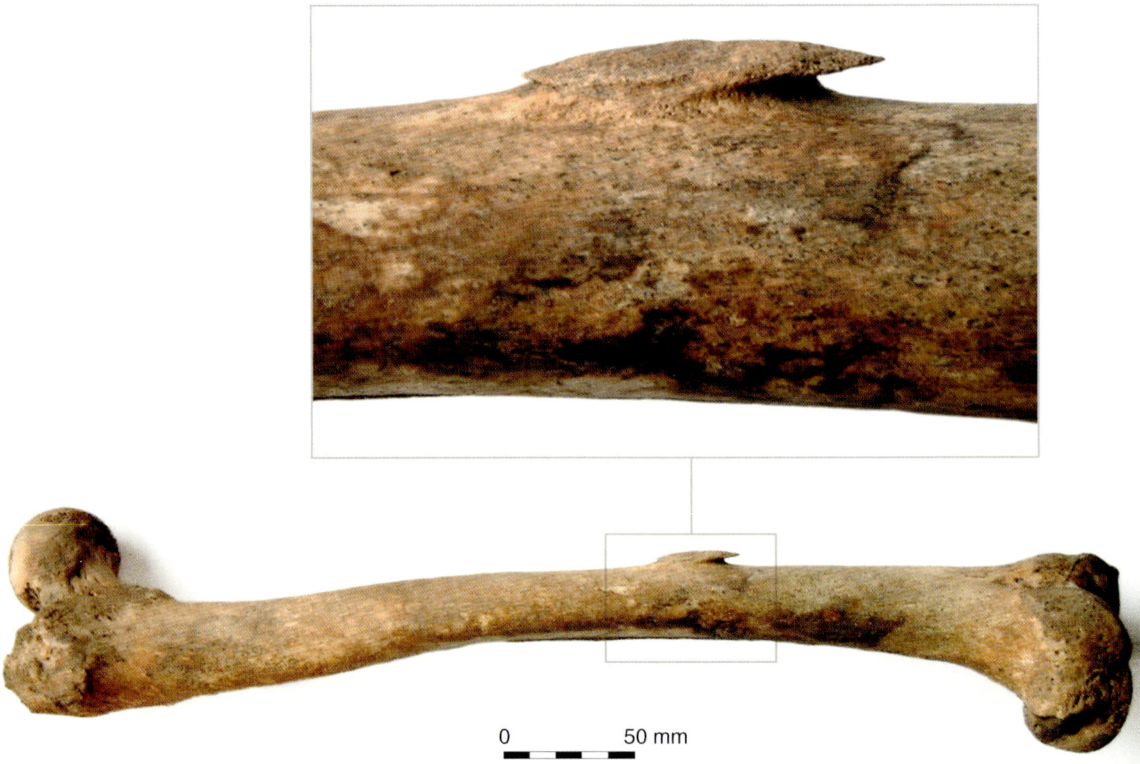
0
50 mm

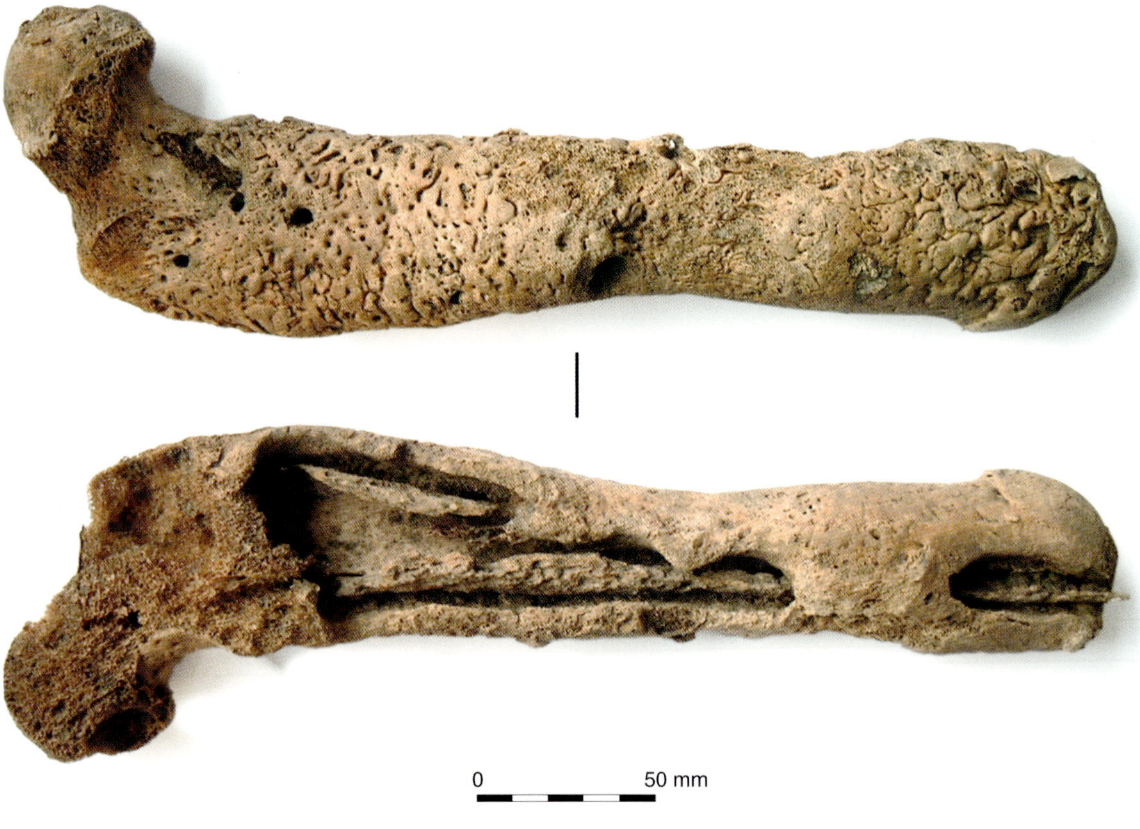
0
50 mm

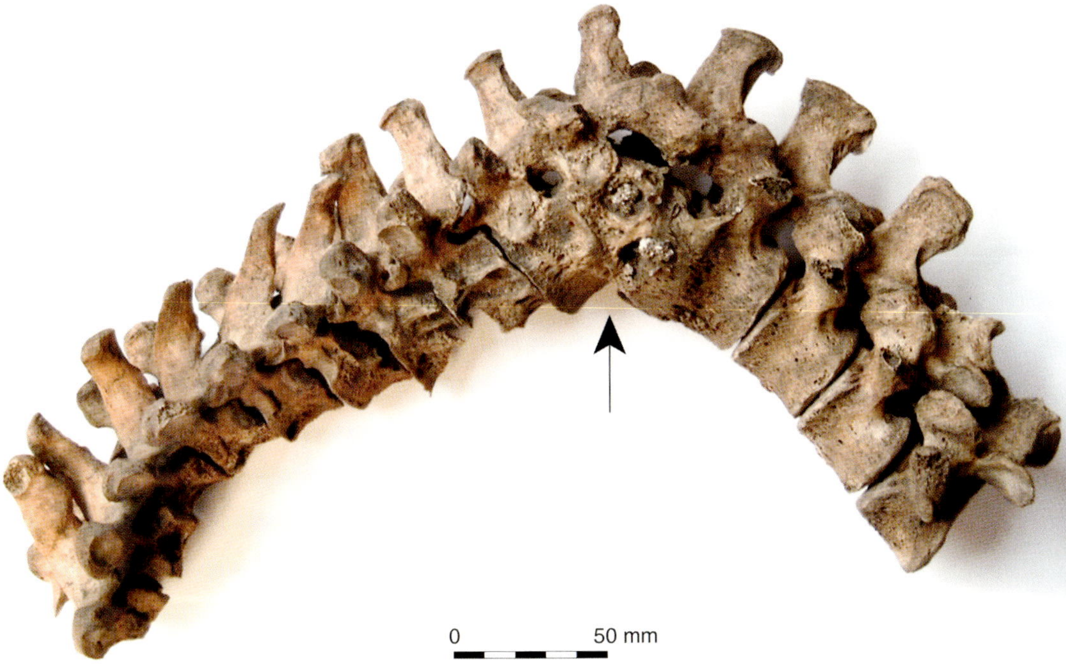
0
50 mm

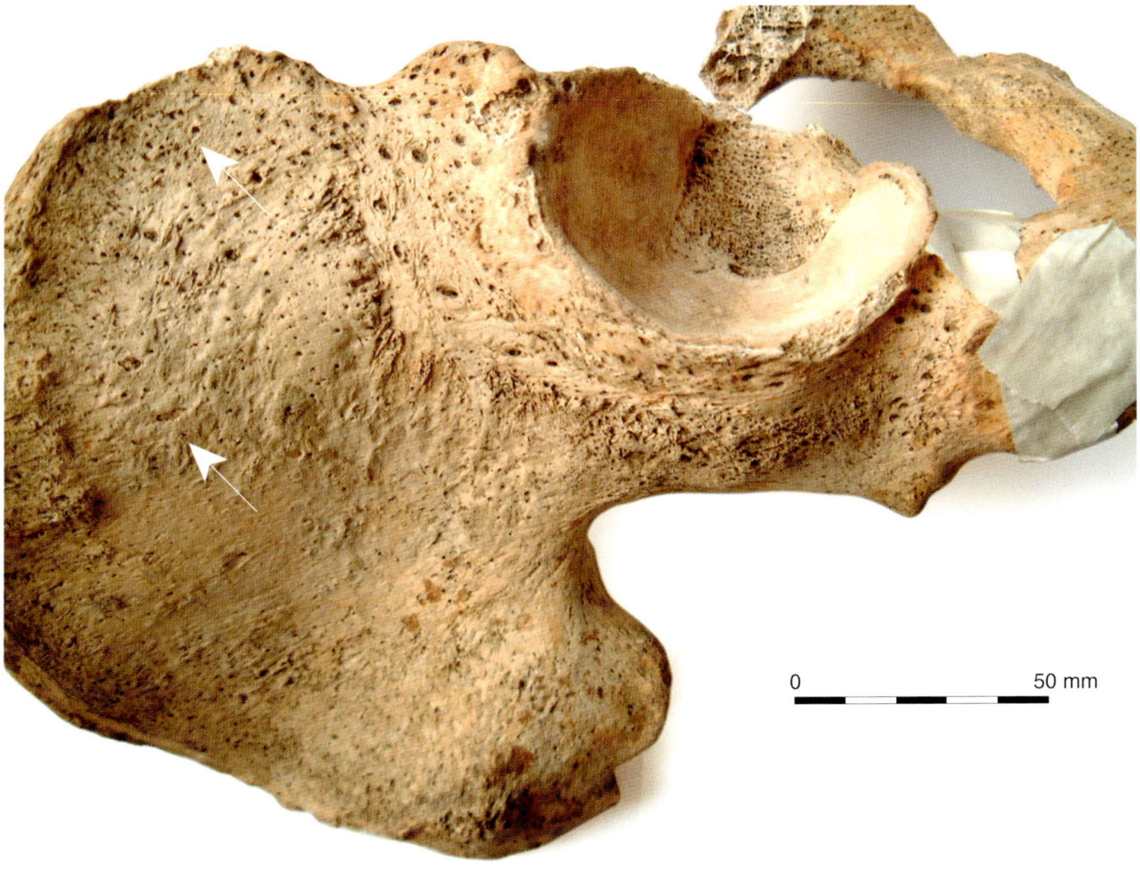
0
50 mm

0 50 mm

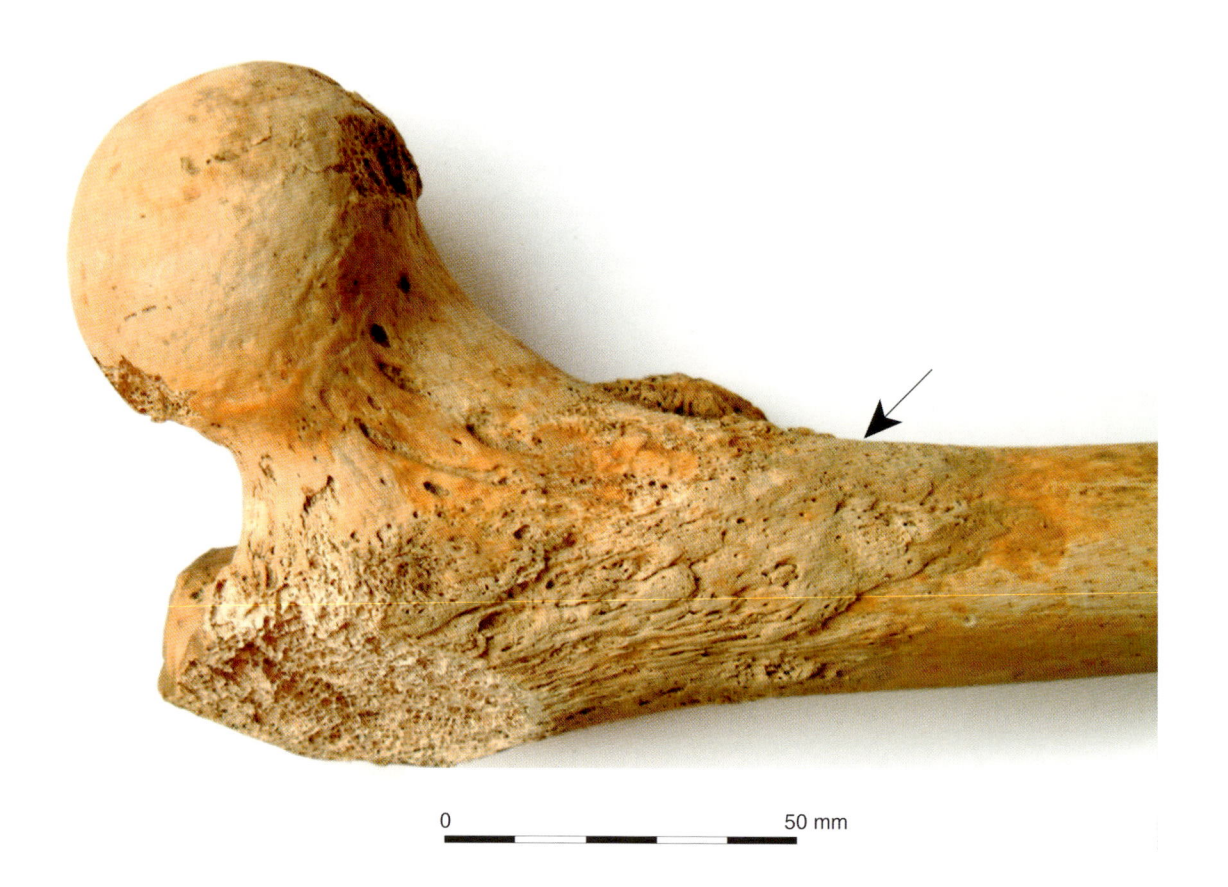

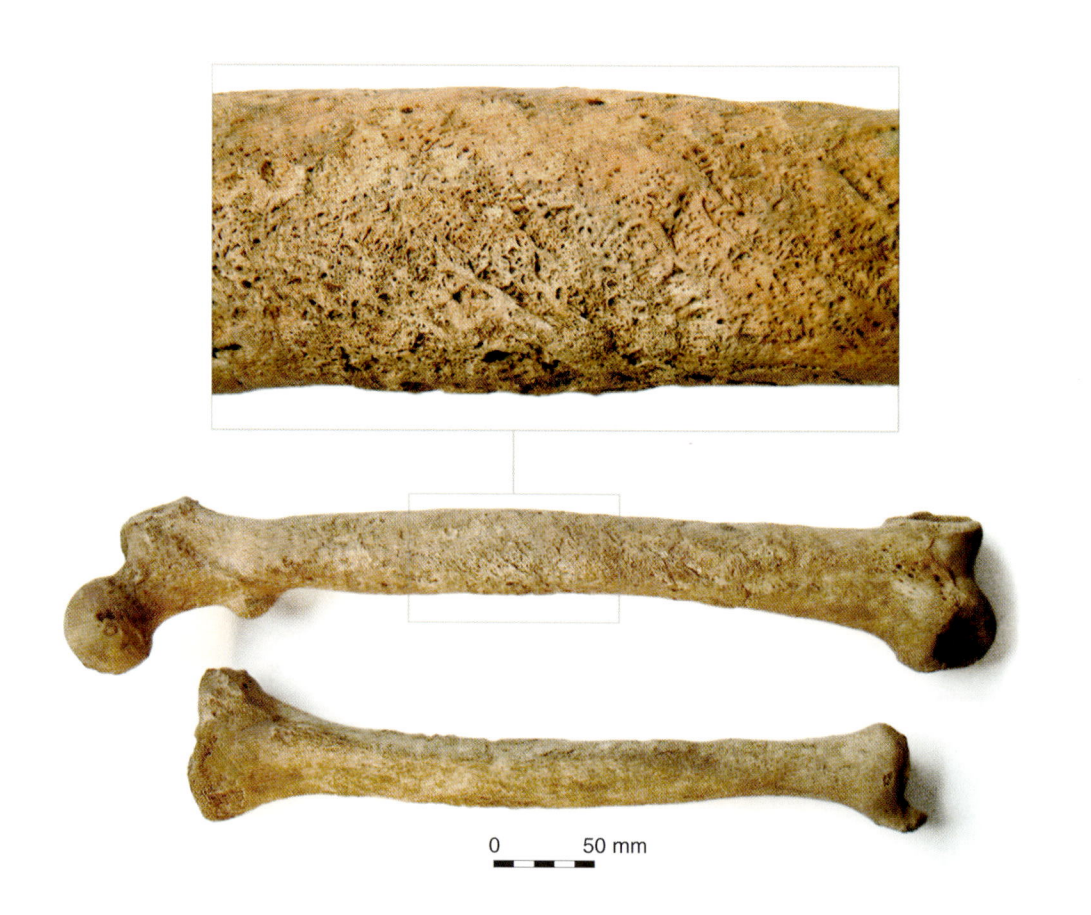

0 50 mm

0　　　　　50 mm

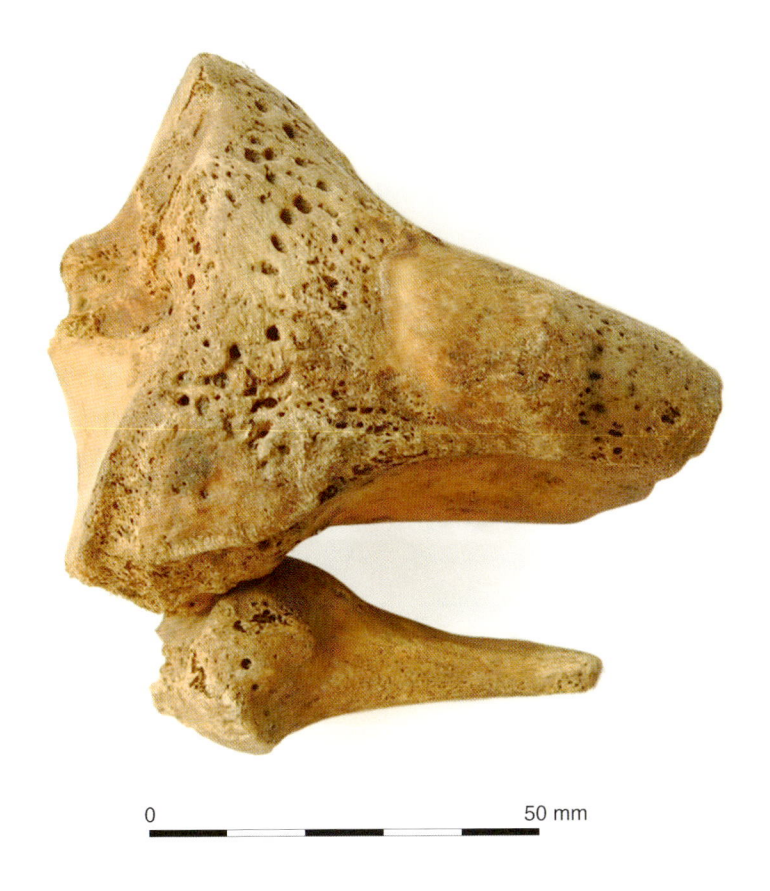

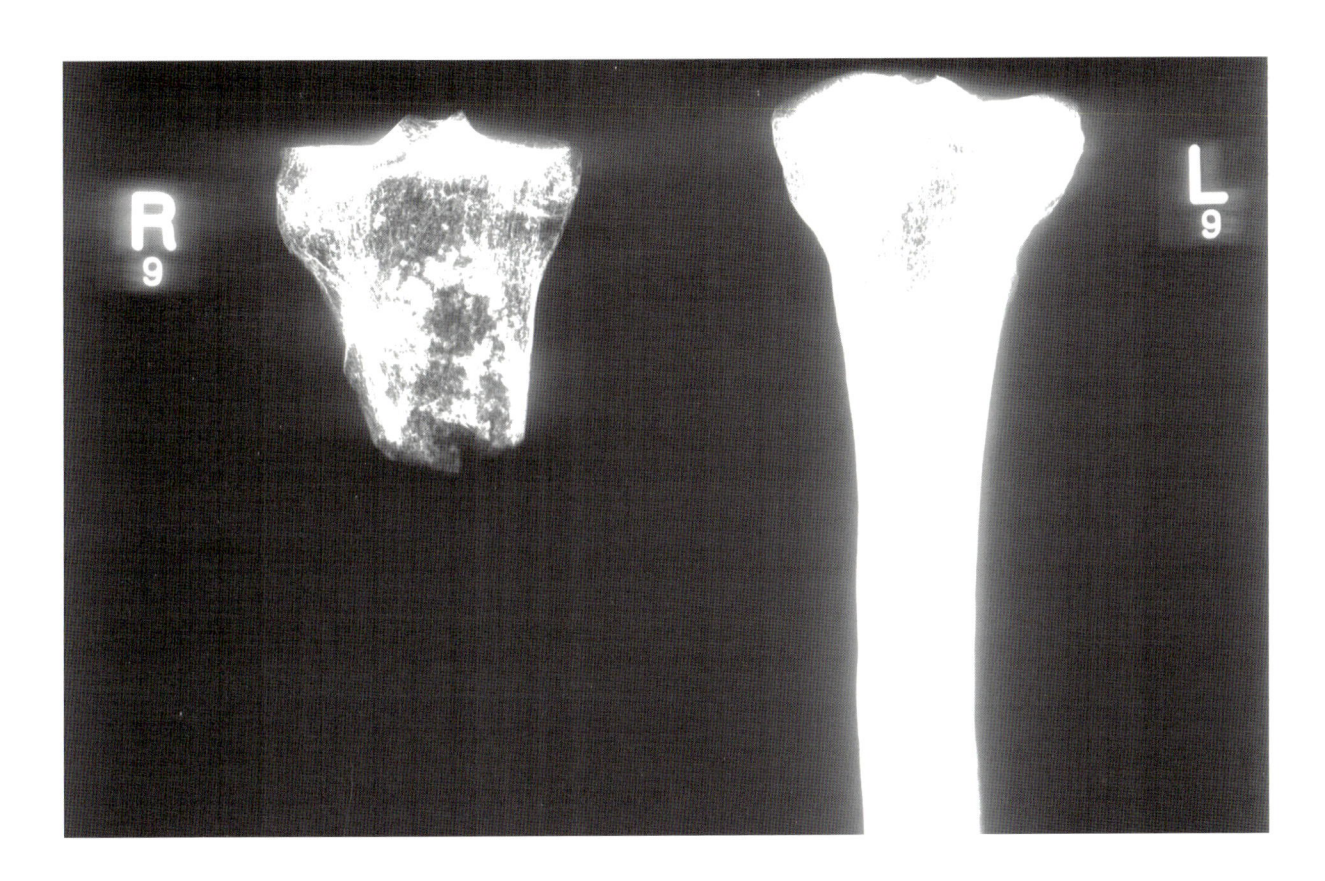

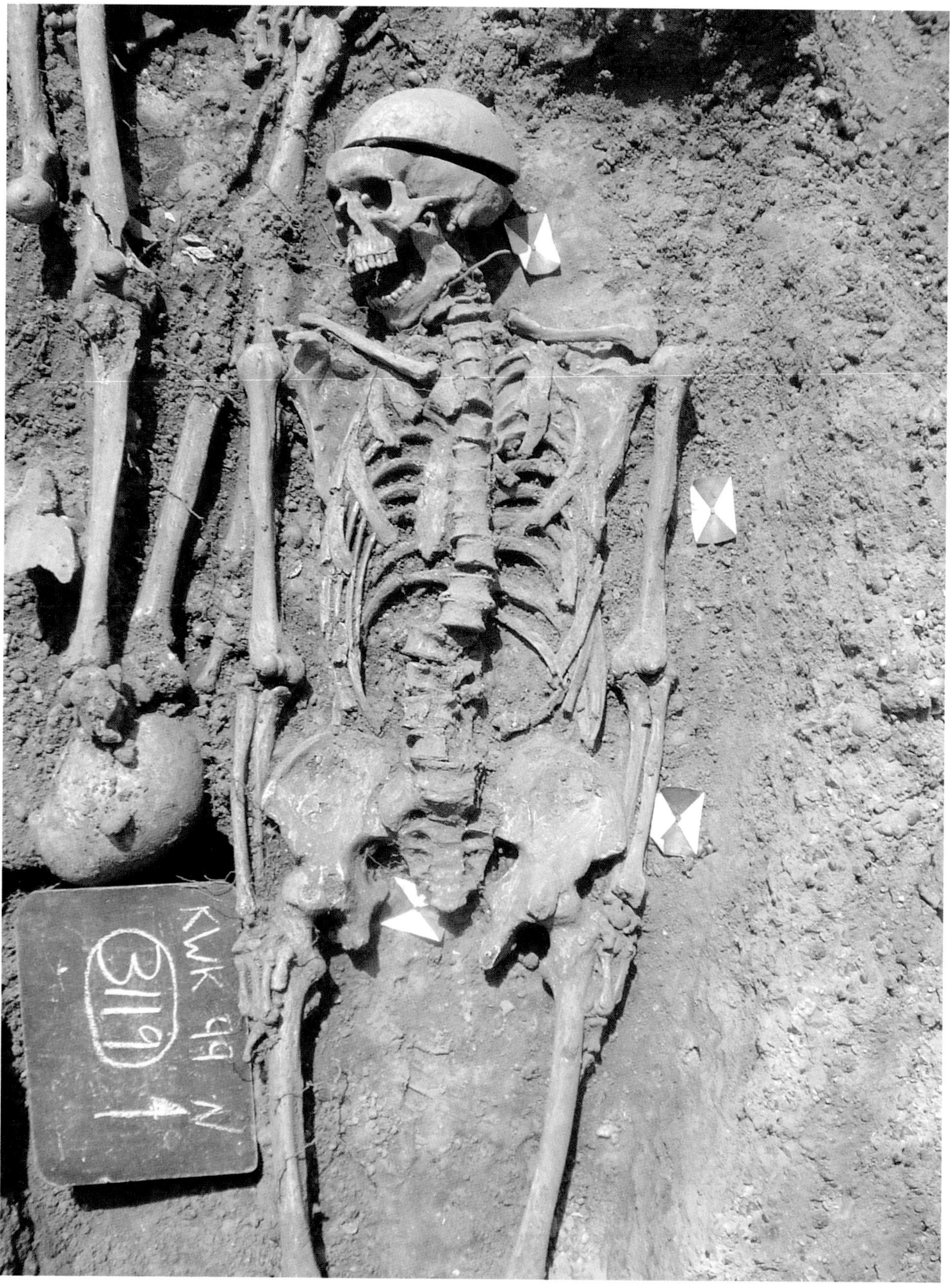
KWK 99
3119
N

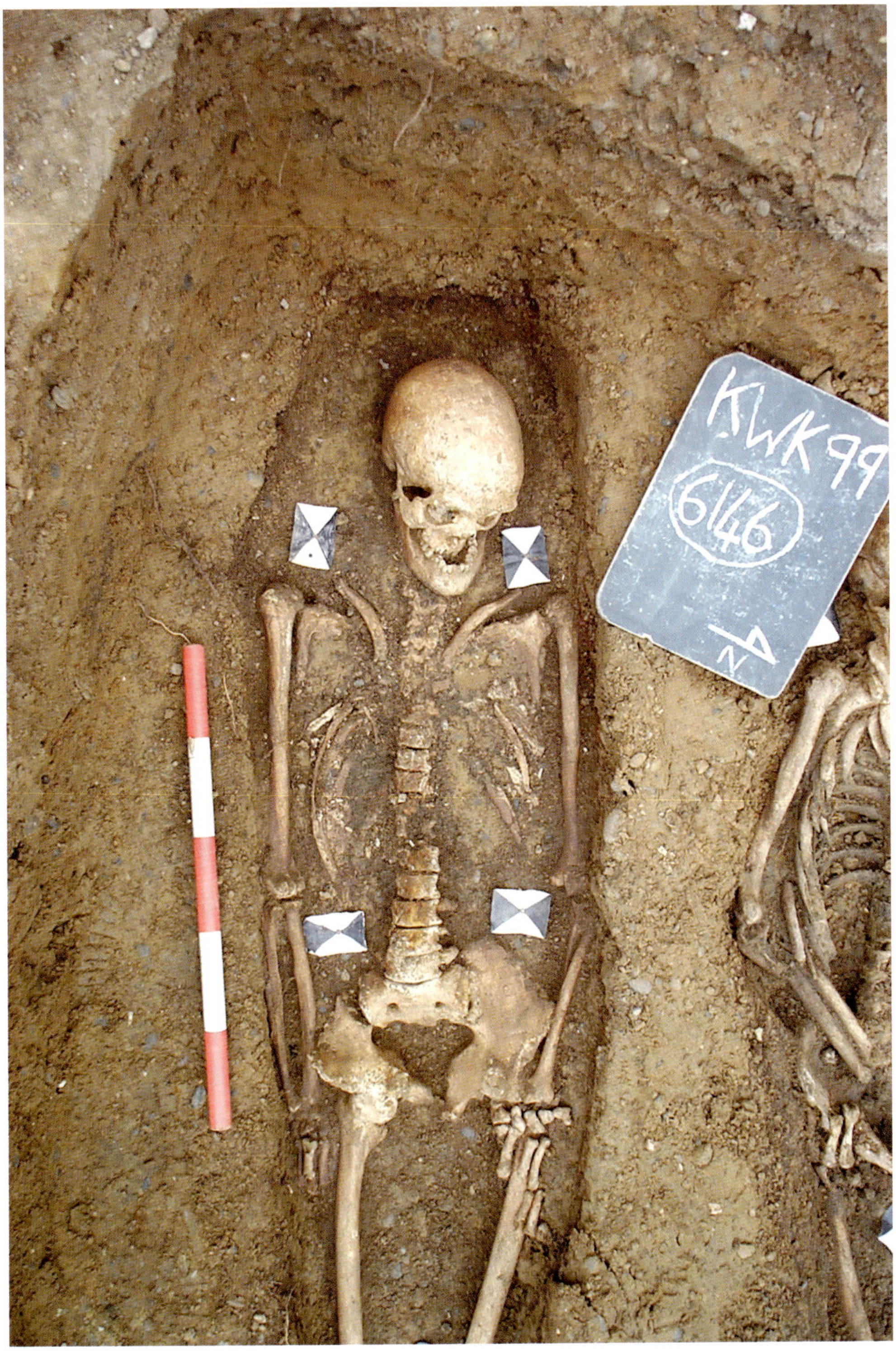
KWK99
6146
N

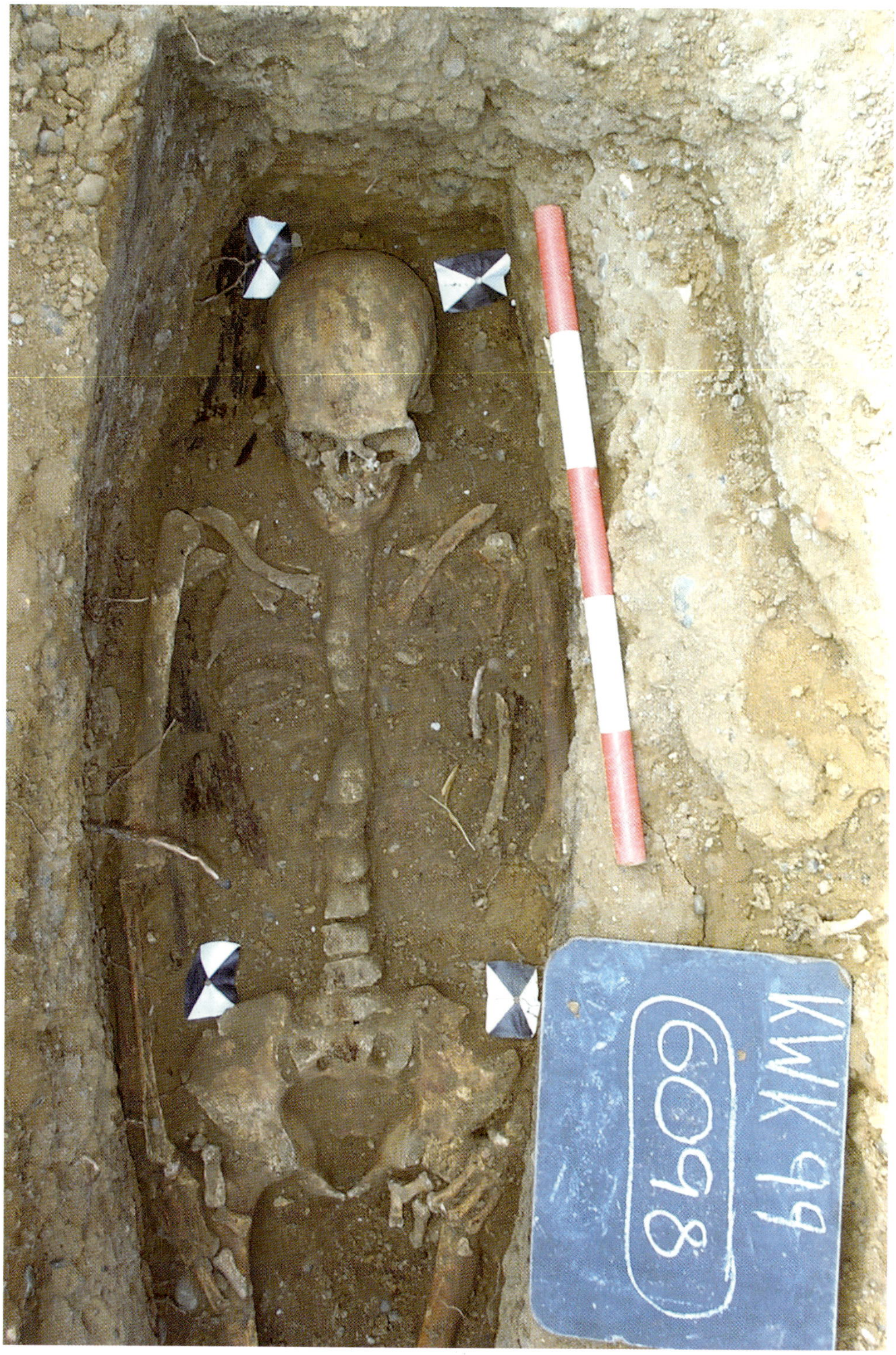
KWK 99
6098

Table 17   Comparison of dental pathology rates per tooth or socket in seven contemporary English assemblages.

Post-medieval assemblages	Ante-mortem tooth loss (n/N)	Peri-apical abscesses (n/N)	Calculus (n/N)	Caries (n/N)	Dental enamel hypoplasia (n/N)
Royal Hospital, Greenwich	44.6% (1172/2624)	7.35% (224/3048)	82.11% (1028/1252)	11.67% (152/1303)	14.37% (178/1239)
St George's Church, Bloomsbury	40.99% (669/1632)	2.82% (46/1632)	70.85% (592/844)	13.39% (110/844)	16.35% (138/844)
St Luke's Church, Islington	36.10% (1762/4883)	1.78% (87/4883)	46.33% (1042/2249)	9.74% (219/2249)	2.18% (49/2249)
Newcastle Infirmary, Newcastle	19.3% (604/3123)	0.9% (29/3123)	55.85% (718/1287)	11% (146/1327)	17% (219/1287)
Christ Church, Spitalfields	19.91% (324/1627)	Data not available	Data not available	19.11% (311/1627)	Data not available
St Martin's church, Birmingham	26.65% (2488/9337)	2.63% (222/8433)	63% (3684/5893)	9.88% (488/4940)	31% (110/1060)
Cross Bones burial ground, Southwark	17.30% (211/1216)	2.30% 28/1216	Data not available	25.93% (161/621)	Data not available

was also sometimes sweetened by sugar or molasses (McDonald 2006, 35), but given the cost of sugar at this time, it is highly unlikely that it was ever consumed in any great quantity aboard ship. Later the oatmeal ration was halved and two ounces of sugar issued instead. It is not unreasonable to assume that sugar consumption by the pensioners before and after their time in the Royal Navy was similar to the civilian working classes of the period.

Another factor that may have reduced the formation of caries was dental attrition, which appeared greater in the Greenwich population than in other post-medieval assemblages, such as St George's, Bloomsbury, and St Luke's, Islington. Unlike these civilian populations, the Haslar Hospital assemblage, comprising principally young and prime adult males on active service, showed a similar pattern to Greenwich, suggesting that accelerated attrition began in early adulthood in the Royal Navy, and its presence in the Greenwich assemblage was not merely due to its older age distribution. Flattening of the enamel folds of the occlussal surface of the molars reduces the risk of food entrapment and hence, of caries. Together with a diet low in simple sugars, this attrition may have contributed to the low caries prevalence amongst the pensioners.

Periapical abscesses

The development of a dental abscess may have many starting points. Bacteria may enter the pulp cavity through dental caries, excessive attrition or trauma to the crown, as well as through dental surgery. An abscess may also develop when a periodontal pocket is formed by the accumulation of bacteria within the pulp cavity, and infection tracks down to the root apex. As pus accumulates within the dental socket and surrounding alveolar bone, local pressure builds, and eventually precipitates the formation of a hole or sinus in the jaw, through which the pus drains into the overlying soft tissue of the gums (Roberts and Manchester 1995, 50). In this advanced stage, the abscess is visible as a small hole on the surface of the maxilla or mandible.

The prevalence of periapical abscesses was calculated by dividing the total number of abscesses with the combined total of teeth lost ante mortem, teeth lost post mortem and permanent dentition. In total, 224 abscesses were recorded out of a possible 3048 sockets observed in the total population (n = 107) giving a TPR of 7.35%. A total of 224 periapical abscesses were recorded (7.35%, n = 107), six of which were present in adult females, and 106 in adult males. In pensioners, 3.7% of sockets were affected, whilst 6% was calculated in adult females. None were observed in adolescents 3132 and 3249 or in the unsexed adult 6017.

A TPR of 7.35% is considerably higher than those observed in the contemporary assemblages displayed in Table 17, which ranged from 0.9% to 2.82%. The reason for this difference is unclear, but like calculus and ante-mortem tooth loss, it is probable that advanced age and poor oral hygiene played significant roles.

Ante-mortem tooth loss

The loss of permanent dentition before death is the end result of several disease processes. Calculus deposits irritate the soft tissue and the underlying bone, which may lead to the reduction of the bone (periodontal disease) and ante-mortem tooth loss (AMTL) (Roberts and Manchester, 1995, 45). Teeth may also be lost by periapical abscesses formed through the exposure of the pulp cavity, caused by caries or excessive attrition coupled with localised resorption of the alveolar margin. Dental extraction for painful teeth was also a common practice at this time. In the Greenwich assemblage an additional pathology that appears to have contributed to AMTL was scurvy (see above). AMTL is regarded as a degenerative disease where the main contributory factors are old age and poor oral hygiene. In this aged population, it is thus not surprising that AMTL was high (44.73% in the total population (n = 107). This figure is higher than the contemporary assemblages shown in Table 17.

This rate was calculated by dividing the total number of teeth lost ante mortem by the combined total of the permanent dentition, teeth lost ante mortem and post mortem (empty sockets). In the adult male population, the AMTL rate was 44.6%, (1172/2624), in adult females 55.34% (57/103), the unsexed adult had lost all but one tooth (31/32), and the two adolescents had suffered no tooth loss (0/58). The prevalence for the total population was therefore 44.73% (1260/2817).

Dental calculus

Calculus consists of mineralised plaque composed of microorganisms that accumulate in the mouth and become imbedded in a matrix of protein and saliva. Sugar in the diet accelerates this process (Hillson 1996, 254–55). There are two types of calculus: supragingival calculus situated above the gum line and subgingival calculus found below the gum line on exposed roots. More heavy calculus deposits are commonly seen on teeth nearest to the saliva glands (Roberts and Manchester 1995, 55). Regular tooth brushing removes plaque deposits, thereby preventing the formation of calculus. In an archaeological context, some calculus may be inadvertently removed during post-excavation processing and handling.

Calculus deposits were recorded by tooth and by location on the tooth. The size of the deposit was also recorded according to the universal standards set out by Brothwell (1981), in which the deposits were scored as slight, medium or heavy. However, such detailed data are beyond the scope of this report. The prevalence of calculus was calculated by dividing the number of teeth affected by the total number of teeth present. Calculus was observed on the crowns of 981 of a total of 1150 teeth of adult males (TPR 85.3%), in 44 of 45 teeth of adult females, and in two of 56 teeth of the two subadults- a TPR of 82.11% (1028/1252 teeth) of the total population (Table 17). Although not quantified in this analysis, the general impression was that in the majority of cases, the calculus was slight.

A high prevalence of calculus is reflected in other assemblages of this time period (Table 17), but is greatest in the Greenwich assemblage, followed by St George's, Bloomsbury, assemblage (the next oldest population). This picture probably reflects the general lack of regular dental hygiene (such as tooth brushing) in the Greenwich sailors, as well as their advanced age, as calculus is accumulative. Different criteria between observers may also account for some of the wide differences in prevalence of calculus between the assemblages.

Periodontal disease

The principal predisposing factor in the development of periodontal disease is the accumulation of calculus in dental pockets. The disease begins as gingivitis (an inflammation of the soft tissues), which is transmitted to the jaw itself. Resorption of the bone commences, followed by tooth loss. There are two different ways in which this disease expresses itself. These are horizontal and vertical bone loss. In horizontal bone loss, more than one tooth is involved and often the whole of the dental arcade. All walls surrounding the teeth are lost uniformly. In vertical bone loss, the lesion is localised around one tooth or possibly two. The bone loss around the tooth is irregular and generally without horizontal bone loss (Hillson 1996, 263–65). In modern populations, there is a strong correlation between advancing age and the prevalence of periodontal disease, which is also the case with archaeological populations. However, the aetiology is multifactoral with genetic predisposition, environment, diet and hygiene being all predisposing factors in the development of the disease (ibid.).

Periodontal disease was recorded as being present or absent, and did not include the number of teeth or parts of the jaws affected. The severity of the disease was scored using the standards set out by Brothwell (1981). This method uses three grades namely slight, medium and considerable. Periodontal disease was recorded on 74 adults (including those with no teeth and incomplete records), and on the two subadults. In this group, a prevalence of 93.42% was recorded (71/76). The CPR for the adult population was 67.62% (n = 105), and for the total population was 66.36% (n = 107).

Periodontal disease was observed in 20% of the named individuals of St Luke's Church, Islington (Boston and Witkin 2005, 210), and in 50% of the named assemblage of St George's crypt, Bloomsbury (Boston and Witkin 2006). Considering the relationship between the disease, increasing age and oral hygiene, the high rate seen in the Greenwich assemblage is hardly surprising.

Dental enamel hypoplasia

Dental enamel hypoplasia (DEH) may manifest on the buccal surface of the tooth crown as pits, horizontal lines or lines of pits (Buikstra and Ubelaker 1994). These defects are caused by thinning of the enamel, and reflect an interruption or slowing of the normal deposition of enamel during crown formation in the first six or seven years of life (Goodman and Rose 1990; Hillson 1996, 165–66). DEH is thought to result from prolonged episodes of illness or malnutrition lasting at least three weeks (ibid.), but Roberts and Cox (2003, 311–312) wrote that food adulterations, used widely in 18th- and 19th-century London and other cities, may also have played a role in the interruption of normal tooth development. DEH is most apparent when normal dental development recommences following such an insult. Unlike bone, enamel does not remodel throughout life and so remains as a permanent indicator of such stress episode in the early years of life. The presence of DEH in the teeth of an individual represents an individual who was compromised physiologically, but who recovered.

In the analysis of the Greenwich assemblage, the type of defect (groove, line or pit) and the numbers of lines or grooves were recorded for each tooth. This level of detail has not been quantified here. The prevalence of DEH was calculated per crown visible, excluding crowns where the buccal surface was obscured by calculus, or where the tooth had suffered marked attrition or carious formation. Of 1239 teeth observed in the total population, 178 displayed DEH (TPR 14.37%, n = 107). In the adult males, the prevalence was 13.3%, in the adult females 24.4%, and in the two adolescents 25.86%.

Compared to DEH rates in the four other 18th- to early 19th-century populations displayed in Table 17, the Greenwich assemblage rate was higher than the named middle class assemblage from St Luke's, Islington, but lower than the other three assemblages, including the two other working class assemblages of the Newcastle Infirmary and St Martin's, Birmingham. It is, however, considerably higher than the average prevalence of 0.6% that has been reported for British post-medieval assemblages (Roberts and Cox 2003, 327). Such wide variation in the prevalence of DEH may well reflect inter-observer differences in identifying DEH, but it should be noted that much of the osteology on the St George's, St Lukes' and Greenwich assemblages was undertaken by the same observer, Annsofie Witkin, and hence, it has to be assumed that the differences observed between the populations are genuine. It is somewhat surprising that the DEH prevalence in the Greenwich assemblage was fairly low, given its known working class origins, and the prevalence of other indicators of childhood stresses, such as cribra orbitalia and low adult stature.

Dental wear

Dental attrition was recorded on the molars of the Greenwich assemblage but was not quantified in this study. The general impression, however, was that the Greenwich seamen and marines suffered considerably more attrition than other contemporary assemblages, such as St George's, Bloomsbury and St Luke's, Islington. Tooth wear was more consistent with the general pattern observed in the Haslar Hospital assemblage, suggesting that seamen of this period suffered greater tooth wear than civilians. Attrition of the molar occlusal surfaces reflects the coarseness of the diet, and in archaeological populations is heavily influenced by the amount of grit introduced into food during by processing. The daily diet of seamen aboard ship included unrefined flour (milled commercially), pulses, 'hard tack' and salted meat and cheese. The last three were often very hard and deteriorated with keeping. Fremont-Barnes (2005, 25) describes how seamen would carve and polish objects out of the salt meat, and make buttons from the cheese. It is probable that the hardness of this food was responsible for the greater attrition observed in the two Royal Navy populations.

Gibson (2002) studied extra-masticatory wear on 90 individuals from the Greenwich assemblage (which included females and one subadult), and observed dental chipping of the anterior dentition, pipe notches, microscopic lingual and labial grooves and wear. Dental chipping, particularly of the anterior dentition, was the most common of the four, with 65 chips found on 42 teeth, or 17.78% skeletons. Although some may have been dietary, Gibson ascribed most to trauma, incurred either through inter-personal violence or from accidents aboard ship. Tearing of the tough paper casing containing the gunpowder charge of a musket using the teeth may have also been responsible for some dental chipping, especially amongst marines. This prevalence was higher than observed in his study of samples from the Newcastle Infirmary (14.29%) and also amongst material from the Methodist burial ground on Carver Street, Sheffield (5.45%) (Witkin 2001).

Twenty-four pipe notches were seen in 14 individuals in this sample, predominantly on the right side of the dental arcade. Most individuals had one notch, but one individual had four. The habit of tobacco smoking was probably acquired after leaving the Royal Navy and is discussed more fully above (see Chronic respiratory disease).

Under microscopy, thick and fine linguo-labial grooves were observed on the tooth crowns. Eight thicker grooves were seen on seven teeth of the sample. Gibson (2002) attributed these grooves to wear caused by hemp fibres held in the mouth during the making of cordage, which was used to splice ropes to prevent fraying. Finer grooves (particularly on the canines) were attributed to sewing, when the thread is bitten off in the mouth. As he pointed out, sewing was an important aspect of a seaman's life, especially the repair and maintenance of the sails. In their free time, seamen were fond of embellishing their clothes with embroidery, rosettes and ribbons (Fremont-Barnes 2005, 45), which they proudly displayed when in port or on those rare occasions of being granted leave. Similar grooves were observed on the dentition of he Newcastle Infirmary sample also examined by Gibson (2002).

Gibson (2002) also observed labial and lingual wear on the dentition of the Greenwich sample. Vertical lingual wear on the anterior dentition in three individuals (skeletons 3024, 6056 and 6078) was consistent with bruxism, the habitual grinding of the teeth during sleep. The severity of the wear was consistent with a longstanding habit in all these individuals.

DISCUSSION

Although relatively small, the Greenwich assemblage is a rare example of a specialist population, in which the age, sex and occupation of this group of skeletons is historically known. Royal Navy records of the 18th and 19th centuries have enabled historians to reconstruct many aspects of the lives of these seamen and marines. Like most records of the lower strata of a society, however, the evidence for the common ratings is often indirect, incomplete and frequently tainted with generalisations and misconceptions. The opportunity to examine the physical remains of 97 skeletons from Greenwich was a golden opportunity to interrogate another strand of evidence in order to reconstruct an accurate picture of the lives of these individuals, whose role in the defence of the realm against the French Republic, the Dutch, Spanish and ultimately, Napoleon, was so crucial to Britain's national interests.

Osteological analysis of the Greenwich assemblage revealed that the vast majority of the population comprised adult males of advanced age, with seven older females and two adolescents, probably dependants. This is consistent with the limited historical research undertaken on Greenwich Pensioners for this study. The evidence of a sample of 100 Trafalgar veterans, who were also Greenwich in-pensioners, gave a mean age at death of 70.1 years.

One interesting aspect of the assemblage was the identification of two adult males of probable negroid ancestry. Although a suite of cranial and post-cranial measurements were undertaken on all skeletons as part of the osteological analysis, further work is required in order to identify the ancestry of these and other skeletons. Forensic databases, such as FORDISC and CRANID, have yet to be utilised. Isotope work on diet and childhood origins will also be a powerful tool in addressing the question of the origins of these seamen. This highlighted the diverse national origins of the ratings of the Royal Navy in late 18th and early 19th centuries.

Historical records indicated that most ratings were working class in origin, with the majority of occupations on entering and/or leaving the Royal Navy being skilled and unskilled labourers and artisans. Given the harsh living conditions endured by the working classes of this period, it is not surprising that there were relatively high prevalences of skeletal indicators of childhood depravation in the Greenwich assemblage. Mean male stature was 5 ft 5 in (167.9 cm), most similar to the pauper assemblage of the Cross Bones burial ground, Southwark, and 2–3 cm lower than mean stature of middle class assemblages of the period. The prevalence of childhood deficiency diseases, such as cribra orbitalia and rickets, were likewise high, but the latter did not appear to have continued into adulthood. Surprisingly, dental enamel hypoplasia was not consistent with this picture of childhood depravation.

The Greenwich in-pensioners represent a select and lucky few chosen for admission by virtue of prolonged service in the Royal Navy and the extent of their physical handicap. Many out-pensioners were only admitted to the hospital in the last few years of their lives. As Lewis (1960, 416) poetically commented 'they were mostly the picked, brine-pickled survivors of a gruelling existence', and it is therefore not surprising that the skeletal assemblage contained such high rates of pathology, particularly of trauma and infection, but also of degenerative joint disease and osteoarthritis. Life at sea was dangerous and arduous, with falls, crush injuries and injuries in battle being commonplace. Although a surgeon and his assistant, or assistants, were aboard all Royal Navy ships, the high number of poorly reduced fractures indicated that setting of bones was not a priority. Six amputations were present in the Greenwich assemblage. All but one appeared healed, the exception showing severe chronic infection that was ongoing at the time of his death. Interestingly, bone resorption in the amputated limb of all of the lower limb amputees suggested that none of the amputees used the peg leg prosthesis so frequently depicted in illustrations. Indeed, two above knee amputees showed bony changes tentatively suggestive of under arm crutch use.

Isolated from the rest of society, a Royal Navy ship was a little world of its own, with its own language, customs, in-fighting and friendships. Although the Navy made considerable efforts to enforce a surprising degree of cleanliness for the time period, infectious diseases and epidemics remained a constant source of morbidity and mortality, not surprising considering the close proximity in which hundreds of men lived and worked. Although most of these diseases were acute, some, like tuberculosis, thrived under these conditions, and were observed in the Greenwich assemblage.

After 'fevers', scurvy has been cited as the greatest single cause of death amongst 18th-century sailors. Skeletally, a differential diagnosis of scurvy is highly problematic, as many bony changes (such as subperiosteal bleeding, orbital lesions and ante-mortem tooth loss) may be attributed to a range of other conditions. Periostitis was found on multiple elements in 53 skeletons (50.48%) of adults. It is impossible to know how many of these were scorbutic in nature, but it is highly probable that many can be attributed to this disorder. Of twelve skeletons displaying pitting on the greater wing of the sphenoid, eight also had periostitis, five had orbital lesions and five had porotic hyperostosis. The prevalence of AMTL was 10% higher than in the rest of the adult male population. Although a small sample, this tentatively suggests that a more holistic approach may facilitate our identification of scorbutic individuals. Identifying scurvy using biochemical markers may be a valuable avenue of future research.

Although in many ways isolated from the wider world, seamen and marines of the Royal Navy did have intermittent contact with the outside world, and diseases rife in ports were transmitted aboard. Venereal diseases were one group of infectious diseases historically known to afflict large numbers of seamen. Venereal syphilis is the only sexually transmitted infection to be recognised skeletally, and treponemal disease was seen in three adult males of the Greenwich assemblage. Although it was impossible to distinguish between venereal syphilis and yaws in this assemblage, a prevalence of 2.8% in this population was still much higher than the CPR of 0.77% calculated for this period by Roberts and Cox (2003, 341). When one considers that bony involvement occurs in approximately 10–12 % cases of syphilis (Roberts and Manchester 1995, 152), in reality the prevalence of this disease amongst seamen would have been very high indeed.

Both historical records and osteological ageing techniques concur that the majority of the Greenwich population were ageing adults. Unlike most other archaeological populations of lesser longevity, a number of diseases more prevalent in older age groups were observed in the Greenwich assemblage. These included DISH, a high prevalence of degenerative joint disease, osteoarthritis, osteoporosis, neoplasms, and two probable cases of pulmonary hypertrophic osteoarthropathy.

Cortical defects and enthysophyte formation were not systematically recorded in the Greenwich assemblage. The overall impression was that these changes were marked in the Greenwich assemblage, particularly in the upper limbs, probably as a consequence of prolonged pulling on ropes. Alterations in the joint surfaces also may have developed in response to this hyperflexion of the elbow joint, but requires more detailed analysis.

CONCLUSION

In conclusion, the small skeletal assemblage from the ratings burial ground of the Royal Hospital Greenwich, has proved a rich alternative dataset on the lives of the seamen and marines of the Royal Navy of the mid- to late Georgian period, a period during which the Royal Navy played a pivotal role in Britain's wars with the Dutch, Spain, America, the French Republic, and Napoleon. The wide range of pathologies present reflected the origins, activities, diet, and hardships of life aboard ship, and the physical effects of advancing age. The osteological analysis discussed above was undertaken in a commercial archaeology setting, in which resources of time and money were restricted, and all results are presented with the full understanding that the analysis was far from exhaustive. Considerably more work is warranted on this unique and extremely interesting specialist assemblage, and it will undoubtedly prove a valuable resource in research in the future.

Chapter 5: Coffins and Coffin Fittings

INTRODUCTION

The remains of 86 coffins were recovered during excavation, largely represented by surviving metal fixing nails and coffin furniture or fittings, and by slight darkening of the grave backfill around the skeleton. From better preserved sand shadows (Plate 29), it was evident that coffins were of the single break variety ubiquitous in this time period (Litten 1991).

Overall, the coffins were simply furnished with all but one being made of iron, the most inexpensive metal in use for this purpose. Due to corrosion, most coffin fittings were poorly preserved, and although there were at least 22 breastplates, it was not possible to identify the names of any of the deceased. Results of the analysis of the coffin fittings are discussed below, and are summarised by context in Appendix 4.

HISTORIC BACKGROUND

18th- to 19th-century funerary practices

The later 18th and early 19th centuries are remarkable for the profound social significance attached to giving the dead 'a good send off'. Contemporary literature again and again reflects the yearning for a decent funeral and respectable burial, that was felt by all classes, and reiterates the attitude that social status should be expressed in funeral and memorials (Curl 2000, 197). During this period, funerals became a vehicle for social display with funerals of the well-to-do frequently involved processions of black draped hearses, black plumed horses, mutes and chief mourners, a complex symbolism surrounding appropriate mourning dress and behaviour, grand memorials and, of course, the heavily decorated coffin itself.

Financial investment in funerary panoply grew over the course of the 18th century, reaching its zenith in the 1840s. Even amongst the poor, the importance of providing a decent burial was keenly felt (May 2003; Curl 2000, 197). Writing in 1843, Edwin Chadwick estimated that whilst persons of rank or title might expend between £500 and £1500 on a funeral, the middle classes spent between £60 to £100, tradesmen between £10 to £12, whilst a adult 'of the labouring classes' could be decently put to rest for £5, and a child for 30 shillings (May 2003, 7-8). To those on low incomes, however, this comparatively modest sum was often ruinous (Curl 2000, 197), and many families were plunged in considerable financial distress in their attempt to 'do right' by their dead. Amongst the poor, many put aside a nest egg they could ill afford for this purpose, whilst others contributed weekly to friendly or other societies, which often included a funeral benefit paid out on the death of a member (May 2003, 11). This guaranteed that the individual was not subjected to the shame of 'dying on the parish' and thereby avoided the ignominious and dreaded fate of their remains being used for dissection in an anatomy hall (ibid.).

By 1700-20, the funeral furnishing trade was a firmly established business, providing wooden coffins and fittings for all classes of people and at various costs, depending on the status and wealth of the deceased (Litten 1991). Grips were produced by casting, but the rest of coffin fittings comprised thin sheets of metal stamped using dies (ibid.). Between 1720-30, these were produced by hand-operated die stamping machines, but after this such machines became power-assisted. Coffin fittings could then be produced en masse and were financially accessible to all but the most indigent by the mid- to late Georgian period (ibid.).

In the early Victorian period, this excessive expenditure and ostentation of funerals began to be regarded as vulgar and in poor taste. From the 1840s onwards simplicity in funerary display once again became the vogue, a practice that persists to this day (May 2003, 7). The coffins from the Royal Hospital burial ground date to the heyday of the Georgian/early Victorian funerary tradition, but in keeping with their modest incomes and social status, the coffins excavated at Greenwich were relatively simple. What is unclear is whether the these coffins were issued by the Hospital or whether they were purchased by surviving relatives and fellow veterans keen to give the deceased the best possible 'send off' that they could afford.

COFFIN CONSTRUCTION AND DECORATION

Coffin

In the later post-medieval period, coffins were of the flat lidded single-break type, and those recovered from the Royal Hospital burial ground were no exception. Little of the original wood of these coffins had survived, being almost exclusively fragments preserved on the reverse of metal coffin fittings, particularly upholstery studs, and on the shafts of coffin nails. Burial 6098 (grave 6069) was slightly better preserved, with small fragments of wood overlying the chest and arm regions (Plate 30). The limit of the coffins showed up as a darkening of the grave fill surrounding the skeleton, and in some cases, for example coffin 6147 (skeleton 6146, grave 6084: Plate 29), the single break coffin shape could be discerned;. Often the presence of coffins was attested by coffin fixing nails and fittings alone.

No analysis of the taxa of surviving coffin wood was undertaken. Historically, elm is known to have been the most popular coffin wood in this period, being valued for its quality of water resistance (Litten 1991) and it is probable that most of the coffins were constructed of this wood.

During the Georgian and Victorian periods, coffins varied considerably in construction and material. They ranged from the simplest unadorned wooden coffins used in pauper funerals, to the triple layered affairs heavily adorned with velvet and encrusted with elaborate metal fittings used in the burial of the wealthy. The cheapest coffins were simple constructions of a single layer of wooden planks, nailed together with iron nails at the corners and along the coffin length. Planks could also be held together by joinery (especially mortice and tenon joints), as seen in the Baptist coffins from the Vancouver Centre excavations, Kings Lynn (Boston 2004).

Iron fixing nails were recovered from 73 coffins (84.88%) at Greenwich. Most were complete but some were corroded and fragmented. Wood adhered to a high proportion of the shafts. Nails were counted by the number of heads so as to avoid duplication. The number of nails per coffin ranged from one to 75, a mean of approximately 16 per coffin. It is highly probable, however, that recovery of nails during excavation was not complete, and may account for the wide variation between the nails found in different graves. It is possible, of course, that joinery rather than nailing was used to secure the planks of the coffin instead.

More expensive coffins also included a metal shell, most commonly of lead, but occasionally of zinc or iron (Litten 1991). This shell usually encased an inner wooden coffin. No such shells were found within the ratings burial ground, but probably were used in many officers' burials in the adjoining cemetery.

From the late 17th century onwards, it became customary to cover the exterior of the coffin with upholstery of baize or velvet, and to decorate the lid and side panels of coffins with studs and metal coffin fittings. A full suite of fittings comprised one to four departum plates (an inner and outer breastplate, a headplate and a footplate), lid motifs, escutcheons, grips and grip plates. In addition, brass or iron studs, originally used to secure the upholstery to the wooden case, became a decorative device, being arranged to create complex patterns on the lid and side panels of the coffin. More humble coffins sported some but not all of the above furnishings. The most common fittings found in poorer coffins were grips and grip plates, then breastplates and simple upholstery stud decoration.

Excavations of the 18th- to 19th-century churchyard and crypt of Christ Church, Spitalfields, London, undertaken in the 1980s, revealed large numbers of coffin fittings. The taxonomy compiled from these fittings (Reeve and Adams 1993) forms the basis for identification of the styles in vogue throughout this period. The coffin fittings from the ratings burial ground were compared to this catalogue wherever preservation was sufficiently good to identify a style. No parallels could be made in any fittings, bar grips from nine coffins.

Upholstery stud-work

18th- to 19th-century wooden coffins were usually upholstered in either velvet or baize (depending on cost), and secured with iron or brass upholstery studs. Once purely functional, by the Georgian period upholstery studs had become a decorative device. Complex patterns were created using studs on the lid and side panels of coffins. Single or double rows of studs commonly delimited the margins of the lid and side panels and often divided up these surfaces into smaller panels. At Greenwich, unlike examples from St George's crypt, Bloomsbury (Boston 2006) and St Luke's church, Islington (Boston 2005), the studs comprising these rows were often widely spaced (2-3 cm apart). Studs were also arranged together in circles or triangles, often in the corners of panels. Eight coffins appeared to have been decorated in this simple way.

At Greenwich, upholstery studs were made exclusively of iron, and like all the furnishings had suffered considerable corrosion (Appendix 4). Wood adhered to the reverse of the studs in many cases. Upholstery studs were recovered from 46 coffins (53.49%), and ranged in number from two studs (coffin 6015, skeleton 6014, grave 6002), three studs (coffin 3121, skeleton 3119, grave 3118) and five studs (coffin 3228, skeleton 3107, grave 3074; and coffin 3153, skeleton 3152, grave 3131) to over 500 studs (coffin 3043). At least 3,346 studs were present, an average of 72 or 73 studs per coffin. Given their small size and the extent of corrosion and concretion onto pebbles and soil of the grave fill, however, many studs were probably missed during excavation, and the true number was probably much higher.

The studs of two coffins (3043, skeleton 3044, grave 3041; and 3111, skeleton 3102, grave 3091) were painted black, tentatively suggesting that the upholstery baize was another colour. Unfortunately, textile survival was very poor, and one only example of upholstery cloth was recovered attached to the reverse of a stud. This was a fairly loose weave, but was very fragmentary.

Breastplates

Breastplates are commonly found overlying the chest area of post-medieval skeletons. These plates, originally attached to the coffin lid, identified the deceased, commonly displaying the name, age-at-death and date of death of the deceased. They occasionally provide additional biographical information, such as titles, professions and family affiliations. As such, they are a vital resource in reconstructing the identity of the deceased, on both an individual and a community scale. The breastplates, or fragments of breastplates, recovered during the excavation could be identified with 25 or 27 coffins; three plates were from multiple burials and could not be ascribed to a specific coffin with confidence (Appendix 4). Unfortunately, none of the plates were sufficiently well preserved to be legible.

Breastplates of more opulent coffins were commonly of lead or brass, with biographical details inscribed onto the surface of the plate. Inscription was not possible on the cheaper iron breastplates. Instead, the plate was often painted black, and the name and details were painted on in a contrasting colour, usually white. In the working class burials from St Hilda's churchyard, South Shields, Northumberland, three such breastplates were discovered (Brian Dean pers. comm.), whilst a number were recovered during excavation of a post-medieval burial ground at the Salisbury Art Centre site by AC Archaeology (Sharon Clough pers. comm.). In the Greenwich Hospital assemblage, flecks of black paint were identified on a few breastplate and grip plate fragments, but no contrasting paint for lettering was identified.

All the breastplates from Greenwich were composed of stamped iron sheets. The thinness of the sheets made the fittings very vulnerable to corrosion and disintegration. Breastplates were often largely whole when revealed during excavation, but fragmented on lifting. Due to this poor preservation, it was not possible to match these stylistically to the Christ Church Spitalfields taxonomy. Some details, such as borders and motifs of drapery and foliage were identified, and are noted in Appendix 4.

Grips and grip plates

Once solely functional, the grips with which mourners supported and steadied the coffin, became stylistically elaborate during this period, as did the grip plates by which the grips were attached to the coffin. Needing to be robust, the metals used for grips were restricted to iron and brass, whereas a greater variety of materials was used for grip plates.

Grips were recovered from 42 coffins in the ratings' burial ground, but only 22 coffins had grip plates. This difference is almost certainly a factor of preservation. Like breastplates, grip plates comprised thin sheets of stamped iron, and were very vulnerable to corrosion and disintegration. Grips were more solidly constructed, and hence survived better. They were, however, still vulnerable to rusting, and preservation varied from very poor to moderate. In the former, no recognition of styles was possible, but nine better preserved grips could be matched to the Christ Church Spitalfield's (CCS) taxonomy. Three examples of CCS type 1; three examples of CCS type 2a, and three of CCS type 3b were identified. All three of these styles are very simple, lacking motifs, such as flowers, cherubim and swirling foliage, so popular for grip styles of this period. Due to the longevity of use of the three styles, it was not possible to date these interments from the grip styles other than that they were loosely 18th- or 19th-century in date.

Grip plates were too fragmentary to discern many motifs or design details. One sunburst motif was identified (coffin 3087, skeleton 3086, grave 3028), but no further details were evident. Iron grip bolts were recovered from five graves.

Lid motifs and escutcheons

Lid motifs and escutcheons are thin sheets of metal stamped with a range of motifs, and used to decorate the upholstery on the lid and side panels of the wooden case. Lid motifs are larger than escutcheons and tend to be located centrally in the chest and knee areas of the coffin lid. Escutcheons are most commonly found in the corners and along the margin of the upholstery stud-work panels of the coffin lid and side panels of the outer wooden case. Several grave fills contained the fragmented remains of stamped iron sheets, but it was unclear whether they originated from breastplates, grip plates or lid motifs. None showed the small-scale detail common to escutcheons.

DISCUSSION

The coffins and coffin furnishings discovered within the graves in the rating's burial ground were very simple, with a complete lack of ostentation that characterised more wealthy burials of this period. Although little wood survived, it is reasonable to assume that all of the single break coffins were constructed of single thickness wooden planks. The exterior of some had been upholstered, although too little survived to identify the textile. All of the coffin fittings were made of iron, which was the cheapest material available. It is difficult to confidently ascertain how many coffins originally had coffin fittings, particularly breast plates and grip plates as iron preservation was exceedingly poor. Three different styles of grips were identified- all of very simple design. The assemblage is typical of a working class population of this period.

It is unclear whether coffins were issued by the Hospital on the death of one its inmates, or whether they were independently procured by the deceased before his death or by surviving well wishers. Certainly, they appeared more ornate than the Royal Navy coffins recovered from the Paddock of Haslar Hospital, which were almost entirely lacking in coffin furniture (Boston 2005). Further documentary research may shed more light on this issue, but is beyond the scope of this report.

CONCLUSION

Although this assemblage comprised only a tiny sample of the estimated 20,000 Greenwich pensioners buried within the rating's burial ground of the Hospital, it has nevertheless provided a unique window into the lives of 18th- and early 19th-century seamen and marines that comprised the Navy in the 'Age of Sail'. In bringing together the diverse but related disciplines of archaeology, osteology and history it has been possible to interpret this group more holistically than is possible for most archaeological assemblages, and in so doing has suggested many new avenues of research that may be explored. The richness of this data is such that this report can only be viewed as an overview or preliminary report from which considerably more research may be undertaken.

Appendix 1: Selected Trafalgar Veterans Who Died in the Royal Hospital, Greenwich

Summary of a sample of 100 Seamen and Marines who fought at Trafalgar and who were buried at Greenwich Hospital before 1858. This is a selection from data in Ayshford and Ayshford, 2004.

Surname	Forename	Rating	Age at Trafalagar	Birthplace	Age at death	Year of death	Length of service	Injuries	Trade on enlisting	Trade after discharge
Addison	Dominick	AS	26	Toulon	73	1853	15.4	-		Mariner
Allen	Robert	PRM	19	Crompton, Somerset	65	1841	3.1	Right leg amputated		
Anderson	Archibald	LM	22	Greenock, Renfrewshire	77	1855	11	'blown up' (T)	Cooper	
Armstrong	Samuel	Clerk	22	Clommell, Tipperary	68	1850	5	-		Clerk
Ayre	Thomas	OS	35	Southwark	71	1849	6.5	-		Lighterman
Babb	Daniel	LM	21	Hunstum, Devon	62	1845	11.75	-	-	
Baker	John	LM	36	Hambleton, Surrey	71	1839	9	-	Labourer	
Balcot	Robert	Carpenter's crew	32	York	70	1841	24	-		Carpenter
Barnes	William	PRM	32	Stratford, Wilts	64	1838	12.5	lost 4th finger	Farm labourer	
Beal	James	LM	23	Deal, Kent	62	1841	8	-		-
Bell	Henry	Quarter gunner	28	Manchester	48	1825	20	Right cheek (T)		-
Bendick	Ralph	AS	34	London	72	1841	17.8	-		-
Birton	William	Boy RM	17	Hinkley, Lancs	66	1853	11.1	Injured left side		Frameworker
Bound	William	AS	35	Portsmouth	81	1851	21.8	Head wound (T)	Mariner	
Bowles	James	OS	30	Gorlseston, Suffolk	73	1848	30.2	-		Mariner
Bray	William	AS	24	Kingsand, Devon	64	1844	25.4	Head wound (T)		-
Brown	Jacob	PRM	21	Sudbury, Glouc.	71	1854	15.2	Wounded (T)		-
Brownrigg	John	LM	23	Dublin	73	1855	12			Tobacconist
Bucklin	Allen	PRM	24	Reigate, Surrey	65	1844	12.5	-	Labourer	
Bunning	William	Boy 3rd Class	11	Sheerness, Kent	63	1853	41	-		Sailmaker
Burn	Edward	OS	22	West Ham, Essex	66	1850	17.5	Head wound off Russia		Silk weaver (A)
Burne	James	AS	23	Littlehampton, Sussex	77	1855	11.1	-		Mariner (A)
Burnes	Peter	LM	25	St Kitts, W. Indies	61	1843	11.8	Blinded in accident		Sackmaker (A)
Burton	William	LM	25	Fakenham, Norfolk	61	1843	11.8	Fractured left handL hand		
Bush	John	OS	21	Norfolk	61	1845	11.5	Gunshot to knee; Splinters many parts of body; Wound to back & loins (T)	-	-

(continued on next page)

Appendix 1 (*continued*)

Surname	Forename	Rating	Age at Trafalagar	Birthplace	Age at death	Year of death	Length of service	Injuries	Trade on enlisting	Trade after discharge
Calanso	Ralph	AS	32	Penzance	74	1847	18.1	Broken shoulder	-	Stonemason
Capell	Jacob	PRM	25	Queen Charlton, Somerset	73	1849	17.75	Wounded (T)	Labourer	Labourer
Carney	Thomas	PRM	30	Dublin	79	1854	-	1805-fever	Labourer	-
Catherine	Joseph	PRM	24	Paul, Cornwall	66	1847	16	Wounded (T)	Labourer	-
Chant	Isaac	AS	50	London	85	1841	11.2	-	-	Waterman
Chapman	Thomas	PRM	27	Bradford, Wilts	74	1851	12.2	Gunshot to head, jaw and cheeks	Dyer	Clothworker
Chapman	George	PRM	28	Westminster	74	1852	19	Wounded (T)	Taylor	-
Charnley	William	LM	26	Walton-le-Dale, Lancs.	79	1857	18	Hurt left foot	Weaver	-
Cherry	Peter	AS	22	Calais	71	1857	6.3	-	Labourer	-
Christian	Francis	AS	28	London	82	1855	20	Loss of hearing	-	Mariner
Church	James	LM	22	Plymouth dock	66	1849	-	-	-	-
Clancy	Edward	LM	23	Wexford	70	1852	16.5	-	-	-
Clowden	Daniel	AS	26	London	74	1849	10.9	Wounded left leg (T)	-	Shoemaker
Coggan	George	PRM	18	Brushford, Somerset	67	1854	21.75	-	Labourer	-
Coil	Michael	OS	25	Waterford	61	1841	15	Lost right eye	-	-
Connor	James	PRM	17	Dublin	56	1843	14.9	Wounds to breast, shoulder, knee (T); diseased liver (discharged 1820)	-	-
Connor	John	PRM	26	Dublin	65	1844	-	Lost right arm above elbow (T)	-	-
Cook	Charles	OS	23	Hartford	56	1843	21.9	Lost sight	-	Cabinetmaker
Cooke	John	LM	25	London	69	1846	15	-	-	-
Coombs	James	PRM	19	Shepton Mallett, So.	59	1841	18	Wounded (T), 'ruptured'	Labourer	-
Cornish	John	AS	27	Plymouth	52	1828	12.75	Contused ankle; wounded left arm in action	-	Printer
Court	Henry	PRM	21	Midsomer Norton, So.	71	1851	30.75	Wounded in head	Collier	Miner
Creer	William	LM	23	Castletown, Isle of Man	71	1855	11.9	-	-	Millwright
Crews	John	Quarter-master's Mate	30	Plymouth	64	1838	15.9	-	-	-
Crofton	Thomas	PRM	27	Dublin	52	1825	17	Both legs wounded (T)	Tailor	-
Crooney	John	LM	28	Cork	69	1845	11.83	-	-	-
Curly	Henry	LM	30	Dublin	68	1852	12.08	Wound to loins	-	Whipmaker
Dailey	Owen	OS	30	Tarrough, Co Meath	69	1831	17.3	Wounded left arm (musket ball)	-	Labourer
D'Armaro	Rafle	LM	22	Naples	73	1854	13	-	-	Labourer
Darnells	Thomas	PRM	27	Somerset	75	1853	10.42	-	Farm labourer	-

Appendix 1 (*continued*)

Surname	Forename	Rating	Age at Trafalagar	Birthplace	Age at death	Year of death	Length of service	Injuries	Trade on enlisting	Trade after discharge
Davis	Hugh	AS	32	Dolgelly, N Wales	71	1845	17	'Ruptured' (T)	-	Leather dresser
Davis	William	PRM	24	Corsley, Wilts	64	1842	7.25	Lost palate & injured left shoulder in fall	Cloth dresser	Sheerman
Day	Edward	PRM	21	Southgate. Exeter	74	1857	19.3	Discharged-debility	Tailor	Tailor
Dennis	Phillip	PRM	3	Plymouth	81	1856	17.1	-	Tailor	-
Dodd	Christopher	OS	52	Willock, Salop	81	1844	16.5	-	-	miner
Edwards	George	OS	22	Liverpool	67	1850	12.5	Head wound (T)	-	Mariner
Elvine	John	OS	22	London	66	1849	26.8	Wounded left foot (T)	-	Silk weaver
Emmerson	John	OS	27	London	76	1854	-	-	-	-
Endsor	Thomas	OS	26	Tamworth	73	1857	14	-	-	-
England	William	OS	30	London	68	1838	14	Injury 1st joint right thumb (accident)	-	Labourer
English	John	LM	23	Dublin	68	1850	25	-	-	Mariner
Everitt	James	PRM	21	-	73	1854	11.25	-	-	Farm labourer
Eyles	Samuel	PRM	24	Stapleton, Devon	76	1855	21.17	-	Whitesmith	Labourer
Faig	Mathew	AS	30	Dover	76	1854	19	-	-	Labourer
Fear	William	OS	25	Tiverton, Devon	69	1850	11.9	-	-	Labourer
Fergusson	Patrick	AS	36	Dublin	79	1848	-	-	-	-
Fetterman	William	Yeoman of the Powder Room	29	Brancaster, Norfolk	64	1831	19	Wounded in back by splinters (T)	-	Seaman
Forest	George	LM	22	Southwark	73	1856	-	Considerable ulceration of leg (1805 admitted to Haslar Hospital)	-	-
Frankpit	William	PRM	22	Tiverton, Devon	67	1847	9.83	Injured foot	-	Labourer
Gaffney	William	LM	21	Dublin	74	1856	15.6	-	-	Labourer
Gale	Robert	AS	27	Shipton, Yorks	74	1845	11.25	Wounds to breast, leg & back	-	Mariner
Gamsby	George	AS	33	Cork	71	1837	25	Wounded left hip (T). Fell from hatchawy to cockpit. Use of limbs impaired	-	Labourer
Gardner	William	OS	25	Bristol	72	1852	13.5	-	-	Brazier
Gillett	William	LM	21	Axminster, Devon	73	1855	11.25	-	-	Baker
Goree	John Henry	Quarter gunner	49	Spain	71	1828	14	Hurt in back (T)	-	-
Gostry	Henry	OS	34	Co. Cork	79	1847	14.9	Injured left foot	-	Labourer
Graham	Thomas	LM	24	London	67	1851	11	-	-	Labourer

(*continued on next page*)

Appendix 1 (continued)

Surname	Forename	Rating	Age at Trafalagar	Birthplace	Age at death	Year of death	Length of service	Injuries	Trade on enlisting	Trade after discharge
Gray	Henry	OS	22	Harrington NB, Midlothian	69	1855	23.75	Wound to left knee	-	Labourer
Gray	Henry	Gunner's mate	33	Durham	69	1842	12.83	-	-	-
Gray	Joh	AS	24	Salisbury	71	1852	-	-	-	-
Green	James	Gunner's mate	32	Weymouth	90	1855	42.25	Hurt in head, contusion	-	Mariner
Green	Thomas	AS	30	Cork	73	1841	18.75	Exposed tibia with splinters, gunshot (T)	-	Labourer
Greenslade	John	LM	32	Chudleigh, Devon	84	1857	16.6	Hurt left leg	-	Labourer
Griffiths	Richard	LM	25	London	58	1838	13.5	Loss of hearing (T)	-	Gunmaker
Grimes	Samuel	PRM	18	Manchester	64	1850	10.83	Wounds in action	Weaver	Weaver
Hagan	John	OS	40	Armagh	78	1841	13.67	Wounded left leg	-	Barber
Hammond	Isaac	AS	28	Sheffield	73	1852	18.08	Lost forefinger & ruptured right side (T)	-	Labourer
Harfett	Joseph	PRM	27	Midsommer Norton, So.	58	1827	18	Fractured head, wounded arm, varicose veins	Labourer	-
Harris	John	LM	26	Dantzick, Prussia	78	1857	12.5	Lost sight (active service)	-	Tailor
Healey	Patrick	LM	22	Cork	69	1851	11.33	'Ruptured' at Trafalgar	-	Coppersmith
Hill	Josh	OS	35	Manchester	88	1853	14.5	Lost right forefinger (on board)	-	Mariner
Hill	William	OS	40	Kennington, Devon	81	1846	9.67	-	-	-
Hines	James	PRM	23	Watton-under-Edge, Glos.	70	1853	-	Compound fracture of arm	Shoemaker	-
Hollicock	Josh	PRM	17	Yardley, Worcs.	67	1855	9.08	-	Vice maker	Whitesmith
Holloway	James	OS	29	London	65	1840	20	-	-	-
Totals			Average age at Trafalgar (years) 26.4		Mean age at death (years) 70.01		Mean years service incl. Merchant Navy 15.7			

Abbreviations: AS = able seaman; OS = ordinary seaman; LM = landman; PRM = private Royal Marine; (T) = injury sustained during the Battle of Trafalgar

Appendix 2: Grave Catalogue

by Brian Dean, Lorraine Lindsay-Gale and Ceridwen Boston

The skeletal evidence from the excavated graves described below is contained in Appendix 3: Skeletal Catalogue.

1999 EVALUATION

The skeletons found in graves uncovered during the 1999 evaluation were not removed but recorded *in situ*. Graves were revealed in Trenches 10, 11 and 12, which lay within Areas 1 and 2, and which were excavated in 2001. Trenches 13 and 14 produced no evidence of graves. The results of the evaluation are briefly discussed in Chapter 3 above. For full details see the evaluation report (OA 1999c).

ARCHAEOLOGICAL WATCHING BRIEF – STUDENT ACCOMMODATION (TRENCH 15)
(Fig. 7)

Trench 15 was excavated in February and March 2000, subsequent to the 1999 evaluation and after the preparation of the evaluation report (OA 1999c). Two, possibly three, graves (1564, 1571 and 1568) were located. Details of the skeletons from graves 1564 and 1571 can be found in Appendix 3 below.

Group 1563 - Grave 1564 (Fig. 7, plan 1504)

Grave 1564 was rectangular and contained an adult male inhumation (skeleton 1565). The grave had vertical sides, a flat base, and measured 1.4 m long and 0.7 m wide and was immediately above grave 1571. Part of the grave lay beyond the limit of the excavation. The grave fill (1566) was similar to the fill (1573) of grave 1571 and was dark grey-brown with orange patches, and a small amount of ceramic building material.

Skeleton 1565 was in a good state of preservation and 76–100% complete. It was a male aged as 50+ years, and had a stature of 167 cm. The skeleton was laid out in a supine position, with head to the west and feet to the east. Seven coffin nails (SF1501) were present within the fill (1566) and a further two nails were found with the skeleton.

Group 1567 - Grave 1568 (Fig. 7, plan 1504)

The western end of a sub-rectangular grave (1568) was revealed but only partly excavated. The grave was excavated to a depth of 1.6 m, but not bottomed. No skeleton was found. Most of the grave lay beyond northern limit of the trench.

Group 1570 - Grave 1571 (Fig. 7, plan 1505)

Grave cut 1571 contained an adult possible male inhumation (1572). The skeleton was beneath skeleton 1565, and the grave cut continued the line of the cut of grave 1564. It measured 1.4 m long, 0.7 m wide, and overall was 1.6 m deep. The grave fill (1573) was dark grey-brown with orange patches, and contained a small amount of ceramic building material. There was no discernible difference between the fills (1566 and 1573) of graves 1571 and 1564.

Skeleton 1572 was in good condition and was 76–100% complete. It was a possible male aged 40–50 years at death, and had a stature of 167 cm. It had been laid out in a supine position, with head to the west and feet to the east. The skeleton lay within the remnants of a coffin, indicated by the presence of five iron grips (SF1502–SF1506).

EXCAVATION OF THE ELECTRICAL SUB-STATION

Group 2003 - Grave 2004 (Fig. 11)

Grave cut 2004 contained a single adult female inhumation (skeleton 2005). The grave was rectilinear with vertical sides and a flat base. It measured 1 m long, 0.55 m wide, and was 0.80 m deep. The foot of the grave extended beyond the eastern limit of the trench. The fill (2006) was friable mottled sandy clay with 30% mixed gravel and stone.

Skeleton 2005 was in a good state of preservation, but was only 26–50% complete. It was an adult female, aged 50+ years at death, with an estimated stature of 166 cm. The skeleton was aligned SW-NE, and lay in a supine, extended position. Coffin nails (SF2000–SF2007) and studs were recovered.

PROPOSED CONFERENCE FACILITY – AREAS 1 & 2

The finds from the 2001 excavations include both iron and copper alloy objects. The iron objects, which include predominantly coffin fittings - breastplates, grips and grip plates, studs and coffin nails – are not well preserved, but are catalogued in summary form in Appendix 4. The copper alloy finds, which include some buttons and a number of shroud pins, are catalogued in Appendix 5.

AREA 1 (Fig. 6)

Group 3020 (Pile Trench 3001) - Grave 3107

Group 3020 comprised grave 3107 containing three burials (skeletons 3019, 3016 and 3024) positioned one above the other. The sub-rectangular grave cut measured 2.10 m long, was 0.4 m wide at the east end and 0.62 m wide at the west end, and was 1.28 m deep. It had vertical sides and a flat base. The fill (3018) was mottled dark brown and yellow silty sand. Finds recorded within this fill were animal bone, pottery, shell, glass and clay pipe.

Skeleton 3024 was the earliest inhumation. It was the skeleton of an adult male, aged 35–45 years, and 166 cm in stature. It was 76–100% complete and in excellent condition. It was laid out in a supine position with arms extended, head to the west and feet to the east. There was no wood surviving from associated coffin 3025, but iron studs and fixing nails were recovered from the head and torso area.

Skeleton 3016 was the second inhumation in grave 3107. The skeleton was that of an adult male, aged 45+ years at death, and 173.7 cm in stature. It was 76–100% complete, and in poor condition. The ribs and vertebrae were poorly preserved. It was laid out in a supine position with the head to the west and feet to the east. The associated coffin (3015) was marked by a coffin stain in the grave fill (3018). It was impossible to distinguish between the coffin of skeleton 3016 and that associated with the overlying skeleton 3019 (see below), and it was not possible to determine which iron nails were part of which coffin. A single context number (3015) was allocated to the coffin stain associated with the two burials; in reality each individual would have been interred within his own coffin.

Skeleton 3019 was the final inhumation in grave 3017. It was in poor condition and was 76–100% complete. The skeleton was that of an adult male was aged 40–45 years at death, and had a stature of 163 cm. The skeleton was lying in a supine position, arms extended, with head to the west and feet to the east. The upper part of the body was slumped, and the skull rolled back. An associated coffin stain 3015 and iron nails were found, but could not be distinguished from the coffin associated with skeleton 3016 (above).

Group 3050 (Pile Trench 3009) – Grave 3041

Group 3050 comprised a sub-rectangular grave (3041) containing three inhumations (skeletons 3068, 3057 and 3044). There was no evidence of any recut. The grave had a flat base, and vertical sides, and measured 2.10 m long x 0.52m/0.37 m wide x 1.34 m deep. The fill (3042) was loose, dark brown with patches of yellow silty sand. Fragments of pottery, bone, glass and metal within the fill were probably residual. All three inhumations were adult males.

Skeleton 3068 was the earliest burial, was in excellent condition and 76–100% complete. Skeleton 3068 was a male aged 45+ years at death, and had a stature of 183 cm. The skeleton was in a supine position with the head to the west and feet to the east. The associated coffin remains (3067) consisted of a coffin stain (single break type), Fe studs, fixing nails and a fragmented breastplate. Four shroud pins were found with the skeleton (SF3004–3005, 3008–3009: see Appendix 5, nos 4–7).

Skeleton 3057, the second inhumation, was in a good condition and 76–100% complete. The ribs were damaged, possibly due to the presence of the Fe coffin plate. The individual was a male aged 40+ years at death, and had a stature of 168 cm. The skeleton was in a supine position with the head to the west and feet to the east. The associated coffin (3059) was defined by a coffin stain, a breastplate, Fe fixing nails and studs. Clusters of four studs were identified in the corners of the side panels of the coffin. The coffin was of single break type. A single shroud pin was recorded (SF3001: Appendix 5, no. 3).

Skeleton 3044 was the latest burial in this grave. It was in good condition and 76–100% complete. The individual was a male aged 50+ years at death, and had a stature of 166 cm. The skeleton was in a supine position with the head to the west and feet to the east. The associated coffin (3043) was of single break type, and more ornate than most. The evidence comprised a coffin stain, with a single row of Fe upholstery studs following the outline of the lid, fixing nails, grips at the head and foot and on the long axis of the coffin (n= 6), and a badly corroded and fragmentary breastplate. A shroud pin was recorded associated with the skeleton (Appendix 5, no. 2).

Group 3240 (Pile Trench 3005) - Grave 3028

Grave group 3240 comprised four adult male inhumations (skeletons 3029, 3032, 3039 and 3086) within a double grave cut (3028). All skeletons were found lying in a supine position with their heads to the west and feet to the east. Skeletons 3039 and 3086 formed the earlier pair and had been laid alongside one another. They were overlaid by skeletons 3029 and 3032 respectively. Interestingly, amputee skeletons 3032 and 3086 were stacked one above the other. The grave cut (3028) was rectangular and measured 2.20 m x 1.35 m, and 1.2 m deep. Slight curvature of the southern cut tentatively suggested a recut, although this was not clear. The fill (3027) comprised loose sandy gravel with occasional inclusions of ceramic building materials. It probably represents the fill of the last two burials (skeletons 3029 and 3032), and contained the disturbed backfill of the earlier burials (3039 and 3086).

The artefacts recovered from the fill – pottery, glass, iron nails, bricks, clay pipe, and animal bone – it may have come from either grave. They included a complete copper alloy looped button (see Appendix 5, no. 8).

Grave 3028 lower burials

Skeleton 3039 was one of the two early skeletons and had been laid in the southern half of the grave. The skeleton was in a poor condition, and was 76–100% complete. The ribs, hands and feet were missing. The skeleton was a male aged 50+ years at death, and was 169 cm in stature. The skeleton was in a supine position with the head to the west and feet to the east. Iron coffin nails and grips at the ends represented the associated coffin (3048).

Skeleton 3086 was the second early inhumation and had been laid in the north half of grave 3028. The skeleton was 51–75% complete and was in a poor condition. The left femur was amputated above the knee. The individual was a male 40+ years of age, and was 174 cm in stature. The skeleton was in a supine position with the head to the west and feet to the east. The associated coffin (3087) was fairly ornate compared with other burials. The breastplate (3089) was present, as were fairly ornate grips, grip plates and nails. Sections of the margin of the coffin lid were decorated with widely spaced iron studs. The coffin outline revealed a coffin single of break type, measuring 1.8 m long and 0.39 m wide at the shoulders. A copper alloy shroud pin (SF3006) was found wrapped with shroud fabric inside the mouth, and a fragment of shroud textile with fragments of pin (SF3007) was found by the right clavicle (see Appendix 5, nos 9–10).

Grave 3028 upper burials

Skeleton 3029 was a later inhumation located on the south side of the grave above skeleton 3039. It was 76–100% complete, with some ribs and the left foot missing. Bone preservation was poor. The left side may have been mixed with skeleton 3039, because of slumping. Skeleton 3029 was a male 40+ years at death, and had a stature of 171 cm. The skeleton was in a supine position with the head to the west and feet to the east. The associated wooden coffin (3031) measured 1.75 m x 0.35 m. The lid and side panels were heavily decorated by studwork, and a very fragmentary and illegible breastplate was present. There is a possibility that these remains represent fittings of both coffin 3031 and the earlier coffin 3048 (skeleton 3039).

Skeleton 3032 was located on the north side of the grave above skeleton 3086. It was 76–100% complete and in good condition, except for slight damage to the skull. The individual was a male 50+ years at death, and was 171 cm in stature. The left leg had been amputated above the knee. The skeleton was in a supine position with the head to the west and feet to the east. The associated coffin (3033) was identified from iron fixing nails, one grip and a coffin stain. The stain suggests a trapezoid coffin, 1.75 m long x 0.4 m at the head.

Group 3250 (Pile Trench 3015) - Grave 3247

Grave cut 3247 contained two inhumations, an adult male (skeleton 3255) and a late adolescent possibly male (skeleton 3249). The grave was sub-rectangular with vertical sides and a flat base. The dimensions were 2 m long x 0.75 m wide. The fill (3248) was compact, dark brown sandy silt with frequent rounded stones, occasional charcoal and fragments of degraded oyster shell.

Skeleton 3255, the earlier inhumation, was poorly preserved but 76–100% complete. The remains were those of an adult male, aged 35–40 years, with a stature of 171 cm. The body was laid out in a supine extended position. Fe fixing nails and studs represented the associated coffin (no context number allocated).

Skeleton 3249, the later burial, was in a good state of preservation and was 51–75% complete. The remains are of a late adolescent, aged 16–18 years, possibly male. The body was laid out in a supine extended position. Fe fixing nails alone identified the associated coffin (no context number assigned).

Group 3260 (Pile Trench 3006) - Grave 3036

Rectangular grave 3036 contained two inhumations: skeleton 3035 and 3051, with the former overlying the latter. The grave had a flat base and three vertical sides and one with a 70° slope towards the base, and measured 2.30 m long x 1.12 m wide x 1 m deep. Both skeletons were adult, one male and one a possible male, laid out in a supine position, with heads to the west and feet to the east. The fill (3034) was firm, dark brown silty sand with 40% gravel and 1% charcoal inclusions. There was no discernible difference in the fill to indicate a re-cut for the burial of upper skeleton 3035. Finds include a copper alloy cartridge case (Appendix 5, no. 11).

Skeleton 3051 was the earlier burial and was in a good condition and 76–100% complete. There was slight damage to the front of the skull, the vertebrae and the pelvis. The ribs were not present, possibly due to the presence of the heavily corroded iron coffin plate (3052), which had removed in fragments from this area. Skeleton 3051 was a possible male, aged 50+ years at death and had a stature of 168 cm. The skeleton was in a supine position with the head to the west and feet to the east. The coffin remains (3049) comprised a coffin stain that measured 1.8 m in length, a very corroded and fragmented rectangular iron breastplate, six iron grip plates and grips located at the head, feet, and right and left sides of the chest and legs. A single row of iron upholstery studs outlined the margin of the lid.

Skeleton 3035, the later burial, was in good condition and 76–100% complete. The vertebrae and ribs were poorly preserved, the remaining bones in a fair to good condition. The hands were resting on the pelvis, and the left foot was on top of the right. This male individual was 50+ years at the time of death and had a stature of 164 cm. The skeleton was in a supine position with the head to the west and feet to the east. The associated coffin remains (3053) comprised a faint and discontinuous coffin stain and iron fixing nails.

Group 3330 (Pile Trench 3008) – Graves 3064 and 3047

Group 3330 comprises grave 3064 (skeleton 3061) and grave 3047 (skeleton 3045) which truncated the upper fill of grave 3064. Both skeletons were adult males, and interestingly, both were amputees.

Ovoid grave 3064 had a flat base and vertical sides, and measured 2.2 m x 0.8 m. Its fill 3063 was compact mid-brown sandy-silt containing numerous pebbles. Residual finds included pottery, animal bone, metal, wood and clay pipe stems.

Grave 3047 was sub-rectangular in shape and measured 2.2 m x 0.8 m x 0.6 m deep. Its fill 3046 was soft mid-brown silty sand, containing sub-angular and rounded gravel pebbles and a small proportion of charcoal.

Grave 3064

Skeleton 3061 was in excellent condition, and was 76–100% complete. The feet and hands were missing. The individual was a male aged 30–40 years at death, and had a stature of 163 cm. The body was laid in a supine position, head to the west and feet to the east. Remains of the associated coffin (3066) comprised a coffin stain (a single break type), a Fe breastplate, grips (located along the long axis of the coffin) and fixing nails.

Grave 3047

Skeleton 3045 was 76–100% complete and was in good condition. The individual was a male aged 35–45 years at death, and had a stature of 161 cm. The body was laid in a supine position, head to the west and feet to the east. The associated coffin (3062) was only discernible from a coffin stain (single break type), Fe grips at the head and sides, and Fe fixing nails.

Group 3380 (Pile Trench 3007) - Graves 3127, 3093, 3381 and 3833

This group comprised four graves and at least two phases of burial. One grave (3127) contained two pairs of inhumations; the other graves contained single inhumations. There were seven burials in all.

The earliest grave 3127 contained two pairs of burials: skeletons 3191 and 3212, which lay below skeletons 3162 and 3211, respectively. The grave cut was sub-rectangular with vertical sides and a flat base, and measured 1.15 m E-W x 2.2 m N-S x 0.6/0.7 m deep.

Grave 3093 truncated the upper fills of grave 3127, and contained a single inhumation (skeleton 3101). The grave was rectangular with vertical sides and a flat base and measured 2 m long x 0.60 m wide x 0.35 m deep. Finds included a penny possibly of George II (SF3000: Appendix 5 no. 12).

Grave 3381 was located immediately to the south of grave 3093. The relationship between the graves was uncertain. Grave 3381 contained a single individual (skeleton 3083) in a sub-rectangular cut, measuring 2.2 m long x 0.30 m wide x 0.10/0.20 m deep. Grave 3383 truncated this grave. The fill (3382) was grey brown sandy silt with stony inclusions.

Grave 3383 contained skeleton 3385, and the grave cut was rectangular, and measured 2 m long x 0.4 – 0.50 m wide. The fill (3384) was a firm mid orange/brown sandy silt with occasional round and angular stones and charcoal.

Grave 3127 lower burials

Skeleton 3191 was in a good state of preservation, and was 76–100% complete. The remains were those of an adult male, aged 50+ years at death, of estimated stature of 166 cm. The skeleton was in a supine position with the head to the west and feet to the east. No coffin or fittings were recorded.

Skeleton 3212 was also in a good state of preservation and was 76–100% complete. The remains were of an adult male, aged 40+ years at death, and estimated stature was 172 cm. The skeleton was in a supine position with the head to the west and feet to the east. A slight coffin stain and fragments of breastplate, nails, studs and grips defined associated coffin 3225. A shroud pin was found with this burial (SF3013: Appendix 5, no. 14).

Grave 3127 upper burials

Skeleton 3162 was in a poor state of preservation, but was 76–100% complete. The remains were those of an adult male aged 50+ years at death, and with an estimated stature of 165 cm. The skeleton was in a supine position with the head to the west and feet to the east. The associated coffin (3165) comprised a faint coffin stain and a few fragments of wood (single break type). Fe fixing nails and grips were also present. A fragment of shroud fabric and a pin were also recovered (SF3011: Appendix 5, no. 15).

Skeleton 3211 was in a good state of preservation and was 76–100% complete. The remains were those of an adult male age 40+ years of estimated stature of 163 cm. The skeleton was in a supine position with the head to the west and feet to the east. No coffin stain was recorded but Fe nails and studs were recovered in the backfill (3128). No context number was assigned.

Grave 3093

Skeleton 3101 was well preserved, and was 76–100% complete. The individual was a male aged 35–40 years. Its stature was 166 cm. The skeleton was in a supine position with the head to the west and feet to the east. No associated coffin was recorded, but a fragmentary shroud pin with textile fragments was found (Appendix 5, no. 13). A possible George II penny was also found (Appendix 5, no. 12).

Grave 3381

Skeleton 3083 was a later burial. The human remains were in a good state of preservation and were 51–75% complete. The remains were those of an adult male age 50+ years at death, with a stature of 170 cm. The skeleton was in a supine position with the head to the west and feet to the east. Iron fixing nails were present within the cut, but no other evidence of a coffin was recovered (no context number was assigned).

Grave 3383

Skeleton 3385 was the latest burial in the sequence. These remains were well preserved and the skeleton was 51–75% complete. The remains were those of an adult male aged between 40+ years at death, and a stature of 163 cm. The skeleton was in a supine position with the head to the west and feet to the east. The associated coffin was known only from iron fixing nails (no context number was assigned).

Group 3390 (Pile Trench 3009) - Grave 3239

Sub-rectangular grave 3239 contained three adult male inhumations (skeletons 3272, 3269 and 3241). The grave had vertical sides and a flat base, and was truncated by a concrete slab. The dimensions were 2 m long x 0.7 m wide x 0.7 m deep. The fill (3238) of the grave was loose, mid-brown sandy silt with 5% gravel and 1% CBM, which had been markedly disturbed as a result of root activity. A shroud pin (SF3016: Appendix 5, no.16) was found in the grave fill.

Skeleton 3272, the earliest burial was in good condition and was 76–100% complete. The individual was a male aged 40–45 years at the time of death, with a stature of 160 cm. The skeleton was laid in a supine position. The evidence for the coffin (3273) comprised only Fe coffin nails.

Skeleton 3269, the second burial, was in an excellent state of preservation, and was 76–100% complete. This male individual was aged 50+ years at the time of death, with a stature of 162 cm. The skeleton was laid in a supine position. The only evidence for associated coffin (3271) was a small quantity of Fe nails. Shroud pins were also recovered.

Skeleton 3241, the latest of the three burials, was in a good state of preservation and was 76–100% complete. This male individual, of stature 166 cm, was aged 50+ years at the time of death. The skeleton was laid in a supine position. The only evidence for a coffin (3242) associated with this burial was Fe nails.

Group 3410 (Pile Trench 3010) – Grave 3131

Sub-rectangular grave cut (3131) contained three inhumations (3132, 3144 and 3152). One of these burials (3132) was an adolescent of undefined sex, whilst the two others were adult males. The grave had vertical sides and a flat base. The dimensions were 2 m x 0.56 m x 0.89 m. The fill (3129) consisted of loose, mid-grey sandy silt with yellow lenses and included 5% gravel and 1% CBM. Some disarticulated bone (3171) that may have been charnel or the disturbed remains from skeleton 3168 was recovered from the east end of the grave.

Skeleton 3132, the earliest of the burials, was in a poor state of preservation and was 76–100% complete. The skeleton was an adolescent, aged 12–14 years. Sex could not be identified. The associated coffin (3172) was poorly preserved, but Fe fixing nails (unnumbered) and a very corroded Fe breastplate were identified.

Skeleton 3144, the middle inhumation, was in a good state of preservation, and was 76–100% complete. The remains were of an adult male aged 50+ years at death, with a stature of 168 cm. The coffin (3145) was identified only from the presence of ten Fe nails.

Skeleton 3152 was the most recent of the three burials. It was in a good state of preservation, and was 76–100% complete. The remains were those of an adult male aged between 40+ years at death, with a stature of 167 cm. Associated coffin 3153 was identified by Fe fixing nails alone.

Group 3450 (Pile Trench 3011) - Grave 3074

Rectangular grave 3074 contained four adult male inhumations (3107, 3106, 3105 and 3072) stacked one above the other. The grave had vertical sides and a flat base. It measured 2.22 m east to west x 0.74 m north to south, and was 0.95 m deep. The fill (3073) contained animal bone, CBM, pottery, shell, glass, clay pipe, and Fe coffin fittings.

Skeleton 3107 was the earliest inhumation in grave cut 3074. The skeleton, which was 76–100% complete and in good condition, was an adult male aged 40+ years at death, with a stature of 166 cm. The skeleton was laid in a supine position with head to the west and feet to the east. Associated coffin (3228) was defined by a coffin stain and Fe studs, four grips, and fixing nails.

Skeleton 3106 was interred above skeleton 3107. The skeleton was 76–100% complete and in a good condition, and was a male, aged 40+ years at death, with a stature of 163 cm. Some mixing with the small bones of skeleton 3107 may have occurred. The skeleton was laid in a supine position with head to the west and feet to the east. Fe fixing nails and studs recovered from the fill defined the associated coffin (3104). A very corroded breastplate and grips were also recovered, although it is uncertain whether these were originally part of coffin 3104, or coffin 3071 (burial 3072) (see below).

Skeleton 3105 was above skeleton 3106 and was 76–100% complete, although mixing of elements with other skeletons may have occurred. The skeleton was in a good condition. It was a male aged 45+ years at death, and had a stature of 172 cm. The skeleton was laid in a supine position with head to the west and feet to the east. The associated coffin (3104) was defined by the presence of Fe coffin fittings with some wooden coffin edge and a badly corroded breastplate. Again, mixing may have occurred.

Skeleton 3072 was the latest inhumation in the sequence. It was 76–100% complete and in poor condition. The skeleton was an adult female aged 40+ years. It had slumped badly onto skeleton 3105. The grave had been heavily disturbed by root action. The skeleton was laid in a supine position with head to the west and feet to the east. The associated coffin (3071) was defined by wood fragments and a faint coffin stain, plentiful Fe studs, grips and a possible breastplate. Possibly mixed with the fittings of coffin

3104. A copper alloy shroud pin with attached fabric was found at the top of the occipital bone on the left side of the skeleton (SF3003: Appendix 5, no. 17).

Group 3480 (Pile Trench 3015) – Graves 3078 and 3091

This group comprised two grave cuts. The earliest grave (3078) contained a single inhumation (skeleton 3102), and was truncated by grave 3091. Grave 3091 contained four adult male inhumations (3164, 3103, 3108 and 3139). The cut measured 2.3 m long x 0.7 m wide x 0.35 m deep. It was oval in outline and had a flat base and vertical sides. Grave 3091 cut an earlier grave (3078) to the west. Disturbed material from the truncated grave was re-deposited within grave 3091. Pottery, bone, glass, metal and wood fragments were present.

Grave 3078

Skeleton 3102, the earliest skeleton, was in grave 3078 (which had been cut by grave 3091). The skeleton was 51–75% complete, and in good condition. The skeleton was a possible male, aged 40–45 years, with a stature of 163 cm. The body had been laid in a supine position, with the head to the west and feet to the east. The evidence of an associated coffin (3109) included a fragmentary breastplate, fragments of grips and grip plates as well as Fe fixing nails.

Grave 3091

Skeleton 3164 is the earliest burial in 3091, was well preserved and 76-100% complete. The remains were of a 30–40 year old male, with a stature of 170 cm. The skull showed green staining on the right mandible, possibly from a brass shroud pin. The body had been laid in a supine position, with the head to the west and feet to the east. An incomplete coffin stain and Fe fixing nails, studs, and fragments of iron breastplate represented associated coffin 3163.

Skeleton 3103 was the second burial, was in good condition and was 76–100% complete. The burial was a male aged 50+ years, with a stature of 164 mm. There was possible co-mingling with the later burial skeleton 3108 (see below) due to slumping. The body had been laid in a supine position, with the head to the west and feet to the east. Associated coffin 3111 was represented by Fe coffin nails, five grips (located at the head and sides) and a breastplate.

Skeleton 3108 was the third burial, was in a good condition and was 76–100% complete. The individual was a male aged 30–40 years at death, with a stature of 174 cm. The body had been laid in a supine position, with the head to the west and feet to the east. The associated coffin (3138) was represented by Fe fixing nails, studs and a breastplate. It is possible that due to slumping this burial had become a little mixed with the earlier burial skeleton 3103 (above).

Skeleton 3139, the fourth and latest burial overlay skeleton 3108, was in a good state of preservation and was 51–75% complete. The remains were of an adult male aged 40–45 years, with a stature of 165 cm. The body had been laid in a supine position, with the head to the west and feet to the east. No coffin remains were recorded.

Group 3490 (Pile Trench 3015) - Grave 3114 and Charnel pit 3233

Grave 3114 was contained two adult male inhumations (skeletons 3115 and 3229), which overlay a charnel pit (3233). Grave 3114 measured 1.75 m east to west x 0.7 m north to south. It was 0.5 m deep. It appeared that inhumation 3115 was stacked directly above 3229, and that the grave had been back-filled in a single event.

The rectangular charnel pit 3233 measured 0.6 m east to west x 0.56 m north to south, and was 0.15 m deep. It had vertical sides and was truncated at the top by the cut of grave 3114. The fill (3113) of grave 3114 contained a relatively high concentration of disarticulated human bone, which probably derived from the charnel pit.

Skeleton 3229 was in good condition and was 76–100% complete. The individual was an adult male of 45+ years at death and had a stature of 169 cm. The body had been laid in a supine position, with the head to the west and feet to the east. The presence of a coffin (3231) could only be inferred from Fe fixing nails and studs.

Skeleton 3115 was 51–75% complete and in poor condition. This individual was an adult male of 60+ years at time of his death and had a stature of 173 cm. The body had been laid in a supine position, with the head to the west and feet to the east. The associated coffin (3116) was inferred by the presence Fe coffin fixing nails.

Group 3550 (Pile Trench 3015) - Grave 3118

Rectangular grave cut 3118 contained a single inhumation (skeleton 3119). The sides of grave 3118 were vertical and the base flat. It measured 1.8 m east to west x 0.65 m north to south, and was 0.43 m deep. It was filled by 3120. Grave group 3550 overlay Groups 3490 (above) and 3560 (below).

Skeleton 3119 was well preserved and was 76–100% complete. The skeleton was that of an adult male 40+ years at the time of death and had a stature of 174 cm. The body had been laid in a supine position, with the head to the west and feet to the east. The presence of associated coffin 3121 was indicated by Fe fixing nails and two grips.

Group 3560 (Pile Trench 3015) - Grave 3123

Sub-rectangular grave (3123) contained a single possible adult male inhumation (skeleton 3124). The grave cut measured 0.65 m east to west x 0.54 m north to south x 0.42 m deep. The associated coffin (3125) was represented by Fe coffin fittings including a breastplate (3226).

Skeleton 3124. The bone condition was good, but because of truncation by structure 3626, only the head and torso were visible (0–25% complete). This individual was a possible adult male aged 30–50 years at death, and had a stature of 163 cm. The skeleton lay in a supine extended position.

Group 3570 (Pile Trench 3014) – Grave 3095

Sub-rectangular grave 3095 contained two adult male inhumations (skeletons 3098 and 3099), the latter overlying the former. The grave measured 2.10 m long x 0.58 m wide x 0.22 m deep, and had a flat base and vertical sides. It had been truncated by cut 3142. The fill (3096) was loose mid brown silty sand with 15% rounded pebble inclusions, and some pottery and glass fragments. There was extensive root intrusion throughout.

Skeleton 3098, the earlier inhumation, was in an excellent state of preservation and was 76–100% complete. This individual was an adult male of 45+ years at the time of death and had a stature of 174 cm. The skeleton was in a supine position, head to the west and feet to the east; some of the hands and feet bones may have become mixed. The associated coffin (3097) was identified as the single break type from a coffin stain, a fragmented Fe breastplate, Fe fixing nails, studs and grips.

Skeleton 3099, the later inhumation, was in an excellent state of preservation and was 76–100% complete. The skeleton was an adult male of 35–45 years at the time of death. He had stature of 169 cm. The skeleton was in a supine position, head to the west and feet to the east; it is possible that the hands and feet bones had become mixed. The associated coffin (3134) was identified as a single break type from a coffin stain and Fe fixing nails.

Group 3580 (Pile Trench 3014) – Grave 3142

Grave 3142 contained one adult male inhumation and one possible adult male (skeletons 3143 and 3189). The grave was sub-rectangular with vertical sides and a flat base. The dimensions were 2.18 m long x 0.55 m wide x 0.62 m deep. It cut three earlier grave groups: 3510, 3840 and 4090. In turn, the group was cut by 3156 (part of group 3870) to the east. The fill (3141) consisted of loose, marbled (mid-brown/orange brown) silty sand with 15% rounded pebbles and 0.5% flint inclusions.

Skeleton 3189, the earlier inhumation, was in a poor state of preservation, and was 51–75% complete. The remains were of an adult male aged 50+ years at death, with an estimated stature of 167 cm. The burial was aligned W-E, and was laid out in an extended and supine position. The associated coffin (3188) was identified from the presence of iron fixing nails only.

Skeleton 3143, the later inhumation, was in a good state of preservation and was 76–100% complete. The remains were those of a possible adult male aged 40+ years, with a stature of 165 cm. The burial was aligned W-E, and was laid out in an extended and supine position. The associated coffin (3161) was identified from a coffin stain and a severely corroded Fe breastplate, nails and studs.

Group 3590 (Pile Trench 3012) - Grave 3149

Sub-rectangular grave 3149 contained three inhumations (skeletons 3176, 3151 and 3148) located directly one above the other. All three were adult male skeletons. The upper fill of the grave had been heavily truncated by modern construction. The grave cut measured 2.1 m east to west x 0.6 north to south x 0.4 m deep. The fill (3133) was firm dark brown silty sand with 15–20% rounded pebbles.

Skeleton 3176, the earliest skeleton, was 76–100% complete and in good condition. This individual was a male 45–55 years at the time of death, and had a stature of 174 cm. The skeleton was laid out in a supine position, with the head to the west and feet to the east. No coffin details recorded.

Skeleton 3151, the second inhumation, was in excellent condition and 76–100% complete. This individual was a male 35–45 years old at the time of death and had a stature of 168 cm. The skeleton was laid out in a supine position, with the head to the west and feet to the east. No coffin details recorded.

Skeleton 3148 the latest inhumation was in a good state of preservation and was 76–100% complete. This adult male was 50+ years at the time of death, and had a stature of 177 cm. The skeleton was laid out in a supine position, with the head to the west and feet to the east.

Group 3600 (Pile Trench 3013) - Grave 3207

Grave 3207 contained two adult male inhumations (skeletons 3208 and 3213). The grave was sub-rectangular in shape, with vertical sides and a flat base. Its dimensions were 2.20 m long x 0.70 m wide x 0.50 m deep. The fill (3206) consisted of a loose mid-brown sandy silt with 5% gravel and 1% CBM. The grave was truncated by later grave group 3610 (see below).

Skeleton 3213, the earlier inhumation, was excellently preserved and was 76–100% complete. The individual was an adult male, aged 45–55 years at death, with a stature estimated at 171 cm. The skeleton was laid in an extended supine position and oriented W-E. The associated coffin (3214) was evident from Fe fixing nails only.

Skeleton 3208, the later inhumation, was in a good state of preservation and was 76–100% complete. The skeleton was an adult male, aged between 40–50 years at death, with an estimated stature of 164 cm. The skeleton was laid in an extended supine position and oriented W-E. The associated coffin (3209) was identified from Fe fixing nails only.

Group 3610 (Pile Trench 3013) - Grave 3175

Grave 3175 contained a single adult female inhumation (skeleton 3174). The cut measured 2.05 m x 0.65 m x 0.20 m deep.

Skeleton 3174 was 76–100% complete and the preservation was excellent. This female was 50+ years at time of death, and had a stature of 159 cm. The burial had been laid out in a supine position with the head to the west and feet to the east. The evidence for the associated coffin 3173 comprised a coffin stain, Fe fixing nails, Fe grips and grip plates (at the foot and on sides), studs, and a very corroded and fragmentary breastplate. The coffin was of single break type.

Group 3620 (Pile Trench 3015) - Graves 3631, 3627 and 3621

This group comprised three single inhumation burials (graves 3631, 3627 and 3621) that had been dug one above the other.

Grave 3631 (skeleton 3632) was the earliest in the sequence. It was a lozenge-shaped cut with a flat bottom measuring 0.72 m long x 0.38 m wide x 0.15 m deep contained skeleton. Grave 3627 truncated the grave and the foundation trench (3625) for wall footing 3626 obscured its east end.

Grave 3627 (skeleton 3628) was also lozenge-shaped, and measured 0.80 m long x 0.48 m wide x 0.5 m deep. The remains were orientated west-east and lay in a supine extended position. Grave 3621 truncated the grave and the foundation trench (3625) destroyed its east end.

Grave 3621 (skeleton 3623) had a truncated sub-rectangular grave cut (3621), which had vertical sides and a flat base. It measured 0.88 m long by 0.7 m wide. The east end of the grave was lost to the foundation trench (3625) for wall footing 3626.

The fills of all three graves were similar and described as friable, orange/brown silty sand with 20% mixed gravel.

Grave 3631

Skeleton 3632 was in a good state of preservation but was only 26–50% complete. Truncation resulted in the absence of the lower limbs. The individual was male, aged 40+ years, with a stature of 169 cm. No associated coffin was recorded.

Grave 3627

Skeleton 3628, although in a good state of preservation, was only 26–50% complete because the lower limbs were missing. The remains were those of an adult male, aged 40+ years, with a stature of 168 cm. No evidence for a coffin was recovered.

Grave 3621

Skeleton 3623 was in a good state of preservation, but was only 26–50% complete. The lower arms and torso and the legs had been truncated by the foundation trench for wall 3626. The individual was an adult male, aged 50+ years at death, of unknown stature. The coffin was represented by a partial coffin stain (3622).

Grave Group 3630

Ovoid grave 3179 contained the single inhumation of an adult male (3182). The grave cut had slightly sloping sides and a flat base and measured 2.3 m long x 0.8 m wide x 0.4 m deep. The fill (3181) was a soft, yellowish brown with occasional charcoal fragments.

Skeleton 3182 was well preserved and was 76–100% complete. The individual was an adult male, aged 50+ years at death, and with a stature of 159 cm. The inhumation lay in a supine extended position. The coffin (3183) of single break type was defined by slight staining and by Fe nails, a grip (at the foot of the coffin) and a fragment of breastplate.

Group 3690 (Pile Trench 3014 - Grave 3219

Grave 3219 contained a possible female adult inhumation (skeleton 3223). The sub-rectangular grave had vertical sides with a sharp break of slope leading to a flat base. The recorded dimensions were 1.85 m long x unknown width x 0.21 m deep. The fill (3221) was a loose, mid-brown sandy silt with 10% rounded pebbles.

Skeleton 3223 was poorly preserved and was 51–75% complete. Much of the right side of the skeleton had been disturbed by truncation by a later grave 3215. The skeleton was that of a possible female, aged 40+ years at death, and had a stature of 157cm. The skeleton was laid in an extended supine position. The associated coffin (3222) of single break type was represented by a coffin stain, corroded fragments of Fe breastplate, corroded Fe fixing nails, Fe studs and coffin grips at the foot and along left side of the coffin.

Group 3700 (Pile Trench 3014) - Grave 3236

Grave 3236 contained the single inhumation of an adult female (skeleton 3245). The grave cut was sub-rectangular with vertical sides and a flat base. Its dimensions were 2.22 m long x 0.38 m deep. The fill (3237) was firm dark to mid-brown silty sand with 10–15% rounded pebbles.

Skeleton 3245 was poorly preserved and only 51–75% complete. The remains were those of an adult female, aged 35–45 years, of unknown stature. The skeleton was aligned W-E, and laid out in a supine, extended position. A single break wooden coffin (3246) contained the above skeleton. The coffin evidence comprised a clear coffin stain (dimensions: 1.65m long x 0.45 m wide at shoulders), Fe fixing nails and studs, a breastplate, and five grips (at the head, foot and sides of coffin).

Group 3800 (Pile Trench 3012) - Grave 3198

Grave 3198 contained three inhumations (3253, 3243 and 3201). The three inhumations were adults, two males and one of undefined sex. The grave was an elongated oval shape in plan, with vertical sides, a sharp break of slope and a flat base. It measured 2.12 m long x 0.66 m wide x 0.30 m deep. Some truncation had occurred during machine excavation. The fill of this cut (3199) consisted of a soft, yellowish brown silty sand with 10% rounded pebbles. Grave 3198 cut grave 3257 (group 4070) and grave 3185 (group 3810).

Skeleton 3253, the earliest of the three inhumations, was in a good state of preservation and 76–100% complete. The remains were those of an adult male aged 50+ years at death, with an estimated stature of 168 cm. The burial was oriented W-E in a supine extended position. An associated coffin (3254) was identified from Fe fixing nails. A shroud pin was found with this burial (SF3014: Appendix 5, no.18).

Skeleton 3243, the second burial, was in a good state of preservation and was 75–100% completeness. The remains were those of an adult male aged 40+ years with an estimated stature of 171 cm. The burial was oriented W-E in a supine extended position. The associated coffin (3244) was identified from Fe fixing nails.

Skeleton 3201 the last burial in the sequence appeared to have suffered prior disturbance but was described from field notes as being in good condition. The skull, hands, feet and left leg were missing. On site recording indicated an adult of undetermined sex. The burial was oriented W-E in a supine extended position. There is no evidence for an associated coffin, possibly as a result of truncation of the burial mechanical excavation. This skeleton was not included in the skeletal assemblage.

Group 3810 (Pile Trench 3012) - Grave 3185

Grave 3185 contained a single adult male inhumation (skeleton 3187). The grave cut had been heavily truncated, but was sub-rectangular with very shallow sides and a flat base. The dimensions were 1.6m long x 0.5m wide x 0.10m deep. The fill (3186) was firm, dark greyish brown sandy silt with 10–20% small stones.

Skeleton 3187 was in a good state of preservation and was 26–50% complete. The individual was an adult male aged 40+ years, with a stature of 178 m. The skeleton had been laid out W-E in a supine extended position. No evidence for a coffin was recovered.

Group 3870 (Pile Trench 3014) - Grave

Grave 3156 contained a single adult male inhumation (3159). The sub-rectangular grave cut had vertical sides and a flat base. Its dimensions seem to have been 1.10 m long x 0.6 m wide x 0.38 m deep, but it extended beyond the eastern limit of the excavation. The fill (3157) was loose silty sand with rounded pebbles.

Skeleton 3159 was in a good state of preservation and was 51–75% complete. It was the skeleton of an adult male aged 45+ years at death, and had a stature of 166 cm. The skeleton had been laid out in an extended supine position. Fe fixing nails, studs and three coffin grips (at the head and shoulders) represented the associated coffin (3158). No coffin wood survived but a single break shape could be discerned from the coffin stain.

Group 4050 (Pile Trench 3010) - Grave 3167

Sub-rectangular grave (3167) contained two inhumations (skeletons 3168 and 3177). The grave had vertical sides and a flat base. The dimensions were 2 m long x 0.7 m wide x 0.91 m deep. Both skeletons were adult males. The fill (3166) consisted of loose, mid-brown sandy silt with 5% gravel and 1% CBM. The group was truncated to the west by grave group 3410, and to the east by an unnumbered and unexcavated grave.

Skeleton 3177 was the earlier of the two burials. It was in a good state of preservation and was 51–75% complete. The remains were of an adult male aged 45–55 years, with an estimated stature of 174 cm. Laid out supine extended and oriented W-E.

Skeleton 3168, was the later burial. Preservation of the bone was excellent, and the skeleton was between 79–100% complete. The remains were those of an adult male aged 50+ years, with an estimated stature of 168 cm. Some disturbed bone was assigned to this skeleton. Laid out supine extended and oriented W-E. The associated coffin (3169) was defined by Fe nails only.

Group 4060 (Pile Trench 3010) - Grave

Grave 3193 contained two adult male skeletons (3194 and 3202). The grave cut was sub-rectangular with vertical sides and a flat base, and measured 2.1 m long x 0.8 m wide x 0.75 m deep. The fill (3192) was a loose, mid greyish brown sandy silt with 5% gravel and 1% CBM.

Skeleton 3202 was the earlier of the two burials. It was in a good state of preservation and 76–100% complete. The remains were those of an adult male aged 40+ years at death, of stature 163 cm. Laid out in a supine extended position and broadly aligned W-E. Associated coffin (3203) was defined by the presence of Fe fixing nails but no coffin furniture or wood was extant.

Skeleton 3194 was the later burial. Its preservation was excellent and it was 76–100% complete. The remains were of an adult male, aged 40+ years, with a stature of 166 cm. Laid out in a supine extended position and broadly aligned W-E. Only Fe fixing nails suggested the presence of an associated coffin (3195).

Group 4070 (Pile Trench 3012) - Grave 3257

Grave cut 3257 contained two adult male inhumations (skeletons 3258 and 3261). The grave was sub-rectangular with vertical sides and a flat base. It measured 1.80 m long x 0.40 m wide by 0.25 m deep. The fill (3256) was a loose mid-brown sandy silt with 5% gravel and 5% CBM.

Skeleton 3258 was in an excellent state of preservation, and 51–75% complete. The individual was an adult male, aged 40+ years at death. The estimated stature was 162cm. The associated coffin (3259) was represented by Fe fixing nails. No other elements survived.

Skeleton 3261 was well preserved and was 76–100% complete. The remains were those of an adult male aged between 30–40 years at the time of death. The stature was 174 cm. Two Fe fixing nails represented the coffin (3262) associated with this burial.

Group 4090 (Pile Trench 3014) - Grave 3215 and Charnel pit 3234

Grave 3215 contained an adult male inhumation (3218) and a quantity of charnel (3235) in a pit (3234). The sub-rectangular grave had vertical sides with a flat base and measured 2.03 m long x 0.67 m wide x 0.18 m deep. The fill (3216) was loose mid-brown silty sand with 15% rounded pebbles. The skeleton 3218 had been laid out in a supine extended position.

Beneath the skeleton a charnel pit 3234 was located within the eastern part of grave 3215. The relationship between grave and pit was uncertain: pit 3234 may have been contemporary with, or cut by, 3215. The cut for the charnel pit was rectangular with vertical sides and a flat base. The recorded dimensions were 0.63 m long x 0.23 m wide x 0.11 m deep. The charnel deposit (3235) was assigned to skeleton 3223. No coffin remains were recovered with the charnel.

Skeleton 3218 was in a good state of preservation and was 76–100% complete. The remains were those of an adult male aged 50+ years at death, with a stature of 160 cm. The associated coffin (3217) of single break type was represented by a coffin stain, a fragmented Fe breastplate, Fe studs, six grips (located at head, foot and sides) and Fe fixing nails.

Group 4100 (Pile Trench 3009) - Grave 3263

Double grave 3263 contained two pairs of adult inhumations (skeletons 3268 and 3276; and 3265 and 3274), one pair above the other. The grave cut was rectangular and measured 2.30 m long x 1.28 m wide x 1.15 m deep. It had vertical sides and a flat base. The fill (3264) was composed of graveyard soil and natural river gravels with 10% CBM. One piece of prehistoric pottery and some glass were found within the fill.

Grave 3263, lower burials

Skeleton 3268, was one of earlier inhumations. It was in excellent condition and was 76–100% complete. This possibly male individual was 35–45 years at the time of death, and had a stature of 168 cm. Body laid out in a supine position, with head to the west and feet to the east. No associated coffin was recorded.

Skeleton 3276 was the second earlier inhumation. It was in poor condition, and was 51–75% complete. This male individual was 50+ years at the time of death, and had a stature of 158 cm. Body laid out in a supine position, with head to the west and feet to the east. A few Fe nails defined the associated coffin.

Grave 3263, upper burials

Skeleton 3265, was in good condition, and was 76–100% complete. This male individual was 50+ years at the time of death and had a stature of 159 cm. Body laid out in a supine position, with head to the west and feet to the east.

Skeleton 3274 was the second of the later burials in grave 3263. It was in good condition and 76–100% complete. This possible male was 30–40 years at the time of death and had a stature of 154 cm. Body laid out in a supine position, with head to the west and feet to the east.

AREA 2 (Fig. 7)

Group 6020 (Pile Trench 6002) - Grave 6002

Grave 6002 had an unusually deep sub-rectangular double grave cut, and contained the inhumations of four adults buried in two pairs (skeletons 6017 and 6019, and 6003 and 6014), the former overlaying the latter. The cut (6002) had vertical sides and a flat base. It truncated north-south ditch 6008. The loose sandy fill (6001) of redeposited natural contained animal bone, pottery and clay pipe.

Grave 6002 lower burials

Skeleton 6019 was the earlier inhumation located on the south side of grave 6002. It was 76–100% complete and in good condition. The individual of unknown sex was aged 50+ years at death. Stature could not be determined. Body laid out in a supine position, with head to the west and feet to the east. A clear coffin stain (single break type) defined the associated coffin (6021) that measured 1.69 long, and the presence of Fe fixing nails.

Skeleton 6017 was the other early inhumation and was located on the north side of grave 6002. It was 76–100% complete and in good condition. The male individual was 40+ years at death, and had a stature of 169 cm. Body laid out in a supine position, with head to the west and feet to the east. A clear coffin stain (single break type) that measured 1.80 m long and 0.41 m at the shoulders defined the associated coffin (6018). Fe fixing nails were also present.

Grave 6002 upper burials

Skeleton 6003, the upper inhumation, located in the northern part of grave 6002. It was 76–100% complete and in poor condition. The right shoulder and ribs were missing. The male individual was aged 40–50 years at death, and had a stature of 156 cm. Body laid out in a supine position, with head to the west and feet to the east. The associated coffin (6004) was identified from a clear coffin stain (single break type) that measured 1.70 m by 0.55 m at the shoulders. Fe grips (x 4, located along the long axis), an illegible breastplate, Fe upholstery studs (outlining the edges of the lid) and Fe fixing nails were present.

Skeleton 6014, the upper inhumation located in the southern part of grave 6002, was 76–100% complete and in a good condition. It had slumped badly, and the ribs and vertebrae were decayed. The male individual was 40+ years at death, and had a stature of 168 cm. Body laid out in a supine position, with head to the west and feet to the east. The associated coffin (6015) was identified from a coffin stain (single break type), which measured 1.85 m x 0.40 m at the shoulders, and Fe fixing nails.

Group 6040 (Pile Trench 6000) - Grave 6062

Rectangular grave 6062 was a double grave containing four adult male inhumations buried in two pairs (skeletons 6073 and 6103, and 6063 and 6096), one above the other, respectively. The grave cut measured 2.10 m x 1.35 m x 1.50 m deep, and had vertical sides and a flat base. It was excavated by machine, and only one piece of clay pipe was retrieved from the fill.

Grave 6062 lower burials

Skeleton 6073, the earlier inhumation on the south side of the grave was 76–100% complete and in a good condition. The mail individual was aged 50+ years at death, and had a stature of 161 cm. Fe fixing nails and studs (although some may have originally belonged to an unexcavated grave to the north) represented the associated coffin (6074).

Skeleton 6103, the earlier inhumation on the north side of the grave, was 76–100% complete and in poor condition. The male skeleton was aged 50+ years at death, and had a stature of 171 cm. The associated coffin (6104) was identified from Fe fixing nails.

Grave 6062 upper burials

Skeleton 6063, the upper inhumation on the south side of the grave, was 76–100% complete and in a good condition. The male individual was 50+ years at death, and had a stature of 168 cm. It had slumped badly at the northern end. The associated coffin (6064) was identified from Fe fixing nails.

Skeleton 6096, the upper inhumation on the north side of the grave was 76–100% complete and in a good condition. It was also badly slumped to the northern end. The left arm was disarticulated from the shoulder, probably post-mortem. The male individual was 50+ years at death, and had a stature of 179 cm. The associated coffin (6097) was identified from a coffin stain, ornate studwork, a grip, and Fe fixing nails.

Group 6070 (Pile Trench 6001) - Grave 6009

Rectangular grave 6009 contained two adult male inhumations (skeletons 6013 and 6016), positioned one above the other. The grave cut measured 2.4 m x 0.65 m and 1.7 m deep, and had vertical sides and a flat base. The fill (6011) contained large pieces of CBM, occasional coal and charcoal, animal bone, pottery, glass and oyster shell.

Skeleton 6016, the lower and earlier inhumation, was 76–100% complete and in a good condition. The male individual was aged 45–60 years at death, and had a stature of 166 cm. Body laid out in a supine position, with head to the west and feet to the east. The associated coffin (6031) was identified from a coffin stain and Fe coffin-fixing nails.

Skeleton 6013, the upper inhumation, was 51–75% complete and in a poor condition. Root action had caused significant damage: the skull was largely destroyed and the right side of the body much disturbed. The bones were soft and friable. The male individual was aged 40–50 years at death, and had a stature of 167 cm. Body laid out in a supine position, with head to the west and feet to the east. A coffin stain (single break type) that measured 1.80 m x 0.45 m at the shoulders defined the associated coffin (6012). Fe coffin fixing nails were also present.

Group 6120 (Pile Trench 6003) - Grave 6032

This group comprised a grave (6032) containing two adult male inhumations (skeletons 6092 and 6094), the first positioned directly above the second. The rectangular grave cut measured 2.48 m x 0.66 m x 1.7 m deep. CBM, pottery, shell, glass and clay pipe were found within the fill (6033).

Skeleton 6094, the earlier inhumation, was 51–75% complete and in poor condition. The male individual was 40–50 years at the time of death and had a stature of 162 cm. Body was laid out in a supine position, with head to the west and feet to the east. The associated coffin (6095) was defined by a coffin stain (dimensions 1.75 m long x 0.38 m at shoulders), and Fe fixing nails. A very fragmentary and corroded copper alloy shroud pin (SF 6008) was recovered, but no details of its precise location were recorded (Appendix 5, no.19).

Skeleton 6092, the later inhumation was 51–75% complete and in poor condition. This individual was adult male aged 40+ years, and had a stature of 160 cm. Body laid out in a supine position, with head to the west and feet to the east. The associated coffin (6091) was identified from Fe fixing nails and fragments of coffin wood. The coffin stain was incomplete.

Group 6150 (Pile Trench 6004) - Grave 6026

A rectangular double grave 6026 contained four adult inhumations buried in two pairs (skeletons 6056 and 6058; 6027 and 6053), placed one on above the other. The skeletons comprised two males, one possible male and one possible female. The grave cut measured 2.55 m long x 1.54 m wide with no depth was recorded.

Grave 6026 lower burials

Skeleton 6056, one of the earlier inhumations, was a male, 76–100% complete and in good condition. The male individual was aged 50+ years at death, with a stature of 170 cm. Body laid out in a supine position, with head to the west and feet to the east. The coffin stain (single break type), measuring 1.8 m long, and 0.4 m at the shoulders identified the associated coffin (6057). Small traces of decayed wood present. Fragments overlying skeleton indicated lid. Fe fixing nails and a grip were present. A copper alloy shroud pin was recovered (SF 6003: Appendix 5, no.21) in association with the coffin stain.

Skeleton 6058, the second lower inhumation, was a 50+ year old possible male. The skeleton was 76–100% complete and in excellent condition. The stature was estimated to 179 cm. The arms were folded across the chest and abdomen. Body laid out in a supine position, with head to the west and feet to the east. The associated coffin (6059) was represented by Fe fixing nails and one grip.

Grave 6026 upper burials

Skeleton 6027 lay directly above skeleton 6056, and was 76–100% complete and in good condition. A deluge mid-recovery had washed away some of the small hand and feet bones. The skeleton was a possible female, aged 50+ years, with a stature of 159 cm. Body laid out in a supine position, with head to the west and feet to the east. The associated coffin (6028) was represented by a coffin stain (single break type) that measured 1.80 m long x 0.40 m at the shoulders, and some wood fragments that were possibly part of the base of the coffin. Fe fixing nails, studs and a grip (some with wood fragments attached) were present. A copper alloy shroud pin was recovered in association with the coffin stain (SF 6000: Appendix 5, no.20).

Skeleton 6053 lay directly above skeleton 6058. It was the skeleton of a 40+ year old male, 76–100% complete and in good condition. Stature was 168 cm. Body laid out in a supine position, with head to the west and feet to the east. The associated coffin (6054) comprised a coffin stain (single break type) and wood fragments, including part of the base, much of which was washed away in a deluge. The coffin measured 1.8 m long x 0.35 m at the shoulders. One Fe grip, studs and fixing nails were also recovered.

Group 6250 (Pile Trench 6005) - Grave 6025

Sub-rectangular grave 6025 contained two adult male inhumations (skeletons 6023 and 6105), the former overlying the latter. Grave cut 6025 had vertical sides and a flat base, and measured 2 m east/west x 0.4 –0.5 m north/south x 1.80 m deep. The fill contained pottery, animal bone, CBM, shell, charcoal and coal.

Skeleton 6105, the lower, earlier inhumation, was 76–100% complete and in a good condition. The skeleton was a male of 40+ years age, and a stature of 158 cm. The right arm lay beneath the pelvis, and the left above it. Body laid out in a supine position, with head to the west and feet to the east. The associated coffin (6106) was represented by Fe fixing nails, a breastplate and a coffin stain (single break type) that measured 1.75 m x 0.40 m at the shoulders.

A small find of a Cu alloy shroud pin (SF 6011) was found on the mandible (Appendix 5, no. 22).

Skeleton 6023 was 76–100% complete and was in a poor condition. Male individual aged 50+ years at death, with a stature of 176 cm. Body laid out in a supine position, with head to the west and feet to the east. The associated coffin (6022) was identified from a coffin stain and Fe fixing nails as a single break type.

Group 6270 (Pile Trench 6006) - Grave 6039

Sub-rectangular grave 6039 contained two adult male inhumations (skeletons 6035 and 6037). The grave cut had vertical sides and a flat base and measured 2.40 m long x 0.62 m wide x 1.82 m deep. The fill (6034) was a firm, light orange/brown, sandy silt with frequent gravel and rounded pebbles inclusions and a small quantity of ceramic building material (CBM).

Skeleton 6037, the earlier inhumation, was in a good state of preservation, and was 76–100% complete. The remains were those of an adult male, aged 45–55 years at death, with an estimated stature of 160 cm. The skeleton was laid out in an extended, supine position. Fragments of poorly preserved leather (SF6005) were discovered beneath the back and around the right side in the torso region of the skeleton. The leather was poorly preserved to identify the garment with any confidence. They could have been the remnants of a leather waistcoat or stays, but is perhaps more likely that they had a medical function perhaps as a truss worn for long-term rupture (see above Chapter 4; see also Appendix 5, no. 25). A coffin stain (single break type), measuring 1.77 m long x 0.38 m at the shoulders represented the associated coffin (6038). Fe fixing nails, some of which had wood fragments adhering to them, were present. As well as the fragment of leather (SF6005), two shroud pins (SF6004, SF6006) were associated with burial 6037 (Appendix 5, nos 26–27).

Skeleton 6035, the later inhumation, was in a good state of preservation, and 76–100% complete. The remains were those of an adult possible male, aged 35–45 years at death, with an estimated stature of 168 cm. The skeleton was laid out in an extended, supine position. Fragments of poorly preserved leather or textile (SF602) were discovered around the right side in the torso of the skeleton, possibly the remains of a garment or coffin lining (see Appendix 5, no. 24). A shroud pin (SF: 6001) was also recovered (Appendix 5, no. 23). The associated coffin (6036) was represented by a coffin stain, measuring 1.83 m long x 0.4 m at the shoulders, together with Fe nails and studs. The coffin was of single break type.

Group 6410 (Pile Trench 6009)

Group 6410 was not a grave but an earlier non-archaeological geotechnical test pit (probably test pit 4 of the OA watching brief in 1999). The rectangular cut (6065) measured 2.17 m x 1.0 m, and was filled by 6065. This fill contained debris from the excava-

Group 6420 (Pile Trench 6009) - Grave 6075

Rectangular grave 6075 contained one male adult inhumation and one possible male inhumation (skeletons 6089 and 6078). The grave had vertical sides and a flat base. The dimensions were 2.28 m long x 0.66 m wide x 1.26 m deep. The fill (6076) was loose, light brown gravelly sand with 15% larger gravel inclusions.

Skeleton 6089, the earlier inhumation, was in a good state of preservation and was 76–100% complete. The remains were those of an adult male, aged 35–45 years at death, with an estimated stature of 165 cm. The skeleton was laid out in an extended supine position. The associated coffin (6088) was represented by a coffin stain (single break type), a fragmented Fe breastplate (on which foliage motifs were observed), Fe fixing nails, studs and four grips (located at head and along sides of coffin). Cu alloy shroud pin was recovered (SF 6007: Appendix 5, no. 29).

Skeleton 6078, the later inhumation, was in a poor state of preservation and was 51–75% complete. The remains were those of a possible male adult, aged 40+ years at death, with an estimated stature of 168 cm. The skeleton was laid out in an extended supine position. The coffin (6077) was represented by an incomplete coffin stain (single break type), two Fe grips (located at foot and left side) and Fe fixing nails.

Group 6430 (Pile Trench 6009) - possible Grave 6099

This feature was a rectangular cut (6099) with vertical sides and a flat base (dimensions of 2.05 m long x 0.72 m wide x 1.50 m deep). The fill (6101) was firm orange/mid-brown sandy gravel with occasional roots. No articulated skeleton, disarticulated human remains or coffin remains were recovered. Bone within the fill proved to be four fragments of cattle long bone shaft.

Group 6460 - Grave 6084

Rectangular grave cut 6084 contained the four adult male inhumations in two pairs (6146 and 6151; and 6085 and 6142), the former pair being earlier. All lay in a supine position, with their head to the west and feet to the east. The grave cut (6084) measured 1.95 m long x 1.20 m wide.

Grave 6084 lower burials

Skeleton 6146 was 76–100% complete and in good condition. This male individual was 50+ years at the time of death, and had a stature of 175 cm. This skeleton lay beneath skeleton 6142. The associated coffin (6147) was represented a coffin stain (single break type). Fe fixing nails, grips, grip plates, studs and a breastplate (with wood fragments adhering to the reverse) were recovered. Copper alloy shroud pins were found with this burial, one (SF6013) to the right of the mandible, and the second (SF6014) under the chin (Appendix 5, nos 31–32).

Skeleton 6151 lay directly beneath skeleton 6085. The former was 76–100% complete and in a good condition. This male individual was 45+ years at the time of death and had a stature of 165 cm. Associated coffin 6152 was identified from a coffin stain (single break type), measuring 1.76 m x 0.4 m at the shoulders, Fe fixing nails, studs and grip plates (with wood fragments attached). Three shroud pins were found with this burial, one (SF6015) by the right temporal bone, another (SF6016) under the left temporal bone, and the third (SF6017) beneath the skull (Appendix 5, nos 33–35).

Grave 6084 upper burials

Skeleton 6085 was located in the northern part of grave 6084 on the same level as skeleton 6142. The former was in good condition and was 76–100% complete. The skull was damaged. This male individual was 50+ years at the time of death, and had a stature of 166 cm. The associated coffin (6086) was represented by an incomplete coffin stain (single break type) and Fe studs with wood fragments adhering, fixing nails, grips and a poorly preserved breastplate.

Skeleton 6142 was 75–100% complete and in good condition. This male individual was 50+ years at the time of death, and had a stature of 174 cm. A coffin stain (single break type), measuring 1.90 m long and 0.40 m the shoulders represented the associated coffin (6143). Fe grips, studs and fixing nails were present. A copper alloy shroud pin (SF 6012) was found on the mandible (Appendix 5, no. 30).

Group 6540 (Pile Trench 6012) - Grave 6069

Sub-rectangular grave (6069) contained two adult male inhumations (skeletons 6128 and 6098), the former lying below the latter. The grave cut measured 2.37 m x 0.82 m x 0.76 m deep. It had vertical sides and a flat base. The lower fill (6121) had a depth of 0.52 m, and the upper fill (6071), a depth of 0.7 m.

Skeleton 6128, the earlier inhumation, was 51–75% complete and in a poor condition. This male individual was 50+ years at the time of death, his stature unknown. The body was laid out in a supine position, with the head to the west and feet to the east. The associated coffin (6129) was identified from a coffin stain (measuring 2.2 m long x 0.4 m at the shoulders) and Fe fixing nails. The coffin appeared trapezoid in shape.

Skeleton 6098, the later inhumation was 76–100% complete and in a poor condition. This male individual was 50+ years at the time of death, and had a stature of 166 cm. The body was laid out in a supine position, with the head to the west and feet to the east. Severely decomposed wood and Fe fixing nails represented the associated coffin (6072). The edges of the coffin revealed a single-break type, and remnants of the collapsed lid directly overlay the skeleton the length of the coffin. Fragments of the base were also preserved. The coffin measured 1.80 m long by 0.38 m at the shoulders. It was possible to conclude that it had been constructed of wooden slats or narrow planks. Two shroud pins were found closely associated with the skeleton. One pin with a piece of cord, and shroud fabric in a possible clump of human hair (SF6009) was found at the right mandibular ramus, and a second shroud pin (SF6010) with a fragment of cord was found by the left hand mandibular ramus (Appendix 5, nos 36–37).

Group 6550 - Grave 6131

Grave 6131 contained a single adult female (skeleton 6132). The grave cut measured 1.95 m x 0.60 m x 0.08 m deep. It was heavily truncated by machine excavation.

Skeleton 6132 was 76–100% complete, and in an excellent condition. This female individual was 40–50 years at the time of her death, and had a stature of 162 cm. The skeleton lay in a supine position with head to the west and feet to the east. The associated coffin (6133) was represented by an incomplete coffin stain (single break type), Fe studs, fixing nails, three grips (located along the long axis of the coffin) and fragments of a breastplate.

Group 6560 (Pile Trench 6007) - Grave 6081

Sub-rectangular grave 6081 contained two adult male inhumations (skeletons 6082 and 6113). The grave had vertical sides and measured 2.30 m long x 0.80 m wide x 1.45 m deep). The fill (6079) comprised a loose yellow sand with grey patches, containing inclusions of 25% gravel.

Skeleton 6113, the earlier inhumation, was in a good state of preservation and was 76–100% complete. The remains were those of an adult male aged 50+ years at death, with an estimated stature of 172 cm. The skeleton was laid out in an extended supine position. The associated coffin (6114) was represented by Fe fixing nails only.

Skeleton 6082, the later inhumation, was in a good state of preservation and was 76–100% complete. The remains were those of an adult male aged 40+ years, with an estimated stature of 170 cm. The skeleton was laid out in an extended supine position. A slight coffin stain and Fe fixing nails represented associated coffin 6083.

Appendix 3: Skeletal Catalogue

by Nicholas Marquez-Grant and Annsofie Witkin

Key for dentition
/ - lost PM
X - Lost AM
B - Broken
C - caries
PC- peri-apical cavity/ dental abscess
NP- Not present
R- Root only
U - Unerupted
E - Erupting
PE - Partial eruption
PU - Pulp exposed
- - Jaw not present
H - Hypoplasia
cc - Calculus
P - Periodontal disease

Abbreviations
DISH - diffuse idiopathic skeletal hypertosis
DIP - distal interphalangeal joint

Skeleton Number: 1565   **Grave group:** 1563
Completeness: 76–100%   **Preservation:** Good
Age: 50+ yr   **Sex:** Male   **Stature:** 162 cm
Summary of pathological conditions: Spinal degenerative joint disease, Schmorl's nodes, DISH, Degenerative joint disease of right and left shoulder, elbow, hip and knee joints, ribs, metacarpals and hand phalanges. Possible septic arthritis on left ulna, Periostitis on left fibula. Fractures of left tibia, left fibula and five ribs, Cribra orbitalia. Dental caries, Enamel hypoplasia, Dental calculus, Periodontal disease

R							Dentition							L
		PU							PU					
		P	P	P	P			P		P	P			
		cc	cc	cc	cc			cc		cc	cc			
					H			H	C	H	H			
X	X	6	5	4	3	X	/	1	2	3	4	X	X	X	X
X	7	/	5	4	3	2	1	1	2	3	4	5	X	X	8
	C														C
	cc		cc	cc	cc	cc	cc	cc	cc	cc	cc	cc			
	P		P	P	P	P	P	P	P	P	P	P			P

Skeleton Number: 1572   **Grave group:** 1570
Completeness: 76–100%   **Preservation:** Good
Age: 40–50 yr   **Sex:** Male?   **Stature:** 167 cm
Summary of pathological conditions: Spinal degenerative joint disease, Schmorl's nodes, Degenerative joint disease of right and left shoulder, elbow, wrist, hip and knee joints, and on ribs, carpals and phalanges, Periostitis on left and right tibia, Fractures of nasal bones, frontal bone and two ribs, Lumbarisation of sacrum. Dental caries, Enamel hypoplasia, Dental calculus, Periodontal disease, Periapical cavity.

	R							Dentition								L
		P	P	P									P			
		cc	cc	cc									cc			
				C												
X	X	6	5	4	X	X	X	X	X	/	X	X	6	X	X	
X	X	X	X	X	3	X	X	X	2	3	X	X	X	X	X	
					H				C							
					P				P	P						
					PC											

Skeleton Number: 2005
Completeness: 26–50%
Age: 50+ yr **Sex:** Female
Grave group: 2003
Preservation: Poor
Stature: 166 cm
Summary of pathological conditions: Spinal degenerative joint disease, Degenerative joint disease of right and left hip joints

	R							Dentition								L
-	-	-	-	-	-	-	-	-	-	-	-	-	-	-	-	
-	-	-	-	-	-	-	-	-	-	-	-	-	-	-	-	

Skeleton Number: 3016
Completeness: 76–100%
Age: 45+ yr **Sex:** Male
Grave group: 3020
Preservation: Poor
Stature: 173.7 cm
Summary of pathological conditions: Spinal degenerative joint disease, Degenerative joint disease of right hip and right and left knee joints, Porotic hyperostosis, Fracture of L1 vertebra, right femur and right foot phalanx, Button osteoma, Possible scurvy. Dental calculus, Impacted tooth

	R							Dentition								L
X	X	X	X	X	X	X	X	X	X	X	X	X	X	X	X	
X	X	X	X	X	X	X	X	X	X	3	X	X	X	X	X	
										cc						

Skeleton Number: 3019
Completeness: 76–100%
Age: 40–45 yr **Sex:** Male
Grave group: 3020
Preservation: Poor
Stature: 163 cm
Summary of pathological conditions: Spinal degenerative joint disease, Schmorl's nodes, Degenerative joint disease of right and left shoulder joints, both hip joints and left knee joint, Periostitis on right and left tibiae and fibulae, Fractured nasal bones, right zygomatic, left humerus, left third metacarpal, one rib, left tibia and left navicular. Periapical cavity, Periodontal disease

	R							Dentition								L
									PC							
X	/	X	X	X	/	X	X	X	X	X	X	/	X	X	X	
X	X	X	5	X	X	X	X	X	X	X	X	X	X	X	X	
			P													

Appendix Three

Skeleton Number: 3024   **Grave group:** 3020
Completeness: 76–100%   **Preservation:** Excellent
Age: 35–45 yr   **Sex:** Male   **Stature:** 166 cm
Summary of pathological conditions: Spinal degenerative joint disease, Periostitis on ten ribs, Possible scurvy. Dental caries, Dental calculus, Periapical cavity, Periodontal disease

R							Dentition							L
P	P	P	P	P	P	P	P		P	P	P	P	P	P
cc	cc	cc	cc	cc	cc	cc	cc		cc	cc	cc	cc	cc	cc
		C				PC							C	
8	7	6	5	4	3	2	X	1	/	3	4	5	6	7	8
8	7	X	5	4	3	2	1	1	2	3	4	5	6	7	8
					H					H					
cc	cc	cc	cc	cc	cc	cc	cc	cc	cc	cc	cc	cc	cc	cc
P	P	P	P	P	P	P	P	P	P	P	P	P	P	P

Skeleton Number: 3029   **Grave group:** 3240
Completeness: 76–100%   **Preservation:** Poor
Age: 40+ yr   **Sex:** Male   **Stature:** 172 cm
Summary of pathological conditions: Spinal degenerative joint disease, Degenerative joint disease of right and left humeri, both acetabula and right metatarsal, Periostitis on right and left tibia, Fracture of frontal bone and left fibula, Possible scurvy, Possible osteochondritis dissecans. Dental calculus, Periodontal disease

R								Dentition							L
P	P	P	P	P	P	P	P	P	P	P	P		P	P	P
cc	cc	cc	cc	cc	cc	cc	cc	cc		cc	cc		cc	cc	
8	7	6	5	4	3	2	1	1	2	3	4	X	6	7	8
8	7	6	5	4	3	2	1	1	2	/	4	5	6	7	8
cc	cc	cc	cc	cc	cc	cc	cc		cc		cc	cc	cc	cc	cc
P	P	P	P	P	P	P	P	P	P		P	P	P	P	P

Skeleton Number: 3032   **Grave group:** 3240
Completeness: 76–100%   **Preservation:** Good
Age: 50+ yr   **Sex:** Male   **Stature:** 164 cm
Summary of pathological conditions: Spinal degenerative joint disease, Schmorl's nodes, Degenerative joint disease of right and left shoulder joints, left sternoclavicular joint, metacarpals, hand phalanges and metatarsals, Sharp blade injury to right mandible, fractured neck of left femur, Amputation of left femur. Dental caries, Dental calculus, Periapical cavity, Periodontal disease

R								Dentition							L
					P		P	P		P		P		P	
								PC	PC	PC	PC	PC			
												cc			
								C							
X	X	X	/	/	3	/	1	1	/	3	/	5	X	7	X
X	X	X	X	X	X	X	X	X	X	3	/	5	X	X	X
										P		P			

95

'Safe moor'd in Greenwich tier'

Skeleton Number: 3035   **Grave group:** 3260
Completeness: 76–100%   **Preservation:** Good
Age: 50+ yr   **Sex:** Male   **Stature:** 164 cm
Summary of pathological conditions: Spinal degenerative joint disease, Schmorl's nodes, Degenerative joint disease of right and left shoulder joints, left sternoclavicular joint, both hip joints and DIP joint, digit 1 of right hand, Periostitis on left fibula and right tibia, Porotic hyperostosis, Cribra orbitalia. Dental caries, Periapical cavity, Periodontal disease

```
 R                        Dentition                          L

       P   P
           P   PC                       PC
       C   C
   X 7 X 5 X X X X | X X X X / X X X
   X X X X X 3 X X | X X X X X X X X
               P
```

Skeleton Number: 3039   **Grave group:** 3240
Completeness: 76–100%   **Preservation:** Poor
Age: 50+ yr   **Sex:** Male   **Stature:** 169 cm
Summary of pathological conditions: Spinal degenerative joint disease, Schmorl's nodes, Degenerative joint disease of left shoulder joint, both elbow joints, both wrist joints, both hip joints, both knee joints, right and left carpals and metacarpals, Periostitis on right fibula, Maxillary sinusitis, Porotic hyperostosis, fracture of left nasal bone, left fibula and right fifth metatarsal. Periapical cavity

```
 R                        Dentition                          L

                 PC  PC
   X X X X X X X X | X X X X X X X X
   X X X X X 3 X 1 | 1 X 3 4 X X X X
```

Skeleton Number: 3044   **Grave group:** 3050
Completeness: 76–100%   **Preservation:** Good
Age: 50+ yr   **Sex:** Male   **Stature:** 166 cm
Summary of pathological conditions: Spinal degenerative joint disease, Schmorl's nodes, Degenerative joint disease of right shoulder joint, right and left sternoclavicular joints, right elbow joint, both wrist joints, right and left carpals, metacarpals, hand phalanges and metatarsals, Cribra orbitalia, fracture of left clavicle and right second and third metacarpals.

```
 R                        Dentition                          L

   X X X X X X X X | X / X X X X X
   X X X / X / 2 X | / / X X X X X X
```

Skeleton Number: 3045   **Grave group:** 3330
Completeness: 76–100%   **Preservation:** Poor
Age: 35-45 yr   **Sex:** Male   **Stature:** 161 cm
Summary of pathological conditions: Spinal degenerative joint disease, Schmorl's nodes, Degenerative joint disease of right and left temporo-mandibular joints and left hip joint, Periostitis on left tibia, Osteomyelitis on right femur, Amputation of left femur, Porotic hyperostosis, Fracture of right and left nasal bones. Dental caries, Dental calculus, Enamel Hypoplasia, Periapical cavity, Periodontal disease

Appendix Three

R								Dentition							L
P	P	P	P	P	P	P	P		P	P	P	P	P	P	P
								PC		PC	PC				
	cc	cc	cc		cc		cc		cc	cc	cc	cc	cc		
											C			C	R
8	7	6	5	4	3	2	1	X	X	3	4	5	6	7	8
8	7	6	5	4	3	2	1	1	2	3	4	X	X	7	X
										C	C				
			H	H	H				H	H	H				
			cc		cc	cc	cc	cc	cc	cc					
P	P	P	P	P	P	P	P	P	P	P	P			P	

Skeleton Number: 3051 **Grave group:** 3260
Completeness: 76–100% **Preservation:** Good
Age: 50+ yr **Sex:** Male? **Stature:** 166 cm
Summary of pathological conditions: Spinal Degenerative Joint Disease, Schmorl's nodes, Degenerative Joint Disease of right and left hip joints and tarsals, Rickets, Maxillary sinusitis, Fracture of right tibia and fibula. Dental Caries, Calculus, Periodontal disease, Periapical cavity, Impacted tooth

R								Dentition							L
P						P				PC					P
8	X	X	X	X	3	X	X	X	X	X	X	X	X	/	8
X	X	X	X	4	3	2	X	X	2	3	X	X	X	X	X
					C	R									
				cc	cc	cc			cc	cc					
						PC									
				P	P	P			P	P					

Skeleton Number: 3057 **Grave group:** 3050
Completeness: 76–100% **Preservation:** Good
Age: 40+ yr **Sex:** Male **Stature:** 168 cm
Summary of pathological conditions: Spinal degenerative joint disease, Degenerative joint disease of right and left shoulder joints, right and left sternoclavicular joints, both elbow joints, both sacro-iliac joints, both hip joints, right and left carpals and metacarpals, Fracture of left nasal bone and right fibula. Enamel hypoplasia, Dental calculus, Periodontal disease

R								Dentition							L
P	P	P	P	P	P	P	P	P	P	P	P	P	P	P	P
cc	cc	cc	cc	cc	cc	cc	cc	cc	cc	cc	cc	cc	cc	cc	cc
					H					H					
8	7	6	5	4	3	2	1	1	2	3	4	5	6	7	8
8	7	6	5	4	3	2	1	1	2	3	4	5	6	7	8
					H					H					
cc	cc	cc	cc	cc	cc	cc	cc	cc	cc	cc	cc	cc	cc	cc	cc
P	P	P	P	P	P	P	P	P	P	P	P	P	P	P	P

Skeleton Number: 3061 **Grave group:** 3330
Completeness: 76–100% **Preservation:** Excellent
Age: 30–40 yr **Sex:** Male **Stature:** 163 cm
Summary of pathological conditions: Spinal degenerative joint disease, Schmorl's nodes, Degenerative joint disease of right and left temporo-mandibular joints, Periostitis on left tibia, Porotic hyperostosis, Cribra orbitalia, Fracture of right and left nasal bones, Amputation of right tibia and fibula. Dental caries, Enamel hypoplasia, Dental calculus, Periodontal disease

R								Dentition								L
P	P		P	P					P	P	P	P	P			
cc	cc		cc	cc					cc	cc	cc	cc	cc			
									H				C			
8	7	X	5	4	/	/	X	X	/	3	4	5	6	7	X	
8	7	6	5	4	3	/	/	/	/	3	X	X	6	7	8	
	H			H					H				C	R		
cc	cc	cc	cc	cc	cc				cc			cc	cc	cc		
P	P	P	P	P	P				P			P	P	P		

Skeleton Number: 3068 **Grave group:** 3050
Completeness: 76–100% **Preservation:** Excellent
Age: 45+ yr **Sex:** Male **Stature:** 183 cm
Summary of pathological conditions: Spinal degenerative joint disease, Schmorl's nodes, Degenerative joint disease of right and left shoulder joints, both sternoclavicular joints, both elbow joints, both wrist joints, both hip joints, both ankle joints and right and left carpals, metacarpals, hand phalanges, tarsals, metatarsals and foot phalanges, Periostitis on eleven ribs and both tibiae, Porotic hyperostosis, Cribra orbitalia, Fracture of right nasal bone, right humerus, left first and second metacarpals, two left ribs and on left femur, Possible benign ecchondroma. Dental caries, Dental calculus, Periapical cavity, Periodontal disease

R								Dentition								L
PC													PC	PC		
		P	P	P	P	P	P	P	P	P	P	P	P	P	P	
		cc	cc	cc	cc	cc	cc	cc	cc	cc	cc	cc	cc	cc	cc	
		C							C			R				
X	/	X	5	4	3	2	1	1	2	3	4	5	6	7	8	
8	7	X	5	4	3	2	X	1	2	3	4	5	X	7	8	
C												R				
cc	cc		cc	cc	cc	cc		cc	cc	cc	cc	cc		cc	cc	
P	P		P	P	P	P		P	P	P	P	P		P	P	
			PC									PC				

Skeleton Number: 3072 **Grave group:** 3450
Completeness: 76–100% **Preservation:** Poor
Age: 40+ yr **Sex:** Female **Stature:** 157 cm
Summary of pathological conditions: Spinal degenerative joint disease, Degenerative joint disease of right and left temporo-mandibular joints, Periostitis on both femora, tibiae and fibulae, Maxillary sinusitis, Cribra orbitalia, Congenital malformation of first segment of sacrum. Periapical cavity

R								Dentition								L
X	X	X	X	X	X	X	X	X	X	X	X	X	X	-	-	
-	X	X	X	X	X	/	/	/	/	/	X	X	X	X	X	
										PC	PC					

Appendix Three

Skeleton Number: 3083   **Grave group:** 3380
Completeness: 51–75%   **Preservation:** Good
Age: 50+ yr   **Sex:** Male   **Stature:** 170 cm
Summary of pathological conditions: Spinal degenerative joint disease, Schmorl's nodes, Degenerative joint disease of right shoulder joint, both hip joints, both ankle joints, left hand phalax, right and left tarsals, Periostitis on right and left tibia, Fracture of left hand proximal phalanx and left fibula, Possible echondroma on right first metacarpal

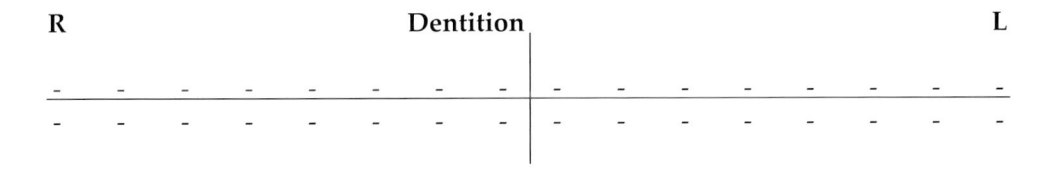

R								Dentition								L
-	-	-	-	-	-	-	-		-	-	-	-	-	-	-	-
-	-	-	-	-	-	-	-		-	-	-	-	-	-	-	-

Skeleton Number: 3086   **Grave group:** 3240
Completeness: 51–75%   **Preservation:** Poor
Age: 40+ yr   **Sex:** Male   **Stature:** 174 cm
Summary of pathological conditions: Healed Type 2 cribra orbitalia of L and R orbits; healed porotic hyperostosis frontal and parietal bones: possible scury; ankylosis of intermeidaite and distal phalanges of R foot possibly secondary to trauma; amputation of L femoral shaft with associated periostitis; ancillary facets on superio-lateral part of greater tubercle and suerio-lateral aspect of lesser tubercle of R and L humeri- possible crutch use

R								Dentition								L
P	P		P	P	P	P	P		P	P	P	P	P	P	P	P
cc	cc		cc	cc	cc	cc	cc		cc	cc	cc	cc	cc	cc	cc	cc
C	C															
8	7	X	5	4	3	2	1		1	2	3	4	5	6	7	8
8	7	6	5	4	3	2	1		1	2	3	4	5	6	7	8
cc	cc	cc	cc	cc	cc	cc	cc		cc	cc	cc	cc	cc	cc	cc	cc
P	P	P	P	P	P	P	P		P	P	P	P	P	P	P	P

Skeleton Number: 3098   **Grave group:** 3570
Completeness: 76–100%   **Preservation:** Excellent
Age: 45+ yr   **Sex:** Male   **Stature:** 174 cm
Summary of pathological conditions: Spinal tuberculosis, Degenerative joint disease of the sternoclavicular and acromioclavicular joints, Periostitis of left and right tibia, Porotic hyperostosis, Cribra orbitalia, Fracture of T1 vertebra and left nasal bone. Enamel hypoplasia, Dental caries, Dental calculus, Periodontal disease. Os acromiale

R								Dentition								L
P	P	P	P	P	P	P	P		P	P	P	P	P	P	P	
cc	cc	cc	cc	cc	cc	cc	cc		cc	cc	cc	cc	cc	cc	cc	
				H												
C	C	C		C												C
8	7	6	5	4	3	2	1	X	2	3	4	5	6	7	8	
X	X	X	5	4	3	2	1		1	2	3	4	5	X	7	X
				C											C	
			cc	cc	cc	cc	cc		cc	cc	cc	cc	cc		cc	
			P	P	P	P	P		P	P	P	P	P		P	

Skeleton Number: 3099   **Grave group:** 3570
Completeness: 76–100%   **Preservation:** Good
Age: 35–45 yr   **Sex:** Male   **Stature:** 166 cm
Summary of pathological conditions: Spinal degenerative joint disease, Schmorl's nodes, Degenerative joint disease on tarsals, right first metacarpal and right first metatarsal, Possible Tuberculosis, Possible Osteitis on left fibula, Fracture of right first metacarpal, Spina bifida, Sacralisation. Dental calculus, Enamel hypoplasia and Periodontal disease

R								Dentition							L
P	P	P	P	P	P	P	P	P	P	P	P	P	P	P	P
cc	cc	cc	cc	cc	cc	cc	cc	cc	cc	cc	cc	cc	cc	cc	cc
H	H	H		H						H		H	H	H	H
8	7	6	5	4	3	2	1	1	2	3	4	5	6	7	8
8	7	6	5	4	3	2	1	1	2	3	4	5	6	7	8
cc	cc	cc	cc	cc	cc	cc	cc	cc	cc	cc	cc	cc	cc	cc	cc
P	P	P	P	P	P	P	P	P	P	P	P	P	P	P	P

Skeleton Number: 3101   **Grave group:** 3380
Completeness: 76–100%   **Preservation:** Good
Age: 35–40 yr   **Sex:** Male   **Stature:** 166 cm
Summary of pathological conditions: Spinal degenerative joint disease, Schmorl's nodes, Degenerative joint disease of right and left shoulder joints, both sternoclavicular joints, both sacro-iliac joints, right and left hand phalanges, Periostitis on right and left tibia and on five ribs, Porotic hyperostosis, Fracture of left scapula and right hand intermediate phalanx, Benign neoplasm on lacrimal bones. Dental caries, Periodontal disease

R								Dentition							L
/	-	-	-	-	-	-	X	/	/	/	/	X	/	X	X	X
/	X	X	5	4	3	2	X	X	2	/	4	X	X	X	X
			cc	cc	cc	cc			cc		cc				
			P	P	P	P			P		P				

Skeleton Number: 3102   **Grave group:** 3480
Completeness: 51–75%   **Preservation:** Good
Age: 40–45 yr   **Sex:** Male?   **Stature:** 163 cm
Summary of pathological conditions: Spinal degenerative joint disease, Degenerative joint disease of right shoulder joint, Periostitis on right and left humeri, on four ribs, right tibia and right fibula possibly reflecting mild treponemal infection

R								Dentition							L
-	-	-	-	-	-	-	-	-	-	-	-	-	-	-	-
8	/	X	5	4	3	2	1	1	2	3	4	5	6	7	8
					C	C	R	C					C	C	
					H					H					
cc		cc	cc	cc	cc	cc	cc	cc	cc	cc	cc	cc	cc	cc	cc
P		P	P	P	P	P	P	P	P	P	P	P	P	P	P

100

Appendix Three

Skeleton Number: 3103   **Grave group:** 3480
Completeness: 76–100%   **Preservation:** Good
Age: 50+ yr   **Sex:** Male   **Stature:** 172 cm
Summary of pathological conditions: Spinal degenerative joint disease, Scoliosis, Degenerative joint disease of right and left shoulder joints, left sternoclavicular joint, both wrist joints, both hip and knee joints, and of right and left metacarpals, hand phalanges, tarsals and metatarsals, Periostitis on left tibia, Fracture of five ribs, both maxillae, both nasal bones, right zygomatic and left clavicle, Rickets

R								Dentition								L
X	X	X	X	X	X	X	X	X	X	X	X	X	X	X	X
X	X	X	X	X	X	X	X	X	X	X	X	X	X	X	X

Skeleton Number: 3105   **Grave group:** 3450
Completeness: 76–100%   **Preservation:** Good
Age: 45+ yr   **Sex:** Male   **Stature:** 172 cm
Summary of pathological conditions: Spinal degenerative joint disease, Schmorl's nodes, Degenerative joint disease of right and left temporo-mandibular joints, both shoulder joints, right sternoclavicular joint, both elbow joints, both wrist joints, both hip joints, both knee joints, both ankle joints, right trapezium, right and left metacarpals, right and left metatarsals, Periostitis on right and left tibia and on left femur, Fracture of both nasal bones and on right tibia. Porotic hyperostosis, Cribra orbitalia. Enamel hypoplasia, Dental caries, Dental calculus, Periodontal disease, Periapical cavity

R								Dentition								L
		PC		PC	PC	PC			PC		PC				
	P	P	P	P	P			P	P	P		P	P		
	cc											cc	cc		
		R	R		C				R						
X	7	6	5	4	3	/	/	1	2	3	X	5	6	X	X
X	X	X	5	4	3	2	1	1	2	3	4	5	X	X	X
					H					H					
		cc	cc	cc	cc	cc	cc	cc	cc	cc					
		P	P	P	P	P	P	P	P	P	P				

Skeleton Number: 3106   **Grave group:** 3450
Completeness: 76–100%   **Preservation:** Good
Age: 40+ yr   **Sex:** Male   **Stature:** 163 cm
Summary of pathological conditions: Spinal degenerative joint disease, Schmorl's nodes, Degenerative joint disease of right shoulder joint, both hip joints, both knee joints, and of right metacarpal, right and left tarsals, metatarsals and foot phalanges, Periostitis on right tibia and fibula, Porotic hyperostosis, Cribra orbitalia. Enamel hypoplasia, Dental caries, Dental calculus, Periapical cavity, Periodontal disease. Evidence of craniotomy

R								Dentition								L
	PC				PC					PC					
	P		P					P	P		P				
	cc		cc					cc	cc		cc				
	C														
X	/	6	/	/	3	/	/	X	2	3	/	/	6	X	NP
8	X	6	5	4	3	2	X	X	2	3	4	5	X	7	X
	C									H					
cc	cc	cc	cc	cc	cc		cc	cc	cc	cc		cc			
P	P	P	P	P	P		P	P	P	P		P			

Skeleton Number: 3107   **Grave group:** 3450
Completeness: 76–100%   **Preservation:** Good
Age: 40+ yr   **Sex:** Male   **Stature:** 166 cm
Summary of pathological conditions: Spinal degenerative joint disease, Degenerative joint disease of right and left temporo-mandibular joints, both shoulder joints, left wrist, right and left carpals and metacarpals, left and right first metatarsal, Porotic hyperostosis, Cribra orbitalia, Fracture of both nasal bones, two ribs, right third metacarpal and two thoracic vertebrae, Button osteoma on frontal bone, Osteochondritis dissecans on first left metatarsal. Enamel hypoplasia, Dental caries, Dental calculus, Periapical cavity, Periodontal disease

R								Dentition							L
							PC	PC							
						P	P	P	P	P					
						cc	cc	cc	cc	cc					
						C	C		C						
X	/	X	/	/	3	/	1	/	2	3	4	X	X	X	X
X	X	X	X	4	3	2	/	/	/	/	X	X	X	X	X
				C	H										
				cc	cc	cc									
				P	P	P									
				PC											

Skeleton Number: 3108   **Grave group:** 3480
Completeness: 76–100%   **Preservation:** Good
Age: 30–40 yr   **Sex:** Male   **Stature:** 174 cm
Summary of pathological conditions: Spinal degenerative joint disease, Schmorl's nodes, Degenerative joint disease of right and left sternoclavicular joints, Periostitis on 11 ribs, both humeri, both radii and ulnae, right and left metacarpals, both femora, both tibiae, both fibulae, left calcaneous and right and left metatarsals and left fibula and right tibia, Porotic hyperostosis, Spondylolysis of L5 vertebra. Enamel hypoplasia, Dental caries, Dental calculus, Periodontal disease

R								Dentition							L
P	P	P	P	P	P	P	P	P	P	P	P	P	P	P	P
cc	cc	cc	cc	cc	cc	cc	cc	cc	cc	cc	cc	cc	cc	cc	cc
					H		H	H		H					C
8	7	6	5	4	3	2	1	1	2	3	4	5	6	7	8
/	7	6	5	4	3	2	1	1	2	3	4	5	6	7	8
	C													C	C
cc	cc	cc	cc	cc	cc	cc	cc	cc	cc	cc	cc	cc	cc	cc	cc
P	P	P	P	P	P	P	P	P	P	P	P	P	P	P	P

Skeleton Number: 3115   **Grave group:** 3490
Completeness: 51–75%   **Preservation:** Poor
Age: 60+ yr   **Sex:** Male   **Stature:** 173 cm
Summary of pathological conditions: Spinal Degenerative Joint Disease, Schmorl's nodes, Degenerative Joint Disease on left temporo-mandibular joint, right ulna and radius, Periostitis on five right ribs and distal right and left humeri, Fracture of second right metacarpal and T12. Periapical cavity, Periodontal disease

R								Dentition							L
X	X	X	X	/	/	X	X	X	X	X	X	X	X	X	X
X	X	X	X	X	/	/	/	X	X	/	X	5	X	7	X
												P		P	
								PC							

Appendix Three

Skeleton Number: 3119   **Grave group:** 3550
Completeness: 76–100%   **Preservation:** Good
Age: 40+ yr   **Sex:** Male   **Stature:** 174 cm
Summary of pathological conditions: Spinal degenerative joint disease, Schmorl's nodes, Degenerative joint disease on right and left acromioclavicular and sternoclavicular joints, right and left hip joints, left ulna, phalanges of right and left metatarsal, Periostitis on right and left femora, roght and tibiae, ribs and right fibula, Porotic hyperostosis, Cribra orbitalia. Enamel hypoplasia, Dental caries, Dental calculus, Periodontal disease. Evidence of craniotomy

R							Dentition							L
		P	P	P	P		P	P	P	P	P	P	P	
		cc	cc	cc	cc		cc	cc	cc	cc	cc	cc	cc	
					H		H	H		H				
					C									
X	X	6	5	4	3	/	1	1	2	3	4	5	6	X	X
/	X	6	5	4	3	2	1	1	2	3	4	5	6	7	X
													C	C	
		cc	cc	cc	cc	cc	cc	cc	cc	cc	cc	cc	cc	cc	
		P	P	P	P	P	P	P	P	P	P	P	P	P	

Skeleton Number: 3124   **Grave group:** 3560
Completeness: 0–25%   **Preservation:** Good
Age: 30–50 yr   **Sex:** Male?   **Stature:** 163 cm (Right humerus)
Summary of pathological conditions: Spinal Degenerative Joint Disease, Schmorl's nodes, Degenerative joint disease on right and left temporo-mandibular joints, Fracture of right and left nasal bones

R								Dentition							L
NP	X	/	X	X	/	X	X	X	X	X	/	X	X	X	NP
-	-	-	-	-	-	-	-	-	-	-	-	-	-	-	-

Skeleton Number: 3132   **Grave group:** 3410
Completeness: 76–100%   **Preservation:** Poor
Age: 12-14 yr   **Sex:** Unknown   **Stature:** -
Summary of pathological conditions: Porotic hyperostosis, Spinal tuberculosis. Enamel hypoplasia, Dental caries

R								Dentition							L
		C				H		H					C		
U	7	6	5	4	3	2	1	1	2	3	4	5	6	7	U
U	7	6	5	4	3	2	1	1	2	3	4	5	6	7	-
						H			H						

Skeleton Number: 3139   **Grave group:** 3480
Completeness: 51–75%   **Preservation:** Good
Age: 40–45 yr   **Sex:** Male   **Stature:** 165 cm (Left ulna)
Summary of pathological conditions: Spinal degenerative joint disease, Schmorl's nodes, Degenerative joint disease of right hip joint, both knee joints and of right and left tarsals, Fracture of left navicular, Osteochondritis dissecans right talus

R								Dentition							L
-	-	-	-	-	-	-	-	-	-	-	-	-	-	-	-
-	-	-	-	-	-	-	-	-	-	-	-	-	-	-	-

Skeleton Number: 3143   **Grave group:** 3580
Completeness: 76–100%   **Preservation:** Good
Age: 40+ yr   **Sex:** Male?   **Stature:** 168 cm (Left)
Summary of pathological conditions: Spinal degenerative joint disease, Schmorl's nodes, Degenerative joint disease of left shoulder joint, right scaphoid and both knees, Periostitis on twelve ribs and both tibiae, Porotic hyperostosis, Fracture of both nasal bones, left zygoma, two ribs, on L3 vertebra, right fifth metatarsal, left navicular and left metatarsals, Avulsion fracture on tibial tuberosity of right tibia. Enamel hypoplasia, Dental caries, Dental calculus, Periodontal disease

R								Dentition							L
P	P	P	P		P	P	P	P	P		P	P	P	P
cc	cc		cc				cc	cc	cc		cc	cc	cc	cc
		R			H	H		H				C		
8	7	6	5	NP	3	2	1	X	2	3	NP	5	6	7	8
X	/	X	5	4	3	2	1	1	2	3	4	5	X	X	X
					C										
					H										
			cc	cc	cc	cc	cc	cc	cc	cc	cc	cc			
			P	P	P	P	P	P	P	P	P	P			

Skeleton Number: 3144   **Grave group:** 3410
Completeness: 76–100%   **Preservation:** Good
Age: 50+ yr   **Sex:** Male   **Stature:** 168 cm
Summary of pathological conditions: Spinal degenerative joint disease, Schmorl's nodes, Degenerative joint disease of right and left temporo-mandibular joints, both acromio-clavicular joints, right elbow joint, both hip joints and right metatarsals and left first metatarsal, Periostitis on left fibula, Maxillary sinusitis, Possible healed scurvy, Fracture of nasal bones, left maxilla, T12 vertebra, right ulna and on eight ribs

R								Dentition							L
X	X	X	X	X	X	X	X	X	X	X	X	X	X	X	X
X	X	X	X	X	X	X	X	X	X	X	X	X	X	X	X

Skeleton Number: 3148   **Grave group:** 3590
Completeness: 76–100%   **Preservation:** Good
Age: 50+ yr   **Sex:** Male   **Stature:** 177 cm
Summary of pathological conditions: Spinal degenerative joint disease, Schmorl's nodes, Degenerative joint disease on right foot, Periostitis on right and left fibula and right tibia, Osteomyelitis on right tibia, Fracture of right tibia, right and left fibula and left rib. Dental calculus, Periodontal disease

R								Dentition							L
		P	P		P	P		P							
		cc	cc		cc	cc		cc							
					R										R
NP?	X	6	5	X	3	2	/	/	2	X	X	X	X	X	NP?
8	X	X	5	4	3	X	X	X	X	X	4	5	X	X	8
															R
		cc	cc	cc						cc	cc				
P		P	P	P						P	P				P

Skeleton Number: 3151 **Grave group:** 3590
Completeness: 76–100% **Preservation:** Excellent
Age: 35–45 yr **Sex:** Male **Stature:** 168 cm
Summary of pathological conditions: Spinal joint disease, Degenerative joint disease on left elbow joint, right and left hand phalanges, right knee joint, right and left first metatarsals, Fracture of left maxilla, five ribs, right third metacarpal, left radius and ulna, right clavicle, treponemal disease (? yaws). Enamel hypoplasia, Dental calculus, Periodontal disease

	R								Dentition							L	
	P	P	P	P		P	P	P	P	P	P	P	P	P		
	cc	cc								cc	cc	cc	cc			
	R									H		H				
	8	7	6	5	/	3	2	1	/	2	3	4	5	6	7	NP
NP	7	6	5	4	3	2	1	1	2	3	4	5	6	7	NP
					H	H	H	H	H	H	H	H	H	H	H	
	cc	cc	cc	cc	cc	cc	cc	cc	cc	cc	cc	cc	cc		
	P	P	P	P	P	P	P	P	P	P	P	P	P		

Skeleton Number: 3152 **Grave group:** 3410
Completeness: 76–100% **Preservation:** Good
Age: 40+ yr **Sex:** Male **Stature:** 167 cm
Summary of pathological conditions: Spinal degenerative joint disease, Schmorl's nodes, Degenerative joint disease of right and left acromio-clavicular joints, right shoulder joint, both sacro-iliac joints and right first metatarsal, Periostitis on both maxillae, three ribs and both tibiae, Possible scurvy, Cribra orbitalia, Fracture of both nasal bones and of T8 vertebra. Spondylolysis. Dental caries, Dental calculus, Periapical cavity, Periodontal disease

	R								Dentition								L
	P		P	P	P	P	P	P	P	P	P	P	P	P	P	P
	cc		cc	cc	cc	cc	cc		cc	cc	cc	cc	cc	cc	cc
												C	C		
	8	X	6	5	4	3	2	1	1	2	3	4	5	6	7	8
	8	7	6	5	4	3	2	1	1	2	3	4	5	6	7	8
																C
	cc	cc	cc	cc	cc	cc	cc	cc	cc	cc	cc	cc	cc	cc	cc	cc
	P	P	P	P	P	P	P	P	P	P	P	P	P	P	P	P

Skeleton Number: 3159 **Grave group:** 3870
Completeness: 51–75% **Preservation:** Good
Age: 45+ yr **Sex:** Male **Stature:** 166 cm
Summary of pathological conditions: Spinal degenerative joint disease, Degenerative joint disease of right and left temporo-mandibular joints and both hip and knee joints, Fracture of right and left nasal bones, left zygomatic and right scapula. Dental caries, Dental calculus, Periapical cavity, Periodontal disease. Evidence of craniotomy.

	R								Dentition								L
					PC											
						P	P	P	P	P	P	P				P
						cc	cc	cc	cc	cc	cc	cc	cc		cc
						H				H	H				
						C	C		C	R	C				
	X	X	X	X	/	3	2	1	1	2	3	4	5	X	X	8
	/	X	6	5	4	3	2	1	1	2	3	4	X	X	X	8
		R	R	C												C
				H	H				H	H					
					cc	cc	cc	cc	cc	cc	cc	cc				cc
			P	P	P	P	P	P	P	P	P	P				P

Skeleton Number: 3162   **Grave group:** 3380
Completeness: 76–100%   **Preservation:** Poor
Age: 50+ yr   **Sex:** Male   **Stature:** 165 cm
Summary of pathological conditions: Spinal degenerative joint disease, Schmorl's nodes, Degenerative joint disease of right and left shoulder joints, both sternoclavicular joints, left elbow joint, both wrist joints, left triquetral, right metacarpal, right sacro-iliac joint, left hip joint, left knee joint, Periostitis on eleven ribs, Fracture of one rib. Dental caries, Periodontal disease

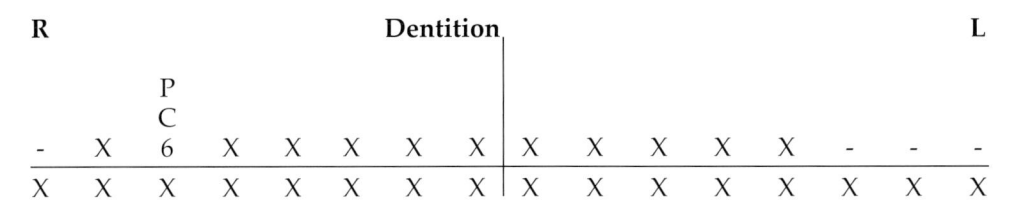

R								Dentition							L
		P													
		C													
-	X	6	X	X	X	X	X	X	X	X	X	X	-	-	-
X	X	X	X	X	X	X	X	X	X	X	X	X	X	X	X

Skeleton Number: 3164   **Grave group:** 3480
Completeness: 76–100%   **Preservation:** Good
Age: 30–40 yr   **Sex:** Male   **Stature:** 170 cm
Summary of pathological conditions: Spinal degenerative joint disease, Degenerative joint disease of left hip, knee and ankle joints, and left tarsals, Periostitis on left zygomatic and on 15 ribs, Porotic hyperostosis, Cribra orbitalia, Fracture of left tibia and fibula. Dental calculus

R								Dentition							L
	cc										cc	cc	cc	cc	
8	7	X	/	4	3	/	/	1	2	3	4	5	6	7	8
8	7	6	5	4	3	2	1	1	2	3	4	5	6	7	X
cc	cc	cc	cc	cc	cc	cc	cc	cc	cc	cc	cc	cc	cc	cc	

Skeleton Number: 3168   **Grave group:** 4050
Completeness: 76–100%   **Preservation:** Excellent
Age: 50+ yr   **Sex:** Male   **Stature:** 168 cm
Summary of pathological conditions: Spinal degenerative joint disease, Degenerative joint disease of left shoulder joint, right hip joint, and right and left first metatarsal, Periostitis on both fibulae, Fracture of left tibia and left third metacarpal, Abnormal bowing of left femur

R								Dentition							L
-	-	-	-	-	X	/	X	X	/	-	-	-	-	-	-
X	X	X	X	4	3	2	1	/	2	3	/	/	X	X	X

Skeleton Number: 3174   **Grave group:** 3610
Completeness: 76-100%   **Preservation:** Excellent
Age: 50+ yr   **Sex:** Female   **Stature:** 159 cm
Summary of pathological conditions: Spinal Degenerative joint disease, Schmorl's nodes, Degenerative joint disease on right and left acromioclavicular joint, Periostitis on left ribs, both tibiae and both fibula, lytic lesions on right and left first metatarsal. Enamel hypoplasia, Dental calculus, Periapical cavity, Periodontal disease

R								Dentition							L
P		P	P	P	P	P	P	P	P	P	P			P	P
cc		cc	cc	cc	cc	cc	cc	cc	cc	cc			cc	cc	
8	X	6	5	4	3	2	1	1	2	3	4	X	X	7	8
8	X	X	5	4	3	2	1	1	2	3	4	X	X	7	8
				R							H				
cc		cc		cc	cc	cc	cc	cc	cc	cc			cc	cc	
P		P		P	P	P	P	P	P	P			P	P	
	PC														

Appendix Three

Skeleton Number: 3176   **Grave group:** 3590
Completeness: 76–100%   **Preservation:** Good
Age: 45–55 yr   **Sex:** Male   **Stature:** 174 cm
Summary of pathological conditions: Spinal degenerative joint disease, Schmorl's nodes, Degenerative joint disease on both hip and knee joints, Porotic hyperostosis, Periostitis on both tibiae and right fibula, Fracture of nasal bones and foot proximal phalanx, Spina bifida, Sacralisation,. Dental calculus, Periodontal disease

```
         R                    Dentition                          L
                                  |              P       P   P
                                  |              cc      cc  cc
  -  X  X  X  X  X  X  X | X  X  /  /  5   X   7   8
  X  X  X  X  X  /  X  X | X  X  3  X  X   X   X   X
                                  |     P
```

Skeleton Number: 3177   **Grave group:** 4050
Completeness: 51–75%   **Preservation:** Good
Age: 45–55 yr   **Sex:** Male   **Stature:** 174 cm
Summary of pathological conditions: Spinal degenerative joint disease, Degenerative joint disease of right first metacarpal and left hand phalanges, Periostitis on one rib, Fracture of rib, left distal hand phalanx, right tibia and right fibula, Soft tissue trauma to right femur, Osteochondritis dissecans

```
         R                    Dentition                          L
                                  |
  -  -  -  -  -  -  -  -  | -  -  -  -  -  -  -  -
  -  -  -  -  -  -  -  -  | -  -  -  -  -  -  -  -
```

Skeleton Number: 3182   **Grave group:** 3630
Completeness: 76–100%   **Preservation:** Good
Age: 50+ yr   **Sex:** Male   **Stature:** 159 cm
Summary of pathological conditions: Spinal degenerative joint disease, Schmorl's nodes, DISH, Ankylosis of sacroiliac joint, Degenerative joint disease of right and left shoulder joints, both sternoclavicular joints, both elbow joints, both knee joints, and of right and left carpals, metacarpals and phalanges, Porotic hyperostosis. Dental calculus, Periodontal disease

```
         R                    Dentition                          L
                                  |      R
  X  X  X  X  X  X  X  X  | X  X  3  X  X  X  X  X
  NP X  6  5  4  X  X  X  | X  X  X  X  X  6  X  NP
        cc cc cc                                cc
        P  P  P                                 P
```

Skeleton Number: 3187   **Grave group:** 3810
Completeness: 26–50%   **Preservation:** Good
Age: 40+ yr   **Sex:** Male   **Stature:** 178 cm
Summary of pathological conditions: Degenerative joint disease of left tibia, Fracture of right tarsals

```
         R                    Dentition                          L
                                  |
  -  -  -  -  -  -  -  -  | -  -  -  -  -  -  -  -
  -  -  -  -  -  -  -  -  | -  -  -  -  -  -  -  -
```

Skeleton Number: 3189 **Grave group:** 3580
Completeness: 51–75% **Preservation:** Poor
Age: 50+ yr   **Sex:** Male   **Stature:** 167 cm
Summary of pathological conditions: Degenerative joint disease of right and left patellae and right first metatarsal, Periostitis on right and left tibia, Porotic hyperostosis, Cribra orbitalia, Fracture of right and left nasal bones, Possible rickets. Periapical cavity

	R							Dentition							L	
									PC							
X	X	X	X	X	X	X	X	X	X	X	X	X	X	X	X	
-	-	-	-	-	-	-	-	-	-	-	-	-	-	-	-	

Skeleton Number: 3191 **Grave group:** 3380
Completeness: 76–100% **Preservation:** Good
Age: 50+ yr   **Sex:** Male   **Stature:** 164 cm
Summary of pathological conditions: Spinal degenerative joint disease, Schmorl's nodes, Degenerative joint disease of right and left shoulder joints, both sternoclavicular joints, both hip joints, left carpals and metacarpals, right hand phalanges, Porotic hyperostosis, Fracture of left hand proximal phalanx, left talus and possibly on T11 vertebra

	R							Dentition							L
-	-	-	-	-	-	-	-	-	-	-	-	-	-	-	-
X	X	X	X	X	X	X	X	X	X	X	X	X	X	X	X

Skeleton Number: 3194 **Grave group:** 4060
Completeness: 76–100% **Preservation:** Excellent
Age: 40+ yr   **Sex:** Male   **Stature:** 166 cm
Summary of pathological conditions: Spinal degenerative joint disease, Schmorl's nodes, Periostitis on both scapulae, both clavicles, right humerus, both *os coxae*, both femora and all ribs present, thus a possible diagnosis being Hypertrophic osteoarthropathy, Porotic hyperostosis, Cribra orbitalia, Fracture of right fibula, Spina bifida. Enamel hypoplasia, Dental caries, Dental calculus, Periodontal disease, Impacted tooth

R Dentition L

```
    cc                      cc  cc      cc          cc
-   7   -   -   -   -   -   -   1   2   -   4   -   -   7   -
8   X   X   X   X   X   X   X   X   X   3   X   X   6   /   X
                                        C
                                        H
cc                                      cc          cc
P                                       P           P
```

Skeleton Number: 3202 **Grave group:** 4060
Completeness: 76–100% **Preservation:** Good
Age: 40+ yr   **Sex:** Male   **Stature:** 163 cm
Summary of pathological conditions: Spinal degenerative joint disease, Schmorl's nodes, Degenerative joint disease of left wrist, both hip joints, both knee joints, right and left carpals, right metacarpal, right and left metatarsals, Porotic hyperostosis, Cribra orbitalia, Fracture of left nasal bone, right foot phalanx, and soft tissue trauma to right femur. Enamel hypoplasia, Dental caries, Dental calculus, Periapical cavity, Periodontal disease

Appendix Three

```
R                           Dentition                               L
                              PC
                              P      P          P
                                                H
NP  X   X   X   X   /   X   1 | 1   X   3   X   X   X   /   NP
─────────────────────────────────────────────────────────────────
NP  7   X   /   4   3   2   1 | 1   2   3   4   5   X   /   NP
    C           R                         C   C   C
                                                  H
    cc          cc  cc  cc    | cc  cc  cc  cc  cc
    P           P   P   P     | P   P   P   P   P
                PC                        PC
```

Skeleton Number: 3208   **Grave group:** 3600
Completeness: 76–100%   **Preservation:** Good
Age: 40–50 yr   **Sex:** Male   **Stature:** 164 cm
Summary of pathological conditions: Spinal degenerative joint disease, Schmorl's nodes, Degenerative joint disease of right and left acromio-clavicular joints, left shoulder joint, right hip joint, both knee joints, left ankle joint, and right metacarpal, Periostitis on both tibiae and both fibulae, Cribra orbitalia, Fracture of left radius, right third metacarpal, L1 vertebra, right fibula, left tibia and left talus. Dental caries, Dental calculus, Periapical cavity, Periodontal disease

```
R                               Dentition                                   L
                                                                    PC
                P   P   P   P                       P   P   P
                    cc  cc  cc                          cc  cc
                R                                               R
X   X   X   5   4   3   2   X   /  |  /   3   4   5   X   -   -
─────────────────────────────────────────────────────────────────────────
8   7   6   5   4   3   2   1   1  |  2   3   4   5   6   7   8
                C   C                       C
cc  cc  cc  cc  cc  cc  cc  cc  cc |  cc  cc  cc  cc  cc  cc  cc
P   P   P   P   P   P   P   P   P  |  P   P   P   P   P   P   P
```

Skeleton Number: 3211   **Grave group:** 3380
Completeness: 76–100%   **Preservation:** Good
Age: 40+ yr   **Sex:** Male   **Stature:** 163 cm
Summary of pathological conditions: Spinal degenerative joint disease, Schmorl's nodes, Degenerative joint disease of right and left shoulder joints, both sternoclavicular joints, both elbow joints, left wrist joint, both hip and knee joints, right ankle joint, and on right metacarpal, right tarsals, metatarsals and phalanges, Periostitis on right and left fibulae, Porotic hyperostosis, Possible rickets, Fracture of right and left nasal bones, three ribs and right proximal foot phalanx. Enamel hypoplasia, Dental calculus, Periapical cavity, Periodontal disease, Impacted tooth

```
R                                   Dentition                                       L
                                                              PC
        P   P                       P   P           P         P   P   P
        cc  cc                      cc  cc          cc            cc  cc
                                                    H             R
NP  7   6   X   X   NP  /   1   | 1   NP  3   X   5   6   7   NP
─────────────────────────────────────────────────────────────────────────────
NP  7   6   5   4   3   2   1   | 1   2   3   4   X   6   7   NP
                                        H   H
    cc  cc  cc  cc  cc  cc  cc  | cc  cc  cc  cc      cc  cc
    P   P   P   P   P   P   P   | P   P   P   P       P   P
```

Skeleton Number: 3212   **Grave group:** 3380
Completeness: 76–100%   **Preservation:** Good
Age: 40+ yr   **Sex:** Male   **Stature:** 172 cm
Summary of pathological conditions: Spinal degenerative joint disease, Schmorl's nodes, Kyphosis, Degenerative joint disease of right and left sternoclavicular joints, left knee joint and right carpal and metacarpal, Periostitis on two ribs, Endocranial lesions, Fracture of right first metacarpal. Enamel hypoplasia, Dental caries, Dental calculus

R							Dentition							L
	cc								cc		cc	cc		
					H				H					
					C							C		
X	7	-	-	-	3	2	1	1	2	3	4	5	6	7	8
8	7	6	5	4	3	2	/	1	2	3	4	5	6	7	8
					H				H					
cc	cc	cc	cc	cc	cc	cc		cc	cc	cc	cc	cc		

Skeleton Number: 3213   **Grave group:** 3600
Completeness: 76–100%   **Preservation:** Excellent
Age: 45–55 yr   **Sex:** Male   **Stature:** 171 cm
Summary of pathological conditions: Spinal degenerative joint disease, Schmorl's nodes, Degenerative joint disease of right and left acromio-clavicular joints, right hip, right knee, right trapezium and right first metacarpal, Osteitis on left tibia, Porotic hyperostosis, Cribra orbitalia, Sacralisation of L5 vertebra. Dental caries, Dental calculus, Periapical cavity, Periodontal disease

R							Dentition							L
							PC							
P	P	P	P	P	P	P		P	P	P	P	P	P	
		cc	cc	cc	cc						cc	cc	cc	
		C												
		R				R								
8	7	6	5	4	3	2	/	1	2	3	4	5	6	X	X
8	7	6	5	4	3	2	/	1	2	3	4	5	/	X	X
	C	R												
		cc		cc	cc	cc	cc	cc	cc	cc	cc	cc		
P	P	P	P	P	P	P		P	P	P	P	P		

Skeleton Number: 3218   **Grave group:** 4090
Completeness: 76–100%   **Preservation:** Good
Age: 50+ yr   **Sex:** Male   **Stature:** 160 cm
Summary of pathological conditions: Spinal degenerative joint disease, Schmorl's nodes, Degenerative joint disease of right and left shoulder joints, both sternoclavicular joints, both hip joints, both knee joints, right trapezium and right first metacarpal, right first metatarsal, Periostitis on left femur, Fracture of T8 and T9 vertebrae, Porotic hyperostosis. Enamel hypoplasia, Dental caries, Dental calculus, Periapical cavity, Periodontal disease. Os acromiale.

R							Dentition							L
									PC					
	P												P	
	cc												cc	
						C	H	H	R	R	R	R		
NP	7	X	X	X	X	2	1	1	2	3	4	5	X	7	-
NP	7	X	5	4	3	2	X	X	/	3	4	5	X	7	NP
					H									
	cc												cc	
	P												P	

Appendix Three

Skeleton Number: 3223 **Grave group:** 3690
Completeness: 51–75% **Preservation:** Poor
Age: 40+ yr **Sex:** Female? **Stature:** 157 cm
Summary of pathological conditions: Degenerative joint disease of hip joint, Fracture of left humerus

R						Dentition							L
-	-	-	-	-	-	-	-	-	-	-	-	-	-
-	-	-	-	4	3	-	-	-	-	3	-	-	-

Skeleton Number: 3229 **Grave group:** 3490
Completeness: 76–100% **Preservation:** Good
Age: 45+ yr **Sex:** Male **Stature:** 169cm (Left tibia)
Summary of pathological conditions: Spinal degenerative joint disease, Schmorl's nodes, Degenerative joint disease on acromio-clavicular joints, Osteomyelitis on right femur, Treponemeal disease (? syphilis, ? yaws), Porotic hyperostosis, Cribra orbitalia, Fracture of right and left femur, Spina bifida, Bifid rib. Enamel hypoplasia, Dental caries, Dental calculus, Periapical cavity, Periodontal disease

R								**Dentition**							L
							PC								
			P	P	P		P	P	P	P	P				
			C							H					
X	X	X	5	4	3	/	1	1	2	3	4	X	X	X	X
NP	/	X	5	4	3	2	1	1	2	3	4	5	X	7	NP
							R					C		C	
		cc	cc	cc	cc		cc	cc	cc	cc	cc		cc		
		P	P	P	P	P	P	P	P	P	P		P		

Skeleton Number: 3241 **Grave group:** 3390
Completeness: 76–100% **Preservation:** Good
Age: 50+ yr **Sex:** Male **Stature:** 166 cm
Summary of pathological conditions: Spinal degenerative joint disease, Schmorl's nodes, Degenerative joint disease of right and left shoulder joints, both sternoclavicular joints, both hip joints, right knee joint, Periostitis on right and left tibiae, nine ribs, Osteomyelitis on right femur, Porotic hyperostosis, Cribra orbitalia, Fracture of right parietal, both nasal bones, right clavicle, right humerus, right and left radius, right pisiform, left first metacarpal, four ribs, right femur, right tibia and both fibulae, Osteoporosis. Dental caries, Dental calculus, Periapical cavity, Periodontal disease

R								**Dentition**							L
										PC					
X	X	X	X	X	/	X	X	X	X	/	X	X	X	X	/
X	X	X	/	4	3	2	/	/	X	3	X	X	X	X	X
				R	R	R				C					
					cc					cc					
				P	P	P				P					
				PC											

Skeleton Number: 3243 **Grave group:** 3800
Completeness: 76–100% **Preservation:** Good
Age: 40+ yr **Sex:** Male **Stature:** 171 cm
Summary of pathological conditions: Spinal degenerative joint disease, Schmorl's nodes, Degenerative joint disease of right and left acromio-clavicular joints, both wrist joints, right metatarsal, Periostitis on eleven ribs, Fracture of right radius

R							Dentition							L
-	-	-	-	-	-	-	-	-	-	-	-	-	-	-
-	-	-	-	-	-	-	-	-	-	-	-	-	-	-

Skeleton Number: 3245 **Grave group:** 3700
Completeness: 51–75% **Preservation:** Poor
Age: 35–45 yr **Sex:** Female **Stature:** -
Summary of pathological conditions: Spinal degenerative joint disease, Degenerative joint disease of right and left sternoclavicular joints and both hip joints. Enamel hypoplasia, Dental caries, Dental calculus, Periapical cavity, Periodontal disease

R								Dentition								L
				PC									PC			
	P			P	P	P	P	P	P	P	P	P		P	P	
	cc			cc	cc	cc	cc	cc	cc	cc	cc	cc		cc	cc	
				H	H	H	H	H	H	H	H					
				R												
NP	7	X	X	4	3	2	1	1	2	3	4	5	X	7	8	
NP	X	X	5	4	3	2	1	1	2	3	4	5	6	X	NP	
												R				
			H	H						H	H					
			cc	cc	cc	cc	cc	cc	cc	cc	cc		cc			
			P	P	P	P	P	P	P	P	P	P	P			

Skeleton Number: 3249 **Grave group:** 3250
Completeness: 51–75% **Preservation:** Good
Age: 16–18 yr **Sex:** Unknown **Stature:** -
  (?Male)
Summary of pathological conditions: Schmorl's nodes. Enamel hypoplasia, Dental caries, Dental calculus

R								Dentition								L
					H	H	H	H	H	H						
PE	7	6	5	4	3	2	1	1	2	3	4	5	6	7	PE	
8	7	6	5	4	3	2	1	1	2	3	4	5	6	7	8	
C				H		H		H		H	H	H			C	C
									cc						cc	

Skeleton Number: 3253 **Grave group:** 3800
Completeness: 76–100% **Preservation:** Good
Age: 50+ yr **Sex:** Male **Stature:** 168 cm
Summary of pathological conditions: Spinal degenerative joint disease with ankylosis, Schmorl's nodes, Degenerative joint disease of right and left shoulder joints, both sternoclavicular joints, both elbow joints, both wrist joints, both hip joints, both knee joints, right and left carpals, metacarpals and hand phalanges, right and left tarsals, Possible scurvy, Fracture of right nasal bone, one rib and left fourth metacarpal

R								Dentition								L
X	X	X	X	X	X	X	X	X	X	X	X	X	-	-	-	
X	X	X	X	X	/	X	X	X	X	/	X	X	X	X	X	

Appendix Three

Skeleton Number: 3255 **Grave group:** 3250
Completeness: 76–100% **Preservation:** Poor
Age: 35–40 yr **Sex:** Male **Stature:** 171 cm
Summary of pathological conditions: Spinal degenerative joint disease, Schmorl's nodes, Degenerative joint disease of left first metacarpal, Trauma on right clavicle, left first metacarpal, left calcaneous, Thickening of skull vault (Paget's condition? Hyperostosis?). Enamel hypoplasia, Dental caries, Dental calculus, Periodontal disease

R						Dentition							L
	P	P	P	P	P		P				P		
	cc	cc	cc	cc							cc		
		H			H								
	C	C											
X	7	6	5	4	3	/	1	X	/	/	/	5	/	/	-
NP	X	X	/	4	3	2	1	1	2	/	4	5	X	X	NP
				C	H						C				
				P	P	P	P	P	P		P	P			

Skeleton Number: 3258 **Grave group:** 4070
Completeness: 51–75% **Preservation:** Excellent
Age: 40+ yr **Sex:** Male **Stature:** 162cm
Summary of pathological conditions: Spinal degenerative joint disease, Schmorl's nodes, Degenerative joint disease of left shoulder joint, both hip joints, both knee joints, right scaphoid, right and left tarsals, Periostitis on eight ribs, Fracture of right scaphoid, two ribs and right fibula

R	Dentition	L
- - - - - - - -	- - - - - - -
- - - - - - - -	- - - - - - -

Skeleton Number: 3261 **Grave group:** 4070
Completeness: 76–100% **Preservation:** Good
Age: 30–40 yr **Sex:** Male **Stature:** 174 cm
Summary of pathological conditions: Spinal degenerative joint disease, Schmorl's nodes, Periostitis on ten ribs, Porotic hyperostosis, Cribra orbitalia, Fracture of left hamate, Amputation of left femur, Osteoporosis. Enamel hypoplasia, Dental caries, Dental calculus, Periapical cavity, Periodontal disease

R								Dentition							L
				PC			PC								
cc	cc	cc	cc	cc	cc	cc		cc	cc	cc	cc	cc	cc	cc	cc
		C	C	R			R								
8	7	6	5	4	3	2	1	1	2	3	4	5	6	7	8
8	7	6	5	4	3	2	1	1	2	3	4	5	6	7	8
C				H				H							
cc	cc	cc	cc	cc	cc	cc	cc	cc	cc	cc	cc	cc	cc	cc	cc

Skeleton Number: 3265 **Grave group:** 4100
Completeness: 76–100% **Preservation:** Good
Age: 50+ yr **Sex:** Male **Stature:** 159 cm
Summary of pathological conditions: Spinal degenerative joint disease, Schmorl's nodes, Degenerative joint disease on right and left temporo-mandibular joints, both shoulder joints, both elbow joints, both wrist joints, both hip and knee joints, right and left carpals, metacarpals, hand phalanges, tarsals and metatarsals, Rheumatoid arthritis, Cribra Orbitalia, Porotic hyperostosis. Enamel hypoplasia, Dental calculus, Periodontal disease

R						Dentition								L
			P cc	P cc H						P cc				
-	X	X	5	4	X	X	X	X	X	X	4	/	X	-	-
X	X	X	5	4	3 H	/	1	X	X	X	4	5	X	X	X
			cc P	cc P	cc P		cc P				cc P	cc P			

Skeleton Number: 3268 **Grave group:** 4100
Completeness: 76–100% **Preservation:** Excellent
Age: 35–45 yr **Sex:** Male? **Stature:** 168 cm
Summary of pathological conditions: Spinal degenerative joint disease, Schmorl's nodes, Degenerative joint disease on right acromioclavicular and sternoclavicular joints, both elbow joints, left hip joint, Periostitis on six ribs, Porotic hyperostosis, Cribra orbitalia, Fracture of left radius and left fifth metacarpal. Enamel hypoplasia, Dental caries, Dental calculus, Periapical cavity, Periodontal disease

R						Dentition								L
											PC P	PC P			
				P cc			P cc	P cc H C	P cc H C	P	P R				
X	X	/	X	4	/	X	X	1	2	3	4	5	/	-	-
8	X	X	5	/	3 C H	/	/	/	/	3	4	/	6	7	8
									H						
cc P			cc P		cc P			cc P	cc P			cc P	cc P	cc P	

Skeleton Number: 3269 **Grave group:** 3390
Completeness: 76–100% **Preservation:** Excellent
Age: 50+ yr **Sex:** Male **Stature:** 162 cm
Summary of pathological conditions: Spinal degenerative joint disease, Schmorl's nodes, Degenerative joint disease of right and left temporo-mandibular joints, both shoulder joints, both sternoclavicular joints, both elbow joint, both wrist joints, right and left carpals, Fracture of right parietal, left cuboid and left fifth metatarsal, Possible benign neoplasm on left fifth metatarsal. Enamel hypoplasia, Dental caries, Dental calculus, Periodontal disease

R						Dentition								L
X	/	X	X	X	X	X	X	X	X	X	X	X	X	-	-
X	X	X	/	4 C cc P	3 cc P	/	/	1 H cc P	/	3 H cc P	X	X	X	X	X

Skeleton Number: 3272 **Grave group:** 3390
Completeness: 76–100% **Preservation:** Good
Age: 40–45 yr **Sex:** Male **Stature:** 160 cm
Summary of pathological conditions: Spinal degenerative joint disease, Schmorl's nodes, Degenerative joint disease of left acromio-clavicular joint, left elbow joint, both wrist joints, both hip joints, both knee joints, right first metacarpal and hand phalanges, left carpal and first metacarpal, right and left first metatarsals and foot phalanges, Periostitis on left maxilla, eight ribs, both tibiae, Porotic hyperostosis, Cribra orbitalia, Possible scurvy, Fracture of right and left nasal bones, three ribs, left foot phalanges (followed by ankylosis). Dental caries, Dental calculus, Periapical cavity, Periodontal disease

R							Dentition							L	
			PC	PC											
			P	P								P			
X	X	X	5	4	X	X	X	X	X	X	X	5	X	X	X
X	X	X	X	X	3	2	/	1	2	3	4	5	X	X	X
						C					C	C			
						cc		cc	cc	cc	cc				
					P	P		P	P	P	P	P			
							PC								

Skeleton Number: 3274 **Grave group:** 4100
Completeness: 76–100% **Preservation:** Good
Age: 30–40 yr **Sex:** Male? **Stature:** 154 cm
Summary of pathological conditions: Spinal degenerative joint disease, Schmorl's nodes, Periostitis on ribs, Maxillary sinusitis, Porotic hyperostosis, Cribra orbitalia, Fracture of left patella, Spina bifida, Enamel hypoplasia, Dental caries, Dental calculus, Periodontal disease

R							Dentition							L	
P	P		P	P	P		P	P					P	P	
	cc		cc	cc				cc					cc		
R															
8	7	-	5	4	3	U	1	1	U	X	X	X	X	7	8
NP	7	6	NP	4	3	2	1	/	2	3	4	NP	6	7	NP
	C	R			H	H	H			H	H		C	C	
	cc			cc	cc	cc	cc		cc	cc	cc		cc	cc	
	P	P		P	P	P	P		P	P	P		P	P	

Skeleton Number: 3276 **Grave group:** 4100
Completeness: 51–75% **Preservation:** Poor
Age: 50+ yr **Sex:** Male **Stature:** 158 cm
Summary of pathological conditions: Spinal degenerative joint disease, Schmorl's nodes, Degenerative joint disease on right and left hip joints, right tibia, Otitis media, Porotic hyperostosis, Cribra orbitalia

R							Dentition							L	
X	X	X	X	X	X	X	X	X	X	X	X	X	X	X	X
X	X	X	X	X	X	X	X	X	X	X	X	X	X	X	X

Skeleton Number: 3385 **Grave group:** 3380
Completeness: 51–75% **Preservation:** Good
Age: 40+ yr **Sex:** Male **Stature:** 163 cm
Summary of pathological conditions: Degenerative joint disease of left third metacarpal, Porotic hyperostosis

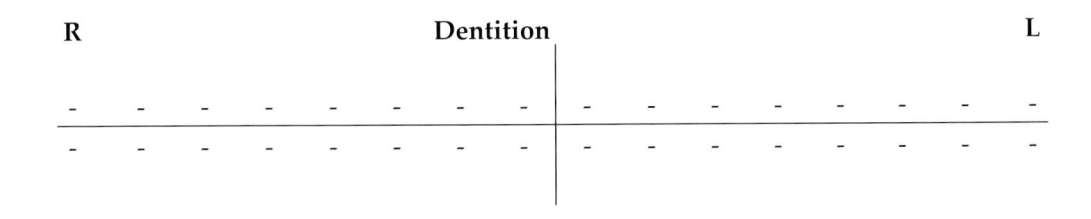

R							Dentition							L	
-	-	-	-	-	-	-	-	-	-	-	-	-	-	-	-
-	-	-	-	-	-	-	-	-	-	-	-	-	-	-	-

Skeleton Number: 3623   **Grave group:** 3620
Completeness: 26–50%   **Preservation:** Good
Age: 50+ yr   **Sex:** Male   **Stature:** -
Summary of pathological conditions: Spinal degenerative joint disease, Schmorl's nodes, Degenerative joint disease of right and left shoulder joints, both sternoclavicular joints, Periostitis on seven ribs, Fracture of left nasal bone and three ribs. Dental calculus, Periapical cavity, Periodontal disease.

	R						Dentition						L		
					PC										
		P	P		P										
		cc													
					R										
NP	7	6	X	X	3	/	X	/	/	X	X	X	-	-	-
X	X	X	5	4	3	/	/	/	/	3	/	/	X	X	X
		cc	cc	cc				cc							
		P	P	P				P							

Skeleton Number: 3628   **Grave group:** 3620
Completeness: 26–50%   **Preservation:** Good
Age: 40+ yr   **Sex:** Male   **Stature:** 168 cm (Right humerus)
Summary of pathological conditions: Spinal degenerative joint disease, Schmorl's nodes, Degenerative joint disease of right shoulder joint, both sternoclavicular joints, Periostitis on eight ribs, Cribra orbitalia, Subluxation of right shoulder, Possible fracture of right clavicle. Enamel hypoplasia, Dental caries, Dental calculus, Periapical cavity, Periodontal disease

	R							Dentition						L	
		PC													
	P	P	P	P	P	P			P	P	P	P			
												cc			
		R			H				H						
NP	7	6	5	4	3	2	/	/	/	3	4	5	X	7	NP
NP	7	6	X	4	3	2	1	1	2	3	4	X	6	7	NP
	C														
	cc	cc		cc	cc	cc	cc	cc	cc	cc	cc				
	P	P		P	P	P	P	P	P	P	P		P	P	

Skeleton Number: 3632   **Grave group:** 3620
Completeness: 26–50%   **Preservation:** Good
Age: 40+ yr   **Sex:** Male   **Stature:** 169 cm (Left humerus)
Summary of pathological conditions: Spinal degenerative joint disease, Schmorl's nodes, Degenerative joint disease of left temporo-mandibular joint, both shoulder joints, both sternoclavicular joints, both elbow joints. Enamel hypoplasia, Dental calculus, Periodontal disease.

```
R                      Dentition                              L

        P           P  P  P   P  P  P
                    H  H  H   H  H  H
8   X  X  /  /      3  2  1   1  2  3   X  /  X  /  /
─────────────────────────────────────────────────────────
8   7  X  5  4      3  2  /   1  2  3   /  /  X  7  /
                    H  H      H  H  H
                    cc        cc cc
P   P     P  P  P   P         P  P  P            P
```

Skeleton Number: 6003   **Grave group:** 6020
Completeness: 76–100%   **Preservation:** Poor
Age: 40–50 yr   **Sex:** Male   **Stature:** 156 cm
Summary of pathological conditions: Degenerative joint disease of left knee, Periostitis on right and left tibia, Cribra orbitalia, Fracture of right parietal and on left tibia and fibula

```
R                      Dentition                              L

-   X  X  X  X  X  X  X   X  X  X  X  X   -  -  -
─────────────────────────────────────────────────────
X   X  X  X  X  X  X  X   X  X  X  X  X  X  X  X
```

Skeleton Number: 6013   **Grave group:** 6070
Completeness: 51–75%   **Preservation:** Poor
Age: 40–50 yr   **Sex:** Male   **Stature:** 167 cm
Summary of pathological conditions: Spinal degenerative joint disease, Schmorl's nodes, Kyphosis, Porotic hyperostosis, Fracture of vertebrae and one rib, Osteoporosis. Dental caries, Dental calculus, Periodontal disease

```
R                      Dentition                              L

                              cc  cc       cc  cc
                              C
-   -  -  -  -  -  -  -   -  -  3  4   -  6  7  -
─────────────────────────────────────────────────────
8   /  6  5  4  3  /  1   1  2  3  4   X  X  X  X
C      C     B  C
    cc                    cc cc cc
P      P  P  P  P         P  P  P  P
```

Skeleton Number: 6014   **Grave group:** 6020
Completeness: 76–100%   **Preservation:** Good
Age: 40+ yr   **Sex:** Male   **Stature:** 168 cm
Summary of pathological conditions: Spinal degenerative joint disease, Degenerative joint disease of right elbow and left hand phalanges, Fracture of right and left nasal bones and eleven ribs. Dental caries, Dental calculus, Periodontal disease

Dentition

R															L
	P	P	P	P	P	P	P		P	P	P	P	P		
	cc	cc	cc	cc		cc	cc		cc	cc	cc	cc	cc		
					R								C		
/	7	6	5	4	3	2	1	/	NP	3	4	5	6	7	NP
NP	7	6	X	4	3	/	X	X	2	3	4	5	6	7	NP
					R								C		
	cc	cc			cc				cc	cc	cc	cc	cc		
	P	P		P	P				P	P	P	P	P	P	

Skeleton Number: 6016 **Grave group:** 6070
Completeness: 76–100% **Preservation:** Good
Age: 45–60 yr **Sex:** Male **Stature:** 166 cm
Summary of pathological conditions: Spinal degenerative joint disease, Schmorl's nodes, Degenerative joint disease of right and left temporo-mandibular joints, both acromio-clavicular joints, both sternoclavicular joints, both hip joints and left knee joint, Porotic hyperostosis, Rickets, Fracture of left parietal, right nasal bone and left first metacarpal. Dental calculus, Periapical cavity, Periodontal disease

Dentition

R																L
						PC										
				P	P		P	P								
					cc		cc	cc								
				R												
-	- -	-	4	3	X	1	1	X	X	X	X	-	-	-		
NP	X 6	5	4	3	2	1	1	2	3	4	5	6	7	NP		
	cc	cc	cc	cc	cc	cc	cc	cc	cc	cc	cc	cc	cc			
	P	P	P	P	P	P	P	P	P	P	P	P	P			
												PC				

Skeleton Number: 6017 **Grave group:** 6020
Completeness: 76–100% **Preservation:** Good
Age: 40+ yr **Sex:** Male **Stature:** 169 cm
Summary of pathological conditions: Spinal degenerative joint disease, Schmorl's nodes, Degenerative joint disease of left knee joint, Porotic hyperostosis, Fracture of three ribs, T6 and T9 vertebra, right tibia and fibula, and left tarsals. Enamel hypoplasia, Dental caries, Periapical cavity, Periodontal disease

Dentition

R																L
X	X	X	X	X	X	X	X	X	X	X	X	X	X	X	X	
X	X	X	X	X	X	2	/	X	X	3	/	5	X	X	X	
										C						
										H						
						P				P		P				
						PC										

Skeleton Number: 6019
Completeness: 76–100%
Age: 50+ yr **Sex:** Unknown
Grave group: 6020
Preservation: Good
Stature: -
Summary of pathological conditions: Spinal degenerative joint disease, Schmorl's nodes, Degenerative joint disease of right and left shoulder joints, right sternoclavicular joint, both wrist joints, both hip joints, left carpals and left first metatarsal, Fracture of right third cuneiform, Osteochondritis dissecans of fibula, Possible congenital dysplasia fn right and left fourth metatarsals

R								Dentition							L
X	X	X	X	X	X	X	X	X	X	X	X	X	X	X	X
X	X	X	X	X	/	X	X	X	X	X	X	X	X	X	X

Skeleton Number: 6023
Completeness: 76–100%
Age: 50+ yr **Sex:** Male
Grave group: 6250
Preservation: Poor
Stature: 176 cm
Summary of pathological conditions: Spinal degenerative joint disease including Ankylosis spondylitis, Schmorl's nodes, Degenerative joint disease of right and left shoulder joints, left trapezium, Periostitis on six ribs and both tibiae, Porotic hyperostosis, Cribra orbitalia, Possible rickets, Fracture of right and left nasal bones. Dental caries, Dental calculus, Periapical cavity, Periodontal disease

R								Dentition							L
						PC			PC	PC					
X	X	X	X	X	X	X	X	X	X	X	X	X	X	X	X
X	X	X	5	4	3	2	X	X	X	3	X	X	X	X	X
		R	R							C					
				H						H					
			P	P	P	P				P					
	PC	PC								PC		PC	PC		

Skeleton Number: 6027
Completeness: 76–100%
Age: 50+ yr **Sex:** Female?
Grave group: 6150
Preservation: Good
Stature: 159 cm
Summary of pathological conditions: Spinal degenerative joint disease, Degenerative joint disease of right and left elbow joints, both knee joints. Periapical cavity

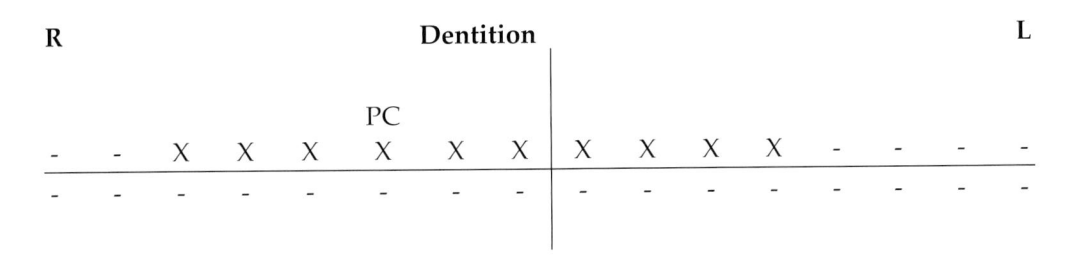

R								Dentition							L
				PC											
-	-	X	X	X	X	X	X	X	X	X	X	-	-	-	-
-	-	-	-	-	-	-	-	-	-	-	-	-	-	-	-

Skeleton Number: 6035   **Grave group:** 6270
Completeness: 76–100%   **Preservation:** Good
Age: 35–45 yr   **Sex:** Male?   **Stature:** 168 cm
Summary of pathological conditions: Spinal degenerative joint disease, Schmorl's nodes, Degenerative joint disease of right carpals, right and left knee joints, right and left tarsals, Periostitis on both tibiae and left fibula, Porotic hyperostosis, Fracture of both nasal bones, left maxilla, five right ribs, Osteochondritis dissecans on right third metacarpal. Enamel hypoplasia, Dental caries, Dental calculus, Periapical cavity, Periodontal disease

R								Dentition							L
			PC												
	P	P	P	P	P	P	P	P		P	P	P	P	P
	cc	cc		cc	cc	cc	cc	cc		cc	cc	cc	cc	cc
					H	H	H	H						
							C					C		
NP	X	6	5	4	3	2	1	1	2	/	4	5	6	7	8
8	7	6	5	4	3	2	1	1	2	3	4	5	6	7	8
C	C			H					H					C	C
cc	cc	cc	cc	cc	cc	cc	cc	cc	cc	cc	cc	cc	cc	cc	cc
P	P	P	P	P	P	P	P	P	P	P	P	P	P	P	P

Skeleton Number: 6037   **Grave group:** 6270
Completeness: 76–100%   **Preservation:** Good
Age: 45–55 yr   **Sex:** Male   **Stature:** 160 cm
Summary of pathological conditions: Spinal degenerative joint disease, Degenerative joint disease of right and left acromio-clavicular joints, both hip joints and right and left first metatarsals, Fracture of one right rib and on L5 vertebra, Rickets, Osteochondroma on left femur

R								Dentition							L
-	-	X	X	X	X	X	X	X	X	X	X	X	X	X	X
X	X	X	X	X	X	X	X	X	X	X	X	X	X	X	X

Skeleton Number: 6053   **Grave group:** 6150
Completeness: 76–100%   **Preservation:** Good
Age: 40+ yr   **Sex:** Male   **Stature:** 168 cm
Summary of pathological conditions: Spinal degenerative joint disease, Degenerative joint disease of right and left tempor-mandibular joints, both shoulder joints, both sacro-iliac joints, both hip joints, both knee joints, left first metatarsal, Periostitis on right tibia, Porotic hyperostosis, Fracture of left nasal bone, left maxilla, right patella, left tibia and right second metatarsal. Dental calculus, Periapical cavity, Periodontal disease

R								Dentition							L
		PC								PC					
						P						P			
X	X	X	X	/	/	2	X	/	/	X	/	5	X	X	X
X	X	X	/	/	X	/	X	X	2	3	4	X	X	X	X
									cc	cc	cc				
									P	P	P				
				PC	PC										

Appendix Three

Skeleton Number: 6056 **Grave group:** 6150
Completeness: 76–100% **Preservation:** Good
Age: 50+ yr **Sex:** Male **Stature:** 170 cm
Summary of pathological conditions: Spinal degenerative joint disease, Schmorl's nodes, Degenerative joint disease of right and left shoulder joints, Periostitis on right and left scapula, both clavicles, both humeri, radii, ulnae, femora, tibiae and fibulae, Porotic hyperostosis, Possible scurvy, Fracture of left nasal bone, right fifth metacarpal, left fourth metacarpal. Enamel hypoplasia, Dental caries, Dental calculus, Periapical cavity, Periodontal disease

R														L
						Dentition								
								PC	PC		PC			
		P	P	P	P	P	P	P	P	P	P	P		
		cc	cc		cc	cc		cc	cc					
					H		H	H		H				
						C		R	R		C			
NP	X 6	5	4	3	2	1	1	2	3	4	5	X	X	X
X	X X	5	4	3	X	1	/	2	3	4	5	X	X	NP
						R								
					H									
		cc	cc					cc	cc	cc				
		P	P	P		P		P	P	P	P			
		PC												

Skeleton Number: 6058 **Grave group:** 6150
Completeness: 76–100% **Preservation:** Excellent
Age: 50+ yr **Sex:** Male? **Stature:** 179 cm
Summary of pathological conditions: Spinal degenerative joint disease, Degenerative joint disease of right and left tempor-mandibular joints, both shoulder joints, both sternoclavicular joints, both elbow joints, left hip joint, both knee joints, right and left carpals, right and left tarsals, metatarsals and foot phalanges, Periostitis on both tibiae and fibulae, Fracture of frontal bone, sphenoid, right nasal bone, left first cuneiform, left metatarsals and right foot proximal phalanx. Dental calculus, Periapical cavity, Periodontal disease

R							**Dentition**							L
									PC					
			P	P	P			P	P	P		P	P	
			cc	cc	cc			cc	cc	cc		cc	cc	
X	X	X	5	4	3	/	X	X	/	3	4	5	/	7	8
NP	7	6	5	4	3	2	/	/	/	3	4	5	X	7	NP
	cc	cc	cc	cc	cc	cc			cc	cc	cc	cc		
	P	P	P	P	P	P			P	P	P	P		
		PC												

Skeleton Number: 6063 **Grave group:** 6040
Completeness: 76–100% **Preservation:** Good
Age: 50+ yr **Sex:** Male **Stature:** 168 cm
Summary of pathological conditions: Spinal degenerative joint disease, Degenerative joint disease of right and left shoulder joints, both elbow joints, left wrist joint, both hip joints, both knee joints, both ankle joints, right and left carpals, right tarsals, left metatarsals, Fracture of right and left nasal bones and maxillae, left radius, both fibulae, right talus, left calcaneous, left navicular, left medial and intermediate cuneiforms. Dental caries, Dental calculus, Periodontal disease. Os acromiale of right scapula

	R						Dentition							L	
						P									
X	X	X	X	X	X	3	/	/	/	X	/	X	X	X	X
X	X	X	5	4	3	2	1	/	/	/	X	/	X	X	X
			C	C			C								
				cc	cc	cc	cc								
			P	P	P	P	P								

Skeleton Number: 6073 **Grave group:** 6040
Completeness: 76–100% **Preservation:** Good
Age: 50+ yr **Sex:** Male **Stature:** 161 cm
Summary of pathological conditions: Spinal degenerative joint disease, Schmorl's nodes, Degenerative joint disease of right and left temporo-mandibular joints, left shoulder joint, left sternoclavicular joint, right ankle joint, right and left metatarsals, Periostitis on left parietal, both tibiae, right and left second metatarsals, Fracture of both nasal bones and maxillae, Benign cyst on right orbital plate (lacrimal and ethmoid affected). Enamel hypoplasia, Dental caries, Dental calculus, Periapical cavity, Periodontal disease

	R							Dentition							L	
					PC											
					P	P	P	P	P	P	P					
					cc	cc	cc	cc	cc	cc						
					R	H				H						
X	X	X	X	4	3	2	1	1	2	3	X	X	X	X	X	
8	7	6	5	4	3	X	1	1	2	3	4	5	6	7	/	
cc	cc	cc	cc	cc	cc		cc	cc	cc	cc	cc	cc	cc	cc		
P	P	P	P	P	P		P	P	P	P	P	P	P	P		
								PC								

Skeleton Number: 6078 **Grave group:** 6420
Completeness: 51–75% **Preservation:** Poor
Age: 40+ yr **Sex:** Male? **Stature:** 168 cm
Summary of pathological conditions: Spinal degenerative joint disease, Degenerative joint disease of right shoulder joint, both hip joints, both knee joints, left ankle joint, right and left tarsals and first metatarsals, Possible case of erosive joint disease on first metatarsals and proximal foot phalanx, Cribra orbitalia, Fracture of left nasal bone. Dental calculus, Periodontal disease

	R							Dentition							L	
P	P		P	P	P	P	P	P	P	P	P					
			cc	cc	cc	cc	cc	cc	cc	cc	cc					
8	7	X	5	4	3	2	1	1	2	3	4	5	-	-	-	
-	7	-	5	4	3	2	1	1	2	3	4	5	-	-	-	
			cc	cc	cc	cc	cc	cc	cc	cc	cc	cc				

Skeleton Number: 6082 **Grave group:** 6560
Completeness: 76–100% **Preservation:** Good
Age: 40+ yr **Sex:** Male **Stature:** 170 cm
Summary of pathological conditions: Spinal degenerative joint disease, Degenerative joint disease of right wrist joint, Periostitis on three ribs, Cribra orbitalia, Fracture of right and left nasal bones, left rib, right scaphoid, left tibia, left fibula and left first metatarsal. Enamel hypoplasia, Dental caries, Dental calculus, Periapical cavity, Periodontal disease

Appendix Three

R							Dentition							L
							PC							
		P					P							
		cc					cc							
NP	7	X	X	X	/	/	1	/	/	/	X	X	X	X	NP
NP	NP	6	5	4	3	2	1	1	2	3	4	5	6	NP	NP
		C					H	H						
		cc	cc	cc	cc	cc	cc	cc	cc	cc	cc	cc	cc	
		P	P	P	P	P	P	P	P	P	P	P	P	
		PC												

Skeleton Number: 6085 **Grave group:** 6460
Completeness: 76–100% **Preservation:** Good
Age: 50+ yr **Sex:** Male **Stature:** 166 cm
Summary of pathological conditions: Spinal degenerative joint disease, Degenerative joint disease on both hip joints, DISH, Porotic Hyperostosis, Cribra orbitalia, Fracture of right radius and ulna, Button osteoma. Enamel hypoplasia, Dental caries, Dental calculus, Periapical cavity, Periodontal disease

R							Dentition							L
							PC	PC						
		P	P	P					P	P		P	P	
		cc	cc	cc				cc			cc	cc		
										R		C	C	
/	X	X	5	4	3	X	/	/	X	X	4	5	X	7	8
X	X	X	X	X	X	X	X	X	X	3	X	X	X	X	X
										H					
										cc					

Skeleton Number: 6089 **Grave group:** 6420
Completeness: 76–100% **Preservation:** Good
Age: 35–45 yr **Sex:** Male **Stature:** 165 cm
Summary of pathological conditions: Spinal degenerative joint disease, Schmorl's nodes, Degenerative joint disease of right and left tarsals, Periostitis on four ribs, left radius, left ulna, both tibiae and fibulae, both tali, Fracture of both nasal bones and maxillae, Amputation likely on left hand. Enamel hypoplasia, Dental caries, Dental calculus, Periapical cavity, Periodontal disease

R							Dentition							L
	PC													
	P	P	P	P	P	P			P	P	P	P	P	
									cc	cc	cc	cc	cc	
	C	H	H	H	H	B				H	H			
X	7	6	5	4	3	2	/	/	/	3	4	5	6	7	X
8	7	6	5	4	3	2	1	1	2	3	4	5	6	7	8
C				H	H				H	H	H		H		
cc		cc	cc	cc	cc	cc	cc	cc	cc	cc	cc	cc	cc	cc
P		P	P	P	P	P	P	P	P	P	P	P	P	P

Skeleton Number: 6092 **Grave group:** 6120
Completeness: 51–75% **Preservation:** Poor
Age: 40+ yr **Sex:** Male **Stature:** 160 cm
Summary of pathological conditions: Porotic hyperostosis, Cribra orbitalia, Trauma on left nasal bone and right tibia

R						Dentition									L
-	-	-	-	-	/	X	X	X	X	-	-	-	-	-	-
X	X	X	X	X	X	X	X	X	X	X	X	X	X	X	X

Skeleton Number: 6094 **Grave group:** 6120
Completeness: 51–75% **Preservation:** Poor
Age: 40–50 yr **Sex:** Male **Stature:** 162 cm
Summary of pathological conditions: Spinal degenerative joint disease, Porotic hyperostosis, Cribra orbitalia, Maxillary sinusitis, Periostitis on right and left fibula, right tibia, Fracture of right fourth metacarpal, right fibula, left femur, left second metatarsal, L3–L5 vertebrae. Enamel hypoplasia, Dental caries, Dental calculus, Periodontal disease

R								Dentition							L
						P		P		P					
-	X	X	/	/	3	X	-	1	-	3	-	-	-	-	-
NP	7	6	5	4	3	2	1	/	/	3	4	5	6	7	NP
	C	C								C	C	C	C		
	H				H					H			H		
	cc	cc	cc	cc	cc	cc	cc								
	P	P	P	P	P	P	P			P	P	P	P	P	

Skeleton Number: 6096 **Grave group:** 6040
Completeness: 76–100% **Preservation:** Good
Age: 50+ yr **Sex:** Male **Stature:** 179 cm
Summary of pathological conditions: Spinal degenerative joint disease, Degenerative joint disease of right and left temporo-mandibular joints, right shoulder joint, right elbow joint, right knee joint, right and left tarsals, Possible cyst on spheoid, Fracture of nasal bones and possibly on left clavicle

R								Dentition							L
X	X	X	X	X	X	X	X	X	X	X	X	X	X	X	X
X	X	X	X	X	X	X	X	X	X	X	X	X	X	X	X

Skeleton Number: 6098 **Grave group:** 6540
Completeness: 76–100% **Preservation:** Poor
Age: 50+ yr **Sex:** Male **Stature:** 166 cm
Summary of pathological conditions: Spinal Degenerative Joint Disease, Degenerative Joint disease of right and left hip joint, left tibia, Fracture of frontal bone, Rickets. Dental caries, Dental calculus, Periapical cavity, Periodontal disease

R								Dentition							L
	P	P				P	P	P	P			P			
	cc	cc			cc	cc	cc	cc	cc	cc	cc	cc	cc		
						C				C	R				
NP	7	6	/	/	3	2	1	1	2	3	4	5	6	X	NP
X	X	6	5	4	3	2	1	X	X	3	4	5	X	X	8
		C	C				C	R							C
		cc	cc	cc	cc					cc	cc	cc			cc
		P													P
		PC													

Appendix Three

Skeleton Number: 6103   **Grave group:** 6040
Completeness: 76–100%   **Preservation:** Poor
Age: 50+ yr   **Sex:** Male   **Stature:** 171 cm
Summary of pathological conditions: Spinal degenerative joint disease, Schmorl's nodes, Degenerative joint disease of right and left shoulder joints, both hip joints, both knee joints, right trapezium, right and left first metacarpals and hand phalanges, left metatarsals, Fracture of left clavicle. Dental caries, Dental calculus, Periapical cavity, Periodontal disease

R							Dentition								L
				PC		PC									
				cc		cc				cc		cc			
											R				
-	-	-	/	4	/	2	/	/	X	/	4	5	6	-	-
X	X	X	5	4	3	2	1	1	2	3	4	/	X	X	X
			R												
			C												
				cc	cc	cc	cc	cc	cc	cc	cc				
				PC											

Skeleton Number: 6105   **Grave group:** 6250
Completeness: 76–100%   **Preservation:** Good
Age: 40+ yr   **Sex:** Male   **Stature:** 158 cm
Summary of pathological conditions: Spinal degenerative joint disease, Schmorl's nodes, Degenerative joint disease of right and left acromio-clavicular joints, right shoulder joint, right elbow joint, right wrist joint, right and left metacarpals, right hand phalanges, Periostitis on right and left tibiae, Porotic hyperostosis, Rickets, Fracture of both nasal bones, two right ribs, right third metacarpal, Button osteoma. Enamel hypoplasia, Periapical cavity, Periodontal disease, Impacted tooth

R							Dentition								L
				PC											
				P		P									
						cc									
				R		H									
X	X	X	5	X	3	X	X	X	X	U	X	X	X	X	X
X	X	X	X	X	X	X	X	X	X	X	X	X	X	X	X

Skeleton Number: 6113   **Grave group:** 6560
Completeness: 76–100%   **Preservation:** Good
Age: 50+ yr   **Sex:** Male   **Stature:** 172 cm (Left humerus)
Summary of pathological conditions: Spinal degenerative joint disease, Schmorl's nodes, Degenerative joint disease of right elbow joint, right hip, right triquetrum, Porotic hyperostosis,, Fracture of both nasal bones, Sacralisation. Dental caries, Dental calculus. Periapical cavity, Periodontal disease

R							Dentition								L
				PC		PC		PC	PC	PC					
	P	P		P											
				R											
X	X 6	5	/	3	/	X	X	X	/	X	X	X	X	X	
NP	/ X	X	X	X	/	/	/	/	/	X	5	6	7	NP	
											C				
												cc	cc		
											P	P	P		
				PC				PC		PC					

'Safe moor'd in Greenwich tier'

Skeleton Number: 6128 **Grave group:** 6540
Completeness: 51–75% **Preservation:** Poor
Age: 50+ yr **Sex:** Male **Stature:** -
Summary of pathological conditions: Fracture of right nasal bone and right maxilla. Dental caries, Dental calculus, Periapical cavity, Periodontal disease

		R						Dentition							L	
				P	P	P				P	P	P	P			
				cc	cc	cc					cc	cc	cc			
X	X	X	5	4	3	X	X		X	X	3	4	5	6	X	X
8	7	6	5	4	3	2	1		1	2	3	4	5	6	7	8
						R									C	R
cc	cc	cc	cc	cc	cc		cc		cc	cc	cc	cc	cc	cc	cc	
P	P	P	P	P	P		P		P	P	P	P	P	P	P	P
															PC	

Skeleton Number: 6132 **Grave group:** 6550
Completeness: 76–100% **Preservation:** Excellent
Age: 40-50 yr **Sex:** Female **Stature:** 162 cm
Summary of pathological conditions: Spinal degenerative joint disease, Schmorl's nodes, Degenerative joint disease on right and left shoulder joints, left elbow joint, right tarsals, left cuboid, Lytic lesion on left lunate

	R							Dentition							L
-	-	-	-	-	-	-	-		-	-	-	-	-	-	-
-	-	-	-	-	-	-	-		-	-	-	-	-	-	-

Skeleton Number: 6142 **Grave group:** 6460
Completeness: 76–100% **Preservation:** Good
Age: 50+ yr **Sex:** Male **Stature:** 174 cm
Summary of pathological conditions: Spinal degenerative joint disease, Schmorl's nodes, Degenerative joint disease on left acromio-clavicular joint, right and left sternoclavicular joints, both hip joints, Cribra orbitalia, Fracture of right nasal bone, Lytic lesions on right ilium. Enamel hypoplasia, Dental caries, Dental calculus, Periapical cavity, Periodontal disease

	R								Dentition							L	
					PC	PC				PC							
			P				P	P	P	P	P		P		P		
					cc	cc			cc	cc							
					H	H			H	H							
			R			R	C				R		R		R		
X	/	/	5	X	X	2	1		1	2	3	X	5	X	7	X
NP	7	X	X	4	3	2	X		X	2	3	4	5	X	7	X
					C	C					C	C	R		C		
				H								H					
	cc		cc	cc	cc				cc	cc							
	P		P	P	P				P	P	P	P		P			
													PC				

Skeleton Number: 6146 **Grave group:** 6460
Completeness: 76–100% **Preservation:** Good
Age: 50+ yr **Sex:** Male **Stature:** 175 cm
Summary of pathological conditions: Spinal degenerative joint disease, Degenerative joint disease on left shoulder joint, left elbow joint, both hip joints, right carpals, Porotic hyperostosis, Rickets, Fracture of left ulna. Dental caries, Dental calculus, Periapical cavity, Periodontal disease

Appendix Three

	R							Dentition							L
PC	PC														
			P	P					P	P	P	P			
			cc	cc					cc	cc	cc	cc			
									R			C			
/	/	/	5	4	/	/	/	/	2	3	4	5	X	X	X
8	7	6	5	4	3	2	1	1	2	3	4	5	6	7	X
		PC											R		

Skeleton Number: 6151 **Grave group:** 6460
Completeness: 76–100% **Preservation:** Good
Age: 45+ yr **Sex:** Male **Stature:** 165 cm
Summary of pathological conditions: Spinal degenerative joint disease, Schmorl's nodes, Degenerative joint disease on right and left temporo-mandibular joints, left shoulder joint, both elbow joints, Porotic hyperostosis, Cribra orbitalia, Possible osteitis on left radius and right tibia, Fracture of nasal bones, right maxilla, left clavicle, two right ribs and L1 vertebra, Ante-mortem perforation on left maxilla, Possible developmental defect on left tibia. Dental calculus, Periapical cavity, Periodontal disease

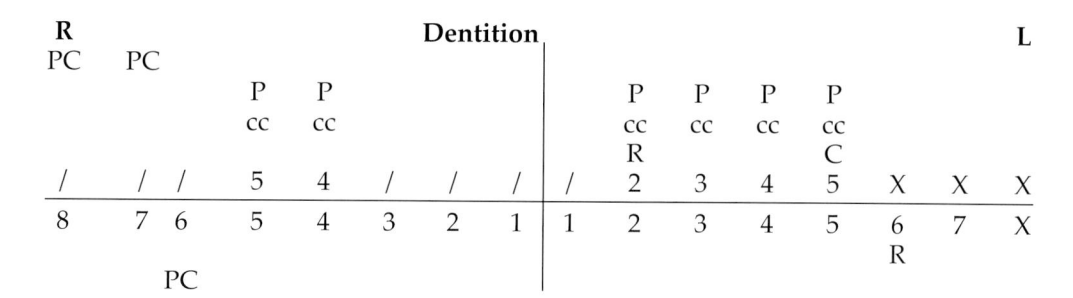

R								Dentition							L
							P	P			P	P			
							cc	cc			cc	cc			
X	X	X	X	X	/	/	1	1	/	X	4	5	X	X	X
X	X	X	X	X	X	X	X	/	X	X	X	X	X	X	X
								PC							

Appendix 4: Coffin Fittings

The appendix is in two parts. The first part - Appendix 4a - is a catalogue of selected grave fittings quantfying and describing the elements recovered. The second part - Appendix 4b - is a summary of the remaining coffin fittings. Both Appendices are ordered by grave cut number (column 1) then skeleton number (column 2). The third column gives the context number for the associated coffin remains where appropriate. The fourth column gives the context number allocated to the finds.

Appendix 4a   Catalogue of coffin fittings and nails from Areas 1 and 2.

Grave	Skeleton	Coffin	Context	Breastplates	Grips	Grip plates	Coffin nails (count)	Upholstery studs (count)	Unidentified metal fittings
3028	3039	3048	3039	-	-	-	-	iron; corroded; wood adhering to reverse. (2)	1 x fragment of corroded iron plate -?? grip plate fragment found near foot
			3048	-	x 5; iron; very corroded; CCS type 1	iron; fragmented; rounded border; type unidentifiable	iron; mixed preservation; wood adhering to shafts. (21)	iron; poor preservation; wood adhering to reverse. (c. 50)	-
3028	3086	3087	3087	-	x 4; iron, very corroded, fragmented	iron; fragments only; sunburst motif -?? CCS3	iron; well preserved; wood adhering to shafts. (42)	iron; mixed preservation; wood adhering to reverse. (190-200)	-
			3089	iron; corroded and very fragmented; drapery & floral motifs discernible	-	-	-	-	-
3028	3029 / 3032	3031 / 3033	fill 3027	-	x 4; iron; very corroded; ? CCS type 1	iron; c. 4 fragments of punched plate associated with grips; type unidentifiable	-	iron; very corroded; wood adhering to reverse. (3)	x 2 iron grip bolts
3028	3029	3031	3031	iron; very corroded and incomplete; tendrils, swirls, rope border motifs seen	x 6-7; iron; very corroded fragmented	iron; fragments of punched plate adhering to grip, type not identified but swirls similar to CCS 13	iron; mixed preservation; wood adhering to shafts; variable sizes. (20)	iron; very corroded; wood adhering to reverse. (292)	x 3 iron grip bolts
3028	3032	3033	3032	-	-	-	iron; incomplete shaft with wood adhering. (1)	-	-

(continued on next page)

Appendix 4a (*continued*)

Grave	Skeleton	Coffin	Context	Breastplates	Grips	Grip plates	Coffin nails (count)	Upholstery studs (count)	Unidentified metal fittings
			3033	-	x 2; iron; concretions ++, very corroded; type unidentifiable	iron; fragments adhering to grip; others loose; no design identifiable	iron; corroded ++; variable sizes. (19)	iron; corroded; wood adhering to reverse. (65)	1 x grip bolt, iron
3036	3051	3049	3049	-	x 4; iron; fragmented; type unidentifiable	-	iron; good preservation; wood adhering to shafts. (29-32)	(330)	x 1; iron; corroded ? knife blade
3036	3051 3035	3049 3053	fill 3034	-	very poorly preserved iron; no and type could not be identified	small fragments of iron plate may be grip plate	iron; mixed preservation; wood adhering to shafts; variable sizes. (10)	iron; corroded; wood adhering to reverse; rows of up to 4 studs. (75)	1 x iron grip bolt
3041	3068 3057 3044	3067 3059 3043	fill 3042	-	-	-	-	-	x 6 small iron fragments -? grip or large nail
3041	3044	3043	3043	iron; multiple fragments; too corroded- no motifs or type identified	x 5; iron; near complete but severely corroded; type not identified	iron; fragments of plate adhering to reverse of grips; severely corroded -type not identified	iron; moderately to severely corroded; wood adhering to shaft. (28)	black enamelled iron; in rows or clusters; severely corroded; wood adhering to reverse. (433 single studs; 34 fragments of 2 studs; 58 fragments of multiple stud clusters)	iron; fragments of punched iron plate- possible lid motif/ escutcheon; measuring 1.5 x 2 cm; severely corroded
3074	3107 / 3106 3105 / 3072	3228 / ?3104 ?3104 / 3071	fill 3073	iron; fragmented & incomplete ; several small fragments (mostly 1 x 1 cm; iron; punched plate; type not identifiable but two parallel lines of a border seen	-	-	iron; varied sizes; moderate to severe corrosion; wood adhering to shafts. (82-87)	iron; moderately to severely corroded;; wood adhering to reverse. (197)	several amorphous iron fragments -? Grips; numerous small unidentified lumps of severely corroded iron
3074	3107	3228	3107	-	-	-	iron; medium-sized, corroded; wood adhering to shaft. (1)	-	-

Appendix 4a (*continued*)

Grave	Skeleton	Coffin	Context	Breastplates	Grips	Grip plates	Coffin nails (count)	Upholstery studs (count)	Unidentified metal fittings
			3228	-	x 8; iron; fairly well preserved; CCS type 2a	No evidence of plates	iron; mixed preservation; wood adhering to shafts; variable sizes. (59)	iron; single corroded studs; wood adhering to reverse. (5)	iron grip bolts attached to grips
3074	3106 3105	?3104	3104	iron; fragmented & incomplete; drapery motif & rope border seen; central panel rectangular or tapered; black painted	x 5; iron; marked concretions on one, others fair preservation; CCS type 2a	fragments of iron plate adhering to reverse of grip	-	iron; corroded; wood adhering to reverse; all single. (8)	1x iron grip bolt
3074	3105	?3104	3105	-	-	-	iron; medium-sized, corroded; wood adhering to shaft. (3)	-	-
3074	3072	3071	3071	-	x 3; iron; 2 complete & one 3/4 complete; severely corroded	-	-	-	-
			3072	-	-	x 1 possible fragment; iron; severely corroded; no motif or type identified	iron; moderately corroded. (1)	-	-
3078	3102	3109	Fill 3079	-	x 1 iron; exceedingly badly corroded & concretions ++; type not identified	iron; fragmented & incomplete; punched decoration but motifs not discernible. ? breastplate ? grip plate	-	(17)	several amorphous iron fragments -? grips
			3109	iron; fragmented & incomplete; central panel appeared oval, surrounded by double border & swirl motifs	x 1; iron; marked concretions; type not identified	-	iron; medium-sized, corroded; wood adhering to shaft. (13)	iron; very corroded; wood adhering to reverse; studs clumping together in groups, or forming double row. (126)	-

(*continued on next page*)

Appendix 4a (*continued*)

Grave	Skeleton	Coffin	Context	Breastplates	Grips	Grip plates	Coffin nails (count)	Upholstery studs (count)	Unidentified metal fittings
3091	3164 3103 3108 3139	3163 3111 3138 -	Fill 3092	iron; very fragmented and corroded	possible x 1; fragments only; border discerned	-	iron; well preserved; wood adhering to shafts. (7)	iron studs, very corroded and concretions ++ (30-40)	x 1 large metal object with large flange and shaft; incomplete; flange 4.3 cm diameter; shaft 9.2 cm length
3091	3164	3163	3163	iron; very corroded and incomplete; drapery motifs seen	-	-	iron; mixed preservation; wood adhering to shafts; variable sizes. (8)	iron; very corroded; wood adhering to reverse; some studs arranged together in clusters. (20)	-
3091	3103	3111	3103	-	-	-	-	iron; corroded. (1)	-
			3111	iron; very fragmented; type not identified	-	-	iron; moderate to severe corrosion; wood adhering to shafts. (31)	black painted iron; severely corroded; often wood adhering to reverse. (58 single studs; x 16 fragments containing several studs in clusters and rows)	lump of amorphous iron, severely corroded
3093	3101	none	3101	-	-	-	iron; medium-sized, corroded. (1)	-	-
3095	3098	3097	3097	iron; very fragmented and corroded; type not identifiable- border & foliage motifs present	iron; very fragmented and corroded- 1 or 2 present; ? CCS 1	-	iron; preservation variable; wood adhering to shafts but no upholstery. (20)	iron studs, very corroded and concretions ++; rows suggest studs delineated margin of lid & side panels; clumps suggest patterns. (c 100)	-
			3098	-	-	-	iron; very corroded. (1)	-	-
3095	3099	3134	3134	-	-	-	iron; mixed preservation; wood adhering to shafts. (22)	iron; poor preservation; wood adhering to reverse. (18-20)	amorphous concretions; one fragment of punched iron plate -? grip plate/ breastplate/ lid motif

Appendix 4a (*continued*)

Grave	Skeleton	Coffin	Context	Breastplates	Grips	Grip plates	Coffin nails (count)	Upholstery studs (count)	Unidentified metal fittings
3107	3024 3016 3019	3025 }3015	fill 3018	-	-	-	iron; mixed preservation; wood adhering to shafts. (30)	-	-
3107	3024	3025	3025	-	-	-	iron; mixed preservation; wood adhering to shafts; variable sizes. (33-35)	iron; very corroded, wood adhering to reverse; small clumps & rows of *c*.3 studs. (118)	3 x iron fragments of thin plate- ? breastplate/ lid motif/ grip plate
3118	3119	3121	3121	-	x 5; iron; 2 complete; moderate to severe corrosion; no type identified	x 3; iron; rusted onto reverse of grips; severely corroded; no type or motifs identified	iron; moderate to severe corrosion; wood adhering to shafts. (15)	iron; severely corroded. (3)	-
3123	3124	3125	3125	x 1 fragment of breastplate; corroded; no motif or type discernible	x 4; iron; incomplete; severely corroded; type not discernible	-	iron; severely corroded; wood adhering to shaft. (5)	iron; severely corroded. (5)	numerous small amorphous fragments of corroded iron; many have wood attached
			3226	iron; very corroded & incomplete; swirl motif seen; upholstery fabric adhering to reverse	-	-	-	iron; very corroded; wood adhering to reverse. (7)	-
3127	3191 / 3212 3162 / 3211	none / 3225 3165 / none	fill 3128	-	x 2; iron; very corroded-type not identifiable	5 x small fragments of iron plate-? grip plate	iron; most well preserved; wood adhering to shaft. (37)	iron; very corroded. (*c.* 5)	numerous amorphous fragments of iron; concretions +++
3127	3191	none	3191	-	-	-	iron; moderately corroded. (8)	-	Circular iron lump, severely corroded
3127	3212	3225	3225	iron; very fragmented & incomplete; tendrils and border identified	x 3; iron; corroded & concretions ++	x 3; iron; adhering to grip; very corroded	iron; mixed preservation; wood adhering to shafts; variable sizes. (20)	-	-
3127	3162	3165	3165	-	x 3; iron; extremely corroded & concreted; type unidentifiable	fragments of iron plate adhering to reverse of grips	-	-	several amorphous iron fragments -?? grips

(*continued on next page*)

Appendix 4a (continued)

Grave	Skeleton	Coffin	Context	Breastplates	Grips	Grip plates	Coffin nails (count)	Upholstery studs (count)	Unidentified metal fittings
3131	3132 3144 3152	3172 3145 3153	3131	-	x 1; iron; exceedingly corroded and concreted; type unidentifiable	-	iron; mixed preservation; wood adhering to shafts. (16-18)	-	numerous amorphous concretions containing iron
			fill 3129	iron; highly fragmented and incomplete; style not identified; nailed to coffin	-	-	iron; preservation mixed; wood adhering to shaft. (7)	-	-
3131	3144	3145	3144	-	-	-	iron; poorly preserved. (1)	-	-
			3145	-	-	-	iron; mixed preservation; wood adhering to shafts. (18)	iron; exceedingly poor preservation; clusters of studs. (10-15)	-
3131	3152	3153	3153	-	-	-	iron; mixed preservation; wood adhering to shafts. (7)	iron; poor preservation; wood adhering to reverse. (5)	-
3142	3143	3161	3161	iron; very corroded & incomplete; no motifs seen	x1; iron; amorphous corroded +++	-	iron; mixed preservation; wood adhering to shafts; variable sizes. (21)	iron; corroded; wood adhering to reverse. (79)	several amorphous iron fragments -?? grips
3149	3176 3151 3148	- - -	fill 3133	-	-	-	iron; well preserved, 2 bent at right angles. (10)	-	-
3156	3159	3158	3158	-	x 4; iron; corroded; CCS type 2a	No evidence of grip plates	iron; mixed preservation; wood adhering to shafts; variable sizes. (21)	iron; corroded; wood adhering to reverse; all single. (12)	several amorphous iron fragments -?? grips
3167	3177 3168	- 3169	fill 3166	-	-	-	-	-	several fragments of thin iron plate; no decoration surviving- corroded ++- ? breastplate/ grip plate/ lid motif
3167	3168	3169	3169	-	-	-	iron; medium-sized, corroded. (3)	-	-

Appendix 4a (continued)

Grave	Skeleton	Coffin	Context	Breastplates	Grips	Grip plates	Coffin nails (count)	Upholstery studs (count)	Unidentified metal fittings
3193	3202	3203	3203	-	-	-	iron; moderately corroded; wood adhering to shaft. (19)	-	-
3193	3194	3195	3195	-	x 1 possible grip, measuring 7 x 2 cm; severely corroded	-	iron; moderately to severely corroded; wood adhering to shaft. (14)	-	x 1 large iron lump with two nails protruding at right angles- possible lid motif or grip
3198	3253 3243 3201	3254 3244 none	fill 3199	-	-	lead; severely corroded; 4 x 2 cm in size	iron; moderately corroded. (13)	-	U-shaped iron hoop, moderately corroded
3207	3208	3209	3209	-	x 1 possible grip, measuring 7 x 2 cm; severely corroded	-	iron; severely corroded; wood adhering to shaft. (14)	-	3 x iron lumps, severely corroded- ? grips
3215	3218	3217	3217	iron; very corroded & fragmented; type not identifiable but swirls of ? foliage & sunbursts seen; border shaped as in CSS 35 or 38	x 5-6; iron; very corroded & fragmented	iron; fragments of plate adhering to reverse of grips	iron; mixed preservation; wood adhering to shafts; variable sizes. (27)	iron; very corroded; wood adhering to reverse; studs together forming rows & triangles. (180-200)	x 1 iron grip bolt
3219	3223	3222	3222	iron; very, very fragmented and incomplete; no patterns discernible	x 6; iron; very corroded; CCS 3b	iron; tiny fragments of plate associated with grip	iron; very corroded. (1)	iron; very corroded; wood adhering to reverse. (20)	-
3239	3241	3242	3242	-	-	-	iron; very corroded; wood adhering to reverse. (10)	-	-
3247	3255 3249	- -	fill 3248	-	-	-	iron; well preserved; wood adhering to reverse. (19 larger nails and 4 tacks)	iron; concretions ++ (4)	-
3247	3249	-	3249	-	-	-	iron; well preserved; wood adhering to reverse. (1)	-	-

(continued on next page)

Appendix 4a (continued)

Grave	Skeleton	Coffin	Context	Breastplates	Grips	Grip plates	Coffin nails (count)	Upholstery studs (count)	Unidentified metal fittings
6002	6019 / 6017 6014 / 6003	6021 / 6018 6015 / 6004	fill 6001	-	-	-	iron; severely corroded. (1)	-	-
6002	6019	6021	6021	-	-	-	iron; moderately corroded. (23)	-	-
6002	6017	6018	6018	-	-	-	iron; severely corroded. (22)	iron; moderately to severely corroded; wood adhering to reverse. (15 single studs)	-
6002	6014	6015	6015	-	-	-	iron; severely corroded. (6)	iron; moderately to severely corroded; wood adhering to reverse. (2 single studs)	-
6002	6003	6004	6004	x 4; fragments of punched plate, largest 5 x 3 cm; severely corroded; no motifs or type discerned	-	-	iron; severely corroded. (18)	iron; moderately to severely corroded; wood adhering to reverse. (132 single studs)	-
6009	6016	6031	6031	-	-	-	iron; moderately corroded. (15)	-	-
6009	6013	6012	6012	-	-	-	iron; moderately corroded. (21)	-	-
6025	6105	6106	6106	-	iron; severely corroded onto grip plate; shape barely discernible	iron; fragmented & corroded onto grip; rectangular in shape, but other detail obliterated	iron; moderately to severely corroded; wood adhering to shaft. (14)	iron; moderately to severely corroded; wood adhering to reverse. (28 single studs; 3 clusters of studs)	x 1 severely corroded lump of iron (4 x 2 cm)- possible grip and grip plate
6025	6023	6022	6022	-	-	-	iron; severely corroded. (8)	-	x 2 amorphous lumps of iron- ?? grips
6026	6056 / 6058 6027 / 6053	6057 / 6059 6028 / 6054	fill 6029	-	x 1; iron; near complete; corroded, type not identified	-	iron; moderately to severely corroded. (9)	iron; moderately to severely corroded; wood adhering to reverse. (49)	-

Appendix 4a (*continued*)

Grave	Skeleton	Coffin	Context	Breastplates	Grips	Grip plates	Coffin nails (count)	Upholstery studs (count)	Unidentified metal fittings
6026	6027	6028	6028	-	x 1; iron; complete; moderately corroded	-	-	iron; moderately to severely corroded; wood adhering to reverse. (11 single studs)	-
6032	6094	6095	6095	-	-	-	iron; mixed preservation; wood adhering to shafts. (5)	-	-
6032	6092	6091	6091	-	-	-	iron; mixed preservation; wood adhering to shafts. (12)	-	-
6039	6037	6038	6037	-	-	-	-	-	x 1; iron; moderately corroded; possible small hinge or bracket
6039	6035	6036	6036	-	-	-	iron; moderately corroded; wood adhering to shafts. (36)	iron; moderately to severely corroded; wood adhering to reverse. (41)	-
6062	6103	6104	6104	-	-	-	iron; moderate to severe corrosion; wood adhering to shafts. (25)	iron; severely corroded; wood adhering to reverse. (8)	-
6062	6096	6097	6097	-	x 3; iron; incomplete and very corroded; CCS type 3b	-	iron; mixed preservation; wood adhering to shafts. (23)	iron; poor preservation; wood adhering to reverse.	amorphous concretions; 5 fragments of punched iron plate -? grip plate/ breastplate/ lid motif
6069	6128	6129	6129	-	-	-	iron; moderate to severe corrosion; wood adhering to shafts. (17)	-	-

(*continued on next page*)

Appendix 4a (*continued*)

Grave	Skeleton	Coffin	Context	Breastplates	Grips	Grip plates	Coffin nails (count)	Upholstery studs (count)	Unidentified metal fittings
6075	6089	6088	6088	-	-	-	iron; mixed preservation; wood adhering to shafts. (25)	iron; poor preservation; wood adhering to reverse. (250-270)	amorphous concretions; 1 fragment of punched iron plate -? grip plate/ breastplate/ lid motif
6081	6113	6114	6114	-	-	-	iron; moderate to severe corrosion; wood adhering to shafts. (23)	-	-
6084	6146	6147	6147	iron; very corroded and fragmented; type not identified but punched border & foliage motif seen	x 4; iron; corroded; CCS type 3b	x 1; iron; very corroded and fragmented	iron; poor preservation; wood adhering to shafts. (6)	iron; very corroded, wood adhering to reverse; multiple studs forming triangle. (80)	-
6084	6151	6152	6152	-	-	x 4; iron; severely corroded, adhering to grips; type not identified but fusiform & small -17.2 x 5.2 cm	iron; poor preservation; wood adhering to shafts. (8-10)	iron; very corroded, wood adhering to reverse; studs spaced *c.* 1 inch apart. (275)	-
6084	6142	6143	6143	iron; severely corroded fragment of punched plate, 2 x 2 cm; possibly breastplate; no motifs or type identified	x 2; iron; 1 complete, one incomplete; moderately corroded- type not identified	-	iron; moderately to severely corroded; wood adhering to shaft. (22)	iron; moderately to severely corroded; wood adhering to reverse. (152 single studs; 15 of 2 studs; 1 row of 4 studs; 3 clusters of studs)	x 1; iron fragment (3 x 1 cm); severely corroded
6131	6132	6133	6133	iron; numerous small fragments of punched plate (2 x 2 cm); possible breastplate; no motifs or type discernible	x 2; iron; 1 complete, one incomplete; corroded; type not identifiable	-	iron; moderate to severe corrosion; wood adhering to shafts. (27)	iron; moderately to severely corroded; wood adhering to reverse. (60)	2 amorphous lumps of severely corroded iron

Appendix 4b   Summary quantification of uncatalogued nails and fittings from burials in Areas 1 and 2.

Grave	Skeleton	Coffin	Context	Breastplates	Grips	Grip plates	Coffin nails	Upholstery studs	Count of metal fittings
3036	3051	3049	3052	present	-	-	-	-	x 50 fe coffin fittings
3041	3057	3059	3059	present	-	-	present	present	x 150 fe coffin fittings
3041	3068	3067	3067	fragmentary	-	-	present	present	x 250 fe coffin fittings
3047	3045	3062	3062	-	present	-	present	-	x 201 fe coffin fittings
3064	3061	3066	3066	present	present	-	present	-	x 50 fe coffin fittings
3093	-	-	3384	-	-	-	-	-	x 8 fe coffin fittings
3127									
3142	3189	3188	3188	-	-	-	nails only	-	x 20 fe coffin fittings
3175	3174	3173	3173	fragmentary	present	present	present	present	x 168 fe coffin fittings
3179	3182	3183	3183	fragment	x1 fe grip	-	present	-	x 138 fe coffin fittings
3185	3187	-	3186	-	-	-	-	-	x 4 fe coffin fittings
3198	3243	3244	3244	-	-	-	nails only	-	x 20 fe coffin fittings
3198	3253	3254	3253		-	-	nails only	-	x 2 fe coffin fittings
			3254						x 50 fe coffin fittings
3207	3213	3214	3214	-	-	-	nails only	-	x 20 fe coffin fittings
3236	3245	3246	3246	present	x 5 grips	-	present	present	x 205 fe coffin fittings
3239	3269	3271	3269	-	-	-	nails only	-	x 3 fe coffin fittings
			3271						x 10 fe coffin fittings
3239	3272	3273	3273	-	-	-	nails only	-	x 42 fe coffin fittings
3247	3255	-	3255	-	-	-	present	present	x 1 fe coffin fitting
3257	3258	3259	3259	-	-	-	nails only	-	x 6 fe coffin fittings
3257	3261	3262	3262	-	-	-	nails only	-	x 1 fe coffin fitting
3257	3258	3259	3256	-	-	-	present	-	x 9 fe coffin fittings
	3261	3262							
3627	3628	-	3629		-	-		-	x 2 fe coffin fittings
6026	6053	6054	6053	-	x1 fe grip	-	present	present	x 1 fe coffin fitting
			6054						x 100 fe coffin fittings
6026	6056	6057	6057	-	x1 fe grip	-	present	-	x 100 fe coffin fittings
6026	6058	6059	6059	-	x 1 fe grip	-	present	-	x 42 fe coffin fittings
6039	6037	6038	6038	-	-	-	nails only	-	x 50 fe coffin fittings
6062	6063	6064	6064	-	-	-	nails only	-	x 12 fe coffin fittings
6062	6073	6074	6074	-	-	-	present	present	x 28 fe coffin fittings
6069	6098	6072	6072	-	-	-	present	-	x 20 fe coffin fittings
6075	6078 / 6089	6077 / 6088	6076	-	-	-	-	-	x 1 fe coffin fittings
6075	6078	6077	6077	-	x 2 fe grips	-	present	-	x 182 fe coffin fittings
6081	6082		6083	-	-	-	nails only	-	x 34 fe coffin fittings
6084	6085	6086	6085	fragmentary	present	-	present	present	x 19 fe coffin fittings
			6086						x 301 fe coffin fittings

Appendix 5: Detailed Catalogue of Selected Metalwork and Textile from Graves

by Lorraine Lindsay-Gale and Ceridwen Boston

INTRODUCTION

The material in this catalogue comprises 33 copper alloy objects, and 4 occurrences of textile fragments. Further small fragments of textile were also discovered adhering to many of the shroud pins. The textile fragments are discussed below.

SHROUD PINS

Most of the metal objects (n=29; 87.9%) were shroud pins, most of which were very corroded and fragile, and many were broken into pieces. In better preserved examples, it was evident that the pins had round, or ball, heads, which appeared to have been soldered onto the shaft.

OTHER METAL FINDS

Four metal finds other than shroud pins were recovered from graves. A worn copper alloy penny (Cat. No. 12) probably minted in the reign of George II (1727–1760) was recovered from the fill of Grave 3093 and associated with skeleton 3101. Both the King's head and the figure of Britannia were facing left. The worn nature of the coin suggests that it had been in circulation long before it was deposited within the grave, and this would seem to be confirmed by the fact that Grave 3093 is not one of the earlier graves on the site.

A copper alloy cartridge case (Cat.No. 11) came from the fill of grave 3036. Finally two buttons were recovered, one from the cemetery soil (Cat.No. 1), and the other (Cat.No. 8) from the fill of Grave 3028. This dearth of buttons suggests that in general the pensioners were not buried in their clothes. The exceptions may be the male burials 6035 and 6037 (both Grave 6039, Group 6270). In 6035 where the remnants of a leather or textile garment (Cat.No. 24) were recovered from the right side of the torso. The remains (Cat.No. 27) from burial 6037 were beneath and around back and right side of the torso. The latter garment was possibly a waistcoat or stays, but perhaps more likely a truss (See Chapter ?? above).

Three other metal objects recovered during excavation have not been catalogued. These are a possible door catch in copper alloy from context 3081, and two objects of uncertain purpose from context 6065. The latter context was the fill of modern machine cut 6066.

TEXTILE

Fragments of loosely woven textile, almost certainly remnants of shrouds or coffin sheets, were found adhering to shroud pins. In some instance it was possible to see where pins had penetrated the fabric.

The type of surviving textile was not investigated, but given the social status and date of the burials, these are most likely to have been either wool or cotton. Earlier burials would have been shrouded in the wool, as the Burial in Woollen Acts (1666, 1678 and 1680) required that all individuals were to be shrouded in wool. By law an affidavit had to be sworn before a justice or clergyman within eight days of the funeral, confirming that the shroud of the deceased was woollen (Stock 1998, 134). Failure to do so incurred the heavy penalty of £5 on the estate of the deceased, £2 10s of which was given to the poor and £2 10s to the informer. This law was only repealed in 1814. After this date there was greater diversity in fabric types used to make shrouds, which included calico, alpaca, cashmere, etamine, flannel, hollands, serge, silk linen and poplin, but by far the most common were plain woven wool or cotton (Janaway 1996, 24). Given the low social status of the ratings it is most probable that cheaper fabrics were used.

The practice of covering the naked or clothed corpse in a loose winding sheet tied at the head and feet was going out of vogue in the mid-18th century and by the 1770s had almost completely disappeared (Litten 1991, 79). The shroud now resembled a backless nightdress often decorated with frills down the centre of the chest. The head of both males and females were often covered with a cap. Coffin sheets were tacked to the sides of the coffin interior, and folded over the dressed corpse, usually leaving the face uncovered whilst it lay in state. These coverings were often tacked or pinned in place over the body. The overall effect was that the deceased was asleep in bed (Litten 1991, 79). It is unclear whether the surviving pins and associated textile fragments found in the graves at the Royal Hospital were part of shrouds or of coffin sheets, although the latter seems more probable. A number of pins were recovered near the mandible of the skeletons, suggesting that these pins originally had secured the sheets around the face.

Catalogue

Area 1 soil horizon

1 **Button**, flat, burnished but undecorated, with fixing loop on reverse. Copper alloy. Dimensions: D: 17 mm. Th: 1 mm. Context 3005, SF3015.

Grave Group 3050 - Grave 3041, skeleton 3044

2 **Shroud pin**, tightly wrapped in shroud fabric found in association with the mandible of inhumation of adult male (skeleton 3044). Pin broken in two, encrusted, with high level of corrosion. Fabric, coarse weave, brown, with green staining. Copper alloy. Dimensions: (1) 35 mm x 20 mm; (2) 12 mm x 10 mm. Context 3044.

Grave Group 3050 - Grave 3041, skeleton 3057

3 **Shroud pin**, wrapped in shroud fabric found at the left mandibular ramus of skeleton 3057. Appears nearly complete but badly corroded and encrusted. Fabric is brown with coarse weave. Copper alloy. Dimensions: L: 35 mm; W: 6 mm. Context 3056, SF3001.

Grave Group 3050 - Grave 3041, skeleton 3068

4 **Shroud pin**, found at the mandibular ramus right hand side with two fragments of fabric. Encrusted and corroded. Copper alloy. Dimensions: L: 12 mm; W: 1 mm. Context 3075, SF3004.

5 **Shroud pin,** found at the medial aspect of the distal left tibia. Badly corroded and wrapped in coarse brown shroud fabric. Copper alloy. Dimensions: L: 12 mm; W: 3 mm. Found with large piece of shroud fabric, brown with green staining *c.* 400 mm x 20 mm. Context 3075, SF3005.

6 **Shroud pin**, found at the mandibular ramus left hand side. Tightly wrapped in coarse shroud brown coloured fabric. Badly corroded and broken. Copper alloy. Dimensions: L: 25 mm; W: 1 mm; Head W: 2 mm. Context 3075, SF3008.

7 **Shroud pin**, found at the medial aspect of distal right tibia. Very fragmentary remains. Copper alloy. Context 3075, SF3009.

Grave Group 3240 - fill of Grave 3028

8 **Button** with hollow centre, formed from two concave sections. Complete, but encrusted, pitted, cracked and bent. There are two small holes on either side of the loop. Copper alloy. Dimensions: D: 15 mm: Th: 7 mm. Context 3027.
  Possibly associated with two most recent burials (skeletons 3029 and 3032) in grave 3028.

Grave Group 3240 - Grave 3028, skeleton 3086

9 **Shroud pin** wrapped with fabric found inside mouth of skeleton 3086. Dimensions: Main section overall (1) 25 mm x 10mm including fabric; (2) 10 mm x 5 mm overall including fabric. Very corroded and encrusted pin broken into three pieces. Dimensions: (1) 30 mm x 4 mm; (2) 10 mm x 3 mm; (3) 10mm x 7 mm. Copper alloy. Context 3077, SF3006.

10 **Shroud textile** found next to right clavicle. Possibly with pieces of shroud pin present. One piece of shroud fabric clearly shows where a pin had been. Dimensions: (1) 10 mm x 2 mm; (2) 5 mm x 2 mm. Context 3077, SF3007.

Grave Group 3260 - fill of Grave 3036

11 **Cartridge case**. Complete, but encrusted, pitted, bent, and laminated. Copper alloy. Dimensions: L: 23 mm; Base D: 15 mm; top D: 11mm. Context 3034.

Grave Group 3380 - Grave 3093, skeleton 3101

12 **Penny,** probably of **George II**, dated 1732. Very worn on both faces with much detail lost, but the king's head facing left can be discerned on the obverse, and the figure of Britannia also facing left can be seen on the reverse. The date of issue is faintly visible beneath the figure of Britannia and appears to be '1732'. Copper alloy. Dimensions: D: 27 mm. Context 3055.

13 **Shroud pin**, very fragmentary and incomplete, with shroud fabric. Dimensions: Pin head: 2mm x 1 mm. Copper alloy. Context 3112.

Grave Group 3380 - Grave 3127, skeleton 3212

14 **Shroud pin**, complete and well preserved, but bent, with rounded head. Copper alloy. Dimensions: L: 25 mm; stem D: 1 mm; Head D: 2 mm. Context 3212, SF3013.

Grave Group 3380 - Grave 3127, skeleton 3162

15 **Shroud pin**, in two pieces. Copper alloy. Dimensions: (1) 15 mm x 2 mm; (2) 6mm x 3mm at head end. Context 3162, SF3011.

Grave Group 3390 - fill of Grave 3239

16 **Shroud pin**. Very corroded and encrusted. Copper alloy. Dimensions: 10 mm x 3 mm. Context 3238, SF3016.

Grave Group 3450 - Grave 3074, skeleton 3072

17 **Shroud pin** and **textile**. Two very small fragments. Found at the top of the occipital, left side of skeleton 3072. Copper alloy. Dimensions 5 mm x 2 mm. Context 3069, SF3003.

Grave Group 3800 - Grave 3198, skeleton 3253

18 **Shroud pin**, tightly wrapped and almost totally obscured by shroud fabric. Pin broken, corroded, and encrusted. Fabric - brown and coarse - found under the skull of 3253. Copper alloy. Dimensions: L: 30 mm; W: 15 mm including fabric. Context 3199, SF3014.

Grave Group 6120 - Grave 6032, skeleton 6094

19 **Shroud pin**. Very fragmented, corroded, and encrusted. Copper alloy alloy. Dimensions: largest fragment: 6 mm x 3 mm. Context 6094, SF6008.

Grave Group 6150 - Grave 6028, skeleton 6027

20 **Shroud pin**, broken and badly corroded and encrusted. Copper alloy. Dimensions: L: 25 mm; head D: 2 mm. Context 6028, SF6000.

Grave Group 6150 - Grave 6026, skeleton 6056

21 **Shroud pin**, found within remains of coffin. Very corroded and encrusted. Two pieces. Fused with fragments of shroud fabric. Copper alloy. Dimensions: 20 mm x 5 mm. Context 6057, SF6003.

Grave Group 6250 - Grave 6025, skeleton 6105

22 **Shroud pin**, found on mandible. Very corroded. Small fragments only. Dimensions: Largest fragment 8 mm x 3 mm. Copper alloy. Context 6105, SF6011.

Grave Group 6270 - Grave 6039, skeleton 6035

23 **Shroud pin**, found at the left mandibular ramus of skeleton 6035. Very fragmentary, in four pieces each approximately 5 mm x 4 mm. Very pitted and corroded. Copper alloy. Context 6041, SF6001.

24 **Leather** or **textile** found under the scapula, ribs and right side of skeleton 6035. Possible leather jerkin or perhaps remains of coffin lining. Dark brown, fragmentary and very fragile. Context 6055, SF6002.

Grave Group 6270 - Grave 6039, skeleton 6037

25 **Leather**, or **possibly textile**. Remains found at the right femur and on right ribs of skeleton 6037. Possible remnants clothing or coffin lining. Dark brown and fragmentary. Context 6067 & context 6068, SF6005.

26 **Possible shroud pin**, fragmentary. Copper alloy. Context 6067, SF6004.

27 **Shroud pin**, two pieces, possibly from two separate pins. Dimensions: (1) 5 mm x 3 mm; (2) 4 mm x 1 mm. Copper alloy. Context 6068, SF6006.

Grave Group 6410 – machine scoop 6066

28 **Probable Shroud textile**. Two fragments. Within the larger piece there was a fragment of copper alloy pin (L: 5 mm). Both pieces are of coarse weave and brown with green staining. Dimensions: (1) 30 mm x 12 mm: (2) 15 mm x 10 mm. Context 3065.

Grave Group 6420 - Grave 6075, skeleton 6089

29 **Shroud pin**, found at right mandibular ramus of skeleton 6089. Pin broken into 5 pieces. Tightly wrapped in shroud material. Badly corroded and encrusted. Copper alloy. Dimensions: 35 mm x 5 mm. Context 6093, SF6007.

Grave Group 6460 - Grave 6084, skeleton 6142

30 **Shroud pin** found on mandible. Corroded and encrusted. Broken, but both head and point present. Copper alloy. Dimensions: L: 30 mm; head D; 2 mm. Context 6142, SF6012.

Grave Group 6460 - Grave 6084, skeleton 6146

31 **Shroud pin**, or **pins**, found on right mandible. Four fragments present. Two fragments belong to one pin, the other two fragments to a finer pin. Copper alloy. Dimensions: (1) 10 m x 3 mm; (2) 5 mm x 3 mm; (3) 5 mm x 1 mm; (4) 3 mm x 1 mm. Context 6146, SF6013.

32 **Shroud pin**, found beneath the chin of skeleton 6084. Broken into three pieces. Very corroded and encrusted. Copper alloy. Dimensions: L: 30 mm; max W: 5 mm. Context 6146, SF6014.

Grave Group 6460 - Grave 6084, skeleton 6151

33 **Shroud pin**, found on temporal lobe right hand side. Very fragmentary. Copper alloy. Dimensions: Largest fragment: 5 mm x 3 mm. Context 6153, SF6015.

34 **Shroud pin wrapped in shroud fabric**, found beneath left temporal bone of skull. Very fragmented and fragile. Copper alloy. Dimensions: 10 mm x 7 mm. Context 6153, SF6016.

35 **Shroud pin** and **fabric** found under skull on the left hand side. Copper alloy. Dimensions: 20 mm x 5 mm. Context 6153, SF6017.

Grave Group 6540 - Grave 6069, skeleton 6098

36 **Shroud pin**, with a piece of cord found in a clump of possible human hair to the right of the

mandibular ramus of skeleton 6098. Broken into 2 pieces. Very corroded and encrusted. Tightly wrapped in fabric and hair. Dark brown, twisted cord appears to be tied around the head of the pin. Dimensions: (1) 200 mm x 3 mm: (2) 8 mm x 3 mm. Copper alloy. Context 6102, SF6009.

37 **Shroud pin**, found at left mandibular ramus of same skeleton, wrapped with fabric and possible human hair, one small section of chord may be present. Very fragmented, corroded and encrusted. Three fragments. Copper alloy. Dimensions overall: 25 mm x 5 mm. Context 6102, SF6010.

Appendix 6: Poetry

by Duncan H Brown

INTRODUCTION

An assemblage totalling 240 sherds (3,568 g) was recovered from 46 contexts. The pottery was sorted by context, ware, vessel type, sherd type and decorative technique and motif, and quantified by rim percent, weight in grams, sherd number and maximum vessel count. Glaze colour and position, and rim diameter, were also recorded. A ceramic terminus post quem for each context is given, based on the earliest date of the latest piece present.

STRATIGRAPHIC ANALYSIS

Table 18 shows the quantities of pottery from each feature type. It is clear that over 90% of the assemblage was recovered from grave fills and is therefore likely to be residual. The range of termini post quem suggested by the pottery for the grave fills covers AD 1250, for context 1313, to AD 1750, for context 2009. Since the cemetery was founded in 1742 it is most probable that nearly all the pottery from grave fills was deposited prior to the digging of any graves. Only one sherd, a white refined earthenware handle with sponged blue decoration from context 2008 (a grave), is possibly later than 1750 in date. It is therefore unlikely that any of the pottery relates to the period of grave digging, as consumption of a wide range of ceramic vessels is not a typical cemetery activity.

It is certain that the finds from the modern backfill deposit, 6065, are residual, and this is probably true of the material from all the other features. Overall, the assemblage is very mixed, with medieval, post-medieval and industrial period sherds all present but not in discrete, coherently dateable deposits of any significant size. The charnel pit, 3021, contained Frechen stoneware and post-medieval redwares dateable from c 1550 to 1700 with a single sherd of 13th/14th-century coarseware. Context 1313, the fill of ditch 1312, produced a single sherd of late medieval Surrey whiteware, which is insufficient to accurately date that feature. Layer 3005 contained 17th- or 18th-century English tin glazed ware and context 1416, the fill of pit 1419 has a similar date range. None of these groups is substantial enough to provide a confident date, nor to give further information on how these deposits were formed.

ASSEMBLAGE COMPOSITION

Table 19 shows the quantities of each ware type present, arranged broadly in chronological order. Post-medieval wares, dating from c 1550 to 1750 are the most common, and a wide range of types is represented. The assemblage is, however, fairly average in character, with no particularly exotic types such as Oriental porcelain. It is perhaps typical of what might be expected from an institution such as the Royal Naval Hospital, from where most of this material presumably derives. There is certainly nothing here that is unusual for London. Post-medieval redware is the most common type, most of which was probably produced locally. Most of the tin glaze wares are plain white or pale blue, although some more elaborate types are also present. The full range of Border wares, including green-glazed, yellow-glazed, brown-glazed and redware are present. There are also London stonewares and Staffordshire earthenwares, while among the Continental products are Frechen and Westerwald stoneware and Werra slipware. There are also medieval imported wares, including Raeren and Siegburg stoneware and a fragment of a North French red-painted whiteware, which is possibly the earliest piece, potentially 12th century, or even pre-Conquest in date.

Table 20 shows the numbers of each particular vessel type that occurs in each ware. The medieval wares take the typical forms of jugs and cooking pots and there is nothing unusual among the range of post-medieval vessel types. Bowls, dishes, jars and jugs

Table 18 Quantities of pottery in each feature type.

Feature Type	Rim Percent	Weight (g)	Sherd Count	Vessel Count
Backfill	9	102	7	7
Charnel Pit	22	102	5	5
Ditch	0	3	1	1
Grave	268	3087	221	202
Layer	0	12	2	2
Pit	12	242	3	3
Unknown	0	20	1	1
Totals	**311**	**3568**	**240**	**221**

Table 19 Quantities of ware types present.

Ware type	Rim Percent	Weight (g)	Sherd Count	Vessel Count
North French red-painted whiteware	0	5	1	1
London ware	0	68	6	6
Medieval coarseware	9	47	4	4
Medieval sandy ware	0	25	4	4
Surrey whiteware	0	10	2	2
Late medieval sandy ware	23	344	13	12
Siegburg stoneware	0	17	2	2
Raeren stoneware	0	11	1	1
Early post-medieval redware	0	20	1	1
Post-medieval earthenware	0	162	6	6
Post-medieval redware	123	1329	70	64
Midland purple	12	99	2	2
Post-medieval black-glazed	0	60	3	2
Border wares	31	381	18	17
Frechen stoneware	0	165	9	8
Post-medieval slipware	0	19	2	2
Staffordshire slipware	0	22	5	4
Werra slipware	10	13	2	2
Tin glazed ware	77	440	67	60
Westerwald stoneware	0	28	4	4
English stoneware	15	163	6	6
English white stoneware	7	26	5	5
English dipped stoneware	0	30	1	1
Flower pot	0	44	1	1
Refined earthenware	0	27	4	3
Burnt pottery	4	13	1	1
Totals	**311**	**3568**	**240**	**221**

Table 20 Maximum vessel count by ware type and vessel.

Ware type	Bowl	Colander	Cooking pot	Dish	Flower pot	Jar	Jug	Mug	Pipkin	Misc	Unidentified	Total
North French red-painted whiteware											1	1
London ware						4	1				1	6
Medieval coarseware			2			2						4
Medieval sandy ware						4						4
Surrey whiteware											2	2
Late medieval sandy ware	6					1				3	2	12
Siegburg stoneware							1				1	2
Raeren stoneware							1					1
Early post-medieval redware			1									1
Post-medieval earthenware						2				1	3	6
Post-medieval redware	10		3	1		5	1			31	13	64
Midland purple						2						2
Post-medieval black-glazed						1				1		2
Border wares	1	3	3	2		1			1	1	5	17
Frechen stoneware							8					8
Post-medieval slipware											2	2
Staffordshire slipware				1							3	4
Werra slipware				2								2
Tin glazed ware	3			10		3				25	19	60
Westerwald stoneware										2	2	4
English stoneware						1	1				4	6
English white stoneware	2									2	1	5
English dipped stoneware								1				1
Flower pot					1							1
Refined earthenware						1					2	3
Burnt pottery	1											1
Total	**23**	**3**	**9**	**16**	**1**	**18**	**19**	**4**	**1**	**65**	**62**	**221**

are the most common identifiable forms. Among the most common ware types, post-medieval redware, tin glazed ware and Border ware, different vessel preferences may be seen. Bowls are the most common form in post-medieval redware and dishes are the most common tin glazed vessel. A wide range of Border ware vessels are represented. The three colanders shown are actually likely to be three sherds from the same vessel, but no definite fit could be established.

This assemblage is modest in size and in the range of types present, as might befit a military institution. All of the material predates the period of use of the cemetery and presumably relates to the hospital.

Appendix 7: Clay Pipes

by Angela Boyle

INTRODUCTION

A small assemblage of clay pipes was recovered, largely from grave fills. The material is summarised in Table 21.

DISCUSSION

The pipe from context 6001, paralleled at Nonsuch, is likely to be redeposited in a later grave fill, since the pipes from Nonsuch are mostly early in date (Davey 1981, 215). The identifiable maker's mark 'IB' is not very helpful: as Oswald lists no less than 54 entries for London ranging in date from the first quarter of the 17th century through to the end of the 19th (Oswald 1975, 131).

Table 21   Summary of clay pipe fragments.

Context no.	Context type	Quantification	Comments
1110	grave fill	11 stems	
2001	post-cemetery demolition layer	part bowl and stem	
2009	grave fill	1 stem	
2030	grave fill	part bowl and stem	
3005	cemetery soil	1 decorated bowl	incised decoration encircles end of bowl
		stems	
		1 bowl and part stem	
3009	construction cut fill	1 bowl and partial stem	part of maker's mark 'B'
3018	grave fill	8 stems	
3021	charnel pit fill	1 bowl and partial stem	maker's mark 'IB'
		5 stems	
3027	grave fill	2 partial bowls	
		1 bowl with unclear mark	
		12 stems	
3034	grave fill	1 stem	
3042	grave fill	1 bowl	possible 'I' or 'E' visible
		2 stems	
3046	grave fill	3 stems	
3073	grave fill	1 bowl fragment	
		9 stems	
3079	grave fill	1 bowl	
		1 stem	
3094	void	1 bowl and part stem	
3096	grave fill	3 bowls	
		2 stems	
3112	grave fill	2 stems	
3113	grave fill	1 stem	
3114	grave fill	1 stem	
3128	grave fill	1 decorated bowl	incised decoration encircles end of bowl
		3 plain bowls	
		7 stems	
3129	grave fill	1 decorated bowl fragment	incised decoration encircles end of bowl
		5 stems	
3141	grave fill	10 stems	
3157	grave fill	1 stem	
3166	grave fill	5 stems	
3192	grave fill	1 bowl	
		1 partial bowl and stem	maker's mark 'IB'
		2 stems	
3199	grave fill	1 decorated bowl	incised decoration encircles end of bowl
		2 stems	
3206	grave fill	2 bowls	
		16 stems	

(continued on next page)

Table 21 (continued)

Context no.	Context type	Quantification	Comments
3216	grave fill	2 stems	
3221	grave fill	1 stem	
3237	grave fill	1 bowl	
		6 stems	
3238	grave fill	5 stems	
3256	grave fill	1 stem	
3264	grave fill	1 decorated bowl	incised decoration encircles end of bowl
		1 plain bowl	
		6 stems	
6001	grave fill	1 bowl with leaf decoration	same as Nonsuch No. 20 (Davey 1981, 279)
		1 virtually complete plain pipe	
6011	grave fill	1 bowl	maker's mark obscured
		11 stems	
6029	grave fill	4 stems	
6033	grave fill	1 stem and part bowl	maker's mark ?`P'
		6 stems	
6034	grave fill	3 stems	
6061	grave fill	3 stems	
6065	modern fill	2 stems	
6076	grave fill	1 part bowl and stem	
		7 stems	
6112	construction cut fill	1 bowl	
		4 stems	
6134	grave fill	1 stem	
unstratified		1 bowl	

Appendix 8: Glass

by Leigh Allen

A total of eight fragments of glass from four contexts were recovered. The fragments are all post-medieval in date. A thick fragment from context 2006 is from the base of a wine bottle with a shallow kick-up. A complete string-rim (and part of the neck) recovered from context 1110 is probably early 18th-century in date. The remaining fragments from contexts 2009 and 2023 are thin green body sherds from a straight-sided wine bottle.

Appendix 9: Ceramic Building Material

by Leigh Allen

A total of 329 fragments of ceramic building material weighing 48,067 g was recovered from the three phases of archaeological investigations. The assemblage was made up almost exclusively of fragments of brick (36,883 g) and roof tile (7,308 g) of late medieval/post-medieval date. Most ceramic building tile appeared residual, originating from building debris of earlier developments. A sample was analysed.

There are no complete examples of roof tiles but there are two examples with an intact width; a fragment from context 1110 had a measurable width of 145 mm and a second example from context 3042 measured 155 mm across. The thickness of the roof tiles was variable across each individual tile but in general it fell within the range 11–13 mm. There are a number of fragments that have traces of peg holes through them but it was not possible to ascertain whether each tile would have had one or two holes. There are 6 fragments of ridge tile with measuring 14–15 mm in thickness but they are very small and abraded. Ditch 6008, which predated the burials, contained one fragment of roof tile. Although it was impossible to date it more precisely, the fabric suggested a later post-medieval date. There were two fragments of possible floor tile measuring 30 and 36 mm in thickness.

There are 17 bricks with measurable dimensions these measurements fell within the range of 60-65 mm (thickness) x 95–105 mm (width) x 200–225 mm (length). The smaller bricks may date to the late medieval period but it is more likely that they are post-medieval in date. Two bricks from context 6065 are frogged, the frogs are rectangular and these bricks are not likely to date before the 19th century. One example has an incomplete stamp impressed in the frog '...BC.....OPRES.....4...' This was probably the identification used at the yard and probably dates to the 19th or 20th century.

Appendix 10: Animal Bone

by Bethan Charles

INTRODUCTION

A total of 330 fragments (4583 g) of animal bone were recovered by hand during the excavation. The majority of the bone was in good condition and evidence of butchery, gnaw damage and pathological changes were observed on the bones. All of the material was found within post-medieval and modern features, although it was almost certainly redeposited and probably predates the period of use of the cemetery.

METHODOLOGY

The calculation of the numbers of species recovered was carried out by using the total fragment method. All fragments of bone were counted including elements from the vertebral centrum, ribs and long bone shafts.

The separation of sheep and goat bone was undertaken employing the criteria of Boessneck (1969) and Prummel and Frisch (1986) in addition to using the reference material housed at OA. However, since no positive identification of goat was made all caprine bones are listed as sheep.

The ageing of the animals was based on tooth eruption and epiphyseal fusion. Silver's tables alone were used to give the timing of epiphyseal closure for cattle, sheep, pigs and horses (Silver 1969). Sheep tooth eruption and wear was measured using a combination of Payne (1973) and the tables of Grant (1982). Cattle tooth eruption and wear was measured using Halstead (1985) and the tables of Grant (1982). Pig tooth eruption and wear was measured using Higham (1967), Bull and Payne (1982) and Grant (1982), defined by Hambleton (1999).

It was not possible to sex any of the animals because of a lack of indicative fragments of bone. The measurements taken were those defined by von den Driesch (1976) and can be found with the primary recording data in the archive.

RESULTS

It can be seen from Table 22 that the majority of the material came from the grave fills at the site. Cattle were the most numerous elements identified from the assemblage followed by sheep and pig. The fallow deer bone identified is likely to have been a rare addition to the menu and implies that there was some variety in the diet of the inhabitants.

It was not possible to age many of the bones. However, two cattle mandibles from grave fill and the charnel pit belonged to young adults and a pig mandible, also from a grave fill was aged to between 21 and 27 months. The epiphyseal fusion rate of the bones cattle and sheep indicate that almost all of the animals were over 3 years of age at death. The pig bones were mostly from young adults and juveniles. It is unlikely that pigs would have been kept beyond 2 years of age since they provided little in the way of secondary products.

The lack of immature and juvenile cattle and sheep identified from the remains may indicate that animals were not bred in the area and that meat was brought in from elsewhere to supply the hospital. There is no clear evidence of the animal husbandry practised during this period, though the ages of both the cattle and sheep indicates that they were probably not bred just for their meat and are likely to have been kept as working animals as well as for dairy products, for dung and for wool.

Only one fragment of sheep bone was identified with evidence of gnaw marks which indicates that the deposition of bone has not been greatly affected by scavengers.

Butchery marks were present on 12% of the assemblage and consisted mostly of chop marks on the long bones of cattle, sheep, pig and deer bones as well as some knife marks typical of de-fleshing and dismembering the animal carcasses as well as breaking up the bones for the marrow. None of the bones from the site had been burnt.

Many of the bones from the main domestic species were large and typical of improved breeds of the late medieval and post-medieval period (all measurements can be found in the archive).

One loose horse tooth was recovered from context 3023.

Both dog and cat bones were present in the assemblage. It is unlikely that they were included in the diet of the inhabitants and as none of the elements had evidence of butchery marks it is assumed that they were natural fatalities.

Two bird bones were identified from within the grave fills; one was a fragment of a long bone shaft and the other part of a beak. The bones were not identified to species.

CONCLUSION

The small number of elements identified to species from the site does not provide detailed information regarding the animal husbandry practices in the area and the diet of the inhabitants during this period. It is clear that the three main domestic species provided the majority of meat and the site was of mid to low status.

Table 22 Number of bones according to feature type and species.

Feature Types	Horse	Cattle	Sheep	Pig	Fallow deer	Dog	Cat	Bird	Unid	Total
Grave Fill	2	48	35	16	1	1	3	2	156	264
Charnel Pit	0	8	8	0	0	0	0	0	10	26
Cemetery Soil	0	4	1	0	0	0	0	0	13	18
Modern Backfill	0	2	1	2	0	0	0	0	7	12
Unstratified	0	2	2	1	1	0	0	0	4	10
Total	**2**	**64**	**47**	**19**	**2**	**1**	**3**	**2**	**190**	**330**

It is probable that the material recovered from the site was not intentionally deposited in the graves and is likely to represent a certain amount of redeposited material that found its way into the features as a result of the site being continually dug for the burial of inhumations. This may have distorted the results due to the fact that the deposits within the feature are unlikely to be securely dated and may contain animal bone from earlier periods of occupation.

However, as much of the material was large and indicative of improved domestic species unlikely to have been found in periods before the mid to late medieval period it is probable that the majority of the material can be assigned to this period of occupation.

Appendix 11: Research Projects undertaken on the assemblage

RESEARCH PROJECTS COMPLETED

Andrews, M 2002 *An investigation of the pathological changes in some of the skeletons excavated from the burial ground of the Royal Naval Hospital, Greenwich*, unpublished report for the Postgraduate Diploma in Professional Archaeology, O.U.D.C.E., Oxford University

Margaret Andrew's report was shortlisted for the Current Archaeology/ RAI Dissertation Award 2004.

Galer, D A 2002 *A biocultural and comparative analysis of fracture trauma at Greenwich Naval Hospital 1749-1857*, unpublished MSc. dissertation, University of Bradford

Gibson, M 2002 *Extramasticatory wear on Royal Navy personnel from Greenwich Naval Infirmary; a comparative study*, unpublished MSc dissertation, University of Sheffield

Lindsay-Gale, L 2002 *Post-excavation report on the burial ground at the Royal Hospital, Greenwich*, Placement 1 Oxford Archaeology report for the Postgraduate Diploma in Professional Archaeology, O.U.D.C.E., Oxford University

Turnbull, A K 2004 *Assessment, analysis and comparison of cranial trauma found at the Greenwich Naval Hospital*; unpublished MSc. dissertation; University of Bradford

RESEARCH PROJECTS IN PROGRESS

Cashmore, L *Hand morphology, hand preference and laterality*, PhD dissertation being undertaken at Southampton University

Bibliography

Adams, J C 1990 *Outline of Orthopaedics,* 11th edition, Churchill Livingstone, Edinburgh

Arrizabalaga, J 2003 Syphilis, in Kiple 2003, 312–317

Aufderheide, A C, and Rodriguez-Martin, C 1998 *The Cambridge encyclopedia of human palaeopathology,* Cambridge UP, Cambridge

Austen, Jane 1818 *Persuasion,* 1818, Folio Society 1975

Ayshford, P, and Ayshford, D 2004 *The Ayshford complete Trafalgar Roll,* compact disc: SEFF, Brussels, Belgium

Baillie, Thomas 1778 *The CASE of the ROYAL HOSPITAL for Seamen at GREENWICH : containing a comprehensive View of the internal Government; in which are stated the several Abuses that have been introduced into that great National Establishment, wherein Landmen have been appointed to Offices contrary to Charter; the ample Revenues wasted in useless Works ; . . . .* (By Captain THOMAS BAILLIE, Lieutenant-Governor.) Royal Hospital, March 2, 1778.

Bashford, L, and Pollard, T 1998 'In the burying place' – the excavation of a Quaker burial ground, in Cox 1998

Beck, S V 1997 Rickets: where the sun doesn't shine, in Kiple 1997, 130–35

BGS 1981 British Geological Survey, Sheet No. 271

Boessneck, J 1969 Osteological Differences in Sheep (Ovis aries Linné) and Goat (Capra hircus Linné), in Brothwell and Higgs 1969, 331–358

Boston, C V 2004 The Baptist burial ground, in Brown, R, *Archaeological excavations at Vancouver Centre, Kings Lynn,* unpublished client report, Oxford Archaeology

Boston, C V 2005 *Archaeological evaluation in the Paddock, Haslar Hospital, Gosport, Hants,* unpublished client report, Oxford Archaeology

Boston, C V, and Witkin, A 2006 The human bone assemblage, in Boston, C V, Boyle, A, and Witkin, A, 2006

Boston, C V, and Boyle, A 2005 Burial practice and material culture, in Boyle, A, Boston, C V, and Witkin, A, *The archaeological experience at St Luke's church, Old Street, Islington,* unpublished client report, Oxford Archaeology

Boston, C V, Boyle, A, and Witkin, A 2006 *In the vaults beneath - archaeological investigations at St George's church, Bloomsbury,* unpublished client report, Oxford Archaeology

Boston, C, Boyle, A, Score, D, and Witkin, A forthcoming *'In the vaults beneath' - archaeological recording at St George's Church, Bloomsbury,* Oxford Archaeology Monograph, Oxford

Boulter, S, Robertson, D, and Start, H 1998 *The Newcastle Infirmary at the Forth, Newcastle Upon Tyne. Volume 2. The osteology: People, disease and surgery,* unpublished client report, Archaeology Research and Consultancy at the University of Sheffield

Boyle, A 1995 *A catalogue of coffin fittings from St Nicholas, Sevenoaks,* unpublished archive report

Boyle, A, Boston, C V, and Witkin, A 2005 *The archaeological experience at St Luke's church, Old Street, Islington,* unpublished client report, Oxford Archaeology

Brickley, M, Buteux, S, Adams, J, and Cherrington, R 2006 *St Martin's uncovered- investigations in the churchyard of St Martin's-in-the-Bullring, Birmingham, 2001,* Oxbow Books, Oxford

Brickley, M, and Ives R, 2005 Skeletal manifestations of infantile scurvy, *American Journal of Physical Anthropology* **129 (2)**,163–172

Brickley, M, Mays, S, and Ives, R 2007 An investigation of skeletal indicators of Vitamin D deficiency in adults: effective markers for interpreting past living conditions and pollution levels in 18th and 19th century Birmingham, England, *American Journal of Physical Anthropology* **132 (1)**, 67–79

Brickley, M, Miles, A, and Stainer, H 1999 *The Cross Bones burial ground, Redcross Way, Southwark, London, archaeological excavations (1991–1998) for the London Underground Limited Jubilee Line Extension Project,* MoLAS Monograph **3,** London

Brickley, M, and Smith, M 2006 Culturally determined patterns of violence: biological anthropological investigations at a historic urban cemetery, *American Anthropologist* **108 (1)**, 163–177

Brooks, S, and Suchey, J M 1990 Skeletal age determination based on the os pubis: a comparison of the Acsádi-Nemeskéri and Suchey-Brooks method. *Human Evolution* **5 (3)**, 227–238

Brothwell, D 1981 *Digging up bones,* 3rd edition, New York

Brothwell, D 2003 Yaws, in Kiple, 2003, 362–65

Brothwell, D R, and. Higgs, E S (eds) 1969 *Science in Archaeology,* Thames and Hudson , London

Browner, B D, Jupiter, J B, Levine, A M, and Trafton, P G 2003 *Skeletal trauma: basic science, management and reconstruction,* Saunders, USA

Buikstra, J E. and D H. Ubelaker (eds.) 1994 *Standards for Data Collection from Human Skeletal Remains. Archeological Survey Research Series* No. **44,** Fayetteville, Arkansas

Bull, G, and Payne, S 1982 Tooth Eruption and Epiphyseal Fusion in Pigs and Wild Boar. In Wilson, B, *et al. Ageing and Sexing Animal Bones from Archaeological Sites,* BAR British Series **109**, 55–71

Burney, William 1815 *A New Universal Dictionary of the Marine, being, a copious Explanation of the Technical terms and Phrases . . . Originally compiled by William Falconer, Author of the Shipwreck, &c. Now Modernized and much Enlarged, by William Burney, LL.D. Master of the Naval Academy, Gosport.* T. Caldell & W. Davies, London

Byers, S M 2005 *Introduction to forensic anthropology- a textbook,* 2nd edition, Allyn and Bacon, Boston, USA

Chamberlain, A 1994 *Human remains*, British Museum Press, London

Chandrasoma, P, and Taylor, C R 1995 *Concise pathology*, second edition, Lange Medical Books, USA

Clayton, T, and Craig, P 2004 *Trafalgar- the men, the battle and the storm*, Hodder and Stoughton, London

Clowes, W L 1899 *The Royal Navy. A history from the earliest times to 1900*, Volume Four, reprinted 1997, Chatham Publishing, London

Clowes, W L 1900 *The Royal Navy. A history from the earliest times to 1900*, Volume Five, reprinted 1997, Chatham Publishing, London

Colvin, H M (ed.) 1982 *The History of the King's Works Vol. IV 1485-1660 (Part II)*, HMSO, London.

Cox, M 1996 *Life and death at Spitalfields 1700–1850*, CBA, York

Cox, M (ed) 1998 *Grave Concerns: death and burial in England 1700–1850*, CBA Res Rep **113**, York

Cox, M 2000 Ageing adults from the skeleton, in Cox and Mays 2000

Cox, M, and Mays, S (eds) *Human osteology in archaeology and forensic science*, Greenwich Medical Media,

Curl, J S 2000 *The Victorian celebration of death*, Sutton, Stroud

Davey, P 1981 *The archaeology of the clay tobacco pipe. VI. Pipes and kilns in the London region*, BAR British Series **97**, Oxford

Denko, C W 2003 Osteoarthritis, in Kiple 2003, 234–36

Dormandy, T, 1999 *The white death- a history of tuberculosis*, Hambledon Press, London

Doyle, D 1986 Clinical aspects of osteoarthritis, in Scott, J T (ed) *Copeman's textbook of the rheumatoid diseases*, Churchill Livingstone, Edinburgh, 846–873

Erickson, C 1996 *Our tempestuous day - a history of Regency England*, Robson Books, U.K.

Evans, J, and Chenery, C 2004 *Strontium and oxygen (and lead) analysis of tooth enamel from sample 3061- Greenwich burial*, unpublished NIGL report no **199**

Ferembach, D, Schwidetzky, I, and Stloukal, M, 1980 Recommendations for age and sex diagnoses of skeletons, *Journal of Human Evolution* **9**, 517–549

Fremont-Barnes, G, 2005 *Nelson's sailors*, Osprey Publishing, Oxford

French, R K, 2003 Scurvy, in Kiple 2003, 295–98

Fryer, P, 1984 *Staying power: the history of black people in Britain*, Pluto Press, London

Galer, D A, 2002 *A biocultural and comparative analysis of fracture trauma at Greenwich Naval Hospital 1749–1857*, unpublished MSc. dissertation, University of Bradford

Gibson, M 2002 Extramasticatory wear on Royal Navy personnel from Greenwich Naval Infirmary; a comparative study, unpublished MSc dissertation, University of Sheffield

Gilbert, B M 1976 Anterior femoral curvature: its probable basis and utility as a criterion in racial assessment, *American Journal of Physical Anthropology* **45(3)**, 601–604

Giles, E, and Elliot, O 1962 Race identification from cranial measurements, *Journal of Forensic Science* **7**, 147–157

Gill, G W, and Rhine, S (eds) 1990 *Skeletal attributes of race: methods for forensic anthropology*, Maxwell Museum of Anthropology, Anthropology Papers 4, University of New Mexico, Albuquerque

Glascock, William Nugent, 1826 *Naval Sketch-Book; or, the service afloat and ashore . . . by an Officer of Rank*, 2 vols, London

Goodman, AH and Rose, J 1990 Assessment of systemic physiological perturbations from dental enamel hypoplasias and associated histological structures; *Yearbook of Physical Anthropology* **33**, 59–110

Grant, A 1982 The Use of Tooth Wear as a Guide to the Age of Domestic Ungulates. In Wilson, B *et al. Ageing and Sexing Animal Bones from Archaeological Sites*, BAR British Series **109**

Grauer, A, and Roberts, C 1996 Paleoepidemiology, healing and possible treatment of trauma in the medieval cemetery population of St Helen's-on-the-Walls, York, England, *American Journal of Physical Anthropology* **100 (4)**, 531–544

Grose, F 1811 *Dictionary of the vulgar tongue*, edition published by Beard Books, 2004

Gunn, D R 1974 Don't sit - squat! *Clinical Orthopaedics and Related Research* 103, 104–105

Halstead, P 1985 A study of mandibular teeth from Romano-British contexts at Maxey, in F Pryor and C French *Archaeology and environment in the lower Welland Valley*, Clo. 1, East Anglian Archaeology Report **27**, 219–224

Hamilton, O, and Hamilton, N 1969 *Royal Greenwich: a guide and history to London's most historic borough*, Dodd and Dodd, London

Harvey, A D 1994 *Sex in Georgian England*, Phoenix Press, London

Harvie, D I 2002 *Limeys- the conquest of scurvy*, Sutton Publishing, Great Britain

Henderson, J 1987 Factors determining the state of preservation of human remains, in A, Boddington, A N Garland and R C Janaway (eds) *Death decay and reconstruction: Asppoaches to archaeology and forensic science*, Manchester University Press, Manchester, 43-54.

Hensinger, R N 1989 Spondylolysis and spondylolisthesis in children and adolescents, *Journal of Bone and Joint Surgery* **71A**, 1098-1107

Hillam, C 1990 *The roots of dentistry*, Dental Association Publication, London

Hillson, S 1996 *Dental anthropology*, 3rd edition, New York

Humphreys, M, 1997 Tuberculosis: The 'consumption' and civilization, in Kiple 1997, 136-41

Iscan, M Y, Loth, S R, and Wright, R K 1984 Age estimation from the ribs by phase analysis: white males, *Journal of Forensic Sciences* **29**, 1094-1104

Janaway, R C, 1996 The decay of buried human remains and their associated materials, in Roberts, C A, and Hunter, J (eds) *Studies in crime: an introduction to forensic archaeology*, Routledge, London, 58–85

Jurmain, R D, 1999 Osteoarthritis and activity: occupational and sports studies, in Jurmain, R D (ed)

Stories from the skeleton- behavioral reconstruction in human osteology, Gordon and Breach Publishers, Netherlands

Kemp, P, 1970 *The British sailor: a social history of the lower deck*, Dent, London

Kiple, K, (ed) 1997 *Plague, pox and pestilence- disease in history*, London

Kiple, K F, 2003 *The Cambridge historical dictionary of disease*, Cambridge UP, Cambridge

Krogman, W M, and Iscan, M Y, 1986 *The human skeleton in forensic medicine*, 2nd edition, Charles C. Thomas, Springfield Illinois,

Latham, R, (ed) 2000 *The illustrated Pepys- extracts from the diary*, Penguin Books

Lavery, B, 1989 *Nelson's Navy. The ships, men and organisation 1793–1815*, Conway Maritime Books, London

Lavery, B (ed.) 1998 *Shipboard life and organisation, 1731–1815*, Naval Records Society, vol. **138**, Aldershot

Lavery, B, 2004 *Nelson's fleet at Trafalgar*, National Maritime Museum, Greenwich, London

Leech, Samuel 1844 *Thirty years from home, or, A voice from the main deck*, Boston, USA

Lefebure, M, 1974 *Samuel Taylor Coleridge: a bondage of opium*, Stein and Day New York

Lewis, M, 1960 *A social history of the Navy 1793–1815*, Allen and Unwin, London

Lewis, M, 2007 *Bioarchaeology of children- perspectives from biological and forensic anthropology*, Cambridge UP, Cambridge

Lindsay-Gale, L, 2002 *Post-excavation report on the burial ground at the Royal Hospital, Greenwich*, Placement 1 Oxford Archaeology report for the Post Graduate Diploma in Professional Archaeology, OUDCE, Oxford University

Litten, J, 1991 *The English way of death- the common funeral since 1450*, Robert Hale, London

Loth, S R, 1995 Age assessment of the Spitalfields cemetery population by rib phase analysis, *American Journal of Human Biology* **7**, 990-999

Lowry, J, 2006 *Fiddlers and whores: the candid memoirs of a surgeon in Nelson's fleet*, Chatham Publishing, London

Lovejoy, C O, Meindl, R S, Pryzbeck, T R, and Mensforth, R P, 1985 Chronological metamorphosis of the auricular surface of the illium: a new method for determination of adult skeletal age-at-death, *American Journal of Physical Anthropology* **68**, 15–28

Lovejoy, C O, Meindl, R S, Mensforth, R P, and Barton, T J, 1985 Multifactorial determination of skeletal age at death: a method and blind tests of its accuracy, *American Journal of Physical Anthropology*, **68 (1)**, 1-14

Lukacs, J R, 1989 Dental pathology: Methods for reconstructing dietary patterns, in *Reconstruction of life from the skeleton*, (eds M Y Iscan and K A R Kennedy), 261-286, New York

Maat, G J R, 1982 Scurvy in Dutch whalers buried at Spitsbergen, in Haneveld, G T, Perizonius, W R K and Janssens, P J (eds), *Proceedings of the Paleopathology Association Middleberg-Antwerpen*, 82–93

Maat, G R J, 2004 Scurvy in adults and youngsters: the Dutch experience. A review of the history and pathology of a disregarded disease, *International Journal of Osteoarchaeology* **14 (2)**, 77–81

Matthews, J, 1991 *Welcome Aboard: the story of the seamen's hospital society and the Dreadnought*, Baron Buckingham

May, T, 2003 *The Victorian undertaker*, Shire Publications

Mays, S, 1998 *The archaeology of human bones*, London

Mays, S, 2006 Spondylolysis, spondylolisthesis and lumbo-sacral morphology in a medieval English skeletal population, *American Journal of Physical Anthropology.* **131 (3)**, 352–362

Mays, S, and Cox, M, 2000 Sex determination in skeletal remains, in Cox and Mays 2000

McIntyre, L, and Wilmott, H, 2003 Excavations at the Methodist Chapel, Carver Street, Sheffield, unpublished site report, ARCUS, Sheffield

McKinley, J I, and Roberts, C A, 1993 *Excavation and post-excavation treatment of cremated and inhumed human remains*, IFA Technical Paper **13**, IFA, Birmingham

Meindl, R S, and Lovejoy, C O, 1985 Ectocranial suture closure: a revised method for the determination of skeletal age at death based on the lateral-anterior sutures, *American Journal of Physical Anthropology* **68 (1)**, 57–66

Meindl, R S, Lovejoy, C O, Mensforth, R P, and Carlos, L D, 1985 Accuracy and determination of error in the sexing of the skeleton, *American Journal of Physical Anthropology* **68 (1)**, 79–85

Meisel, A D, and Bullough, P G, 1984 *Atlas of osteoarthritis*, Gower Medical Publishing, New York

Miles, A E W, 1962 The assessment of age from the dentition, *Proc Royal Society of Medicine* **55**, 881–5

Miles, A E W 1963 The dentition in the assessment of individual age in skeletal material, in D R Brothwell (ed) *Dental Anthropology*, Pergamon Press

Molleson, T, and Cox, M, with Waldron, A H, and Whittaker, D K, 1993 *The Spitalfields Project. Volume 2: The Anthropology - The Middling Sort*, CBA Res Rep **86**, York

Moorees, C F A, Fanning, E A, and Hunt, E E, 1963 Age variation of formation stages for ten permanent teeth, *Journal of Dental Research* **42**, 1490–1502

Musgrave, T, and Musgrave, W 2000 *An empire of plants- people and plants that changed the world*, Cassell Illustrated, London

Newell, P 1984 *Greenwich Hospital - a royal foundation 1692-1893*, The Trustees of Greenwich Hospital

Newell, R L 1995 Spondyloysis: a historic review, *Spine* **20**, No. 17, 1950–1956

Nolan, J 1997 *The international centre for life: The archaeology and history of the Newcastle Infirmary*, Newcastle City Archaeology Unit unpublished client report

OAU 1995 *Greenwich Royal Naval College Historical Appraisal Report. Oxford Archaeological Unit*, unpublished client report

OA, 1999a *The Devonport Buildings, King William Walk, Greenwich. Archaeological Watching Brief Report*, unpublished client report

OA, 1999b *The Devonport Buildings, King William Walk, Greenwich. Archaeological Desk Based Assessment*, unpublished client report

OA, 1999c *The Devonport Buildings, King William Walk, Greenwich- Archaeological Field Evaluation Report*, unpublished client report

Ortner, D J, and Ericksen, M F 1997 Bone changes in the human skull probably resulting from scurvy in infancy and childhood, *International Journal of Osteoarchaeology* **7 (3)**, 212–220

Ortner, D J, Kimmerle, E H, and Diez, M 1999 Probable evidence of scurvy in subadults from archaeological sites in Peru, *American Journal of Physical Anthropology* **108 (3)**, 321–331

Ortner, D J, and Putschar, W G J 1981 *Identification of Pathological Conditions in Human Skeletal Remains*, Smithsonian Institute Press, Washington

Oswald, A 1975 *Clay pipes for the archaeologist*, BAR British Series **14**, Oxford

Ousley, S D, and Jantz, R L 2005 *FORDISC - Personal Computer Forensic Discriminant Functions*, computer programme, University of Tennessee

Payne, S 1973 Kill-Off Patterns in Sheep and Goats: The Mandibles from Asvan Kale. Anatolian Studies, *Journal of the British Institute of Archaeology at Ankara* **23**, 281–303

Phenice, T W 1969 A newly developed visual method of sexing the Os pubis. *American Journal of Physical Anthropology* **30 (2)**, 297–301

Picard, L 2000 *Dr Johnson's London*, Weidenfeld and Nicholson, London

Porter, R 1997 *The greatest benefit to mankind. A medical history of humanity from antiquity to the present*, Harper Collins, London

Porter, R 2002 *Blood and guts- a short history of medicine*, Allen Lane, England

Prummel, W and Frisch, H-J 1986 A Guide for the distinction of species, sex and body size in bones of sheep and goat, *J Archaeol Sci* **13**, 567–77

Reeve, J 1998 A view from the metropolis: post-medieval burials in London, in Cox 1998

Reeve, J and Adams, A 1993 *The Spitalfields Project. Volume 1: The Archaeology - Across The Styx*, CBA Research Report No. **85**, York

Resnick, D, 1995 *Diagnosis of bone and joint disorders*, 3rd edition, W.B. Saunders Company, Philadelphia

Resnick, D, and Niwayama, G, 1995 Degenerative disease of extra-spinal locations, in Resnick, D 1995, 1263–1371

Roberts, C A 1991 Trauma and treatment in the British Isles, in Ortner, D J and Aufderheide, A C (eds), *Human palaeopathology: current synthesis and future options*, Smithsonian Institute Press, Washington

Roberts C A, Boylson, A, Buckley, L, Chamberlain, A C and Murphy, E M 1998 Rib lesions and tuberculosis: the palaeopathological evidence; *Tubercle and Lung Disease* **79 (1)**, 55–60

Roberts, C A and Cox, M 2003 *Health and disease in Britain from prehistory to present day*, Stroud

Roberts, C A and Manchester, K, 1995 *The archaeology of disease*, 2nd edition, New York

Robinson, W, 2002 [Jack Nastyface] *Nautical economy, or forecastle reflections of events during the last war*, 1836, cited from edition published as *Memoirs of an English seaman*, Warner, O (ed.) 1973, reprinted Chatham Publishing, 2002, London

Rodger, N A M 1986 *The Wooden World. An anatomy of the Georgian Navy*, Collins, London

Rodger, N A M 2004 *The command of the ocean. A naval history of Britain, 1649–1815*, Penguin Books

Rogers, J, and Waldron, T, 1995 *A field guide to joint disease in archaeology*, Wiley Press

Rugg, J, 1999 From reason to regulation - 1760–1850, in Jupp P C and Gittings C (eds) *Death in England: an illustrated history*, Manchester UP, Manchester

St Hoyme, L E, and Iscan, M Y, 1989 Determination of sex and race: accuracy and assumptions, in Iscan, M Y, and Kennedy, K A R, (eds) *Reconstructing life from the skeleton*, Alan Liss, New York, 53–93

Schwartz, J H, 1995 *Skeleton keys- an introduction to human skeletal morphology, development and analysis*, Oxford UP, Oxford

Silver, I A, 1969 The ageing of domestic animals, in Brothwell and Higgs 1969, 283–302

Slope, N 2004 *Women in Nelson's Navy - burials on Nelson's Island*, http://www.bbc.co.uk/history/british/empire_seapower/women_nelso_navy_05.shtml

Sournia, J-C, 1992 *The illustrated history of medicine*, Harold Stark Publishers, Cambridge

Spavens, W 2000 *Memoirs of a seafaring life: the narrative of William Spavens pensioner on the Navy Chest at Chatham, 1796*, Rodger N A M (ed), Folio Society, 2000, London,

Standaert, J C and Herring, S J 2000 Spondylolysis: a critical review, *British Journal of Sports Medicine*, **34**, 415–422

Steele, J 2000 Skeletal indicators of handedness, in Cox and Mays 2000

Steinbock, R T 2003 Osteoporosis, in Kiple 2003, 236–38

Stirland, A J, 2000 *Raising the dead- the skeleton crew of King Henry VIII's great ship The Mary Rose*, Wiley

Stirland, A J, 2005 Human remains, in Gardiner, J (ed) *Before the mast: life and death aboard the Mary Rose*, Archaeology of the Mary Rose, Vol 4, Mary Rose Trust

Stock, G. 1998a Quaker Burial: Doctrine and Practice, in Cox 1998, 129–43

Stock, G, 1998b The 18th and Early 19th Century Quaker Burial Ground at Bathford, Bath and North East Somerset, in Cox 1998, 144–53

Strother, E 1725 *An essay on sickness and health; wherein are contain'd, all necessary cautions and directions, for the regulation of diseas'd and healthy persons: in which Dr. Cheyne's mistaken opinions in his late essay, are occasionally taken notice of*. Printed by H.P. for Charles Rivington ..., London

Stuart-Macadam, P, 1991 Anaemia in Roman Britain: Poundbury Camp, in Bush, H, and Zvelebil, M (eds) *Health in past societies*, BAR International Series **567**, 101–114

Sutherland, L D, and Suchey, J M, 1991 Use of the ventral arch in pubic sex determination, *Journal of Forensic Sciences* **36**, 501–511

Bibliography

Todd, T W, 1921a Age changes in the pubic bone. I. The male white pubis, *American Journal of Physical Anthropology* **3 (3)**, 285–334

Todd, T W, 1921b Age changes in the pubic bone, *American Journal of Physical Anthropology* **4 (1)**, 1–70

Trotter, M 1970 Estimations of stature from intact long limb bones, in Stewart, T D (ed.) *Personal identification in Mass Disasters*, Washington, 71–83

Trotter, M, and Gleser, G C 1952 Estimation of stature from long bones of American whites and negroes, *American Journal of Physical Anthropology* **10 (4)**, 463–514

Turnbull, A K 2004 *Assessment, analysis and comparison of cranial trauma found at the Greenwich Naval Hospital*; unpublished MSc. dissertation; University of Bradford

Vipul, R D, Byrne, P, Tawfilis, A R, Kim, D W, and Patel, D, 2006 *Facial trauma, nasal fractures*, Internet site: http://www.emedicine.com/plastic/topic482.htm

Von den Driesch, A 1976 *A Guide to the Measurement of animal bones from archaeological sites*, Peabody Museum Bulletin 1

Waldron, T, and Rogers, J 1991 Inter-observer variation in coding osteoarthritis in human skeletal remains, *International Journal of Osteoarchaeology* **1 (1)**, 49–56

Walker, P L 1997 Wife beating, boxing and broken noses: skeletal evidence for the cultural patterning of violence, in Frayer, D W, and Martin, D L (eds) *Troubled times - violence and warfare in the past*, Gordon and Breach Publishers, USA

Weiss, E, and Jurmain, R 2007 Osteoarthritis revisited: a contemporary review of aetiology, *International Journal of Osteoarthritis* **17 (5)**, 437–450

Wilkinson, D 1992 *Oxford Archaeology Field Manual*, unpublished

Wright, R 2005 *CRANID*, computer programme, available from richwrig@tig.com.au